PATRIOTS, PROSTITUTES, AND SPIES

PATRIOTS, PROSTITUTES, AND SPIES

Women and the Mexican-American War

John M. Belohlavek

UNIVERSITY OF VIRGINIA PRESS
Charlottesville and London

University of Virginia Press

Printed in the United States of America on acid-free paper

First published 2017

ISBN 978-0-8139-3990-2 (cloth)
ISBN 978-0-8139-3991-9 (e-book)

1 3 5 7 9 8 6 4 2

Library of Congress Cataloging-in-Publication Data
is available from the Library of Congress.

Cover art: La Mantilla, hand-colored lithograph by Carl Nebel, 1836.

For my sister, Judy, who shares a love of history

CONTENTS

ACKNOWLEDGMENTS

The study of women's history presents a unique set of opportunities and obstacles. Exploring the lives and contributions of women on both sides of the Rio Grande, most of whom left little in terms of letters or diaries, added yet another challenge. If I have done them justice, that success is in significant part owing to the scholarly assistance and suggestions made by Sidney Bland, Doug Egerton, Julia Irwin, Nat Jobe, and Gary Mormino. Their thoughts on various aspects of the manuscript have improved it immeasurably. I would also like to thank the anonymous readers for the University of Virginia Press, who strengthened the volume by recommending worthwhile additions and deletions, Joanne Allen and Morgan Myers for their keen-eyed copyediting skills, and Dick Holway, my editor for this volume, for his unflappability and counsel.

Numerous archives and libraries, including Historic New Orleans, the Dallas Historical Society, the US Military Academy Library at West Point, LSU's Hill Memorial Library, Special Collections, and the Collections of the University of Texas at Arlington, demonstrated the cooperation and professionalism valued and welcomed by the historian. My colleagues at the University of South Florida expressed their ongoing concern and support for this study, while my wife, Susan, demonstrated endless patience and offered stylistic advice that has made the narrative more readable. To each of them I owe a debt of gratitude. They should share in the credit but assume none of the criticism that may be forthcoming of this work.

PATRIOTS, PROSTITUTES, AND SPIES

Introduction

On a cold February morning in northern Mexico, a stinging rain pelted Lola Sanchez's face, awakening her to the drudgery of yet another day with the army of General Antonio López de Santa Anna. Lola battled the harsh elements for weeks. Her bare feet were bruised from stones on the road, and her arms ached from carrying the cooking pot and a few paltry possessions. With little clothing and no shelter, she survived by hard work, pluck, and no small measure of good fortune. Would Lola find dry firewood? Her desperate search must be successful, for how else would she prepare a breakfast of *atole* or tortillas? The backbreaking labor, danger, and monotony seemed worth the sacrifice, for she loved her country. José, her husband, slogged along with the Mexican forces, which depended upon women such as Lola—the *soldaderas*—for sustenance and medical care on the march. These women were the spine of the army.

A thousand miles away in Indiana, Nancy Conner rose before dawn to light the carefully arranged logs in the fireplace, removing the dank cold from her cabin. She prepared breakfast for her two young daughters, brown bread washed down by fresh milk. Pedestrian fare indeed, but filling and inexpensive. The sun rose quickly in the winter sky, so that Nancy could not waste time entertaining the children. Caleb, her spouse, had enlisted in the volunteers in 1846, to defend his homeland and supplement the family income. In his absence, Nancy's Victorian domestic duties expanded dramatically. The labor and loneliness took a toll, and depression left its mark. What if Caleb never returned?

Lola Sanchez and Nancy Conner were not alone. They symbolized thousands of Mexican and American women, for too long voiceless and invisible, who sacrificed for family and nation. This volume offers that voice by exploring various aspects of the war experience. It ranges widely in an effort to address the struggles and concerns of American women at home, often divided and passionate in their defense of the war or opposition to it. They joined groups that patriotically aided the soldiers by providing clothing and flags. Others expressed their reformist views by speaking and writing tracts that condemned the conflict as immoral and unjust. The same split separated pioneering women journalists, such as Jane Swisshelm and Jane Cazneau, who interpreted the war quite differently in their widely read newspaper columns.

Many women channeled their drive and intellect into the popular culture, composing songs, poems, and plays that captured the hearts and minds of a nation. A smaller number of American women found themselves in Mexico by circumstance, laboring in local factories or traveling with the military. Sarah Bowman became a legend, transitioning from army cook to entrepreneurial hotel owner and madam. A youthful Susan Magoffin suffered the perils of the Santa Fe Trail, while Ann Chase endured the unique challenges of managing her husband's business in Tampico. Both Magoffin and Chase kept extensive diaries revealing their personal strengths and resolution, as well as the dangers each faced.

The narrative also focuses on Mexican women in a similar if not parallel context. They too supported the war through the writing of songs and poems, but more impressively, they traveled with their armies. The *soldaderas* provided essential support. Theirs is a tale of courage, heartbreak, and endurance. The conflict sometimes placed Mexican women in a position of opportunity. Gertrudis Barceló evolved from a Santa Fe gambler of questionable reputation to "Doña Tules," businesswoman and one of the town's wealthiest citizens. Other Mexican women worked for the US Army as it occupied the country, but some found that employment came at a high cost. Women became the objects of male fantasy, which frequently resulted in exploitation and violence.

While the stories of celebrated individuals such as Swisshelm, Cazneau, and Chase, who agitated against the war, promoted expansion, or spied for the Americans, have received scholarly attention, their lives and contributions have been largely marginalized in Mexican-American War scholarship. These women flaunted Victorian conventionality but did not rival Barceló or Bowman, mistresses of thriving saloon and gaming establishments. This work seeks to explore and recognize the courage, spirit, and influence of women heralded and unheralded, of varying backgrounds and nationalities, who powerfully impacted the war that changed the continent.

The Social Worlds of the United States and Mexico

In 1846, two profoundly different societies eyed each other suspiciously across the Rio Grande. Both struggled economically and were fraught with political turmoil. One, however, appeared ambitious and on the move; the other, equally ambitious and in disarray. The United States and Mexico had never clashed. The fledgling republics shared a common border but not a common culture, language, or religion. Moreover, Mexican possessions in the Southwest formed a clear obstacle to US expansion. Given the distinctive points of separation between the countries, the question might be raised whether the war that occurred from 1846 to 1848 was a foregone conclusion. If so, who determined whether that western territory would be acquired peacefully or by force of arms? Was this conflict avoidable, or was it the inevitable product of the evolution of two societies at odds and the entrenched attitudes and goals of their leaders?

By briefly exploring the political, economic, and social nature of the two countries, we can obtain a clearer picture of how they came to clash and determine whether a realistic alternative presented itself. The goal is also to create an awareness of the status and place of women in each culture on the eve of the war. The role women played in the contest itself and how the war altered, or failed to alter, their role and position in both the private and public spheres can be more easily determined.

The United States

By the early 1840s, the United States and Mexico faced many of the same challenges but moved in markedly different directions. Both embraced the eagle as their national symbol, but the American bird seemed to be soaring in full flight. The population of the United States reached 17 million, representing a dramatic increase of almost 33 percent over the census in 1830. The country boasted twenty-six states, and although Americans had a joint claim with Great Britain to the Oregon territory, the westernmost states were Missouri, Arkansas, and Louisiana. No doubt, further expansion was on the horizon. While the size of the cities was sharply increasing, only New York, with a population of more than three hundred thousand, could be described as truly imposing. Baltimore, New Orleans, Philadelphia, and Boston hovered at around one hundred thousand residents each. Most Americans, however, lived in rural areas, and 65 percent tilled the soil. Urbanity had its allure, but the future for many Jacksonian Americans remained on the farm and the frontier.[1]

The young republic's promise hinged upon a restless population with a boundless westward vision. Over the course of the first half century of independence, tens of thousands of pioneers left New England and the seaboard South and headed for the frontier of Illinois or Mississippi. The Frenchman Alexis de Tocqueville, traveling the United States in 1831, quickly became aware of this mobility. "In the United States a man builds a house in which to spend his old age, and he sells it before the roof is on . . . he brings a field into tillage and leaves other men to gather the crop; he embraces a profession and gives it up; he settles in a place which he soon afterwards leaves to carry his changeable possessions elsewhere."[2]

Americans carried more than their possessions. They bore a belief system vested in the likelihood of their own success based on natural superiority and a strong Protestant work ethic. There existed a romantic sensibility about the frontier that allowed the weary mechanic or laborer the opportunity for a rebirth on virgin soil. The West harbored a passionate belief in equality, at least for white men, and a right to rise according to one's level of ambition and ability. For many, this freedom epitomized the Jeffersonian promise of the "natural man" fleeing the greed, immorality, filth, and sloth of the rising city. Progress was inevitable for both the individual and the social order if obstacles were removed and government stood aside. Indeed, Washington might provide situational military assistance, but generally local self-rule was imperative.

In such a society, the major functions of the political structure focused upon guaranteeing liberty and individual rights, protecting the citizenry, and promoting the economy. Exactly how those would be accomplished splintered the generation of the Founding Fathers. The philosophical differences that divided the republic remained as the nation transitioned from a first into a second party system. The accompanying ideological issue of the locus of power—in the national government or within the states—posed an ongoing and divisive challenge.

In the 1780s, under the Articles of Confederation, the champions of states' rights faced rather difficult times economically, politically, and diplomatically. Their failures provided the opportunity for a Constitutional Convention in 1787 and the rise of a more balanced vision that left residual power in the states but now placed significant authority in the hands of the national government. The Federalist Party, which broadly embodied that central viewpoint, found itself repeatedly confronted by disenchanted Americans who felt their constitutional rights were being violated. The ascendency of the opposition Democratic-Republicans failed to resolve the broader question. From the Whiskey Rebellion in Pennsylvania in 1794 to the nullification crisis in South Carolina in 1832, periodic public and political disruptions arose as a means to defy and limit control from the capital.

The emergence of a second party system in the 1820s continued to reflect the division. Jacksonian Democrats, who embraced a more limited view of centralized power, faced the Whigs, who advocated a proactive role for government in promoting economic growth. The Democrats under President Martin Van

Buren suffered a reversal of fortune when an economic collapse—the Panic of 1837—impacted the political landscape. In 1840, the Whigs challenged Van Buren with an innovative and populist campaign that featured the War of 1812 hero William Henry Harrison as their candidate. Harrison's purportedly common-man background enabled him to identify with a "Log Cabin and Hard Cider." The strategy worked. The contest brought out an impressive 80 percent of the eligible male voters. The Whig triumph reflected the competitive split between the parties in battles for both the White House and Congress throughout the decade. Both groups focused on economic issues, as well as the image of their candidates, to increase their support. While rising antislavery forces began to organize as the Liberty Party (1840 and 1844) and later within the Free Soil Party (1848 and 1852), their numbers remained small, as Americans clung to the two major parties.[3]

The role of women in politics also evolved. New Jersey had uniquely offered the suffrage to women in 1797 but repealed that right a decade later. Although denied the vote, by the 1840s women had become engaged in the public sphere and took a more active role in politics. Attending rallies and campaign events, speaking out on behalf of candidates (often Whig), and editing or writing for newspapers, women made their presence known.

The economy remained firmly rooted in agriculture. Nine million farmers constituted 70 percent of the labor force and produced 65 percent of the nation's total exports. Within ten years the number of farms rose to 1.5 million, with an average size of more than two hundred acres. Access was helped by keeping the price of federal land to an affordable $1.25 per acre. Farming continued to hold the greatest promise of an independent lifestyle where a family could acquire property and carve out their destiny. The advent of the "market revolution" transformed the economy over time from one of self-sufficiency and marginal investment to one of borrowing, buying additional land, and planting for profit. Commercial farmers would be aided by Cyrus McCormick's patent for a reaper (1834) and John Deere's manufacture of a steel plow (1837). Technology and science supported the savvy farmer who had capital to invest.[4]

Transportation of goods from country to city and back again was critical. Local wagon roads had been supplemented with the National Road and a series of turnpikes to provide cheap access to markets in the East. An expansive river system also made the shipment of merchandise by flatboat, keelboat, steamboat, and, to a lesser extent, canals profitable. An impressive three thousand miles of railroad track linked East and West but tended to move people rather than commodities. Whether crops were sold domestically or overseas, the American mind-set embraced the idea that only self-imposed limits on hard work could keep a man from success. Accordingly, many whites became convinced that the Indians must be removed and land acquired in the West to allow future generations to hold on to the agrarian dream.[5]

Women served a critical functional role in this evolving economy both on the family farm and in the emerging manufacturing sector. From an early age, rural girls understood the hard, repetitious, and unending nature of their duties inside and outside the cabin. They lived their daily lives in a limited space with a maximum of predictability and a minimum of excitement. Understandably, many would seek the freedom and opportunity to earn wages in an urban environment.

In the early republic, cities along the Atlantic coast grew apace, and women found work as independent contractors, often as domestic help or in sewing garments in their homes, for which they were paid as piecework. These women endured low wages and marginal living conditions, especially if they were unmarried or had been abandoned by their husbands. Some struggling women, along with later-arriving Irish immigrant girls, might turn to prostitution as a livelihood or to supplement their income. The so-called Bowery girls exuded a flair and independence that made them appear more entrepreneurs than victims. The double standard remained very much alive, however, and the young woman who sacrificed her virtue had little future in respectable society. Whether women engaged in prostitution by necessity or by choice, their increased numbers in cities like New York signified yet another aspect of the changing role of women that demanded a response from a troubled society.[6]

Following the War of 1812, new opportunities presented themselves outside the farm and home in the form of the factory system. The Northeast, especially New England, experienced a dramatic growth in industry. Owners took advantage of steam power and the river system to build an extensive web of mills that would marginalize the artisan and craftsman. Machine-oriented tasks often required limited skills and training. While shoes, clocks, and tinware were all manufactured for broad and less expensive consumption, textiles commanded the lion's share of the capital and the labor market.

Desperate for workers, the owners turned to young women from farms and villages in the region. Thousands of women, girls, and children—as many as eight thousand in Lowell, Massachusetts, alone—would spin and weave up to fourteen hours a day for $3.00 per week under a rigid system of bells that dictated their time for work, nourishment, and sleep. They lived in a protective boardinghouse milieu intended to guard their safety and virtue. The system flourished, though many Jeffersonian Americans viewed wage labor and the emergence of women in the workforce outside the home as a betrayal of traditional values. The girls ate, slept, and talked together and developed a sense of independence that challenged and threatened conventional views. If they could function and even prosper in such an environment, then what could be said of female inferiority?

Enduring hard, noisy labor and a restrictive situation, the women earned money that could be saved, perhaps for a dowry, perhaps to start their own business, or perhaps to send home to family. In 1834, when pushed to the limit by the mill owners' efforts to increase the pace of their work while cutting wages by 15 percent, they rebelled by striking—"a turn out." The action, which involved more than eight hundred women, failed. Two years later, the bosses attempted to raise their rents. The second strike involved twice as many women, lasted several months, had community support, and succeeded. The depression that followed, however, exacerbated the tension between labor and management and led ultimately to the operatives' forming the first female union in 1845 and pushing for a ten-hour workday.

Certainly, most "Lowell girls" did not intend to dedicate their lives to factory work; many aspired to the lifestyle of the new urban middle class. They often departed after a few years. But they opened the door to employment outside the home for laboring-class women. Worried factory owners soon turned to Irish immigrants as a more manageable alternative to the increasingly confrontational Americans.[7]

The situation was dramatically different among women in the emergent urban middle and upper classes. Some possessed the capital and education to open small businesses, usually related to an element of fashion, while most assumed their own newly imposed societal responsibilities. The changing cityscape posed both opportunity and danger to the American family. Crime, poverty, disease, and generally bad moral influences had taken hold as the nature of the population and the size of the community increased. Men prepared to go out and meet the challenges and reap the rewards of the business sector, so the role of women—and wives specifically—needed to be altered. As the scholar Keith Melder emphasizes, the functional woman of the countryside became the sentimental and ornamental woman in the city. The view was that women, delicate and sensitive, should be sheltered in the home in a created private sphere, guarded against exposure to the rougher aspects of urban life. Their labor no longer needed, they could provide greater service to the family in a different capacity.[8]

Men anxiously sought to identify such a contributing role, which would help stabilize a culture seemingly gone awry and also obviate the threat to the male-dominated public political and economic sphere. Accompanied by sympathetic women, they devised the notion of "republican motherhood" and the "cult of true womanhood" as defining a proper societal position and appropriate duties. Broadly speaking, these involved emphasizing the place of the mother and wife within the home.

The architecture of the house would be altered to allow more space for the essential and important tasks of childrearing and homemaking. This private sphere would allow the woman to exert her knowledge and moral authority within the family with regard to basic skills, civic responsibility, and the Bible. The "cult" believed that the "true woman," defined as demonstrating the virtues of piety, purity, domesticity, and submissiveness, would channel her feelings into the home. The intent was to respect her emotional feelings and moral station, while acknowledging her physical and intellectual weakness. The strategy met with mixed results.[9]

Education played a critical role in changing the status quo and aiding female advancement. By the 1830s, a system of public schools appeared on the horizon in several states. Two decades later, approximately 90 percent of white men and women were literate. A reading revolution that encompassed newspapers, magazines, pamphlets, and books suggests a more informed citizenry, and it opened doors to women beyond the home. Women of all classes might acquire a primary education, and those of the upper classes could advance further, some enrolling at the newly opened (1837) female college in Massachusetts at Mount Holyoke. A number entered the workforce outside the home as elementary-school teachers. Intelligence and curiosity, however, combined with education and means, and available time in the day, to move women onto the avenue of reform and social change.

Inspired by the revivalist religious outpouring of the era labeled "The Second Great Awakening," many women of the middle class converted and found themselves confronting a series of spiritual and moral challenges. Concerned women first met these difficulties of a culture in fluctuation by gathering to organize prayer groups, stage lectures, distribute literature, and raise funds for worthy causes. Society allowed and even encouraged them to engage in such moral actions.

These activities would soon take them outside the home, however, morphing into more controversial undertakings in the public sphere. Immigration and industrialization brought with them urban problems, while moral issues, including the abolition of slavery, restrictions on alcohol, and world peace demanded attention, as did capital punishment, prison reform, mental health, and juvenile delinquency. And what of rights for women in terms of property ownership, divorce, and child custody? While men generally assumed the leadership roles in the sponsoring organizations, the number of women involved rose exponentially. The stage was set for their activism at the onset of the Mexican-American War.[10]

Mexico

A superficial examination of Mexico circa 1840 reveals many of the same political, economic, and social issues and divisions as its northern neighbor experienced. A more careful reading of the subject, however, exposes deep-rooted problems that placed the nation in a precarious position as it prepared to confront the United States in 1846.

After a decade-long struggle, Mexico won its independence from Spain in 1821. Forces advocating a monarchy briefly triumphed as Agustin de Iturbide claimed the throne for less than a year (1822–23). Opposition elements overthrew the emperor and formed a republic in 1824 that extended as far north as Texas and as far west as California. The huge expanse grew to comprise twenty states and four territories and numbered more than 7 million people. The territories, such as New Mexico (ca. 60,000) and California (ca. 90,000), were lightly populated overall and made up largely of mestizos (of mixed European and Indian ancestry) and *indios* (of Indian ancestry).

In a mirror image of the struggle experienced in Philadelphia in the 1780s, Mexicans hotly debated matters of identity and state power. The federal Constitution of 1824 vested real clout in the states and their officers rather than in the regime in Mexico City. Influence emanating from the capital came from Congress, not the president. While the federalists dominated, the centralist groups, which desired a stronger national state and some even the restoration of the monarchy, continued to push back against the new constitution. Formal political parties did not exist, so the lines of opposition were drawn philosophically and organized around social groups such as the Masonic orders.

As the decade progressed, regionalism persisted in many states, and distance from the capital seemed to encourage independence of action. Accordingly, local populations passed laws reflecting their variant views on subjects such as taxes and religion. The abolition of slavery was the one subject that had the support of virtually all Mexicans, except the new Anglo chattel-owning settlers in the

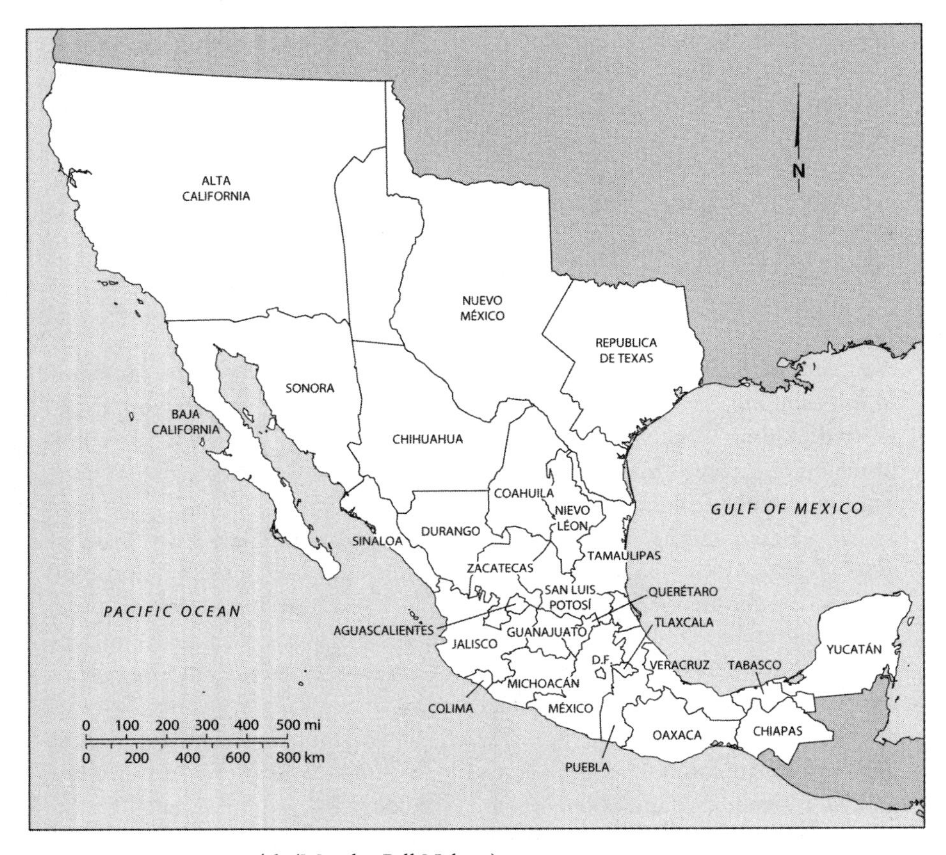

Mexican states in 1846. (Map by Bill Nelson)

northern province of Coahuila y Texas. By 1829, slavery had been eliminated except in that province, where the Texans flaunted the law and the government was too weak to enforce it.

Problematically for the nation, dissatisfaction with the government often manifested itself through the military and its leaders. Antonio López de Santa Anna, a hero of the War of Independence, served as president on eleven different occasions from 1833 to 1855 and symbolized the effort of the army to act as a bridge between Congress and the people. Attacking the legislature as inept, he seized power through the public proclamation *(pronunciamiento)* of Cuernavaca in May 1834 and governed with the authority of a virtual dictator. Angry and frustrated centralists saw this devolution as a threat to the republic and gained control of Congress in 1835. They quickly moved to oust the 1824 Constitution and replace it with the Seven Laws, constitutional reform that brought new and extensive power to conservatives in Mexico City.[11]

Predictably, several states responded violently to attacks on their authority. After a brief conflict, the celebrated 1836 revolt in Texas ended in the establishment of a new country. Less successful uprisings were launched in Zacatecas (1835), New Mexico (1837), the Republic of the Rio Grande (Coahuila, Nuevo León, and Tamaulipas, 1840), Yucatán (1841), and Tabasco (1841). The Chimayo Rebellion in New Mexico involved matters of class and race and received meaningful support from the Pueblo Indians. In Santa Fe, the rebels seized the Palace of the Governors and killed the governor. Manuel Armijo, who assumed the executive duties, crushed the revolt after a few months. Only the upheaval in Yucatán lasted over time (1848). Each insurgency, however, reflected the locals' disillusionment with the central government and the intention in several instances to separate from Mexico. Importantly, badly needed resources were drained from the coffers in the capital, the army tarnished its reputation in many quarters, and commitment to the nation-state took a step backward. In some desperation, with the advent of the war with the Americans, the old Constitution of 1824 was restored in the summer of 1846.

Somehow the economy survived, and aspects of it even grew amid the political chaos. The overwhelmingly rural population (80 percent) lived in small towns or pueblos, on haciendas or ranchos, and worked the fields. The peasantry rarely owned the land they tilled, paying rent and incurring often impossible debts to their wealthy masters in the church or gentry. While agriculture remained generally productive, the farmers struggled to make steady profits or to invest effort in land they could not own.[12]

Mexicans held out great hope for the mining and manufacturing sector. The mines proved the most profitable aspect of the economy, at least for the owners. Silver, and to a lesser extent gold, yielded a majority of Mexico's exports and more than 18 million pesos a year. Yet silver production had dropped sharply because of internal unrest and foreign invasion, and workers benefited little under brutal conditions. Many officials banked their economic future on manufacturing and the prospects of immigration of European and American technology, capital, managers, and, sometimes, experienced workers. The government established the Banco de Avio in 1830 with a capitalization of 1 million pesos as an "assistance bank" to aid those in need of money to launch a project. The cotton fields supplied a burgeoning textile industry if the right elements came together.

Women provided the labor force for these new cloth and cigarette factories, and although the pay was low, it offered an income alternative to demeaning domestic labor. Indeed, employment could be found in the more than one hundred cotton yarn and cloth plants established by 1846. Overall, the confluence of resources proved difficult for individual investors, however, and while the manufacturing sector showed gradual growth in the 1840s, the real industrial revolution lay ahead.[13]

Moreover, the frontier, which held such economic promise for Americans, also drew thousands of Mexicans to the borderlands from California into northern Mexico. The prospect of a new life in ranching, agriculture, or mining stimulated growth but was too often compromised by ongoing conflicts with the Indians. The frontier wars regularly exhausted the financial resources and manpower of the new republic and became an embarrassment for Mexico City. Violence generated by the Apache in New Mexico and the Comanche along the Texas border consumed lives and property, and the central government seemed incapable of squelching the threat. Over time, many in the borderlands, feeling intermittently threatened and ignored by the government, became disillusioned; some even welcomed the arrival of the Americans as saviors. Concurrently, the Mexican government came to disdain the frontier population, especially the mountain peoples *(serranos),* as "barbarians." These divisions took their toll.[14]

Mexican society was implacably bound by race, class, and gender. Position and privilege came with ethnicity and lightness of skin color. The status of a mixed-blood mestizo declined if the bronzeness of his flesh came to resemble that of an *indio.* European-born whites and their *criolla* (Creole) heirs formed a dominant minority who were particularly resistant to any change that might threaten their socioeconomic or political status. They increasingly gravitated to the larger towns and cities for their lifestyle, culture, and education.

The Indians, in contrast, lived essentially in ignorance, poverty, and virtual slavery. They formed the exploited peasantry and the majority of those unwilling soldiers conscripted into the army. A contemporary observer penned *Considerations on the Political and Social Situation of the Mexican Republic, 1847* as a lesson on the failings of his country. There was no reason for the lower classes to sacrifice themselves to defend an uncaring society. He caustically added that the peasantry viewed "everything that can possibly happen to them with the utmost indifference." Following independence, some Mexican leaders hoped to advance the economy and society by educating the citizenry. Congress passed a law in 1842 that made education compulsory for boys and girls aged seven to fifteen. The strategy largely failed. Incremental gains were made, but the vast majority of both men and women remained illiterate. Whether that outcome suited the goals of the ruling class is debatable.[15]

Women found themselves bound not only by a lack of learning but also by a culture, not unlike its Yankee counterpart, in which men attempted to restrict the role of women to the domestic sphere. They largely succeeded. Women of the upper and middling classes maintained their respectability by efficiently managing the home and never venturing out in public unaccompanied. The silk-clad mistress of the hacienda and her daughters spent endless hours at needle-work, light chores, reading, and worship. Labor that calloused the hands was inappropriate. Those duties were carried out by unmarried *indio* girls from the countryside who supplied the domestic help in the cities and manor houses. In the villages, women performed similar household duties, crafting endless numbers of tortillas, minding the children, and maintaining the garden and the animals. Minimal opportunity existed for employment outside the home. In the cities, married lower-class women frequently sold food in local markets and functioned as seamstresses or midwives. The added reals were a critical supplement to the meager wages of their husbands. The aforementioned textile factories also provided an alternative source of income to a restricted number of women, particularly in northern Mexico.[16]

The legal status of women varied from state to state. They might be permitted to own property, and wealthy widows fared best in terms of independence and authority. Most Mexican states lowered the age of majority, the right to marry without parental consent, and emancipation from a father's control *(patria potestas)* to under twenty-five. These changes somewhat empowered single women but did little to help wives and daughters. Mexican women did enjoy greater sexual freedom than their American sisters, however. Adultery was illegal, but extramarital affairs were commonplace. Their discovery usually resulted in no damage to the character or the reputation of the woman involved. Thus, by the early 1840s many Mexican women held some legal rights and experienced sexual freedom but faced limited opportunities in the workplace and virtually no education or political role.[17]

On the eve of war with the United States, Mexico found itself a deeply divided country with a hostile, violent, and corrupt political culture, a stressed economy, and a social structure that offered hope and promise to few. The notion of a common identity remained elusive. "In Mexico, there has not been, nor could there have been, a national spirit," a dour Mexican commented in 1847, "for there is no nation."[18]

And the War Came

On April 25, 1846, the lives of Lola Sanchez, Nancy Conner, and women like them on both sides of the Rio Grande changed dramatically. A reconnaissance party of eighty US troops had been attacked by a larger Mexican force on the north bank of the Rio Grande, some fifteen miles upstream from an outpost named Fort Brown. Seventeen Americans were killed or wounded, and many of the remainder were captured. When word reached the White House on May 8, President James K. Polk lost no time in dubbing this act unprovoked aggression and a cause for war. Five days later, Polk's message persuaded an overwhelming majority in Congress that hostilities were justified.

The ensuing struggle, which cost thousands of lives, and the Mexicans their empire, was of course much more complex than an incidental encounter along the Rio Grande. Polk had been narrowly elected in 1844, defeating the iconic Whig political veteran Henry Clay in a race that produced a virtual draw in the popular vote. Polk, who had taken office in March 1845, had championed US territorial expansion, focusing upon incorporating the Lone Star Republic of Texas and settling the boundary dispute with the British over the Oregon country. These issues had been the centerpiece of his recent campaign. In contrast, Clay, reflecting on the question of slavery and seeking to keep his party united, had waffled on the question of expansion. If elected, Harry of the West likely would have pursued a markedly different, less aggressive course regarding Mexico.[19]

By the summer of 1846, the issues troubling Polk had been resolved. Congress approved a Texas annexation treaty days before he entered the White House, although the southern border with Mexico remained in dispute. A compromise agreement with the Crown in June 1846 placed the Oregon boundary at 49° latitude. Numerous Democrats who had cried "54° 40′ or fight!" in their passion to acquire all of the territory remained embittered, but the president had other, larger issues to deal with.[20]

Polk, who proved to be devious, manipulative, and intelligent, was as ambitious for his nation as he was for himself. Parochial in many ways, the Tennessean was a visionary for his country. Not satisfied with acquiring Texas and a reasonable share of Oregon, the politician labeled "Young Hickory" also targeted the Southwest and California, territories possessed by the new Republic of Mexico. The Santa Fe trade and mineral wealth in New Mexico had already rendered the province's acquisition both desirable and profitable. California held agricultural promise even before the gold rush, and the potential of utilizing ports such as San Francisco to advance US commerce with the Far East—"an empire on the Pacific"—excited northeastern merchants, shippers, and whalers. The president joined many Americans in embracing the sweeping notion of Manifest Destiny, the God-given right of the United States to control North America. He also realized the advantage to national security of expanding to the Pacific Ocean.

Eliminating the danger that might be posed by a weaker Mexican neighbor also would reduce the possibility of an avaricious Britain or France intruding into continental affairs and challenging America's future from sea to sea.

Polk dispatched several diplomats to Mexico in 1845–46, notably the Spanish-speaking Louisiana congressman John Slidell, to determine the Mexican government's willingness to sell its northern territories. Slidell was empowered to offer as much as $25 million for the package. The administration of José Joaquín de Herrera grappled with deep-rooted financial and factional political problems, and Mexican honor and national pride could not be compromised. Herrera refused to officially receive Slidell, while his countrymen rattled their sabers in defiance of the US annexation of Texas. In January 1846, General Mariano Parades y Arrillaga ousted Herrera, and an increasingly irritated Polk dispatched Zachary Taylor's forces from Corpus Christi about 150 miles, to positions near Matamoros on the Rio Grande.[21]

By the end of March, the Americans had raised the flag and built their camp along the riverbank. This provocative act yielded neither military nor diplomatic results. An exasperated Slidell gave the Mexicans an ultimatum of negotiations or hostilities and prepared to return to Washington. The diplomat had failed, and Polk had run out of patience. In early May he spoke with his cabinet about bringing a declaration of war to Congress over $3 million in claims the United States had against Mexico. Whether Congress would have endorsed this rather shameless tactic quickly became a moot point. A late April attack on US troops, about which the president did not receive word until May 9, now enabled him to tear up his existing message and substitute the more forceful charge that the Mexicans had invaded and "shed American blood on American soil."[22]

What followed was an extended three-front war lasting eighteen months. Washington had hoped for a quick conflict, lasting perhaps six months to a year. Volunteers rushed to enlist; no one wanted to miss the great adventure. Although Polk labeled this a defensive conflict resulting from a brazen invasion, acquiring Mexican territory as indemnity was a high priority. To assist in obtaining the desired prizes, he had ordered a small "scientific expedition" of topographical engineers under the command of John C. Fremont, identified as The Pathfinder by the press, to draw maps of northern California and Oregon in 1845–46. Fremont's party was conveniently in the area when in June and July the Bear Flag Revolt of two dozen disgruntled American settlers occurred near San Francisco. Fremont soon assumed command of both elements, the Mexicans yielded, and the independent republic of California immediately gave way to US rule. In a complementary movement, the navy dispatched vessels of

US campaigns in northern Mexico/Southwest. (Map by Bill Nelson)

the Pacific squadron under Commodore John D. Sloat to the coast, where on July 7 he raised the Stars and Stripes over the port city of Monterey and declared himself governor of California.[23]

The War Department in turn ordered Colonel Stephen Watts Kearny's Army of the West, including a group of traders and a battalion of Mormons, to march out of Kansas for New Mexico. His objective was to take Santa Fe, which he did in August 1846 without firing a shot, and then proceed west to southern California. Kearny divided his already small force of sixteen hundred; many remained in occupation in New Mexico, while hundreds under the command of Alexander Doniphan moved south to attack the key city of El Paso and then continue on to Chihuahua. Kearny himself took only three hundred men on a hazardous trek toward San Diego, where in December his troops suffered a stinging defeat in an engagement with Californio lancers. Southern California had been occupied by August 1846, but dissident residents, angry over American policies, staged a four-month revolt that was only crushed when the US military combined its forces in January 1847. The resultant scramble for political power among the Americans, highlighted by Fremont's declaration of himself as governor, embarrassed almost everyone involved and produced a short-lived court martial for Fremont. At least Polk could take comfort in the fact that New Mexico and California were now secure for the Union.[24]

Meanwhile, Zachary Taylor, a crusty, sixty-one-year-old veteran of the Seminole War in Florida, moved quickly to establish his control of northeastern Mexico. Victorious in two engagements in May (Palo Alto and Resaca de la Palma), Old Rough and Ready laid siege to Monterrey, taking the city in late September after days of brutal street fighting. If the Americans expected peace talks to ensue at this juncture, they would be sorely disappointed. Instead, in February 1847 a large force of more than fifteen thousand soldiers under General Santa Anna challenged the US contingent of five thousand near Saltillo. Although many historians view the outcome as a stalemate, Americans hailed the two-day Battle of Buena Vista as a great victory. The Mexicans suffered several thousand casualties and withdrew from the field, enabling the US press to heap more praise upon the increasingly heroic Taylor.[25]

In spite of numerous defeats, the Mexicans were reluctant to negotiate a settlement to the war, prompting Polk to send a second army into the heart of the country. In March 1847, twelve thousand men under the command of General Winfield Scott, "Old Fuss and Feathers," landed outside Veracruz, on the east coast, with the intention of marching 250 miles inland and conquering Mexico City. A refusal to surrender Veracruz was met with a devastating bombardment that killed hundreds of civilians and produced the desired submission.[26]

Scott then tenuously embarked on a four-month march toward the capital, challenged along the way by both local guerrillas and Santa Anna's army. Again, the Americans gained a critical and improbable victory in mountainous terrain on April 18 at Cerro Gordo. Scott rested his men in the highland city of Puebla for three months, giving him the opportunity to refine his strategy. The contest for Mexico City began on August 20. American victories at the bloody Battle of Molino del Rey on September 8 and then the conquest of the castle at Chapultepec on September 12–13 marked the end of organized resistance.

Mexican national pride received a boost when, as the legend maintains, a half dozen cadets from the military academy—*el niños*—died in defense of their country. The last to fall leaped to his death from the castle walls wrapped in the Mexican flag rather than let it fall into the hands of the enemy. All was in vain: on September 14, 1847, American soldiers occupied the main square of the capital.[27]

Demoralized, factionalized, impoverished, and divided by regionalism, class, and race, the Mexicans proved no match for American firepower, leadership, and determination. In spite of Scott's victory, peace talks moved slowly, and the final Treaty of Guadalupe Hidalgo, which gave the Americans the desired western territories (more than 55 percent of Mexico) and the Rio Grande boundary, was not signed until February 2, 1848. In a somewhat puzzling move, Polk gave the Mexican government $15 million for the loss of New Mexico and California. The Americans finally withdrew from Mexico City in June and departed the country by the end of July.[28]

As thousands of men became entangled in the patriotic adventure that was the Mexican-American War, they left behind women like Nancy Conner and Lola Sanchez to assume new responsibilities, make vital decisions, and develop into the mainstays of their families. The conflict placed these women and others like them in roles that challenged and revealed their strengths and weaknesses, their commitment to causes, and their personal moral codes and values. Scholars have touched upon their experiences and acquainted the more engaged reader with some of these characters. In fact, in the last decade numerous works have appeared about the Mexican-American War, especially the military operations and the political significance. Regrettably, however, while women in the American Revolutionary and Civil War eras have drawn scholarly attention, too little effort has been dedicated to the Mexican-American War. No one volume has brought the lives of those who lived in anonymity together with those of the few celebrities. While hardly exhaustive, this work provides an introduction to these women and the issues that touched them in the late 1840s.

The chapters in this volume examine Mexican women in a variety of roles, on the battlefield and as active agents stirring the nationalistic fires of their menfolk. Concurrently, the dark-eyed señorita embodied the fantasy of thousands of American men, who either projected their dream through contemporary literature or attempted to make it a reality during the occupation of Mexico.

Soldiers often struggled with the moral and racial dimensions of their encounters with Mexican women. As proper Victorian men, they wondered whether it was appropriate for them to fall in love with or take advantage of women so "foreign," whose culture was so different from their own. Some men admired the women from afar. Other men revealed their dark side, easily compromising their values to exploit the women who were economically or physically unable to resist their advances. The voices of these men, both of conscience and without, appear regularly throughout the narrative. Their language and behavior, sometimes caring but too often brutal, harsh, and insensitive, should be understood as embodying the attitudes of a generation of Americans toward a people they considered inferior. The viewpoints, tone, and substance of those expressions should be considered as theirs alone.

At home, changing dynamics brought about evolving roles for American women. They bore their own burdens and causes, either championing the war and supporting the troops at home and in Mexico or forthrightly assuming unconventional roles as antiwar activists. The women editors and reporters were among the more determined and aggressive on both sides. Many found themselves close to the front, seizing available opportunities, performing tasks large and small, saving lives, or enriching themselves. Angels of the battlefield rivaled saloon temptresses for the public's attention. The latter had special appeal—dealing cards and caprice, alcohol and illusion, providing respite for the weary soldier, trapper, or trader. They were patriots, prostitutes, spies. Their stories and the impact of their lives, individually and collectively, are worthy of our consideration and deliberation.

1

Women, Reform, and the US Home Front

Americans rejoice in rallying to the colors. Offended by the despicable actions of foreign foes, they experience a rush of patriotic adrenalin and are expected to join as one to defend the nation-state. Such unity knows no gender boundaries. In 1846, most women endorsed the war against Mexico in spirit and effort. They embraced domestic duties of making flags and knitting socks, while many additionally shouldered the economic burdens of home and hearth. Whether it was tilling the fields of a small farm in Ohio or acting as a slave mistress in Louisiana, the role and responsibilities of thousands of women changed dramatically. With the passage of time, loneliness and cynicism enveloped some of them, while others determined that the war's righteousness was in doubt and joined the opposition. This group originated among supporters of the Whig Party in the Northeast, although antiwar sentiment spilled over into the upper South and the Midwest. Women in the world of politics proved somewhat novel and were not welcomed in all quarters. Even so, whether pro- or antiwar, these women made their voices heard and their presence known in the public sphere.

War Fever

On a warm Indiana morning in 1846, the Marion Volunteers stood at attention, awaiting the inspirational oratory that followed. They were not disappointed. Speaker after speaker stirred them to action, but none surpassed Mrs. Bolton, selected by the ladies of Indianapolis to present a handmade American flag to the unit. With great pride and some measure of angst, she encouraged them, "You heard that your country was invaded, you heard her call to arms and simultaneously our hearts responded, 'it is my country, and this army shall defend her.'"

Mrs. Bolton went on not only to praise their patriotism and courage in this time of national crisis but also to add a moral dimension: "In the flush of victory forget not the dictates of humanity; add no unnecessary insult to a fallen foe; let the world see that American soldiers are as generous as they are brave." At no loss for words, Captain Drake, the unit's commander, pledged that the Hoosiers would carry the banner with distinction all the way to the Mexican capital and reassured her, "Nor will we ever forget that generosity is the steady companion of true valor, and that the glory of victory cannot be brightened by deed of revenge and rapacity." Whether such promises could be kept was another matter entirely.[1]

A comparable scene played out in the southern part of the state, where young women had sewn flags and uniforms for departing troops. In Alabama, S. F. Nunnelee, who served in the Eutaw Rangers, well remembered the speeches, the cheering, and the presentation of the flag to the company in June 1846 by the local belle Sarah Inges. The Rangers and the Greensboro Volunteers were the only uniformed soldiers in the First Alabama Regiment. Nunnelee recollected with pride and amusement that the ladies had made his boys cottonade suits with straw hats, while the Greensboro troops received green worsted frock outfits. When they got to Camargo, Mexico, some weeks later, they were issued, no doubt to their relief and delight, navy blue suits, brass buttons, and caps. This caused consternation and jealousy among some other units, "who had a strong prejudice against us partly on this account." Nunnelee puzzled over why they should be viewed with disdain, "since our company, as a whole, was a more intelligent class of men—at least we thought so."[2]

The flags, functional in battle, were usually adorned by the stars and stripes or an eagle, yet they were designed to be attractive, with silk, embroidery, and fringe. In Knoxville, Tennessee, men raised the funds for a banner, allowing sufficient time for the women in the community to display their expertise. Labor on the fabricated standard, "made of the richest materials with exquisite workmanship," took place in Miss Rogers's schoolroom after 3:00 p.m. Rogers herself had the honor of presenting the flag to the unit in December 1847. Richard Edwards proudly noted that the flag flew in the breeze as the regiment marched off "to a foreign land to teach a foreign foe to pay proper respect to our flag and people. Thousands of white handkerchiefs were waved by lily white hands to bid us adieu."[3]

Numerous companies received handmade banners from resident women in elaborate ceremonies accompanied by appropriate inspirational remarks by one of the young ladies. The historian Teri Klassen contends, "Needlework in the form of the flag symbolized a contractual obligation between women, representing the home community, and the men who had volunteered to fight in

Mexico." The seriousness of the event was marked by a La Porte, Indiana, county officer, Robert Fravel, whose sister Marinda had helped sew the flag. Fravel promised that the banner "should be returned if there was left one man to bring it." Hundreds of miles down the Mississippi River, in New Orleans, a delighted Reverend Lewis Leonidas presented a similar fatalistic view, promising the ladies of Soule-Chapel that he wanted "to be buried with the beautiful banner around me as a winding sheet."[4]

The scholar Peggy Cashion raises the ancillary question of the "Spartan mother" in reference to whether sons, husbands, or brothers should die defending the colors rather than bring dishonor upon family, community, and country. The Female Academy in Nashville handed to the thousand men of the First Volunteer Regiment a silk flag sewn with the motto, "Weeping in solitude for the fallen brave is better than the presence of men too timid to strike for their country." After the war, John Blount Robertson vividly remembered the "immense assemblage" that had gathered and the "bright array of beauty" inspired by the senior class leader Miss Irene Taylor, who bestowed upon the men both boon and banner, along with some well-chosen comments. What a proud day for Tennessee! The state's fairest daughters had collected "in all the purity of maidenhood, to express in the strongest, yet most delicate manner" their support for the justice of the cause. That moment emulated the "same spirit that actuated the women of ancient Sparta, [who] had come to send their friends and brothers forth to battle, with the promise of praise to the brave and threats of infamy for him who faltered."[5]

In East Tennessee, Edwards made similar reference to a gathering of young women in Dover. The town was half under water from flooding along the Cumberland River, but the ladies gathered at the upper-floor windows to wave their handkerchiefs and enthusiastically cheer the boys as they sailed off to war. "Since the days of the brave Roman matron," Edwards recalled, "who having prepared shields for her sons and sent them forth to battle, with the injunction to return with them victorious or on them dead, woman has ever held the foremost rank in patriotic devotion and love of country." While this bravado attended numerous farewell ceremonies and was certainly present in the music and poetry of the time, Cashion argues that survival dominated the women's thinking.[6]

The historian Amy Kaplan introduces yet another important element of womanhood and empire in her discussion of the extension of the notion of domesticity. As the United States expanded, the concept of "civilizing" those encountered along the way by white Anglo-Saxon Protestants became a key element of American Manifest Destiny. Whether or not that sense of mission would be realized, women, as the center of the home, played "a major role in defining the contours of the nation and its shifting borders with the foreign." Kaplan argues for an abridgement of the idea of "separate spheres" for women, pointing out that authors on domesticity, particularly Catherine Beecher in her *Treatise on Domestic Economy* (1841), embraced themes relating to nationalism and foreign affairs. In her writing, greater mobility in the idea of the "home" becomes visible if the idea is extended "by imagining the nation as a home." Christian American women, Beecher believed, held the responsibility to promote the virtues of a highly ordered home, in which men would be elevated and reformed and would participate in a worldwide crusade. Women would become unified in this mission to strengthen the domestic sphere and nation internally, while simultaneously extolling the benefits of American values to a waiting world.

As Kaplan points out, the ambitious Beecher wanted to fuse "the boundlessness of the home with the boundlessness of the nation." For the good of the nation, the foreign must be conquered and domesticated. A very thin line existed between Beecher's vision of women and the cultural civilization of a continent and the newspaperman John L. O'Sullivan's notion of expansion, which claimed physical and political mastery of that same space. Although conventional wisdom has it that O'Sullivan coined the term *Manifest Destiny* to describe America's future, some scholars argue that the language was crafted by the expansionist columnist Jane Cazneau.[7]

Women, present at the departures of the troops, were very much aware of the honor culture that drove many soldiers to seek danger in combat and flirt with death. Diaries and letters by the men often reveal the desire to validate their manhood and enhance their image by demonstrating bravery. Such acts raised a man's prospects of both immediate reward in terms of recognition and promotion and, later, as a man of action and a patriot, rewards in business, law, or politics. Women knew that culture was difficult to alter, and found themselves walking a fine line between endorsing extreme and foolish actions in the name of the nation and encouraging the commonsense tactic of survival.

Some men did flee from combat, while others deserted. No doubt, a disgraced soldier could disappear in a large city, but small towns held a longer memory. Mary Gibson, at home in Indiana with four young children, had not heard from her husband, Captain Thomas Ware Gibson, following the Battle of Buena Vista in February 1847. Fearing his death and intensely agitated at his silence, she implored, "O Tommy, I cannot tell you how bad I have felt for the past four or five weeks." Mary had not written, could not write. Then the rumors drifted back to Clark County in April that the Hoosier state's finest had fled the line—they had not—and she demanded to know the truth. "It is said here that the Indiana troops showed themselves great cowards. It is said they all ran when the battle came on. If you did I think a good many of you got shot in the back from the number of officers kild. We all hate that most prodgeously. We would all rather you stood like good soldiers since you have gone there."

Mary's language reflects the common anxiety of many women, that of simply not knowing whether a loved one had survived a celebrated contest with heavy casualties. She evidenced her frustration not only in the judgmental statement about courage in combat but also in the rather cynical aside regarding officers being killed fleeing. Was she perhaps uneasy, too, about her own reputation and that of her family in Charleston should Thomas prove less than valorous? The phrase "since you have gone there" may also reflect Mary's disapproval of her husband's decision to enlist and leave a large family at home. Thomas probably noticed that Mary closed her letter with "good night" rather than a more traditional term of affection.[8]

Loss of reputation was not a problem for the Leland family of Missouri. Their son John died in January 1847, on the march with Stephen Watts Kearny's Army of the West. Leland expired from a fever following a short illness. His fellow soldier Marcellus Ball Edwards attended the funeral along with other members of the unit and complained bitterly about their medical care. Edwards grumbled that the hospital staff could not tell quinine from calomel and said that their lackluster treatment may have contributed to young Leland's demise. He warmly described his late comrade as "a sprightly young man, much esteemed by his company." A letter from his mother was found in his pocket expressing her wish that "she would sacrifice him at the cannon's mouth" rather than find he had deserted. Describing herself as a Spartan mother handing a shield to her son, Mrs. Leland had implored John to "return with it or return upon it—with it or on it."

Such language may well have been intended to steel individual resolve or reaffirm loyalty to the nation, but it rarely reflected the desire of most American mothers to lose their sons in a war with muddled purpose. Mothers and wives encouraged and endured, sometimes evincing a mock-Spartan spirit. When letters did arrive confirming the death of a loved one, the reaction was one of sorrow at the loss, not joy at the cost. As Edwards mournfully observed, "I can well judge of her grief and torture when we return without her boy."[9]

Doubts Arise

In a public plea in November 1846, the Connecticut reformer and antiwar activist D. W. Bartlett magnified the symbolism of the flag issue. The war remained popular, but why so with women? The number of flags and banners they crafted evidenced that ardor. It seemed impossible, a perplexed Bartlett pondered, that a true-hearted woman would love, honor, and idolize a man who had killed innocents. Strange, he thought, "that woman, who should love gentle things, and be full of humanity, strange that she should love war." Bartlett made an appeal for a rejection he believed would bury war: "For the love of God don't receive a murderer into your arms." The extent to which his entreaty met with a positive response is impossible to measure, though it clearly resonated with some women. Even after the war, the Pennsylvania editor Jane Swisshelm could not forgive her old friend Samuel Black for his service. Encountering him on the street, Swisshelm initially refused to take his hand, which she contended was stained with the blood of Mexican women and children, and accused him of murder.[10]

The Boston feminist Caroline Healey Dall responded to the appeal with several of the most scathing critiques of the war. Dall, the oldest of eight children, grew up in a Unitarian household in which education for women was valued. Her father, a wealthy businessman, encouraged his daughter's study of literature, writing, and languages. She felt a strong social and religious responsibility, particularly toward the working-class poor. Healey not only wrote articles voicing the importance of and right to an education and employment for women, but also operated a nursery and engaged in home visitations with destitute families. In 1840, her patronage of Elizabeth Peabody's bookstore, shelves bulging with challenging tracts on European romanticism and literary criticism, led to an introduction to the transcendentalist world of Margaret Fuller. This was heady stuff for the eighteen-year-old Caroline, who found that her brash assertiveness in the weekly group "conversations" was not always welcomed by either Peabody or the regular participant Ralph Waldo Emerson.

Even so, her intellectual growth was undeniable. Compassionate and determined, she found motivation in her faith and release in her social mission. Her marriage to Charles Dall in 1844 seemed to be providential. A community minister and social worker, he shared her values. Their ten-year relationship produced two children; sadly, it also revealed Charles's personal instability and failings as a preacher. In 1855, he accepted an appointment as a missionary to India, rarely returning home over the following three decades.[11]

During the Mexican-American War, Caroline combined her role as minister's wife, teaching and assisting with the parish, with her involvement in the rising tide of feminism. She wrote for the women's-rights magazine *Una* and helped fugitive slaves escape to Canada. In the summer of 1847, her moral opposition to the war yielded two impassioned and challenging expositions. Using the name "Domino," she launched a blistering attack in a piece entitled simply "The War," which was published on July 22 in the *Boston Daily Chronotype.* "No man with the least spark of true patriotism in his soul can look at the present condition of this country without shame, fear and foreboding," she began. Domino proceeded to indict the United States for provoking a war to advance slavery and invading the only country in the world that attempted to imitate its democratic example. In a campaign of conquest the United States had killed women and children and perpetrated "outrages which make men shudder at the recital." The war was unjust and unconstitutional, Domino asserted, and the possibility existed of presidential impeachment for Polk's involvement in "this great national crime." While acknowledging the "efficiency, skill, and courage of our troops" in battle, she contended that the invasion of Mexico would prove more difficult once the army faced the people themselves.[12]

In "Thoughts on War," Dall remarked how easy it had been for Americans to live their daily lives giving little thought to the events transpiring in Mexico until they were reminded by the horrific bombardment of civilians in Veracruz. Wars had been fought, she mused, over ideas, religion, and land. What could be said of this dispute, in which neither side held the high moral ground? She cared not how much the war cost. What if the millions of dollars had been spread over Mexico to dispatch Protestant missionaries to assist in strengthening republican government and providing education? Importantly, she challenged her readers not to blame the government for the slaughter but to accept personal responsibility for supporting the war. As for the veterans, "American woman! What think you of the horrid crimes, inseparable from war, committed by husbands and brothers whom you and I have loved in the Mexican campaign? Can you offer your flushed cheeks in affectionate welcome of brutes and ravishers from their abandoned life?" Better for the men to die on the field, she declared, than to return to the women who loved them "with the stamp of excess, of vice on thy bloated brow and passionate lip." Dall could still accept the soldiers with broken limbs and mangled bodies, but "save us from encountering your depraved hearts, your reeling senses—the monuments of your dead souls."[13]

Bartlett, Swisshelm, and Dall, however, represented a minority of Americans, especially in the first year of the conflict. The patriotic outpouring of women extended beyond flag making to a frenzy of needlework that swept the country. Klassen has painstakingly documented the role of the quilt in endorsing the war and sustaining the soldiers. She convincingly reasons that quilt making "made patriotism, and thus the material expressions of patriotism, especially fashionable." While quilts had little practical value in a war fought in Mexico, through these handcrafted works of art women could enter the public sphere without abandoning their traditional roles. Women could raise funds for worthy causes, interact with nonrelated women, and attend public and semipublic events such as parades, flag presentations, fairs, court days, and camp meetings.[14]

Southern Indiana, the focus of Klassen's study, was a hotbed of Democratic politics, and President-elect Polk received a thunderous response when he visited the area in late 1844. The state volunteered five thousand men in the war, most departing along the Ohio River. The assembling of the enlistees accorded the local population an opportunity to give their heroes a proper send-off. In Madison, Indiana, the ladies of the town donated no quilts but generously provided the soldiers with clothing and other necessities appropriate for their dedication and upcoming privation.

Meanwhile, the quilters would not be outdone. In their nationalistic fervor, they honored the president with a floral pattern in red, green, and white dubbed "Polk's Fancy." Considerable debate still exists over whether elements of the pattern signified support for Manifest Destiny or for Texas annexation. Regardless, Klassen claims that "women used quilt making to bridge personal and public realms, elevating the role of homemaker to that of female citizen." Her point rings true. Five hundred miles away, on Long Island, among much public fanfare, the ladies of Oyster Bay raffled off their quilts to benefit the troops. A local officer stationed in Mexico City had taken along a comforter made by his mother. Unluckily, the bedding had been half-eaten by a hungry mule. He informed his mother that he wanted to purchase several tickets to improve his chances of winning a replacement, a quilt made by his sister.[15]

From farms, towns, and cities across the nation, flushed with patriotism, volunteers such as those in Indiana rushed to enlist. As Polk had boldly emphasized, the Mexicans had brought this conflagration upon themselves by their own aggression. Their "faithless rulers" had rejected the president's repeated olive branches of peace. Now, the Americans found themselves in a defensive war, obliged to take whatever measures were necessary to conclude it.[16]

As the casualties mounted and the war dragged on, however, the romantic perceptions of the nature of combat declined, and so did the number of volunteers. Conscription was never implemented, so rhetoric, martial music, barbeques, parades, ceremony, and song all became standard fare to inspire the departing troops, reaffirm the appreciation of the community, especially the women, and offer hope for the safe return of the men. Still, in 1847 doubt began to spread, and numbers became a concern for the military. Recruiters used a variety of tactics, including attacks on male honor, to sustain the units. One South Carolina enlistee chided his reluctant younger brother, "Mother ought to have made you volunteer."

Communities hastened to raise thousands of dollars to equip and outfit their men. The women in Edgefield, South Carolina, led by Susan Pickens, the daughter of the future governor Francis W. Pickens, evidenced their support by delivering a banner to the company bearing the Spartan-like message "Follow wherever it waves, and bear it aloft in triumph, or perish beneath it in glory." The McDuffie Guards and the Old '96 Boys went off to Mexico, and within a year the caskets began to return to the Palmetto State for burial. Mrs. Anna Maybin, of Columbia, wrote to a soldier in occupation in Mexico about the "considerable feeling" generated by the remains, and her anguished aside spoke for many: "Oh how my heart sikens when I reflect on that war."[17]

The conflict never enjoyed the same popularity in abolitionist New England that it did in other parts of the nation. In Newburyport, the former congressman and minister to China Caleb Cushing faced a challenge in trying to organize the First Massachusetts Volunteers. The Bay State was a hotbed of antiwar activity, and the legislature refused to fund the troops, compelling Cushing to contribute five thousand dollars of his own money to launch the regiment in the winter of 1846. Elected colonel, Cushing made a public appeal to the residents of Old Essex to provide for their boys. The community responded. The industrialist Abbott Lawrence sent shirts, socks, and handkerchiefs. Mary Jackson Smith helped raised two hundred dollars from Newburyport women, and more came in from theater benefits. "Like yourself, [the appeal] is calculated to touch women's souls," Smith flattered Cushing. His new uniform was complemented by a pair of spurs, accompanied by the note, "May they urge you on to deeds of high and noble daring, and never halt, unless in the cause of humanity." He also received a bloodstained sash worn by a British officer in the War of 1812, an ornamented sword, and a horse, which was shipped ahead to New Orleans. The colonel was touched by an elegant ring, "a real Talisman," presented by the ladies of Essex.[18]

The ring became a touchstone for the Unitarian reformer and poet William H. Burleigh's screed in the New York paper the *Emancipator* comparing the fair ladies of New England and the gentle señoritas of Mexico. Burleigh blasted these "recreant Yankee women" for making fools of themselves by hailing their local hero. The gift signaled a public demonstration "of their approval of murder and rapine in the presentation to Col. Cushing of a ring which he bought for himself; and in other ridiculous ceremonies intended to cheer on their townsman to his blood hound's work." In comparison, Burleigh tenderly reminisced about the ministering Mexican angels of the battlefield at Buena Vista, real women with human hearts who had risked their lives to provide sustenance to friend and foe. "The true measure of a nation's advance is found in a rude and savage people," he posited, "who can keep alive the blessed flow of pity and generous philanthropy" while murderous combat raged all about them.[19]

The historian Amy Greenberg illustrates the conflicted nature of the war for many women, even reformers. Greenberg notes that in sharp contrast to Burleigh's condemnation of the bloodshed, the antiwar editor Caroline Kirkland felt obliged to point with pride to the "gallant self-devotion" of American soldiers in holding the field at Buena Vista. Kirkland exemplified the contradiction and anguish felt by many American women. The product of a socially prominent, if not wealthy, New York City family, Caroline attended her aunt's female academy, where she excelled in both academics and the arts. When her father died unexpectedly, she became responsible for her mother and ten siblings. Moving to upstate New York, Caroline taught school and met William Kirkland, a classics scholar at Hamilton College, whom she married in 1828. Their union produced seven children. The Kirklands continued to teach, first at a women's seminary in western New York and then in Detroit.

By the mid-1830s their careers had begun to move in different directions. William became a land speculator, establishing the settlement of Pinckney, while Caroline began to record their adventures on the dreary Michigan frontier. Although his efforts at town-building proved financially unspectacular, her lively and often amusing anecdotes about village life compiled in *A New Home—Who'll Follow?* (1839) earned national acclaim for its satirical style and realism. Two more volumes followed, each enhancing her reputation and winning plaudits from critics such as Edgar Allan Poe, who enthused about her portrayal of the Kirklands' raw, rough-and-tumble backwoods world.

While Caroline enjoyed economic success from her works, William struggled to make Pinckney a profitable venture. A combination of her too candid exposé of their neighbors and the family's monetary issues prompted their return to New York in 1846. Caroline established a girls' school, expanded her writing, and founded a literary salon that included the luminaries William Cullen Bryant and Poe. The enchanted Poe determined that Caroline's "whole countenance beams with benevolence and intellect." Meanwhile, William began editing two newspapers, the *Evening Mirror* and the *Christian Inquirer.* His accidental drowning months later left her in charge of the family and their finances. When the opportunity presented itself to edit a new journal, the *Union Magazine of Literature and Art,* Caroline eagerly accepted.[20]

The *Union Magazine* attracted many of the day's most talented male and female writers, poets, composers, engravers, and artists. Caroline Kirkland provided oversight and contributed to the monthly publication, whose pages could not ignore the war with Mexico. Her editorial hand revealed a patriotic sympathy for the courage and sacrifice of the American soldier, yet a visceral reaction to the brutality and senselessness of war, especially that particular clash. No doubt readers were moved to tears by the promise of a lovers' reunion in the ballad "A Soldier's Departure" or bemused by the snippet about Winfield Scott's chapeau. A tribute to the brave death of Henry Clay Jr. at the Battle of Buena Vista was accompanied by a poignant and touching engraving.

Concurrently, the magazine published a moving etching of a family of modest means that drew the eye to a woman prostate on the wooden floor, her face buried in a crumpled newspaper. The title, "News from the War," was supplemented by a vignette asking, "What shall we say of the wives and mothers who remain quietly at home to endure the prospect of such agony as is here portrayed? Which of the victims excites the deeper compassion? Who needs most the all-sustaining goodness of God, and the tenderest sympathy of man?"[21]

A later issue included a recollection titled "The Gallant Exploit of Lieutenant Schuyler Hamilton," detailing the action of the young officer, wounded and surrounded by Mexicans, who managed to dispatch four of the enemy before miraculously cutting his way through and escaping into the American lines. The daring exploit was supplemented by an engraving depicting Hamilton on horseback shooting a Mexican lancer at point-blank range. Kirkland felt obliged to explain the image to her readers. Clearly memorializing the demise of the valiant Clay and lamenting the plight of a grieving widow was one issue; celebrating the violence of war was quite another. Kirkland clarified in an editorial aside that she did not control the illustrative material in the magazine and did not approve of the content of the Hamilton engraving. She was happy to point out, however, that the artist "consents in deference to her feelings, to refrain from warlike pictures in future." His agreement, she noted with satisfaction, proved "that he was truly a man of peace." Kirkland was not alone in equivocating between humanitarian ideals and patriotic ardor in her commentary on the conflict.[22]

What were American women back home to conclude about the Mexican-American War? Should they adopt the "my country right or wrong" attitude held by many? The causes seemed murky: had the contest been provoked by the Mexicans, as the president declared, or a land grab to advance the institution of slavery? Patriotism ran strong in 1846, but commitment had ebbed by the following year. Relatively few Americans made personal sacrifices. The war lacked a draft of manpower, heavy taxes, or the suspension of civil liberties. Idealism and honor manifested themselves, but many men enlisted for bonus money, employment, and the promise of land. Was the war worth the mounting US casualties and the countless civilian lives lost in Mexico? Humanity itself seemed a casualty as Americans weighed the quarrel from afar. Evidence clearly demonstrates that many wives, mothers, sweethearts, and daughters supported the effort with their hearts, minds, purses, or a combination of all three.

Expectations of a quick victory had been unrealistic. Accordingly, disenchantment with the president and his policies grew rapidly. Poor mail service combined with a rising death toll to heighten anxiety among the waiting women. The US officer corps had a solid number of Whigs and frustrated young men seeking promotion who blamed Polk for their personal plight and the conduct of the war. Their wives and mothers often came to share those views, if they did not hold them in 1846. Young Hickory had miscalculated, and his insensitive blundering, they believed, had cost both the men in the field and their families dearly. Women wanted peace and the return home of troops as soon as possible. An inept Polk should be impeached, some cried, while others were willing to extend the blame beyond the White House to Congress.[23]

Since American arms enjoyed almost unbridled success in combat, the question for many women was neither about victory nor about the causes of the war. Rather they understandably personalized the dispute and impatiently desired a restoration of the status quo ante bellum on the home front. Most women remained in the domestic sphere, though some joined the antiwar movement for philosophical or practical reasons. Many others may have grumbled to their friends or kin, but they continued to either passively or actively support the troops by painstakingly crafting flags, knitting blankets, socks, and shirts, raising funds, and writing letters.

The compassion of women also began to more visibly manifest itself. They became more actively engaged as the army shipped the sick and wounded soldiers to the United States. The plight of these returning troops, maimed, ragged, half-starved, caused an outpouring of sympathy in city after city. In Baltimore, women formed a charitable society to help feed the troops, and in Boston an outraged press demanded to know why soldiers were permitted to "come home, as it were, in disgrace." The importance of the return, especially to troops from small towns, appeared repeatedly in their later letters, diaries, and memoirs. S. F. Nunnelee recalled with muted pleasure his Alabama unit's welcome. "We were glad, and friends were not ashamed of our record as men and soldiers." Whether the women involved actually agreed with the stated purpose of the war is unclear, but apparently many would not callously abandon a loved one in the field nor, it seemed, on their doorstep.[24]

Women and Politics

Other women, some perhaps with less familial risk, became passionately embroiled in opposition to the war, actively engaging in the contest from a political and reformist vantage point. The historian Elizabeth Varon has documented the ties between Whig politics and social activism before the war. Dating back to the rousing support bestowed by women on William Henry Harrison in 1840, the involvement of Virginia women in national campaigns grew over time. More accomplished and celebrated than Harrison, Henry Clay garnered even stronger support from women in the 1844 election. Only weeks after his narrow defeat, several thousand led the effort for the erection of a statue of the Sage of Ashland in Richmond. The Clay Association and its auxiliaries spread throughout the state, and soon funds came from all over the South. Members of the Female Humane Society, the Female Colonization Society, the Mount Vernon Association, and various local poor-relief agencies endorsed the effort. Inevitably, the Democratic press decried the compromise that true Commonwealth ladies made with "the great work of generosity and patriotism" for the sake of partisanship. The women had sacrificed their gender to become rebellious challengers of male authority.[25]

The press weighed in on both sides heatedly debating the appropriateness of women in the political sphere. As Varon emphasizes, however, these women were generally not representative of Virginia's underclasses. Instead, they stood for two primary tenets of Whiggery—social elitism and an emphasis on statesmanship and nationalism. Rejecting the character assassination of the Jacksonians, Whig women firmly believed that Clay manifested traits they found appealing, especially his reluctance to wage war and his skills as a unifier and peacemaker. Ironically, the statue was unveiled in 1860 in a massive celebration on Clay's birthday, April 12, exactly one year before the firing on Fort Sumter that sparked the Civil War. Much earlier, women had become an integral component of the Whig Party, not only as supporters of male ideals but also as welcome decision makers and collaborators with their male counterparts in advancing a common agenda. Thus, even before the Mexican-American War began, women had established a place and a voice within the Whig Party, if not in the Democratic Party.[26]

The scholars Ronald and Mary Zboray exhaustively examined the papers of hundreds of New England women who commented on politics in the antebellum era. They concluded, like Varon, that their white, middle-class subjects were overwhelmingly Whig, opposed Texas annexation, and supported Clay in 1844. The women read newspapers, broadsides, and speeches and wrote letters condemning the prospects of an immoral and unjust struggle to advance the cause of Manifest Destiny. Not especially disturbed about the plight of the Mexicans, men or women, they worried about the moral debility of their own nation. They were antiexpansionist and antimilitarist, and not all were antislavery. While their organizational activities do not seem to parallel those of the women in Virginia, the groundwork for broader action, often in cooperation with reform societies, was laid by the rising tide of awareness and accompanying indignation over the prospects of "Mr. Polk's War."[27]

When the Whigs' worst fears were realized and war commenced, they found themselves divided and in a quandary. While overwhelmingly opposing the hostilities, many felt patriotically obliged not to abandon the boys in the field or the victorious Whig generals. Money for the prosecution of the fighting followed, even when they gained control of the House of Representatives. Others in the party rejected the war at all costs, wringing their hands in despair and doing little to overtly change the direction of the nation's political course.

Fourteen congressmen had voted against the declaration of war. Former president John Quincy Adams and Representative Joshua Giddings of Ohio formed the core of those who steadily used the bully pulpit of Congress to criticize the president. Their predictable remarks often produced groans and sighs from the opposition, but Senator Thomas Corwin's February 1847 speech raised the debate to new levels of vitriol. Corwin delivered a diatribe in which he shocked the chamber by telling his colleagues that if he were a Mexican, he would greet the Americans with bloody hands "and welcome you to a hospitable grave." Had he crossed the line from antiwar patriot to pro-Mexican traitor?

What were the Whigs to do? The Democrats reached back to the Revolution to label them "Tories" and to the War of 1812 to attach the opprobrium "blue-light Federalists." In September, at a Whig gathering purportedly made up of Quaker abolitionists in Wilmington, Ohio, Corwin was the featured speaker. The *Ohio Statesman* reported a tirade blasting his own party for doing nothing to stop the loss of money and flow of blood resulting from "this unrighteous and iniquitous war." Corwin was largely correct in denouncing his mates. The Whigs bounced along confused and divided, but they rode the increasing unpopularity of the war into victory at the polls in 1847.[28]

Most Whig women in the Northeast seemed to reflect the jumbled state of the party. They continued to rail in their diaries and conversations about the inhumanity and unjust nature of the conflict and the mounting casualties, but like their brethren, they did little. Some had naively hoped that Sarah Childress Polk, rumored to be a good person and a positive influence on her husband, could help dissuade him from the path of war. Polk remained undeterred. As expected, when Young Hickory visited New England in the summer of 1847 to drum up support for the cause, they delighted in the chilly reception he received in rainswept Boston. Those truly committed, largely abolitionists, eventually deserted the Whigs for the Liberty Party or rising Free Soil movement.[29]

The Free Soilers, while not dedicated to emancipation, at least pledged not to extend slavery into the territories. For many women, that was not enough. The Zborays recount the political activities of the charming Calista Billings and her friends near Boston in the fall of 1848. The girls yelled slogans, sang songs, and made banners. Seventeen-year-old Calista loved the Whig national campaign and could not get enough of the parades, dances, and speeches. Out of curiosity, she attended a Free Soil rally in Canton featuring Charles Sumner, of Massachusetts, as the featured speaker. Sumner, a rising star in the movement, had already alienated the conservative Whigs by his reference in June 1848 to an alliance between "the lords of the lash and the lords of the loom." When Sumner verbally attacked Calista's uncle, Whig State representative Lyman Kinsley, the girls voiced challenges that Sumner could not ignore. In the resultant exchanges he insulted the young women, driving them to anger and tears. The Free Soilers had indeed lost any hope of conversion, while the girls learned that politics could indeed be a painful business.[30]

The Whigs struggled with a victorious war. How should they deal with a situation that many opposed yet one in which potential Whig candidates won battle after battle and would give the party its next two presidential contenders in Zachary Taylor and Winfield Scott? The leaders clearly understood their sectional dilemma and found a solution in the Hero of Buena Vista. Like Harrison before him, Taylor earned his spurs on the battlefield, not on the hustings. Unlike Old Tip, however, Old Rough and Ready had no recognizable political allegiance, philosophy, or record. This opaqueness made him perfect for the Whigs of 1848.

Clubs were formed, and the usual barbeques, rallies, and organizational meetings held. Taylor's candidacy did create certain problems for antiwar and antislavery supporters, however. The general was the much-lauded victor of numerous bloody battles and a slaveholder. The women looked away. They attended the events but must have struggled to garner the enthusiasm of four years past. At least Taylor was not a Democrat, they rationalized, although they, like some northern "conscience" Whigs, could have entered the ranks of the Free Soil Party with minimal guilt. Taylor triumphed over Lewis Cass and the Free Soiler Martin Van Buren on November 7 but won only a plurality of the Bay State votes; Van Buren finished second.

The general predictably generated strong backing from Whig women in Virginia, who evinced fewer pangs of conscience over his slaveholding and also identified with a man born in the Commonwealth. At the ballot box, he lost the state to Cass. As Varon stresses, however, the Democrats had learned a valuable lesson, and they too embraced women as part of the 1848 campaign. Perhaps their efforts made a difference in the narrow victory in Virginia. Regardless, both parties now saw the value of women's participation within the political sphere, seemingly "without harm to their dignity or to propriety." At least temporarily, victorious Whig women had the upper hand. In the Northeast they savored a bittersweet triumph, joining in the celebration for a man few of them respected.[31]

Women opposed to the war inspired one another through their letters and conversation, by reinforcing old organizations and fostering new ones, and by operating spontaneously. They were certainly motivated to emotional outrage and action by newspaper reports, casualty lists, arriving caskets, and political rhetoric. In other words, they were the audience Corwin hoped to reach with his words of challenge and despair. These women were prospective activists in the ongoing campaign against the war.

Women and Reform

Numerous peace, religious, antislavery, and women's-rights groups joined the antiwar crusade, and many women gathered to voice their opposition spontaneously and independent of any organization. The risks were tremendous. Public pressure equating opposition to the war to treason increased, making the danger even greater for women who pushed the boundaries of political involvement.

Men in both major parties had developed some tolerance, and even acceptance, of women in campaigns and in the public sphere at political events. Assuming a prominent profile, however, by dissenting and attempting to undermine stated national policy pushed the limits. In that capacity, women met to encourage civil disobedience, oppose enlistment, draft and publish protest statements, and circulate petitions. These activities appeared in sharp contrast to what the historian Nancy Isenberg described as the status of being "civilly dead." While the war advocates talked wildly of "extending the area of freedom," they did not intend for the results to include liberty and citizenship for women. Women "became dangerous enemies," Isenberg suggests, "if as political dissidents they placed themselves beyond the protection of men." While many meetings, appeals, and publications seemed designed to reflect a bigendered call to action, in reality the Mexican-American War provided opportunities for courageous women to assert their independence.[32]

Only weeks after hostilities commenced, antiwar caucuses met, and women were clearly evident. In June 1846, the radical pacifist Elihu Burritt solicited a letter from women in Exeter, England, to their compatriots in Philadelphia inviting a commentary on peace. Interestingly, the missive, which drew more than sixteen hundred signees, reflected the looming crisis between Great Britain and the United States over the Oregon boundary, and not the crisis in Mexico. While the English dispute was soon resolved, the women of Philadelphia met, and their quick response focused on broader issues. The rejoinder was widely circulated and in different versions, perhaps the most reliable form appearing in the antislavery *Pennsylvania Freeman.* The omnipresent Quaker reformer Lucretia Mott, along with her friends and fellow abolitionist and women's-rights champions Sarah Pugh and Sarah Tyndale, guided a reply that lacked feminist overtones and leaned heavily on the traditional role of woman as moral guardian and keeper of the religious flame. Their concession to the public sphere mentioned the duty of women "to look with an attentive eye upon the great events transpiring around them." This, of course, was with the intent that they would urge an enlightened mind and a feeling heart "to direct the force of their moral influence against the iniquitous spirit of war."[33]

The women refused to judge the governments involved or the merits of the issues dividing their nations but added that in the case of the Mexican-American War "the principles of justice, mercy and peace" should be instilled. While the pen and the press should be utilized to promote those principles, women must primarily exert their influence within their social circles and especially around the hearth. Some admitted that as mothers they had contributed to the "false love of glory, the cruel spirit of revenge, and the blood thirsty ambition" by buying their sons "tiny weapons" and teaching them to mimic war games. As Isenberg critically emphasizes, this and similar gatherings were significant because while the women addressed the matter in a traditional manner, they dealt with the major issues of the day in the public sphere and had no connection to any particular reform society.[34]

Even so, the handprints of antislavery women clearly marked their activities. The linkage between abolition and the peace movement indeed grew stronger for the logical reason that many in the cause of freedom viewed the war as part of a slaveholders' conspiracy. The crusader Parker Pillsbury shared the outcome of a conclave of the Western Anti-Slavery Society in June 1846 with his ally the Bostonian William Lloyd Garrison. At the conclave, held in a Quaker meeting house in rural New Garden, Ohio, more than a thousand souls assembled to denounce slavery and the war. Pillsbury expressed his disappointment that Garrison and Wendell Phillips were absent but enthused over a number of the speakers present, including the radical Massachusetts abolitionist Abby Kelley and her husband, Stephen Foster. Apparently, no one equaled Jane Elizabeth Hitchcock, an editor of New Salem, Ohio's *Antislavery Bugle,* who spoke on the Constitution with a "surpassing eloquence" that rivaled Cicero. After lengthy, lively, and open discussion that included some opposition, Pillsbury joyfully reported that four hundred members of the convention had signed an antiwar resolution. In contrast, he admitted that "the war spirit is rampant" in the area. Pillsbury had just been invited to several antiwar meetings and quickly found himself surrounded by a large crowd led by a local cleric "in a perfect fury for carnage and slaughter." "I never was so denounced as by that Methodist priest," he confessed. So heated had the language become that the women had feared for Pillsbury's safety and insisted that he remain indoors for the evening.[35]

Radical abolitionism sewed a colorful and increasingly pervasive thread through the fabric of Ohio antislavery. Liberty Party men espoused more conventional political action as a solution, while the followers of Garrison disavowed politics and loyalty to the government and the Constitution. The members of the Western Anti-Slavery Society championed Garrison's values, promoting moral suasion and urging "No Union with Slaveholders." Abby Kelley, a controversial and powerful force in the New England organization, had abandoned the Quakers because of their equivocal stance on slavery. Living a life of self-deprivation, she traveled extensively, preaching the Word. When she arrived in Ohio in early 1846, a soulmate and ally appeared in the person of Betsey Mix Cowles. From Ashtabula County in the northeastern Western Reserve, Cowles invited Kelley and Foster to speak at the Anti-Slavery Society's local meeting in February, and a bond was formed.

Indeed, Abby's radical views and brusque approach did not meet with everyone's favor, but her personal sacrifice and heartfelt message resonated, especially with the aid of the Cowles sisters. The couple worked to persuade Betsey to join the lecture circuit. Intelligent and articulate, she agreed to consider the prospect. Perhaps to sway her decision, they invited her to the national antislavery conclave in New York and a New England gathering in Boston in May. Likely starstruck by the presence of her heroes, the young Cowles drank deeply of the wine of abolition and disunion and also of opposition to the recently declared Mexican-American War. The crowd warmly received the speeches censuring the conflict.[36]

Energized by her experience in the East, Cowles hurled herself into the cause in the fall of 1846. Working closely with her friend and fellow *Bugle* editor Jane Elizabeth Hitchcock, she launched a campaign to repeal the state's restrictive "Black Laws," participated in fundraising, and promoted antislavery fairs. Hitchcock, a transplanted New Yorker, shared Cowles's passion for female education, a cause they continued to work for well beyond the 1840s. The eclectic Cowles lent her talents to criticizing the war, an easy inclusion since she firmly believed that the fracas with Mexico was both a land grab by slave owners and a crime against humanity. She showed her literary acumen, writing antiwar poetry and a bitterly sarcastic playlet titled *Uncle Sam.* Sam admonishes his underling Zachary to be more aggressive in seizing land in northern Mexico from the local population, instructing him to kill those who resist. A reticent Zachary attempts to reason with Uncle Sam but is informed that failure to carry out orders may well result in his own demise. Accordingly, women and children are "all mangled to pieces," and a pleased Sam informs Zachary, "You are the man for me sir, you shall have the Big Chair & the White House as soon as Jimmy's time is up."

The underlying playlet's cynicism, Isenberg suggests, downplays glory for the more tawdry goals of military honor, territorial gain, and political reward. Whether Cowles expressed these feelings for herself alone or intended them for a wider audience remains unclear. Her strong opinions about peace and the Mexican-American War, however, are obvious reflections of a fervency that went beyond the bounds of abolition. Ultimately, Cowles resisted the allure of the eastern establishment and the antislavery lecture circuit and instead remained in Ohio, working strenuously with Hitchcock to promote moral and humanitarian ideals in children's education.[37]

In truth, for Uncle Sam (and President Polk), Zachary's success in northern Mexico in 1846 and an improbable draw at Buena Vista in 1847 did not bring an end to the war. Indeed, the Americans won battle after battle, sometimes in spite of difficult odds, yet the Mexicans would not sue for peace. This puzzling reticence compelled Polk to launch yet a third front in the spring of 1847 that sent Winfield Scott along the 250-mile road from the coastal town of Veracruz to the capital, Mexico City. The lengthy campaign resulted in mounting casualties on both sides.

Betsey Cowles's voice was one among a rising chorus of women's voices in both West and East protesting the contest. In Randolph, Ohio, activists held a peace convention in September endorsed by prominent community women. Concurrently, a southeastern Ohioan named Sarah reacted heatedly to an article in the *St. Clairsville Citizen* blaming Mexican insults and duplicity for causing the war. "I see that this horrible butchery and murdering is, and likely to be still carried on in Mexico," Sarah lamented to her intended, Joel McMillan. "Who that has a half grain of sense does not know that it was our own people that provoked them to war."[38]

Across the state border, in January 1848, the Anti-Slavery Friends of Henry County, Indiana, including women members, drafted a memorial to the Senate asking for a cessation of the war because of its "pre-eminent injustice, wickedness, and barbarity." Not to be outdone, the county's Female Anti-Slavery Society adopted resolutions condemning those (Whig) politicians who denounced the war as "unjust and wicked," language that was increasingly common, while voting for men and supplies. In Farmington, Illinois, Mary B. Davis happily reported a meeting of the Liberty Party in which the group targeted the anticipated candidacy of Zachary Taylor as president. In a foreshadowing of the Free Soil Party, they condemned the feckless Taylor as being demoralized by military life, robbing his slaves of their rights, and prosecuting "an inhuman and unjust war, against an unoffending and semi-barbarous people." On the Wisconsin frontier, Emily Huse blasted Polk and decried the war as "horrid butcherys."[39]

Since the Northeast, especially New England, remained the center of the antiwar movement, pacifists and antislavery and women's-rights advocates frequently conjoined in opposition. For a brief, shining moment the American Peace Society found common ground with northern Free-Soilers and reformers of virtually all stripes. As the historian Valarie Ziegler notes, "These were the headiest of times" for the American Peace Society, but ironically, the organization limited its actions largely to petition drives and print pieces. The society's language echoed the common refrain of the war as "unprincipled depravity and unmitigated sin." Yet, the cautious leadership rejected the notion of public meetings as part of their strategy.[40]

Others stepped up. Rallies were held from Worcester, Massachusetts, to Salem, Ohio. Antiwar women formed an integral part of the committee, drafting protest resolutions at Kennett Square, a borough near Philadelphia. That same month, Lydia Chevalier, of McKean County, Pennsylvania, appealed to women of the free states "who love the human race" to launch petition drives to end "the untold horrors of all war, and the atrocity of the Mexican War in particular." Women had historically saved other nations from impending ruin, Chevalier observed, so would it not be right for them to petition Congress en masse for a withdrawal of American forces and a fair peace settlement? The aging Philadelphia Jewish reformer and philanthropist Rebecca Gratz expressed her sorrow and disgust for the war to her sister-in-law. Reflecting back on the American Revolution, Rebecca wistfully recounted the glory that had accompanied a struggle for liberty and rights. The present controversy challenged her values. "To invade a country and slaughter its inhabitants—to fight for boundary—or political supremacy—is altogether against my principles and feelings and I shall be most happy when it is over."[41]

Others weighed in from abroad. Margaret Fuller continued the assault on expansion and slavery that she had launched before departing for Europe, marriage, motherhood, and a failed revolution. As a strong, independent feminist and reformer with a substantial ego, Fuller had acquired an ample list of friends and associates who admired her intellectual prowess and verbal expression. Perhaps no other American woman could have written *Woman in the Nineteenth Century* (1845). At the same time, some New Englanders were less than enamored of her attitude and elevated status. Unconventional and nonconformist, she might have found some degree of intellectual and ideological compatibility at Seneca Falls in 1848, but the moment arrived too late. In the summer of 1846, wealthy supporters provided partial funding for a trip to Europe, and the *New York Tribune* contracted with her for the balance. As Horace Greeley's foreign correspondent in England and Italy, an assignment she could hardly refuse, Fuller was to write twelve pieces for the paper. She ultimately penned a total of thirty-seven. In her post, she covered cultural and political events in London, but she traveled to Italy as the republican rebellion of 1849 was unfolding.[42]

Although the Mexican-American War had only just begun when she sailed from New York, her feelings quickly appeared in print. In a May 1846 book review for the *Tribune,* Fuller referred to American engagement as "a most unrighteous act," and recent deeds underscored her point that the Mexicans were fighting for their rights, while the Americans battled "for the liberty to do our pleasure." Her cynicism regarding the government, slavery, expansion, and the compromise of national principles only increased over time. In dozens of reports to the *Tribune,* including letters in late 1847 and early 1848, she decried "this horrible cancer of slavery, and the wicked war that has grown out of it." Fuller revealed her heightened disappointment about the decline of the United States from champion of the rights of men to "robber and a jailer; the scourge hid behind her banner." The nation was sinking into a moral abyss, "spoiled by prosperity and stupid with lust of gain." The politicians appeared "selfish or petty," the literature "frivolous and venal." "Her eyes [are] fixed not on the stars, but on the possessions of other men," she wrote. "The spirit of our fathers flames no more, but lies hid beneath the ashes." Tragically, Fuller drowned in a ship disaster less than 100 yards off Fire Island, New York, in July 1850. She was returning to the country she had verbally pilloried, a country whose shape and politics had changed dramatically in her brief absence.[43]

Women on the Home Front

While thousands of American women actively and passively opposed the war, thousands more supported it out of patriotism or self-interest. From a population of almost 21 million, the nation mustered more than eighty thousand men into service from 1846 to 1848. Thus, the number of families directly affected remained rather small. For those with husbands, brothers, or sons in Mexico, however, a casualty rate approaching 25 percent generated increasing anxiety as the war progressed. Peggy Cashion has combed the archives in an impressive effort to examine the reactions of women on the home front. She contends that most women opposed the conduct and the objectives of the war but supported the well-being and safety of the soldiers. Her study also challenges historical wisdom in some circles by emphasizing the durability of the cult of true womanhood and the endurance of the model of piety, purity, domesticity, and submissiveness. Importantly, Cashion points out that the exigencies of war and the unanticipated responsibilities that fell to women often, at least temporarily, changed their view of the cult's tenets, especially submission. Managing a business, a farm, or a plantation required decision making that threatened the patriarchal order but became mandatory for survival.[44]

Officers' wives, some married to professionals with career goals, others wed to volunteers seeking perhaps fame and fortune, found themselves in a unique position. They were often literate, and many enjoyed a more comfortable lifestyle than the wife of a typical enlisted soldier. As a result, their communications with their husbands centered less on physical, and more on emotional, deprivation and on advice about how to continue to operate the farm or plantation effectively. Several women provide very different examples of the difficulties women faced in a managerial role, complicated by the temporary nature of their power. Frances Butler and Edward G. W. Butler had the good fortune to marry each other. Frances grew up on the Woodlawn Plantation in Virginia with the blood of the Custis family flowing through her veins. Her husband, a ward of Andrew Jackson, attended West Point and enjoyed a successful military career until his resignation in 1831. Within the decade, the couple moved to Louisiana, where they owned Dunboyne in Iberville Parish, near Baton Rouge, and managed several other sugar plantations.

When the colonel responded to the call in 1847, management of the family's holdings fell to Frances. Her approach to Edward's absence and the war reflected self-confidence about her ability to direct the family and their properties. She filled here frequent letters to "my beloved husband" with chatty bits of local gossip, as well as attending to the progress and status of the crops. Predictably, kinfolk were an important topic, including her brother's untimely death from "congestion of the lungs." Their youngest daughter, Isabelle, discussed poetry with her father and pleaded with him to find comfort in the Bible. She finished her year at Belmont with the highest honors but worried about the coming fall term. Sharing her views of school life, Isabelle sought Edward's counsel regarding taking courses in mathematics. She had determined to study Spanish but felt that geometry and algebra "were not essential to the education of a girl." Of course, if "her precious father" believed them of value, she would enroll. The proud daughter showed his uniformed daguerreotype to a classmate, who found him very handsome, an observation in which Isabelle enthusiastically concurred. Whether that exchange impacted his views on her curriculum is uncertain. Meanwhile, son Lawrence conjectured that if his father captured the guerrilla leader Antonio Canales, his mission would be accomplished and Edward could come home.[45]

Aware but never maudlin or overprotective about the colonel's health, Frances grew nervous as time passed. Sometimes she imparted an appropriate remedy, telling him, for example, that using red pepper on a snakebite after it had been cauterized was a surefire cure or alerting him to the existence of a French chemist who had invented a disinfecting fluid. When the army dispatched Edward's Third Dragoons on a mission from Matamoros to Monterrey in September 1847, Frances revealed mixed emotions. Finally, she declared with considerable pride, his regiment had received its just tribute, a posting closer to the action. In turn, she acknowledged that the "perils of your brilliant profession" had raised her anxiety to new levels. General Canales and his irregular cavalry lurked in the region, posing a constant threat to American supply convoys and personnel.[46]

The presence of an overseer named Moore complicated matters. An angry Frances dubbed Moore "a serious disadvantage" and complained that she had wearied of his efforts to "flatter and palaver" everyone, including her. Problems on the plantation should not be relayed to the colonel, Moore suggested, since such information would make Edward "uneasy." Frances told her husband in no uncertain terms that she wanted the overseer dismissed and would be much better off without him. She had no confidence in his "judgment, promptitude, activity or forethought." With forceful resignation, however, she reminded Edward, "You invited him, and you need not fear my doing anything to send him away, though I have been sadly tired of him long ago." An intelligent manager, Frances found herself in a power struggle with an individual who had little use for her interference in plantation business.[47]

Moore remained, and Frances was obliged to cooperate with him in a tenuous relationship. The overseer made frequent trips to New Orleans to handle business affairs, but Frances rendered the major decisions regarding the property. Matters related to repairs, purchasing animals, harvesting the cane, and employment of workers fell to her, and she recounted the sugar production and sale in great detail. Financial issues, debts and profits, received her steady, ongoing attention. The Butlers' crop, unlike those of some other plantations in the area, survived a hurricane, and Frances sent Moore "down river" to look for additional hands. Interestingly, he recruited Mexicans, whom after almost two months Frances decided to dismiss. She agreed with neighbors who feared that the Mexicans would set a bad example for the slaves by drinking whiskey when not in the fields. Frances instructed Moore to pay off the Mexicans, accompany them to New Orleans, and arrange to ship them back home.

While raising no objections to the institution of slavery, Frances was incensed when an overseer on her sister Eliza's plantation whipped a boy named Yellow John to death. Harrison, the overseer, attempted to conceal the murder, but the slaves revealed the crime. A post mortem followed, and the killing became a local disgrace. Frances was outraged that the boy "must have died in agony." The ensuing investigation and contradictory testimony by Harrison generated additional grumbling from her.[48]

Frances's judgments were not always in accordance with her husband's wishes, but her presence, self-confidence, and choices yielded a very profitable crop in 1847. The next year's harvest promised as fine a return. As a result, bankers informed the Butlers that the loan they desired would now be easy to obtain. In April 1848 Frances boldly encouraged her husband to incur the debt, buy more slaves, and "render your plantation fully productive." She had grown more self-assured about her knowledge of the sugar, labor, and general operations. Interestingly, Frances repeatedly referred to the crop as "your sugar" and the property as "your plantation."

When Colonel Butler was assigned to the court of inquiry into the conduct of General Scott in early 1848, Frances hoped Edward might be able spend a few days at home. She wanted to know whether he approved of her accomplishments in his absence. "You would do many things that I cannot," she confessed, "though I try my best." Her best was indeed most impressive. Ever focused, in her last letter to Edward in June she emphasized the Louisiana economy, the plantation, the fine crop, and how he needed to bring home with him more slaves and horses from his dragoons, if they were sold inexpensively. As Edward lingered into the summer of 1848 in Mexico, Frances grew more comfortable in her role.

Infrequently discussing war or peace, Frances commented offhandedly in February 1848 that the United States seemed poised to receive New Mexico, California, and the Rio Grande as the result of Nicholas Trist's diplomatic negotiations. She seemed unimpressed. For her, peace meant Edward's safe return to his home and family. Yet, she must have known that the position she had occupied for more than a year would soon be dramatically altered. As her husband reasserted his authority, she would revert to a traditional domestic role.[49]

One hundred miles north, on the Red River, in Rapides Parish, Sarah Hunter struggled with a similar situation, but with a somewhat different attitude and relationship. Sarah Jane Ford was only 16 when she married Robert A. Hunter, two years her senior, in 1830. Robert had grown up on Eden, a plantation eighteen miles from Alexandria. Following in his father's footsteps, he too became a planter and aspiring young politician. Before the war commenced in the spring of 1846, the couple exchanged missives exuding Victorian romanticism and containing language that teetered on desperation at their separation.

Their letters reveal an innocence and commitment to each other that ended only in death. Robert, serving in the state senate in New Orleans, sensed his wife's loneliness and tried to compensate by dispatching several handmade silk dresses, an offering she accepted with gratitude. When Sarah miscarried, her husband tried to comfort her. He, in turn, dealt with his own demons: a serious illness resulting from eating spoiled oysters, an endless legislative agenda, and a troublesome lawsuit filed against him. In May 1846 he enlisted for six months in Andrew Jackson's regiment of Louisiana volunteers. The decision drove Sarah to despair. He had no idea, she reproved him, "of the days and nights of speechless agony that I have endured in your absence, the extent of the sacrifice you now ask me to make. I was just beginning to hope that my trials were nearly over when this last letter arrived."

Thus far in life, Sarah had acted with "fortitude and firmness," but she had her husband to support her. "My love for you has been little less than idolatry," she admitted. In a therapeutic analysis, Sarah dissected their relationship and how she had been "compelled" to share her husband with the world. While Robert had surrounded himself with the bustle and business of New Orleans, she had remained in Alexandria "utterly alone." Now Sarah faced further estrangement and would carry on without complaint. Robert must have noticed, however, her rather stoic declaration that "I will follow your advice as far as I am able."[50]

Sarah's definition of her isolation and loneliness seems somewhat puzzling. Surrounded by her two daughters, her sisters and brother, neighbors, and wives of Robert's fellow officers in Mexico for comfort and consolation, she sunk further into depression. In July 1846 she wailed, "I wish I had never been born, indeed it is too hard." Her nerves were shattered, and life held no pleasure, nor would there be any until her husband returned. He wrote of camp, the absence of discipline among the troops, but most particularly about his feelings for Sarah. When nursed back to health by compassionate Mexican women "of the most forbidding exterior," "I thought of my wife and covered my face and wept."[51]

By January 1847 Robert had returned, but to New Orleans and the legislature. Battling an almost fatal fever and angered by a merchant who had sold his cotton below market price, he confided, "I never wanted to see you as bad in my life as I do at this moment. I would give all I have to embrace you all once more." Their correspondence also shows that during Robert's extended absence and illness, Sarah had taken on more responsibility regarding plowing and planting on the plantation. Her letters speak with coolness about corn, the status of the cotton crop, and her decision not to ship the bales. While she thanked her husband for his trust in her, Sarah remained bereft: "I seriously and candidly do not believe that I could survive you. I cannot bear even to think of such a calamity." Responding to her most recent pregnancy—she had twelve children—Robert insisted that Sarah travel to New Orleans, where she delivered a son in May.

A decade later the family abandoned the plantation for urban life, as Robert became the president of the state board of currency. Tragically, Sarah did not live to make the journey, dying in Alexandria before her fortieth birthday. In many ways, Sarah Hunter had remained a traditional southern woman. Yet, a year of separation had also created an opportunity for a woman whose emotional journey produced a person of skills, strength, and self-reliance.[52]

In Indiana, Thomas Ware Gibson appears to have had some of the same trepidations as E. G. W. Butler in terms of property management. Gibson's wife, Mary, informed him in March 1847 that she was about to allow a lot on their farm to be planted by a man named Fleschman. Apparently, he had worked the property previously, agreeing to also care for adjacent land owned by the Gibsons. Thomas, unhappy with Fleschman's negligence, preferred that the property be planted by another farmer. If Mary decided to contract with Fleschman, however, Thomas insisted that a local fellow named Bill Campbell "make the bargain with him." Like Frances Butler, Mary Gibson could be trusted but should be supervised by a man, especially regarding matters of business and finance.[53]

Most American soldiers, North and South, did not share the Butlers' privileged lifestyle or even the Gibsons' more modest one. They were yeoman farmers, and when they departed, the heavy lifting fell to the women and children. While some wives, especially plantation mistresses, may have benefited from slave labor, most women found themselves operating with little money or support. The situation became more desperate in urban areas, where recruiters lured the poor and recent Irish immigrants into the army with promises of bonuses, a monthly salary, and land. Government guarantees and paydays were erratically met. When cash was available to the troops, the problem of getting it back home was complicated by distance and security. Families could go months without income, leaving them literally destitute and starving during a bitterly cold winter. When possible, concerned wives and mothers dispatched creature comforts—socks, shirts, gowns, handkerchiefs, and blankets—as a patriotic gesture and a way of reminding their men and themselves of the life left behind. As Cashion notes, "Women established appreciation and respect for themselves and the home environment they created."[54]

Women also relished the opportunity to provide ongoing advice about other areas of the lives of male family members, including their health, moral, and, personal behaviors. Cornelia Read Howard, born into a prominent South Carolina family, married into the equally powerful Howard clan of Maryland. She bore only one son before her husband died tragically in 1822 at age thirty-four. Over the next several decades, the "widow Howard" fulfilled the role of consummate doting mother to her twenty-five-year-old son, Captain John Howard. He was her "only treasure in this world," thus her apprehension about his physical and mental state and accompanying counsel knew no bounds. She commented in an informed and unflinching manner about local weddings and funerals, in addition to the death of John Quincy Adams and the French Revolution.[55]

Cornelia followed closely events in Mexico, including military operations and guerrilla warfare. Aware of the oppressive heat, foul water, rancid food, infectious insects, and ubiquitous dirt, Mrs. Howard generally focused her admonitions on John's health. To her thinking, clean clothes and body rendered the best preventative, and so he must remain hygienic. Fresh air and ventilation in his quarters were regenerative, but taking in the night air could be ruinous. She cautioned that, indeed, falling asleep in a current of night air often resulted in deafness and had been the "proximate cause" of his father's death. Advice flowed steadily: Contaminated water might be purified by boiling or mixing with red wine or black tea. A mixed diet of meat and vegetables should be preferred to meat alone, and tea or "a good claret if you can" should be utilized as a beverage.[56]

Mother Howard introduced John to endless remedies and refreshers, from a small tablespoon of heated castor oil to a lemonade concoction made with cream of tartar, sugar, and water. She discussed how an overdose of emetics might be treated by a mixture of flour and water. "The albumen and gluten of these substances will convert the poison into calomel which will pass off," Cornelia patiently explained in a detailed lecture. "The liquid by its bulk distends the stomach and thus produces quick vomiting so as to relieve the stomach by discharging the contents." Cooking without peppers or other stimulants was always wise, and a body wash of spirits and camphor would keep away mosquitoes and gnats. She advocated moderation and was not above the cliché that "an ounce of prevention is better than a pound of cure."[57]

Cornelia's detailed guidance extended to the sublime—some might suggest progressive or strange. If ice became available in Veracruz, it should be ingested sparingly. Overconsumption "causes sudden death in extreme heat," she warned. After consulting with opticians in Baltimore, Cornelia urged John to permit her to send a pair of green or blue sunglasses ("goggles," as she referred to them) to shield his eyes against "the excessive light reflected from the burning sands" and to guarantee a sure aim. She went on at some length about the importance of color and the potential danger of extreme and sudden change in light.

Mrs. Howard also had thoughts about toes. Clipping one's nails was very important, she believed. While on the march, a jagged nail might result in an injury, so Cornelia included file scissors in his trunk. Hair mattered too, and John should leave his "thick" to offer protection against sunstroke. Finally, she communicated wisdom about bathing in polluted harbors and any water that might contain snakes, sharks, or alligators.[58]

Money was no object. The Howards were well off, and Cornelia understood her place in the Baltimore community. "All rich people are aimed at more or less," she counseled her son, while frequently mentioning the behavior and health of the servants. She effectively handled the family's finances during her son's minority and years later looked back with fondness to the time "when the business world gave me credit for good management." It was hardly a distant memory, and Cornelia chided John about potential bank withdrawals or empowering an agent in Baltimore to handle any money matters related to his soldiers. "I wish to be sole Banker," she declared authoritatively. "I wish to be sole Head and you will find it best for your interest. Draw on me. I can always attend to your affairs and do not fear that it will give me trouble." Cornelia repeated the request in numerous letters for emphasis. There should be "no separate authority, which I particularly wish to avoid." Should anyone write to John about business, including the leasing of property, he should refer the person to Cornelia. "There have been some attempts to cheat me," she remarked, "but they did not succeed."

Mrs. Howard operated independently, paying their property taxes ("very high," she grumbled), commenting on the wisdom of buying Baltimore and Ohio Railroad stock, and selling his horse. Thus well situated, her son should spend whatever necessary to enhance his comfort, and that of his men, while in the military, including sending out his laundry to a good hotel that could promise same-day service. She suggested that he limit the cash on his person and establish an account at a bank in New Orleans.[59]

The Howards had influence. Gold pieces and good red wine could be sent from Baltimore whenever and wherever needed, including during the occupation of Veracruz. A horse was important in battle, so Mrs. Howard urged John to purchase a sure-footed animal in Mexico, where he could find one more accustomed to the climate, and make certain to buy a chain bit and bridle that could not be cut in combat. Constantly in fear for his safety, Cornelia warned her son not to trust the Mexicans, who were "as treacherous as Indians," and never to venture out by himself, for fear of murder.[60]

Mrs. Howard did not fail to encourage her son's spiritual and moral side, reminding him of the presence in Mexico of good Jesuit fathers to hear his confession and also reminding him to wear the medal she had given him on his rosary made from the wood of a tree on Mount Olivet. Perhaps he would encounter a Spanish priest who spoke French, in which case they would get along. Should he have little time for prayer, a series of Our Fathers and Hail Marys would suffice. In any case, he should prepare for death in perfect contrition and be at peace with God. Citing Marshall Turenne of France, "one of the few great generals of the world," she encouraged John to make certain that he prayed before going into battle. She appealed daily for her son's well-being but candidly revealed that if God had other plans, she was prepared to meet him in heaven. In the meantime, John must be ever vigilant and "deny yourself what otherwise might tempt you."[61]

Cornelia selectively mentioned women in her letters. She casually noted that a particular lady (Margaret) "is well and unceasing in the interest she takes in you" or "Miss Landry bids me say she prays for your safe return." "Maggy," however, appeared to have a special place in Cornelia's heart and seemingly was targeted for her son's postwar future. On numerous occasions, Cornelia felt obliged to tell John about the woman's affections: "Maggy loves you dearly as you may believe you were her first love"; "Maggy desires her love and best wishes—she loves you"; finally, "Maggy always desires her love to you, perhaps no one but myself loves you as she does." In January 1848, a recently returned Baltimore comrade-in-arms teased John, "I think you can claim the hand of some fair damsel on your return." Ultimately, John married neither "Maggy" nor any other fair Baltimore damsel.[62]

Mrs. Howard served as the surrogate matron for the wives and mothers of the captain's company, acting as the conduit of information between the soldiers and their families. Utilizing her own correspondence with John, she kept them updated on events in Mexico and relayed information and requests, especially regarding specific health and financial needs at home, to his men. Cornelia firmly believed that her son had a preeminent responsibility for the fitness and safety of his troops. Demonstrating a wide-ranging intellect, she cited historical figures such as the seventeenth-century Welsh privateer Captain Henry Morgan, who had preserved the vigor of his crew at Pensacola, while other sailors were carried away by yellow fever. When a soldier in John's company failed to repay a debt, Cornelia urged her son to ignore the repayment, quoting Shakespeare's Polonius: "Loan oft loses both itself and friend." She urged John to give his men cigars to boost their morale. They were accustomed to smoking, and Cornelia saw nothing amiss in terms of their health.[63]

She also knew that her son might be growing weary of her advice and view her "constant and anxious affection" as hectoring. Cornelia tried to reassure him of her good intentions. Though surrounded by wealth, family, and friends, she admitted that jealousy and disaffection had marked her interactions with several female relatives. She felt disrespected by "Aunt Read" and demanded that John have no intercourse with her or his cousin William. They are a "treacherous set," she cautioned. No matter, she told John, "I love no one but you in this world." Seemingly isolated in her affection, Cornelia had developed an obsessive and controlling devotion to her son. John heroically stormed the walls of Chapultepec in September 1847, and his proud mother implored him to send along a daguerreotype of himself in his dress uniform "enclosed properly in a morocco case." She corrected his spelling (checking several dictionaries), reminding him that *artillery* required "two ls." Captain John Howard survived the war, only to die unmarried in 1862—the same year as his mother.[64]

Sisters also served as acceptable conduits for female wisdom. John Hodge, of Ohio, came from a working-class background and may well have enlisted for financial reasons. His concerned sibling, Manorah, offered him practical advice, telling him to save his money, buy a needle and thread, and sew his own clothes. A fall into dissolution, gambling, and drink would be both costly and immoral. With the constant reminder of their dead mother's teachings firmly in place, she cautioned John not to take the first roll of the dice or drop of liquor. Manorah feared his weakness: "If you do, you will repeat it—," she advised. "You know how afraid mother always was that one of her boys would be a drunkard."[65]

American women remained properly concerned about righteous thinking and a sober lifestyle as they came to fear the worst for their men struggling to survive in a strange land. The diaries of the troops do not suggest that religious practice was a mainstay in their lives. Out of curiosity and boredom, many explored the Catholic church at the heart of every town and village and attended services. They sometimes found the ritual and the response of the penitents impressive. "I thought it was the very religion for the people present," an American wrote for the *Washington Daily Union,* "and much more decent and worthy of God's temple, than many of the ranting howling discourses we have at home."[66]

Conversely, the soldiers were angry and repulsed at the wealth of the church and the rich lifestyle of the many priests, while the masses remained in dire straits. The Americans viewed the church as an agency of oppression, feeding the people saints and idols while enriching itself at their expense. As a result, the letters from home that frequently mentioned piety, prayer, and salvation in the face of death may have largely fallen on deaf ears. Whether emotional and spiritual preparation for one's own demise helped erect a moral barrier to prevent a soldier from veering onto the path of vice is debatable.[67]

Religion intersected with morality to form another key component that fell within the female realm during the Mexican-American War. While the US Army enrolled units comprising largely Catholic immigrants, most soldiers practiced a Protestant faith. Within the past decade in the United States, the papacy and its American agents, churches, convents, and monasteries, had come under scrutiny and attack from nativist writers and expositors. In Mexico, a theologically compromised priesthood embraced material wealth and appeared to flaunt mistresses and children. The perceived failure of many Mexican women to embrace Victorian virtue created a moral cesspool in which naive American soldiers might be lured into deserting the tenets of their faith by temptation and easily obtainable vice. The glitter, gold, and ritual of Romanism denied these moral wanderers any hope of salvation. Dangers seemingly were many, and mothers and wives sounded the clarion call.

American women, a thousand miles from the horrors of camp and battle, nonetheless felt the anguish of sleepless nights and the pain of loss. Many patriotically rose to the appeal of their nation, supporting the men in blue in whatever manner possible and praying for their survival. Other women felt the sting of an unjust war and rose to various levels of protest against President Polk and his imperial contest to extend slavery. All of these women, however, enjoyed the advantage of a relatively safe and secure environment where they could write, organize, petition, and demonstrate, either for or against the war, or simply stay silently at home. A number of women were far from mute, as they labored physically, intellectually, and emotionally to assume new roles and manage farms and businesses in the absence of the men in the family.

Mexican women had different options. While they also engaged in creative literary activities, generally in support of their country, thousands found themselves on the battlefield. Their heartrending tales of courage, sacrifice, and suffering have become critical components of the war's reality and mythology on both sides of the border.

2

Soldaderas

MEXICAN WOMEN AND THE BATTLEFIELD

For many Americans, the cloud of Anglo-Saxon superiority floated triumphantly over the conquest of Mexico. An inferior race limited by an ancient Spanish culture and a corrupt Catholic Church, Mexicans should have been grateful for the opportunity to become enlightened. The antiwar poet James Russell Lowell caustically expressed those views in *The Bigelow Papers,* where Birdofredum Sawin, a fictional Massachusetts volunteer under the command of General Caleb Cushing, vents his frustration and disillusionment with the war.

> Afore I come away from hum I had a strong persuasion
> Thet Mexicans worn't human beans,—an ourang outang nation
> A sort o'folks a chap could kill an'never dream on t'arter
> . . . .
> It must be right, fer Caleb sez it's reg'lar Anglo-saxon
> . . . .
> Thet our nation's bigger 'n theirn an' so its rights air bigger,
> An' thet it's all to make 'em free that we air pullin' trigger,
> Thet Anglo-Saxondom's idee's abreakin' em to pieces;
> An thet idee's that every man doos just wut he damn pleases.[1]

Apparently, "wut he damn pleases" spilled over into the exploitation of young Mexican women. As US forces occupied a city, officers employed locals to perform the basic domestic tasks of cooking and cleaning. Samuel Chamberlain, of Massachusetts, claimed that "all the Americans quartered in town, kept house with a good-looking señorita." Indeed, Chamberlain maintained a young married girl, Carmeleita Veigho de Moro, whose husband later had her raped and murdered for comporting with a Yankee. When an American doctor named Morton departed Chihuahua, his mistress dressed as a man and followed him to his new home in Saltillo, where she was observed living in his tent "in the most public manner."

How do we define the image of these women? Are the terms *collaborator, camp follower,* and *victim* fair designations? Many women interacted with the Americans because of economic need or opportunism; they washed clothes and sold food to soldiers in the marketplace. In the minds of many Mexicans, such fraternization with the enemy, which perhaps also included providing "female companionship," sparked predictable resentment. Assuming that every relationship between a Mexican girl and an American soldier had a sexual dimension would be highly presumptive, since engaging in questionable behavior with young Hispanic women would be taboo in both the northern and the southern society. Still, the line seems to have been crossed with disturbing ease.[2]

The Mexican Army

The idea of the United States' racial and cultural superiority played out in many ways in Mexico, largely on the battlefield, where Americans expected their skill, size, courage, and ethnicity to triumph. The Anglo perception that dark-skinned, diminutive Mexican men were more effeminate and therefore inferior tore at the scab of a country trying to heal its national wounds. The Mexican soldier, typically an illiterate peasant impressed into service, too often had little loyalty or commitment to the state, which was riddled by political factionalism and revolution. Only a quarter century from independence, there was a struggle between those Mexicans who envisioned a centralized union and those who envisioned a federal one. In many ways, it was not unlike the situation the Founding Fathers faced in Philadelphia during the summer of 1787 and in the following decades.[3]

The historian Mark Wasserman contends that three factors—a chronic lack of funds, inadequately trained soldiers, and poor leadership—led to the defeat of Mexico. The Mexican government attempted to provide uniforms and arms to equip a substantial military, and did so with Napoleonic-era surplus weapons purchased from Great Britain. The armaments were obsolete and substandard, the Americans owning a particular advantage in terms of artillery. Too many men were conscripted. Pay was poor (a few centavos a day), instruction minimal, and discipline uneven. No wonder. The officer corps, made up of Creole social and economic elites, relished their privilege and status. They habitually neither identified with their men nor generally cared about their well-being. Caught up in the turmoil that could affect their power and position, officers monitored the politics of the capital as closely as they did the movements of the American forces. The scholar David Clary maintains that "the Mexican officer corps was unschooled, corrupt, incompetent and heavy with generals." Wasserman agrees: "The officers, Santa Anna in particular, were irresolute, inconsistent, and often distracted by personal vindictiveness and political scheming, which at crucial times led to costly mistakes in battle."[4]

Their harsh estimation of the officers may spark debate among historians, but certainly the question of the leadership and character of the president and commanding officer, Antonio López de Santa Anna, prompts heated controversy. Self-styled as the Napoleon of the West, the fifty-two-year-old general had fought Mexico's enemies, including the rebellious Texans, for more than a decade and lost a leg in resisting the French in 1838. The severed limb later received an elaborate burial in Mexico City. Elected president initially in 1833, Santa Anna would be in and out of power for the next twenty years. Timothy J. Henderson deems him "the indispensable man of his generation," while struggling to explain his survival in Mexican politics. "Vain, corrupt, incompetent and untrustworthy," Santa Anna was also a genuine hero, dashing, dynamic, and charismatic with an unrivaled personal flair. K. Jack Bauer suggests that he "had difficulty separating opportunism from love of country." His wealth and roguish lifestyle, including an unabashed affection for gambling and women, blended with an image of decisiveness and serious sense of purpose that inspired confidence. While he was no friend of democracy or the masses, the nation repeatedly turned to him in a crisis—and the American invasion posed such an emergency.

In August 1846, Santa Anna returned to Mexico from exile in Cuba. Utilizing his own financial resources and drafting his peons into service, the general rushed to assemble a fighting force to hurl back the Yankees. Clearly, the Mexican forces already in the field seemed unprepared. Lieutenant Manuel Balbontín bewailed the condition of the men in his command in July as they marched to confront Zachary Taylor in northern Mexico. "The state of drunkenness of the troops and the teamsters was unbearable." Predictably, morale among the rank and file suffered.[5]

Numerous historians remark that the Mexicans did possess one area of superiority—the band. Common soldiers carved wooden flutes for camp enjoyment, while every army had its own large brass band, prepared to play everything from Indian pueblo melodies to songs from *The Barber of Seville*. Soldiers fatalistically embraced an old whimsical tune, "La cucaracha" (The cockroach), as the comic symbol of unsympathetic superiors: "La cucaracha, la cucaracha, ya no puede cambiar" (The cockroach, the cockroach, it can never change).[6]

The *Soldaderas*

The soldiers' cynicism was well placed. For the average *soldado,* forced to march hundreds of miles, often with minimal food and water, music, gambling, and *pulque,* a thick juice fermented from the agave plant, offered the major avenues for entertainment and vice. With virtually no organized quartermaster corps to deliver sustenance or medical corps to provide balm for injury, the military relied upon an essential element of every Mexican army—the *soldaderas.* Unlike the Americans, who made limited use of women in their camps, typically as laundresses, the Mexicans traditionally embraced the concept of women in the capacity of critical support. The historian Donald Frazier refers to them as "a shadow army" and "the supply system" of the Mexican military. In the villages and towns, and especially on the march, hundreds, sometimes thousands, of wives, girlfriends, mothers, and sisters assembled their worldly possessions, as well as their children, to trudge along behind the troops. They functioned as nurses, cooks, and laundresses, as well as foraging and providing vital services to family members. Their role was critical. A decade earlier, as many as fifteen hundred *soldaderas* and their children had accompanied the army of Santa Anna on his campaign into Texas. While only three hundred women had reached San Antonio, many dying or simply dropping out of the column, the strength of the women and their cause became legendary. Efforts to end the custom proved fruitless, and the generals grudgingly accepted the invaluable contributions of the women in providing comfort and deterring desertion. Where the officers failed their men, the *soldaderas* supplied essential needs and boosted the morale of their loved ones.[7]

Whether in the city or the countryside, the women suffered along with their men. After the fight for Matamoros in June 1846, a US soldier could not but notice "a most disagreeable stench" emanating from a house. He entered to find "on the floor lying without covering . . . fifty Mexicans wounded in the late engagements, attended by some 10 or 12 women. The smell of the place was insufferable and I had to leave it. The next door was the same and so on for about 20 houses."[8]

On the road, blistering heat, sandstorms, and drought could quickly change into enervating cold, rain, or snow. Rarely possessing adequate food or water, the *soldaderas* tramped on, "dead with fatigue and with their killing burdens of wood." After the action at Cerro Gordo in April 1847, John Peoples, of the *New Orleans Bee,* rode along the five-mile column of paroled Mexican prisoners and their entourage. He took particular interest in the camp women, those "devoted creatures" who trailed their men through good times and bad. Peoples referred to them as "slaves" of affection and grieved to see them "worn down with fatigue, moving at a snail's pace, with their heavy burdens almost weighing them to earth." He described a scene painful to witness yet somehow filled with an admirable loyalty and devotion. Struggling with bedding and clothing on their backs, the women carried food and the utensils to prepare the meals. The reporter acerbically pointed to the exhausted women cooking dinner while their unworthy mates slumbered. "The woman of sixty or more years—the mother with her infant wrapped in her rebosa—the wife . . . the youthful señorita frisking along with her lover's sombrero upon her head; even the prattling girl who had followed padre and madre to the wars." The verb *frisking* connoted an innocent moment, while Peoples accurately described their lives of daily drudgery.[9]

The sterner reality of the plight of the *soldaderas* was reflected in the forced march of hundreds of miles of Santa Anna's army in February 1847 to confront Taylor at Buena Vista. With few rations, shabby clothing, and inadequate weapons, the Mexican Army, numbering more than twenty thousand, departed San Luis Potosí on a brutal trek that would cover almost three hundred miles of desert in just three weeks. Bitter winter weather, freezing temperatures, exhaustion, and starvation took a heavy toll. No firewood was available to warm either the troops or their women. Almost a quarter of the Mexican Army failed to report for roll call on the eve of the contest. Before firing a shot, Santa Anna had lost five thousand soldiers. Many dispirited men simply faded into the night. Others suffered a more tragic fate on a road lined with "dead men and women feasted on by coyotes, along with broken wagons, dead livestock, and deserters scattered in the brush."[10]

On February 22, Santa Anna's exhausted army commenced the attack on Taylor's vastly outnumbered force near Saltillo. The wooden-legged Napoleon of Mexico had traveled in a chariot driven by eight mules, accompanied by "a bevy of wanton women" and a baggage train that included his fighting gamecocks. Lacking in elegance but not preparation, Taylor's five thousand soldiers held their ground. After two days of fighting, the Americans claimed victory. Santa Anna likewise declared himself the winner, then hurried off to attend to the renewed political chaos in the capital. In what can most judiciously be labeled a costly stalemate, Mexican casualties reached sixteen hundred, not including an inexplicable eighteen hundred missing. The Americans suffered about seven hundred killed and wounded. Santa Anna left the *soldaderas* to explore the devastated field, hoping to find the form of their family member intact. A Mexican observer noted, "Here a woman sobbing over the body, now lifeless, of her husband, and there, another ministering to hers, tortured with his wounds."[11]

After the encounter on February 24, Taylor detailed a dozen men, including Samuel Chamberlain, to approach Santa Anna's camp with a flag of truce. Chamberlain's portrayal of the Mexican site revealed the horror of war: stench, filth, dead men and animals everywhere. The men found themselves surrounded by a large party, many "almost witchlike" women, "old, bleary eyed, skin a mass of wrinkles, the color of oak bark." These "fearful hags" thought that the Americans were prisoners and, taking pity, offered them handfuls of rice. Chamberlain realized that the "poor wretches possess the true woman's heart." Though starving themselves, they evidenced kindness toward the enemy. Recognizing their generosity, the Americans opened their haversacks and distributed what supplies they had brought with them to the women. Chamberlain commented with admiration on the burdens and self-sacrifice of the *soldaderas,* who carried on without praise, rations, or pay and endured the severe treatment of their "indolent husbands."[12]

Tragically, not only did the Mexicans withdraw from the field at Buena Vista but the retreat across recently traveled ground marked the deaths of thousands more. The wounded unable to walk, as well as uncounted women and children, abandoned to the animals, endured putrid food, brackish water, and the bone-chilling cold. So extensive was the disaster of the campaign that residents of the town of San Luis Potosí decried the devastating "disappearance" of so many of its women.[13]

The agonizing outcomes repeated themselves in Winfield Scott's campaign on the road to the capital in the summer of 1847. Incompetence and rivalry among the Mexican generals led to the additional slaughter of their troops. The proximity of the women to combat, the chaos of cavalry assaults, and the air filled with bullets and artillery shot yielded a foreseeable outcome. Following one clash, an American officer described the revulsion of burying too numerous *soldaderas* who had died with their soldiers. A Mexican reporter bemoaned the "chaos and terror" of another encounter in which "screaming women ran back and forth like furies. United States cavalry charged through the terrified masses, slaughtering left and right." An American trooper moaned, "The most distressing of all was the sight of hundreds of dead *soldaderas* scattered among the bodies of their men."[14]

The Angel of the Battlefield

While the careful derogation of Mexican men did occur, especially *off* the battlefield (there is little glory in defeating an unworthy opponent), the place of the Mexican woman was quite another matter. Not only their beauty and their plight but their courage and sacrifice emerged as common themes in both letters and the popular literature. Perhaps the most well known and most heartrending image of a Mexican woman materialized from the engagement at Monterrey. The tragic scene was first depicted in a letter written by a soldier on October 7, 1846, sent to the *Louisville Courier,* and then republished for a wide readership in a December issue of Baltimore's *Niles' National Register.*

The missive recounted the clash on September 21 and the actions of a young woman moving about the ground that evening, carrying bread and water to the wounded of both armies and binding their injuries with articles of her own clothing. She returned to her cottage and reappeared on the field later that evening to continue her mission of mercy. Then, the soldier continued, "I heard the report of a gun and saw the poor innocent creature fall dead! I think it was an accidental shot that struck her. I would not be willing to believe otherwise. It made me sick at heart, and turning from the scene, I voluntarily raised my eyes towards heaven, and thought, great God, and *is this war?* The next day her body still lay where it had fallen, with the bread and a few drops of water in a gourd beside her. As the cannon shot and grape continued to fly around them, the American soldiers buried 'the angel of Monterrey.'" Only a few months into the conflict, newspapers far and wide, large and small, recounted this tale of a woman's courage and self-sacrifice under headlines such as "The Horrors of War: A Sad Case" and "A Mexican Woman: Her Noble Conduct and Sad Fate."[15]

The antiwar press, especially in New England, rallied to a vision of the senseless demise of a compassionate woman who only moments earlier had been "holding her pitcher of cooling drink to the feverish lips of the dying." Verse and song quickly followed. In January 1847, the accomplished McConnelsville, Ohio, poet Frances Gage, described as "one of the most gifted daughters of our Buckeye state . . . who has written much, and acquired for herself a reputation high amongst the first female writers of our age," crafted her tribute to the "angel," published along with the account of the incident in the *Ohio Statesman.* The paper noted that the piece would be "read with interest by every admirer of good poetry and correct sentiment." After retelling the maid's brave deeds, Gage's poem concluded with these lines:

> Thy horrors war—oh! who shall tell?
> Struck by a random ball or shell;
> That brave, that noble woman fell
> None died that day more gloriously.
> . . . .

Genius will sing the soldier's name
And give his daring deeds in fame,
For her a holier meed we claim,—
The heart shall shrine her memory.

"Correct sentiment" indicated that due deference should be granted the courage of the soldier; however, a higher place in the heart and heaven would be the reward of the brave maiden. Victorian Americans established a special elevated emotional station in both literature and reality for the fair, blonde, virginal woman, although exceptions could be made for the heroic darker-tressed woman. Should her virtue or honor be threatened or, worse, taken from her, death was to be preferred. Those women who positioned themselves in harm's way or sacrificed for spouse, family, or humanity writ large by performing acts of kindness as designated within the proper women's sphere were memorialized in poem and song.[16]

In this vein, the Episcopal minister the Reverend James G. Lyons composed "The Heroine of Monterey," which was quickly put to music for voice and piano accompaniment. The four-verse song became increasingly more graphic and creative as the angel ministered amid booming shot and flaming shell "thick as winter's driving sleet." Lyons crafted a final scenario for the martyred maid:

They laid her in her narrow bed, the foemen of her land and race;
And sighs were breathed, and tears were shed, above her lowly resting place—
Ay! glory's crimson worshippers wept over her untimely fall,
For deeds of mercy, such as hers, subdue the hearts and eyes of all.[17]

Politicians seized upon the tragedy. In February 1847, Senator Thomas Corwin delivered his powerful speech attacking the morality of the war and the image of the United States among the Christian nations of the world. The "bloody hands" passage, however, overshadowed his remarks about the "angel of Monterrey." Corwin also recalled the benevolence and "robust courage" of the young woman who delivered water to the parched lips of the dying "amid the falling houses and shrieks of war." Suddenly, as an American officer looked upon her, "a cannon ball struck her and blew her to atoms." Clearly, by the time the story of the "angel"'s actions reached antiwar circles in Washington, the story of her death had taken on more dramatic dimensions and varied markedly from the account in the original Louisville letter.[18]

After the war, the legend still would not die. The New York native John Hill

Hewitt gained fame as a composer of minstrel ditties, songs of the South, and in the Civil War era, ballads such as "All Quiet Along the Potomac." In 1851, however, Hewitt made his mark with a song for voice and guitar entitled "The Maid of Monterey." The music was up-tempo, and the lyrics created a very different scene for the maid. As dusk fell and quiet encompassed the bloody ground, she went about her acts of mercy. Hewitt wanted his audience to be aware of her sacrifice, but appears to have been uninterested in the maudlin nature of her death or burial.

> For tho she loved her nation, and pray'd that it might live
> Yet for the dying foemen, she had a tear to give
> Thus here's to that bright beauty, who drove death's pang away
> The meek-eyed señorita, the maid of Monterey.

Some thirty years after the war, the maid was granted a more interesting rebirth in the mind of Luis P. Senarens, the son of a Cuban tobacco merchant and an American mother, who wrote fantasy fiction for teenage boys. In 1886, Senarens created a short story entitled "Old Rough and Ready, or The Heroine of Monterey," which rekindled the image for a younger generation.[19]

From campaign to campaign, "angels" abounded thereafter. The Charleston, South Carolina, *Southern Patriot* reported an incident involving the wanderings of an American soldier, Gwin Bernard of Illinois, after the Battle of Buena Vista. Suffering from fractured ribs and separated from his mates, a feverish and starving Bernard stumbled upon a shack made of reed, mud, and leaves. He entered, desperate, only to find a young woman grieving with her rosary over the body of a family member recently killed. Bernard explained that while her eyes flashed with hatred, the tender nature of her gender and race ultimately prevailed. She provided him with water and a few kernels of parched corn and bound his wounds. Her poverty and dark complexion signaled that nothing more would come of their encounter; "her swart features were beautiful in their ruggedness by an air of fervent devotion." She wept bitterly, but the soldier had no words of consolation as he departed the cottage. He realized, however, that he had been saved by his own angel.[20]

Americans seemed consumed with the anthem of the tender, tragic Mexican maid providing nourishment and relief. Several possible explanations can be offered for the fascination. The heroic woman, whether martyred on a humanitarian mission or on the field of combat, confirmed the Anglo concept that Mexican women were more patriotic, more fearless, and more steadfast than their male counterparts. Gwin Bernard's nameless savior exemplified the depth of compassion of the Mexican woman who in her time of grief and despair afforded comfort and nourishment to her enemy. For the war's survivors, common decency, at least among women, still prevailed. This was in sharp contrast to the bluff and bravado of politicians, generals, and their supporters, who justified the fight as extending the boundaries of liberty and civilization.

An added prompt emanated from the war zones, so far removed from everyday existence for Americans, which gave few Anglo women the opportunity to contribute or sacrifice. Inserting the gender dimension certainly humanized the conflict by demonstrating that actions fought around villages, towns, and cities could well endanger the lives of Mexican women and children. The resultant deaths, the individual woman senselessly shot down by a single bullet or a family crushed by the walls of a falling building, provided fodder for those who saw the killing of Mexican civilians as a barbaric product of a needless quarrel.

The antiwar poet John Greenleaf Whittier seized on the theme in his widely heralded "The Angels of Buena Vista," published in the *National Era.* Whittier took aim at the American political and military leaders who had dragooned the nation into an unholy contest. His sympathies went to the innocents on both sides of the Rio Grande. Inspired by the sentiment of earlier poems and songs of Monterrey, Whittier penned a lengthy, moving scenario of "sisters" witnessing the bloody American victory in February 1847 and hastening onto the field to tend to the wounded with a sip of water and a prayer:

> Whispered low the dying soldier, pressed her hand and faintly smiled;
> Was that pitying face his mother's? did she watch beside her child?
> All his stranger words with meaning her woman's heart supplied;
> With her kiss upon his forehead, "Mother!" murmured he, and died!

And as the day ended,

> The noble Mexic women still their holy task pursued
> Through that long, dark night of sorrow, worn and faint and lacking food.
> Over weak and suffering brothers, with a tender care they hung,
> And the dying foeman blessed them in a strange and Northern tongue.[21]

Several weeks later, in March 1847, Major John Corey Henshaw came across yet another real-life "angel" near Veracruz. As his command moved through a wooded area, Henshaw soon discovered a dead woman, about twenty-eight years old, dressed in white. She had been shot through the right breast and apparently died without a struggle, evidently the target of an American rifleman. In each hand she tightly held a small basket containing provisions, which she obviously had hastily thrown together. Probably, he opined, she was in the act of escaping to the forest "when the messenger of death arrested her flight." Henshaw concluded with the dispassion of a veteran, "Her clothes and body were completely crimsoned with her blood."[22]

Not surprisingly, the Mexicans propagated several of their own "angels of Monterrey." Yolanda García Romero suggests that María Josefa Zozaya was a composite figure. The initial version of her story, published in 1848, has Zozaya engaged in activities, albeit courageously, that seem acceptable to traditional cultures in both Mexico and the United States. Interestingly, however, she was most certainly *not* the "angel of the Monterrey" bringing succour to all the afflicted, but a bona fide Mexican patriot who moved nimbly about the rooftops of the city aiding her countrymen with much-needed food and munitions. A young woman, "as beautiful as the protective goddesses sculpted by the Greeks," she taught her compatriots "how to despise danger" and gave them the pluck necessary to face the challenge of the invading Yankees. The second depiction portrays Zozaya as a much older woman leading on the battlefield and dying in combat. Yet another version, which the historian Elizabeth Salas endorses, parallels the story related in the American press: Zozaya brings relief and comfort to men of both armies until felled by a bullet. While her identity remains obscured in legend, Mexicans seemed to prefer Zozaya as an active patriot, while the "angel" image resonated north of the Rio Grande.[23]

Women in Combat

Women traditionally constituted a key support element of the army, but their emergence in the line of fire, while not unknown, had been unusual. Precedents did exist. In the nineteenth century both Latin and American cultures held a restricted view of women in the public sphere. However, traumatic events in a nation's history sometimes demand the exceptional, and the crucible of war creates unusual heroes. For the United States there was a composite figure called "Molly Pitcher," first bringing water to parched Revolutionary War soldiers and then, when her husband fell, taking his place by his cannon. Almost a century later, Barbara Fritchie, an octogenarian resident of Frederick, Maryland, defied the Confederate general "Stonewall" Jackson to "shoot if you must this old grey head, but touch not your country's flag." In Mexico, the figures of

María Zozaya and Doña Jesús Dosamentes make up a critical component of Mexican legend.

When Monterrey fell to the Americans in September 1846, Zachary Taylor allowed his defeated opponent to withdraw from the city in rank order. Two American officers commented on the unfolding drama. Abner Doubleday watched the procession and derisively recorded seeing "the Mexican forces file by in all their disgrace. They were accompanied by a perfect army of females on horseback." Daniel Harvey Hill also took note of the scene, praising the appearance of the Castilian-looking officers, while demeaning the regular soldiers as "inferior looking men." A large number of women on horseback, apparently officers' wives, followed the army, and trailing behind on foot trudged a host of women carrying packs. "I did not see a good looking woman among them all," he remarked, offhandedly describing their appearance rather than their burden.[24]

A Scotswoman, Frances Calderón de la Barca, observing a similar formation in Santa Anna's army some years earlier, in 1841, concurred with Hill. While remarking about the Indian *soldaderas* following the army, carrying the shoes and clothing of their husbands, de la Barca focused with scorn on a body of "masculine women with serapes or mangas, and large straw hats tied down with various colored handkerchiefs." These "mounted Amazons," she sniffed, "looked like very ugly men in semi-female disguise." Elizabeth Salas rebuts that such disparagement typifies the emergent Victorian view in the West regarding the proper place for women in warfare. Women in a dangerous supportive role most certainly did not meet with the approbation of de la Barca or her peers, who failed to understand both the culture and the needs of the Mexican Army.[25]

Indeed, the environment appeared desperate in 1846, when the Joan of Arc of Mexico first made her appearance, documented in both US and Mexican sources. On September 19, 1846, General Pedro Ampudia, commander of the forces in defense of Monterrey, wrote a short and most unusual letter to the minister of war. A young señorita, Doña Jesús Dosamentes, had reported to him dressed as a captain "and mounted to fight the unjust invaders." Ampudia seized the moment. Recognizing the impact that her audacity might have on the army, rather than brushing the presumptuous woman aside, he received her with the affection "that her heroic behavior deserves" and sent her out to ride the line and inspire the troops. She carried an order from him, however, "so that all would show the respect due to her."

Ampudia dispatched his Joan of Arc to the Third Brigade, where Colonel José Uraga savvily comprehended his part and how the army might utilize its new enthusiastic volunteer to best advantage. He knew that such an opportunity was "rare in the annals of history," and it "moved him to joy and enthusiasm." Before any fighting had occurred, Ampudia and Uraga referred to Doña Jesús as an "intrepid heroine" committed to repelling "the infamous usurpers." Uraga explained to her the dangers and privations, suggesting that a safer environment might be suitable. She remained steadfast. Doña Jesús wanted to be "where the enemy bullets will whistle first and where there will be more glory, even if greater risk." Uraga also wisely understood that he could employ her courage to great effect among his men and ordered that they accord "her all the deference due to her sex" and her patriotic conduct. Grateful that "this delicate señorita" was willing to die for Mexico, Uraga assured his superior that Doña Jesús's praiseworthy conduct would not be "buried in oblivion" and had tremendous potential to impact the morale and enthusiasm of the soldiers.[26]

Doña Jesús Dosamentes would have her Joan of Arc moment, and she would not disappoint her nation. Several months later, in a column for the New York paper *Spirit of the Times,* George Wilkins Kendall included part of a letter from a young Irish deserter from the US Army, "G de L," who had witnessed the lengthy contest for Monterrey. He described the tale of a young woman, known as Dos Amades, who, "seized with a patriotic spirit, unsexed herself and dressed in the full suit of a captain of lancers." She swore that she would drive the "Northern barbarians" from the land or shed her last drop of blood in the effort. Prior to leading a charge on September 21, Dos Amades rode along the line of her troops, exhorting their patriotism and challenging their manhood. The charge failed, and many of her lancers died that day, but the legend of Dos Amades was born. The Irishman praised the courage of the Amazon warrior and her lancers. "There's an example," he exclaimed, "of heroism worthy of the days of old. It has remained for Mexico to produce a second Joan d' Arc, but not, like her successful." Kendall postscripted these comments, declaring that rumors held the young officer to be the daughter of the former governor of Nuevo León. She continued to fight and was almost captured in the city by Texas Rangers. When Monterrey fell, a saddened Dos Amades put her uniform aside and returned to her family and temporary obscurity.[27]

The fact and mythology that surround both María Josefa Zozaya and Doña Jesús Dosamentes inform us about the role of certain Mexican women during the war. We know very little about either individual in terms of her background or fate following the actions during the Monterrey campaign. Doña Jesús was, importantly, the daughter of a high-ranking government official, upper class, and light skinned. It seems unlikely that a poor peasant girl would have access to the tent of the commander of the Army of the North and demonstrate the impudence of demanding a role in the field. When General Ampudia consented to the notion of this female warrior, he clearly saw the inspirational possibilities, but did he indeed envision a martyr or an ongoing symbol? We may never know.

Certainly, less-heralded women risked life and limb defending their country and their men. The Spanish-born writer Niceto de Zamacois stirred and incited Mexicans with his short story published in October 1847 about the martyrdom of the twenty-eight-year-old patriot and intellectual Luis Martínez de Castro at Churubusco, near Mexico City. Zamacois embellished the tale of his doomed hero by creating a fictional love interest, sixteen-year-old Matilde. In the dramatic conclusion, as the Yankees stormed the heights, Mexican resistance stiffened and the valiant Martínez de Castro suffered a ball to the chest, prompting all but his faithful flag-bearer to abandon him. As the Americans closed in and were about to deliver a fatal saber blow, the flag-bearer removed his cap, allowing two long braids to fall, and proclaimed, "Wound, wound this unhappy woman from whom you have taken the only treasure she had in the world." Martínez de Castro recognized the voice and opened his eyes a last time to gaze on his beloved. Life without him had no meaning, however, and the girl soon died of spotted fever, which "came from her constant weeping and suffering." While Martínez de Castro's sacrifice marked "the true way to glory," his friends protested that the romance compromised the actions and the character of the real man.[28]

In December 1846, the US colonel Alexander Doniphan's command of five hundred men had its first skirmish at Bracito, near El Paso. In the brief encounter, a Mexican force of nearly twelve hundred unsuccessfully attacked Doniphan, resulting in no loss of American lives and perhaps a few dozen Mexican casualties. As the Americans sifted through the residue of the melee that remained on the field, a soldier reported with considerable glee, "The Mexican women were gloriously represented in this fight." The rumor abounded that two women had crewed a cannon and that a rifle ball had struck one in the forehead, instantly killing her. Her friend had bravely carried her off the field. "I do not doubt it," the soldier explained, "the women have much more courage and even sense than the men." Another source reported, however, that Missouri volunteers had actually found the woman beside her cannon.

A skirmish at Taos had a more positive ending. As an American dragoon contemplated slaying a Mexican soldier, she managed to save her own life "by an act of the most conclusive personal exposure." Outside Mexico City, US soldiers stumbled upon the tombstone of Doña María Vicario de Quintana. The inscription subtly noted that "she preferred to leave her convent and join the standard of her country, under which she performed many feats of valor." These snippets of patriotism offer insight into what were likely broader, unrecorded sacrifices.[29]

Whether in front leading the soldiers or behind in support, women remained highly visible to the army. That visibility cut both ways. Women expected their men to uphold the honor of the Mexican people and their nation. When American columnists and novelists derided the diminutive size and effeminate nature of Latin men, the women reacted strongly to such language and challenged their men. D. H. Hill observed that after the fall of Monterrey in September 1846, Mexican women, including his very patriotic landlady, doffed mourning garb and draped their houses in black for three days, as the church bells rang funereal tolls. The ladies then proceeded to paint pictures of Mexican officers engaged in sewing and other "feminine occupations," while American officers in full dress looked on.[30]

The indignation of Mexican women regarding the conduct of the war appeared early and expressed itself in broadsides and posters. Legend, hearsay, and reality commingled to create an image of Mexican women engaged in acts of heroism, danger, and self-sacrifice—as well as opportunism—during the contest. Some women emanated from the upper classes, and their deeds, while often real, were intended to inspire patriotism among the sometimes reluctant masses. The extent of their success is elusive, but their status in Mexican history is well established.

Mexicans remain conflicted about the role of women in their turbulent past. Certainly, some women did collaborate with Maximilian's French forces of occupation in the 1860s, as they had with those of Taylor and Scott. The numerous nameless *soldaderas* carry a particular burden, since their motives for collaboration or patriotism varied so dramatically. Many were simply forced into service. For others, money, employment, independence, marriage, or desperation provided the enticement. Salas blasts a minority as "parasitical camp followers." Far more, however, enacted the centuries-old responsibility of giving sustenance and support to their men and their country. Lacking any parallel within the national experience, Americans have too often marginalized their role or simply derogated the *soldaderas* as servants or slaves. Such harsh judgment fails to appreciate the impact they had on the army and what it reveals about gender and Mexican culture.[31]

3

On the Santa Fe Trail

The smoke from a *cigarrito* curled around the woman's face, obscuring her expression. No matter. All eyes focused on her hands, fingers deftly firing out cards onto the wooden table. A crowd of interested and inebriated traders, trappers, and soldiers looked on. Cries of despair and oaths of disgust quickly rose, as the woman swept the gold dust and coins toward her. With little hesitation, the cards were back in play. Gertrudis Barceló proved once again that she had no peer at the monte tables of New Mexico. The road she had traveled from a childhood in Sonora to become Doña Tules of Santa Fe paralleled two decades of economic growth that had transformed the Santa Fe Trail. Political and economic chaos in Mexico had intervened, highlighted by the disruptive war years and the American occupation. New Mexico had endured an invasion by Stephen Watts Kearny and the US Army, supplemented by a battalion of Mormons, with their own goals and destiny.

The military received the aid of merchants such as Samuel Magoffin, whose wagon train followed the army along the trail. Magoffin's young wife, Susan, recorded her views in a revealing diary of their rugged and strange journey into Mexico. Susan met many locals, but none as extraordinary as Doña Tules. The past and future economic interests of the United States and the Magoffins intersected with those of Mexico and Doña Tules in New Mexico in 1846. Neither would be the same.

The Economics of New Mexico

Huzzas filled the air from Lexington, Massachusetts, to Lexington, Kentucky, at the news of General Andrew Jackson's improbable triumph over a formidable British army at New Orleans on January 8, 1815. The War of 1812 had formally ended some days earlier with the signing in Europe of the Treaty of Ghent. The beleaguered American people accrued no tangible benefits, save their heightened national pride and patriotism. While the masses celebrated their hero and the soldiers that symbolized their image, resourceful businessmen and politicians moved to revitalize a country worn down by a generation of economic warfare. Within a decade, the looms at Slatersville and Lowell would hum and rattle, and plows in Illinois and Alabama would furrow and channel the soil for seed.

Traditional Jeffersonians wrestled with the concepts of investment, debt, and global trade, while a generation of "New Republicans," led by Henry Clay and his "American System," pressed for a market revolution that involved significant risk and profit. Indeed, some might argue that this expanded capitalism had its losers, exploited New England girls at spinning wheels or displaced Indians shuttled off to Oklahoma and Kansas, as well as winners, mill owners and farmers. Whether Americans exported their textiles, cotton, and grains to Europe, Latin America, or the Far East, most businessmen and agrarians struggled with the absence of one key component in trade and investment—hard metal specie.

A severe depression, the Panic of 1819, exposed the weakness of the US economy. No significant deposits of gold or silver would be discovered in the United States until a rush began in 1829 near Dahlonega, Georgia. Too late to contribute to the financial recovery, the limited quantity of gold produced could not keep up with the demand of rejuvenated markets, opening the way for the investment of European, especially British, capital. Many Americans also faced the dilemma of utilizing the currency of unreliable state banks or supporting the Second Bank of the United States, whose recent policies had tainted its reputation. For American merchants in the West or those who imported goods from the East Coast across the Mississippi River, help came from a most unexpected source.

Mexico had secured its independence from Spain in 1821 and unlocked its northern provinces to US trade. The prospect of making money from a newly opened venue and having those items paid for by Mexican silver excited and inspired US merchants, particularly in the specie-starved West. They willingly endured the tedium of the Santa Fe Trail, almost eight hundred miles from Independence, Missouri, to New Mexico, for the promise of real profits. The danger posed by Indians, animals, thirst, heat, and rain only added to the challenge.

The commerce began modestly enough in 1821, when the frontiersman William Becknell stumbled into the sale of a small quantity of goods in Santa Fe. Over the course of a quarter century the trade reached $1 million a year, much of it extending beyond the Santa Fe Trail, south along the Camino Real, and

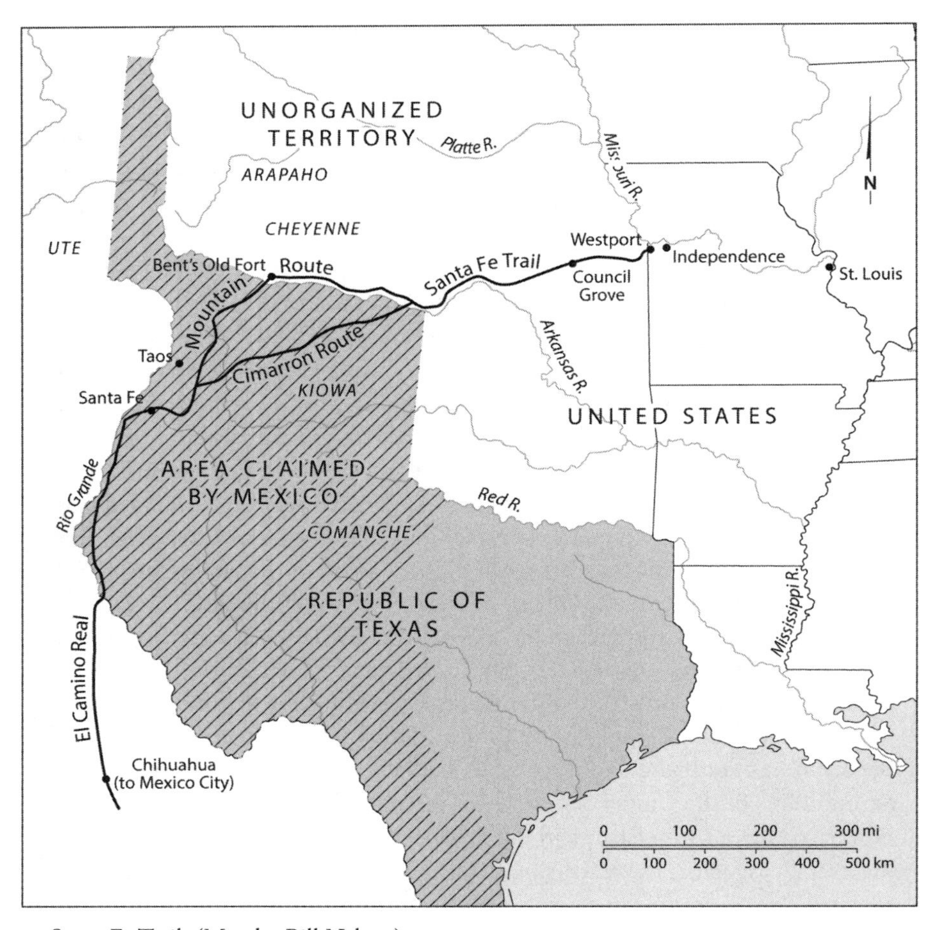

Santa Fe Trail. (Map by Bill Nelson)

reaching Chihuahua. With fifteen thousand inhabitants, Chihuahua was triple the size of Santa Fe, and its thirty smelting plants yielded vast quantities of silver. American businessmen swiftly adjusted to include the interior markets in their calculations. They piled their oxen-pulled Conestoga wagons high, with up to two tons of textiles (cottons, fabrics, and cloth), and returned with somewhat lighter loads of precious metals. Specie, gold dust, silver bars, and coins secured in rawhide packages were the principal element of the exchange, but mules also proved to be a valuable commodity, carrying the bounty back to Missouri.[1]

Traders were not the only American entrepreneurs finding their destiny in New Mexico. Fur trappers, on the heels of the pioneering Lewis and Clark expedition of 1804–6, recognized the opportunity for wealth provided by beaver pelts in the Rocky Mountains. The trappers also ventured south, and by the 1830s, small but growing communities of American men emerged in Santa Fe and Taos. The more ambitious and accomplished men obtained land grants and adapted to the culture, learning Spanish, marrying local women, and becoming Mexican citizens. Among the leading early pioneers, Charles Bent and his brother William established a supply store and depot, Bent's Fort, on the Santa Fe Trail in Colorado. The one-building, one-story compound, made of mud and unburned brick, was about fifty yards square with an inner courtyard. Fireproof and virtually impregnable to Indian attack, it became the gathering spot for both traders and trappers. The fort's success led to an expansion of the firm—Bent and St. Vrain—in Santa Fe and Taos. Charles Bent, a Virginian and West Point graduate, wed the prominent María Ignacia Jaramillo and moved to Taos. He soon became one of the most powerful men in the territory, much to the consternation of Mexican officials.[2]

In 1840, Governor Manuel Armijo objected to the destructive nature of the Americans, harboring robbers in their forts, arming Indians, and promoting illicit trade. Bent, whose growing influence magnified his arrogance for individuals and the law, found the governor equally annoying. For Bent, Armijo exacerbated the downward spiral in the relationship by wrongly slandering him. The sensitive American made a host of enemies in Taos and dedicated a good deal of time defending his reputation.

In 1841, Juan B. Vigil wrote the governor, accusing Bent and a comrade of plotting to annex New Mexico to the Republic of Texas. An attack followed in which Vigil was soundly whipped and Bent placed under house arrest by the alcalde (mayor). The outraged American explained his actions to US Consul Manuel Álvarez in Santa Fe, claiming that the affront had been personal and should be settled as a matter of honor. "I had rather have the satisfaction of whipping a man that has wronged me than to have him punished ten times by the law," he informed Álvarez. "The law to me for a personal offence is no satisfaction whatever, but Cowardes and wimen must take this satisfaction." Bent adroitly used his clout to bribe officials to reduce the taxation rate on the wagons of compatriots arriving from Missouri. A good word and a well-placed peso from "don Carlos Bent" could help mightily in adjusting the six-hundred-dollars-per-wagon duties. When the war began in the spring of 1846, Americans like Bent, for better or worse, were firmly encamped in New Mexico.[3]

The Mormon Battalion and the Borderlands

Since the outbreak of hostilities threatened New Mexican commerce, sharp-eyed merchants found solace in the prospects of a continuation of their trade in spite of the conflict and the more satisfying possibility of US annexation of the Southwest. In June 1846, President Polk, a man whose imperial vision reached to the Pacific Ocean, ordered General Stephen Watts Kearny and his 1,600-man Army of the West to take and occupy Santa Fe on their way to the conquest of California. Kearny's command, 1,350 of whom were rough-and-tumble Missouri volunteers, was supplemented by the Mormon Battalion, an assemblage of about 500 men, women, and children, some headed for California, others bound for the isolation of the Great Salt Lake of Utah. Along the trail, American merchants with hundreds of wagons laden with goods for the extended Mexican markets joined the procession.

Secretary of War William L. Marcy instructed Kearny to adopt a conciliatory policy toward the Mexican people, encouraging their allegiance to the United States, establishing civilian government, promising democratic rule, and maintaining uninterrupted trade. With so few soldiers available for garrison duty, Marcy had little choice but to craft the image of the Americans as a benevolent victor. This strategy appeared conceptually sound but would prove operationally problematic.[4]

Polk's motives in recruiting the Mormons remain murky. Only two years earlier, Prophet Joseph Smith had been murdered by a mob in Illinois, his leadership post taken by the inspirational Brigham Young. Young had moved many of his flock westward to Council Bluffs, Iowa, a stopover on their way to the promised land in the Rockies. Was Polk testing the loyalty of the Mormons, or did he simply recognize the need for additional manpower? Regardless, the appearance of American soldiers in the Mormon camp at Mount Pisgah on June 26 caused quite a stir. Anxious men reached for their weapons, and women and children hid until the mission of the dragoons became clear. They were empowered to recruit five companies of "Saints" for one year to battle the Mexicans. Each company could take along four women as cooks and laundresses. The women would earn seven dollars a month, a private's salary.[5]

The proposal met with mixed reactions among the faithful. A majority rejected the offer, suspicious of the administration's intentions. Many women saw the request as "unfair," saying that "the Saints had given enough and owed the government nothing." Melissa Coray, however, was more positive. "She didn't see why women must always stay behind and worry about their husbands when they could just as well march beside them." The men ultimately took their cue from "Brother Brigham." Lieutenant Colonel James Allen visited with Young, and the resulting conversation convinced the Mormon leader that enlisting would prove their loyalty to Washington, and the soldiers' pay would add to the church's coffers. The Prophet addressed his flock on July 6, and the corner was turned; within three weeks the reluctant but dutiful fell in line. Clearly, the Mormons participated as a matter of faith, not for the defense of the nation, and with the promise that they all would soon rendezvous in the Great Basin of Utah. Anguished sons said their farewells to aging parents, husbands to their wives and children, as the band played "The Girl I Left Behind." One diarist caustically remarked that a young volunteer from Illinois "probably was the only man eager to enter the military service."[6]

Ultimately, 543 men would be mustered into service, joined by 32 married women, aged eighteen to forty-nine, and 51 children. Captain Jefferson Hunt took along his two wives, Celia and Matilda, four sons, and three daughters. Few Mormons had such luxury. The separation of families was particularly painful for the approximately 150 wives and numerous children remaining in a barren environment with little shelter or sustenance. Tragically, their worst fears were too often realized. Margaret Phelps recalled her husband, Alva, disappearing in the middle of the night, leaving her and the children "homeless, without a protector." The family scrambled to survive, building a "wretched hovel" with a dirt floor into a hillside. Pelted with rain over a cold winter, the dirt turned to mud three inches deep. Food was scarce, and the tiny house was heated by wood the children gathered, but the wood was so green that the room filled with smoke. Compounding the depression of the bedridden Margaret's endless winter was the news of her husband's death along the Santa Fe Trail.

Other wives told similar tales of privation. Louisa Sprague was parted from her husband, Richard, for two and a half years. Her ten-year-old daughter, with only rags on her feet, trudged through deep snow to cut and drag wood back to their cramped quarters on Mosquito Creek. The community had one spinning wheel, which everyone used to spin carded wool for their clothing. The church bishop milked his cow each day and shared the meager bounty with Louisa and her family.[7]

Inadequate housing, tattered clothes, and precious little food formed a pattern that arguably caused greater suffering for the women near Council Bluffs than for those headed southwest. Angry and puzzled, Margrett Scott unleashed a tirade on her brother James, who had recently enlisted in the battalion. She confessed that he had "acted so differently to what I had expected" and feared that his innocence and lack of self-control would make him an easy target for "designing men." Margrett admitted, too, that the conduct of the church leadership in support of the Polk administration was "beyond my comprehension." James assured her that he was part of the Army of Israel, servants of God. Yet she was mystified about how a legion of Christians could be "sent out voluntarily with muskets and bayonets" to affect God's will.[8]

Life along the Santa Fe Trail had its own travails. In an effort to save time and reach New Mexico directly, the Mormons traveled the shorter but more desolate Cimarron route. A teamster described the problems with thirst encountered in crossing a desert eighty miles wide carrying a limited supply of water. Bones of dead animals abounded, accompanied by the occasional human skull. When husbands could not provide transportation for their wives on wagons or mules, the women were obliged to walk along with the men. Pregnant women especially suffered. Sickness and death abounded, with fevers taking a toll on soldiers, mothers, and newborn infants. Unfortunately, their leader, Lieutenant Colonel Allen, became an early casualty, succumbing on August 23 at Fort Leavenworth. Kearny found a replacement in a man whom he trusted but the Mormons disliked, the West Pointer Philip St. George Cooke. Providentially for most of the women, the adventure ended after a few months. Their arrival in Santa Fe on October 12, almost two months after Kearny had occupied the town, began with a warm reception in the plaza, including handshakes, from a throng of Mexican women who appeared genuinely delighted to see them.[9]

Hastily, Cooke assessed the reality of the situation: the family approach simply would not work. He decided that the Mormons were too old, too young, too feeble, undisciplined, and "embarrassed by many women." They were worn down by the travel from Nauvoo, Illinois. Marching an additional eleven hundred miles on foot to the Pacific with ill-fed, lightly clad women and children, not to mention the broken-down mules, seemed a recipe for disaster, and he had no money or clothes to relieve their condition.

As a military force, the Mormons were obedient, but they had never been drilled, lacked order, and evidenced "great heedlessness and ignorance, and some obstinacy." Cooke determined to send ill soldiers and families 180 miles to Pueblo, Colorado, where a band of Mississippi brethren had already camped for the season. Several husbands groused that they could not "retain their manhood" and allow their wives to go on without them. Colonel Alexander Doniphan calmed the situation by permitting the distraught husbands to accompany their wives to Colorado.

Eventually, three detachments, including eighty-six men, twenty-eight women, and many of the children, made the trip, supposedly for their health and safety. The hardships continued. They wintered in Pueblo, where the women grappled with the weather extremes and lack of food and water before departing for Fort Laramie, Wyoming, in May 1847, and then on to the Great Salt Lake. Meanwhile, the battalion, battling climate and weather but rarely Mexicans, marched through New Mexico and Arizona (where the Pima Indians provided welcome victuals) before reaching San Diego in late January 1847.[10]

The Mormons had their first extended exposure to Mexican women during their stay in Santa Fe in October 1846. Cooke encouraged his troops to socialize with the community and get to know and appreciate their culture. The results were decidedly mixed. Albert Smith and his son Azariah attended Catholic Mass, where the father delighted in the beauty of the statues and the music, while the son enjoyed the ladies, "some of which looked very pretty; others looked like destruction." The Americans appeared at a dance, a fandango, ill-prepared for the color and drama of the occasion. Sergeant William Coray reluctantly went with his wife and later carped that "the whole event sickened me." While he could tolerate the music, "the ill manners of the females disgusted me."[11]

Not everyone appreciated the plight and sacrifice of the Mormons. The Missourian George Gibson noted that "a more ragamuffin-looking set would be hard to find out of New Mexico," describing the men from officers on down generally as appearing shabby and having bad countenances. Observing the Mormon and Mexican women at a fandango, Gibson concluded that "it was hard to tell which had the advantage of the other." When the Mormons exited Santa Fe, the young lieutenant admitted that their departure did thin the ranks but said that their presence had only "created confusion and disturbance." "The States have lost nothing by the Mormon emigration," he decided, "and California gains as little, for the state of Illinois makes a good bargain to get shut of them at any cost."[12]

When the sixty-seven mule- and oxen-pulled wagons rolled out of Santa Fe in late October, the party comprised only 350 men and 5 women: the aforementioned Melissa Coray, a bride of only three weeks at the commencement of the excursion; Lydia Hunter, the pregnant wife of Captain Jesse Hunter; Phebe Brown, the wife of Sergeant Ebenezer Brown and mother of son Zemira, an aide to the battalion; Susan Davis, the wife of Captain Daniel Davis and his six-year-old son, Daniel Jr.; and Sophia Gribble, the wife of Private William Gribble. Four women, including Melissa Coray, and one boy made the entire crossing to California. Only Gribble did not complete the trek, joining her husband with a third detachment headed for Pueblo. The difficulties mounted as they headed out of Albuquerque bound for San Diego. The relentless rain soaked their clothes and muddied the roads. The difficult terrain obliged Colonel Cooke to lighten the loads of the wagons, reducing each mess to one camp kettle. Twelve private wagons formed part of the train. To help pass the time, Melissa Coray joined Lydia Hunter on her wagon, where they sang hymns and popular songs of the era, such as "Lucy Long." This situation ended unhappily when Captain Hunter protested that his animals were not fit enough to pull Melissa's added weight.[13]

Most Mexicans had never seen an Anglo woman, so they attracted attention at every town and village along their route. The soldiers grumbled that the natives sold them fruit (watermelon remained a special treat), corn, and wine at ridiculous prices but obliged the American ladies, presenting them with apples as a gift. Obtaining foodstuffs remained tricky, and the Americans relied heavily on supplementing their diets with Mexican edibles. The Mormon women exchanged clothes, brass buttons, and other unique items with the local women for food. Scarcity, however, drove a desperate Phebe Brown to scavenge the burnt bread from the company to feed her son. Recognizing the pitiful state of the Mormons, the locals made certain to move their flocks of sheep and goats out of the path of temptation.[14]

For the four Mormon women who survived the arduous passage to California, their arrival in San Diego in January 1847 held a final tragedy. Lydia Hunter gave birth to a son, Diego, the first child to be born to American parents in the city, only to be struck within the week by a fever, tremors, and delirium. "She suffered greatly" and died on April 26. Melissa Coray remained the only other Mormon woman in San Diego until her husband departed for Los Angeles in early May, while Susan Davis and Phebe Brown had already traveled there with their husbands. Susan and Phebe caused quite a stir upon their entrance into Los Angeles, representing a rare Anglo presence. Captain Hunt staged a dress parade to impress the citizens, but by all accounts the soldiers bungled the exercise because of his mistakes. Twenty elegant Creole women were on hand for the occasion, prompting one soldier to remark, "They were the most richly dressed of anything I have seen yet." The ladies likely dismissed the military amateurism; they attended to chat with the American women.[15]

While the women may well have bonded, the American men were left to ponder a troubling reality across the Mexican borderlands—the paucity of Anglo women. Middle-class Victorian America not only broadly proscribed premarital sex but, just as important, remained equivocal about racial boundaries. Marriage between Anglos and Latinos had been limited in both number and geography. A few adventurous merchants established trading houses in Veracruz or cotton factories in northern Mexico and wed local women. A similar situation emerged with veterans of the Santa Fe trade, who saw the advantage of melding destinies with genes from prominent families in New Mexico. The historian Deena Gonzalez emphasizes, however, that such unions remained the exception rather than rule. The 1850 census revealed that in Santa Fe, a community of more than 4,000, 100 of the 239 Euro-American males had married Spanish Mexican women. Gonzalez contends, "Santa Fe remained a Spanish-Mexican town, and most Spanish-Mexicans continued to marry each other."[16]

Texas in the antebellum era demonstrated a somewhat similar pattern. Jane Dysart examined civil marriage records in antebellum (1837–60) San Antonio and discovered that only 10 percent (88) of Mexican women chose to marry Anglos, while more than 900 wed Mexican men. Perhaps not surprisingly, half the Anglo marriages involved upper-class Mexican women and rarely paired an Anglo woman with a Mexican man. Many of the Anglo men were like Jim Bowie, the knife-wielding hero of the Alamo, who came from rather common roots and married Ursula Veramendi, the daughter of a governor of Texas. For landed Mexicans, an Anglo son-in-law, though of undetermined class, might well preserve or provide access to business and social influence, as well as salvage some vestige of political power swept away by the Anglos in the postwar Southwest. Prominent Tejano families, such as the Seguins, the Navarros, and the Cassianos, each of whom held more than twenty thousand acres, tactfully sought the salvation of the wedding vow. The Anglo man also benefited, generally enhancing his social position as well as profiting from the inherited property that customarily fell equally to both daughters and sons.[17]

The scholar Ana Carolina Castillo Crimm traced the path of the wealthy and powerful de León family of Victoria. The de Leóns, led by the matriarch Patricia de la Garza, conducted what can best be described as a soap-opera quest to preserve their family and vast estates amid the turmoil of the period, including the Texas Revolution, the Mexican-American War, German immigration, child adoption, and unending lawsuits. Manipulative, perhaps cunning, the sage grand dame weaved her way through the changing world of Tejano-Anglo relations in the post–Mexican-American War era. Women of her stature held power within the family and the community; her position brought her unquestioned respect and authority. Influencing social relationships, especially involving godparents, women such as Doña Patricia could affect business and family ties. While intermarriage did not play a major role in their dealings, her family befriended the region's powerful Linn clan, whose political and legal might were brought to bear in their behalf.[18]

In California, American seafarers and fortune hunters reinvented themselves in port cities from San Diego to San Francisco. Since no Anglo women were in residence, the racial rules were bent, if not broken. Francis Brown took an "Indian" woman named Magell Mancheeta for his bride, while a Captain Barker wed a "California lady" in a Catholic ceremony. Thomas Wrightington, perhaps the second American to settle in San Diego, arrived on a whaler in 1833 via the Sandwich Islands. A one-eyed shoemaker from Fall River, Massachusetts, Wrightington became a modestly successful businessman, the owner of a one-room adobe grog shop and dry-goods store, and part-time politician. His courtship of Doña Juana Machado Alipaz in 1840 met the needs of both parties. Doña Juana had married a soldier, Domasio Alipaz, who was killed in Sonora in 1835, leaving her a widow at 21 with three small children and property. The couple soon added four more children.[19]

The Mexican-American War brought opportunity to the growing Wrightington household. Following the December 1846 Battle of San Pasqual, in which Kearny's small force was roundly defeated, the American wounded received care at Doña Juana's home. Thomas volunteered for the California Battalion, was named justice of the peace, and added a wing to their adobe. Sadly, he died under mysterious circumstances in 1853. Some sources contend that while traveling to the rancho of a friend, he wandered off into the night and was found dead. The author Richard Henry Dana, who revisited San Diego in 1859, claimed that Thomas "fell from his horse when drunk, and was found nearly eaten up by coyotes."

Doña Juana proceeded to carve out her own remarkable career, earning the endearing label "the Florence Nightingale of Old Town." Riding into the back country with the Catholic priest Father Antonio Ubach, Doña Juana provided care, comfort, and midwifery services to the local Indians, as well as to the residents of San Diego. Her mastery of three languages (Spanish, English, and Native American) facilitated her ability to move easily within a broader community. In part because of her linguistic and nursing skills, she delivered Diego Hunter in January 1847 and helped his mother, Lydia, through her tragic final days. Diego's father, Jesse, on the march toward Los Angeles and unable to look after a newborn, entrusted the child to the care of the midwife. Doña Juana lived until 1901, and, notably, all four of her daughters married Anglo men.[20]

By early 1847 it was clear that the Americans had pacified California and the services of the Saints were no longer required. They petitioned the army for a discharge, and in July 1847 their wish was granted. After a grueling year in military service, a number of Mormons, including the Corays and the Browns, headed north to try their luck in the gold fields. The Corays bought a wagon and horses and joined a party of other Mormons bound for Monterey. Melissa gave birth to a son, William, but the child lived only a few days. They pressed on to San Francisco and then to Sutter's Mill, where they panned for enough gold to equip them for the expedition to Utah. The Browns stayed somewhat longer, not departing California until August 1848. Phebe was the last of the three surviving women to make the entire trek and leave California for the Great Salt Lake.[21]

While the Mormon Battalion never engaged in combat, their amazing journey of thousands of miles through brutal cold and blistering heat, challenged by snakes, Indians, mountains, and deserts, merits recognition. As the men traversed southern New Mexico and Arizona, they built a wagon road so perfectly constructed that it served as the foundation for the route of the Southern Pacific Railroad. Their pioneering legacy included the erection of forts and flour and sawmills, as well as their ambitious and sometimes successful activities in the gold fields.[22]

Susan Magoffin and the Santa Fe Trail

As the battalion mustered out in California in the summer of 1847, the Mexican-American War exploits of Susan Shelby Magoffin come to a close. Magoffin's tale as a pioneering woman on the Santa Fe Trail shares commonality with the travails of her Mormon counterparts but is also marked by its own unique qualities. In early 1846, Susan Magoffin spent six glorious months honeymooning in New York and Philadelphia. The romantic eighteen-year-old Kentucky belle married a man more than twice her age, Samuel Magoffin, who had made his fortune in the Santa Fe trade and knew how to impress his young bride.

Her adolescence as the privileged daughter of a renowned Bluegrass family, however, hardly prepared her for the great adventure that soon followed those joyous days filled with the bustle of East Coast urbanity. Instead, Susan embarked on a fifteen-month expedition with her husband's wagon train that led through Kansas and Colorado before cutting into New Mexico and Chihuahua. When she finally exited Mexico via Monterrey in September 1847, the innocent teenager had matured into a savvy young woman with exposure to new cultures and encounters to be long remembered. While Susan experienced a highly unusual lifestyle during the passage, she challenged the notion that an Anglo woman could make the crossing at all. The usual dangers posed by Indians, animals, and the environment were compounded by the presence of American forces in New Mexico bent upon conquest.[23]

Susan Magoffin, pioneer woman traveler on the Santa Fe Trail. Daguerreotype, 1845. (Courtesy of Missouri History Museum)

Susan found herself in capable hands for such an exciting quest. Her tough, tall, raw-boned spouse was the younger brother of James Wiley Magoffin, a leading trader along the Santa Fe Trail for the past two decades. He had been named US consul in Saltillo by John Quincy Adams in 1825 but soon decided that greater profits could be made in Chihuahua. Magoffin, or "Santiago," as he was widely known, wisely learned Spanish, married Doña María Gertrudis Valdez de Beremende, the daughter in a Mexican family of substance, and became a naturalized citizen. Although spending much of his time in Chihuahua, he also served on the El Paso town council. Magoffin had taken his family back to a farm near Independence in 1844, while continuing in the trade. Both brothers engaged in a lucrative exchange of furs and silver for drugs, dry goods, and a variety of consumer items whose value reached into the millions of dollars.

After more than six weeks on the trail, James arrived in Missouri from Chihuahua in late May. His most recent effort had been very rewarding. Dozens of wagons hauled about $350,000 in specie back to Independence; Magoffin's cut was a handsome $40,000 for his efforts. A quick turnaround had another caravan scheduled to depart from Independence in June 1846, part of a well-established commercial pattern now jeopardized by war between the United States and Mexico.[24]

With serious profits at risk, James received a letter from an old friend, the Missouri senator Thomas Hart Benton, urging him to hasten to Washington to meet with the president to discuss ways to bypass the conflict. They met on June 15, 1846, when James proposed, and Polk agreed, that Magoffin act as a government agent and attempt to negotiate a peace with the New Mexicans to avert bloodshed. Thus the large train of Conestoga wagons, animals, and people constituted more than a routine commercial venture. They followed only days behind a diplomat whose mission was to encourage a quick end to the war with neither disruption of trade nor threat to the life or liberties of the locals.[25]

Sam Magoffin carried his goods in fourteen oxen-drawn wagons. The cracking of the whips, braying of the mules, and profanity-laced whooping and hollering by the teamsters marked too many miles of the trail. In stark contrast, Susan rode in her mule-drawn carriage and commanded three servants, José, Sendeval, and Tabino, and Jane, her maid, who had her own wagon. A separate baggage cart contained their conical tent, "a grand affair" crafted by an army tentmaker in Philadelphia and furnished with carpet, bureau, stools, and bed. Combined with her books, writing implements, and sewing materials, aided by her servants, and comforted by her white-and-brown greyhound, named Ring, Susan rightly referred to herself as "a wandering princess."[26]

As the caravan labored across Kansas and down through Colorado, the daily routine of the "princess" assumed a much less royal air. The world opened to her in ways she could never have imagined in Danville. She fed the chickens and the mules, picked berries, and took daily siestas with Sam—"mi alma" (my soul)—under the sun on buffalo skins. The prairie became treeless, unending, and the weather unpredictable. Summer heat and the omnipresent dust turned rapidly to cold and rain. Mirages mystified, while prairie dogs amused and wolves frightened her. The relentless attacks of the millions of mosquitoes, a "winged pestilence" she determined "equal to any of the plagues of Egypt," stung her body and made her ill. Susan feared bugs of all types and was especially repelled by a long green form she dubbed "an alligator in miniature." She found such critters, along with worms and snakes, to be "the only disagreeable parts of my prairie life"—at least in the first three weeks.[27]

Increasingly observant and sensitive to her environment, Susan stoically approached life's inconveniences and often evidenced good humor. After dealing with downpours and wagons mired in the mud of a riverbed, she remarked that every place has rainy days and that her endurance likely matched that of the Oregon pioneers. Concurrently, she deplored the whipping of the oxen, which left their heads, necks, and backs a bloody mess. Since the sojourners brought their own stores but also lived off the land, boiled chicken, rice, beans, and local berries often dominated their diet. Susan also sampled a variety of foods for the first time. She had never had better meat in Eastern hotels than buffalo ribs, and the thighbone marrow yielded the sweetest butter and most delicate oil she had ever tasted.[28]

Susan's first encounter with New Mexican cuisine, in August, however, left her virtually breathless. Blue corn tortillas served with cheese and a mixture of meat, green peppers, and onions proved far too spicy. After a few bites, she dispatched Sam to retrieve some roasted corn, soup, and a fried egg. Within a few months, her palate had adjusted, and Susan described in detail the tradition and labor involved in constructing a quality tortilla. "They are fine, indeed they are," she stated with satisfaction. When they are accompanied by a dish of frijoles (pronounced "freeholders" by most Americans), "one does not eat a bad dinner." She developed a particular affection for flan, egg custard with cinnamon and nutmeg, always a welcome dessert.[29]

Susan attempted with some success to adjust to an ever-changing world and culture, but her health proved continually problematic. While she was a woman of physical substance, she had been plagued by one malady or another before their departure from Missouri. The fresh air of the plains had done little to improve her condition. Fortunately, a Belgian doctor, Philippe Masure, accompanied the train. The personable physician had some expertise in "female complaints," and Susan's discomfort related partially to her pregnancy. At Bent's Fort in late July, the pain compelled her to lie down almost constantly. Seeking to relieve the suffering, Dr. Masure provided medication and performed an abortion, which ended her agony. The religious Susan sorrowfully, but philosophically, pointed to the interposition of "the hand of a mighty Providence" for the outcome. She could not help but remark, however, on the birth of a fine healthy baby to an Indian woman in a room downstairs. Amazingly, within a half hour of the delivery the mother walked to a nearby river to bathe herself and her child. Susan noted the custom with approval, cautioning that too many ladies "in civilized life" became far too careful about their postpartum condition. But, seemingly cursed, when she gave birth to a son in Matamoros in September 1847, he died soon thereafter.[30]

Susan Magoffin walked through a good part of New Mexico. Covered with dust until she was brown, she hoped that exercise would help restore her health. When their party arrived in a village, such as San Gabriel or San Miguel, she instantly became an object of local fascination regardless of her color. Dozens of children, men, and women swarmed around probably the first Anglo woman they had seen. Convinced that Sam could have charged to behold "the monkey show," Susan indulged the awkwardness, although she confessed that she felt relieved to be out of town and "unmolested by the constant stare of these wild looking strangers." Her view of the locals as unrefined shifted when she heard one woman refer to her as a *bonita muchachita* (a pretty little girl). With some amusement, Susan concluded that they were "a quick and intelligent people." She, in turn, determined to improve her Spanish, which did improve markedly during her stay in Mexico.[31]

In her willingness to develop her language skills and her overall openness and positive attitude toward New Mexican society, Susan Magoffin stood in marked contrast to many of her male peers. Most American observers could not overcome their perceptions of the poverty, servile nature, and treacherous behavior of the people. The world *craven* was often used to describe them.

Surely, Susan was aware. She could not help but notice the sharp contrast between herself and Mexican women of all classes and racial backgrounds. The village women made her blush and keep her veil down in the presence of gentlemen. The women skillfully maneuvered their rebozos and breast-fed their children while smoking *cigarritos.* They "slapped about," with their arms, necks, and bosoms ("they are none the prettiest or whitest") exposed. Shockingly, their skirts extended only down to the calf, and when they crossed a stream, they would pull the hem up above their knees and paddle like ducks. While the women of the upper classes certainly appeared more discreet and elegant in their fashion, they went to extremes with makeup. Susan disapprovingly commented that a Spanish beauty preparing for a fandango had so much flour paste on her face that she appeared as if "from the tombs." Another applied such a generous amount of rouge that Susan thought it was blood.[32]

The Women of New Mexico

The men made the usual distinctions between the fairer Creole women and the darker mestizas and Indians. Many Americans were also highly critical of the morals of New Mexican women, perhaps because the soldiers attempted to engage them in relationships and sexual liaisons that would have been out of bounds in Victorian society. Many, ironically, exploited poor women and then railed about their lack of virtue. Traders and trappers, fresh from weeks of isolation, lauded their beauty and welcomed their company but did question their morals. The explorer Zebulon Pike joined the merchant Josiah Gregg in praise of "their small feet and handsome figures." Pike, however, was sharply critical of their vanity and shallowness. He blamed such behavior on the male objectification of the women, who in turn focused on music, dress, and "voluptuous dissipation." Gregg attributed the immorality to forced marriage, sometimes as early as age fifteen, which later propelled the women into infidelity. Eager and unsuspecting Americans became easy targets. "Coquetry with them was an instinct," one historian noted, "not just a trick."

The New Orleans reporter G. W. Kendall held a higher opinion, lauding their character and "the kind dispositions and tender sympathies exhibited by all classes of the women." He found them modest and generous. Their nonchalance in rejecting the restrictive corseted costume of their northern contemporaries had much more to do with comfort and climate than with morals. In many ways, Kendall reasoned, the dress and easy manner of Mexican women was more alluring than their Yankee counterparts'. After extolling at considerable length the qualities of a fifteen-year-old New Mexican girl, the reporter marveled, "The prettiest girl I ever saw was standing on a mud wall in Albuquerque with a pumpkin on her head."[33]

Quite often, the commentary reflected the impressions of the infatuated teenage traveler and author Hector Lewis Garrard: The ladies were sirens. Smoking enhanced their charms, "their magically brilliant eyes the meanwhile searching one's very soul." A keen-eyed Garrard noted, too, "Their particular style of dress displays the form to advantage . . . they indeed formed a picturesque and pleasing sight." The "prodigal display" of legs, shoulders, and bosom by a chemise that was "too low necked" shocked and captivated Garrard. He deemed the exhibition "uncomely, and, in fact, satiating." Musing about the superficiality of the widely held notion of actually taking a Mexican wife, Garrard allowed that the pleasures to be drawn from such a relationship were of the basest sort. Mexican women, he determined, received a "depraved moral education" and lacked the quintessential element of a true woman—modesty. He thoughtfully acknowledged that "woman *is* woman the world over, no matter where she is found." Mexican women greeted him with a smile, food, lodging, and "a fragrant *cigarillo.*" The smoke, he assured his readers, was obtained "from a Castilian-descended señorita."[34]

"A New Englander" writing for the American press in 1847 echoed similar language. He sharply criticized the lifestyles and morals of New Mexicans generally as squalid and degraded. Properly trained, they would make excellent servants but "are worse than useless if left to themselves." In contrast to the men, however, the women were "kind and affectionate in their disposition, mild and affable in their deportment, and ever ready to administer to the necessities of others." They were also ignorant and superstitious, and their chastity and virtue were woefully deficient. Frank Edwards, who campaigned with Alexander Doniphan, agreed. The women of Santa Fe, he observed, were poor, dirty, and badly clothed, with little awareness of virtue or modesty. Admittedly, those with white blood were pretty, but they could be found only among the upper class and were outnumbered a hundred to one. Edwards, however, joined virtually every American in his rapture over the use of the rebozo, as well as the pretty feet, graceful walk, and free carriage of the Mexican woman. As for the omnipresent *cigarrito,* he cautioned against the custom of taking an already moistened shuck from a Mexican, saying that "their general use of garlic does not improve the flavor."[35]

Regrettably, many Americans contended, attractive women were found still wanting. They never exercised beyond the dance floor and possessed little intellectual or musical prowess. The *New Orleans Picayune* reporter Matt Field lamented that the women "are but slightly removed from Indians. They are all dark complexioned, some of them pretty, but many of them plain, and most of them ugly." Richard Smith Elliott found Mexicans generally "a very dirty people." How disappointing to socialize with a finely clad señorita at a ball, only to discover her the next day clad in an unhooked frock, revealing her "unmentionable garments" and a *camisa* that once had been white. "How would you like to marry out here, reader? Elliott rhetorically queried. "Do you think you could do better? Perhaps so."[36]

Field recounted the tale of a young American smitten at a fandango by the classic raven-haired beauty with piercing dark eyes and "a purely Grecian face." After a dance, which stimulated his desire, each attempted to exchange pleasantries in the other's language, and they partook in the customary *cigarrito.* The lady inhaled deeply and exhaled a cloud through her nostrils that engulfed her unsuspecting admirer. The American's passions promptly went up in smoke. Lieutenant George Gibson summed up the jaded view of too many Americans: "Throughout all of Mexico there is a want of virtue, even in the upper ten thousand, but there is not that low-flung exhibition of it which you meet with daily and almost hourly in New Mexico."[37]

More than foreign flavors and bad behavior disaffected the Americans. They found the countryside to be alien, barren and arid with few trees and little water. The villages were made up of mud huts. What lure existed for the American farmer? With a population of only several thousand, Santa Fe disappointed visitors with a series of colorless, unimpressive adobe buildings. Lieutenant Gibson considered his letdown after the long trek from Missouri: "The town was shabby, without either taste or a show of wealth—no gardens that deserved the name, the fields all unenclosed, the people poor and beggarly." The trader James Josiah Webb remembered the streets as narrow, filthy, and unpaved. "The houses were nearly all old and dilapidated . . . and the people, when in best attire, not half dressed." Matt Field described a dreary town plaza, three hundred yards square, with three sides dedicated to houses rented to American merchants for ten to twenty dollars a month.[38]

On August 1, 1846, General Kearny had dispatched twelve dragoons, led by then Captain Cooke and accompanied by James Wiley Magoffin, with a letter to Governor Armijo urging his peaceful withdrawal from Santa Fe. Armijo considered the military options and yielded. Two weeks later, the Americans occupied the city without firing a shot. As the Yankees marched into the plaza, a fearful mother asked an officer whether she should leave "to save her daughters from dishonor." Many did depart, at least temporarily, for safety in the nearby mountains. The absence of some of the town's elite ladies did not deter Mexican officials from holding a small, hastily organized fandango for the Americans on August 19. It proved awkward at best. Lieutenant Gibson noted the absence of the capital's small female aristocracy and added that those women in attendance "were far from handsome." A fellow officer entered the smoke-filled room to find two dozen women sitting cross-legged on the couches puffing *cigarritos.* Since the women spoke no English and the Americans no Spanish, the assemblage simply laughed, smoked, and danced.[39]

The orchestra—a singer, two violins, and a guitar—played about a dozen melodies that became very familiar to the Yankees. Whether at a soiree, a Mass, or a funeral, the bands repeated the same songs at different tempos. An effort at an accompanying supper fell flat. Gibson judged the food served—fried chicken, hashed beef, and boiled mutton—unequal to what one would get in any farmer's house in the United States. The coffee also was not very good, but everyone agreed that the sponge cake was the best they had ever eaten.[40]

General Kearny responded with his own conciliatory fandango on August 27 at the Palace of the Governors. The supper and dance, with liquor brought in from El Paso, apparently succeeded. With almost five hundred in attendance, congeniality reigned, and the festivities lasted into the early morning hours. The

American officers wore their finest uniforms, and the Mexican women appeared genteel, a few in satin and richly dressed. Lieutenant Gibson had a closer look at Santa Fe's women and determined that "a few were good looking if not handsome. As a general thing their forms are much better than the women in the States." The soldiers discussed the ball the next day and acclaimed it a triumph, noting that the modesty and conduct of the women present met with their approbation. Captain Cooke also attended and agreed that the "ball went off harmoniously" and the women were "comely." Like most American officers, he pointed out the women's "remarkable" small hands and feet. Cooke critically noted, however, that while the women were superior to their male counterparts, "nowhere else is chastity less valued or expected."[41]

Doña Tules and the Occupation of Santa Fe

In a fortnight, brother James Magoffin welcomed Susan and Samuel with an unlikely meal of champagne and oysters. What better way to celebrate the American conquest than a gala? The fandango appalled and intrigued the Kentucky woman. On September 11, Susan attended the dance, critically pronouncing the fashion vintage Henry VIII or Elizabeth I and the ballroom "a menagerie." "Doña Tula," as Susan called her, the leading madam and gambling house owner in Santa Fe, drew attention. Susan described her as "a stately dame of a certain age, the possessor of a portion of that shrewd sense and fascinating manner necessary to allure the wayward, inexperienced youth to the hall of final ruin." Two weeks later, primed for such a soiree held at the Palace of the Governors, Susan appeared dramatically clad in a scarlet crepe shawl and prepared to charm the American officers, if not puff on a *cigarrito.* She now summarily dismissed Doña Tules as "the old woman with false hair and teeth," while adjudging her own efforts at socializing as "not ineffectual."[42]

Susan Magoffin perceptively evaluated the strengths and prowess of the woman widely recognized as Doña Tules but could not have been aware of her struggles and successes. The biographer Mary J. Straw Cook provocatively claimed, "Fruit and young girls ripen early in the sultry Bavispe Valley of east-central Sonora." Around 1800, the valley was the birthplace of Gertrudis Barceló, while Tules, reflecting her curved figure, became her more commonly known and titillating nickname. Cook suggests that the intelligent and savvy young woman was conscious of her power to manipulate men—"she was a genius at the art"—before the family moved to New Mexico in 1815.[43]

The ongoing threat of Apache raids, unpredictable storms, and potentially

Gertrude Barceló—"Doña Tules"—Mexican gambler and hotel owner. *Harper's Monthly Magazine,* April 1854. (Courtesy of the Palace of Governors Photo Archives, NMHM/DCA, 050815.)

devastating flooding made life difficult for women of the Bavispe Valley. While the wealthy Creole elite dominated the lives and culture of the remote villages, Tules's father, a Catalan, apparently neither shared in the largesse nor achieved a social and economic position. Juan Ignacio, a farmer or miner, partnered with his wife, Dolores Herrero, in raising three children in a hostile environment. The family toiled, and Tules honed her survival skills in a society that relished gambling, particularly cards, horse racing, and cockfighting. Juan Ignacio could not ignore the tales of opportunity in New Mexico and joined a caravan north to provide a better, safer life for his wife and children.[44]

The Barcelós settled into an old hacienda in Valencia, near Santa Fe, that had belonged to Juan Ignacio's grandfather. While the prospects sound rather elegant and suggest a dramatic move upward in lifestyle, their situation was dramatically compromised by the ever-present threat of Indian raids. The Apache had devastated the area, burning crops, stealing horses and mules, killing the men, and abducting the women and children. Juan Ignacio had died by 1820, and his eldest daughter, Gertrudis, married soon thereafter into the prominent Sisneros family. Tules was four months pregnant when she and Manuel wed in June 1823, but heartbreakingly, she lost two infant sons, José and later Miguel, in rapid succession to disease. The couple tried to assuage their grief by adopting an orphan, Refugio, as their daughter in 1826. Frustrated by her inability to fulfill her traditional domestic duties, Tules sought other avenues for her talents and energy.[45]

In the 1820s, the first western gold rush enveloped the mountainous mining camp of Real de Dolores, about twenty-five miles southwest of Santa Fe. As men flocked into the camp in an exhaustive search for their fortune, they desired relaxation in the form of women, gambling, and alcohol. Tules Sisneros had discovered her destiny. Card games became a passion among all classes of Mexicans, and Tules no doubt learned how to deal and wager as a girl. Refining those skills, she probably made her way to Real de Dolores in the winter months of 1826 to try her luck at cards with the miners. Her presence was recorded by the local justice, who fined Tules forty-three pesos for gambling. The official received a kickback of twenty-one pesos. Her husband, Manuel, who served as her male security in the camp, was also punished.

The region continued to produce hundreds of thousands of dollars in specie yearly, sending along a goodly amount on the Santa Fe Trail to Missouri and investing in the lucrative trade that had opened in 1821. Tules and Manuel shared in the profits, by 1833 moving to Santa Fe, where they adopted more orphaned children and expanded the family's business horizons. Over the decade, Tules labored. Good luck came and departed, but she courted and successfully developed personal and business relationships with individuals who could provide both protection and information. It was widely rumored that one of those partners, Manuel Armijo, who was the governor of New Mexico on three separate occasions, became her lover.[46]

By the early 1840s, Tules had moved from dealing at hotels to operating her own profitable gambling salon in Santa Fe's Burro Alley. The establishment offered its guests pier-glass mirrors, elegant Brussels carpets, and heavily candled chandeliers. Large parties for local officials and high society were by invitation only. As Tules built a fortune, her reputation as a woman not to be trifled with grew accordingly. When the violent Indian fighter and slave trader James Kirker failed to pay her the four hundred pesos he lost in a card game in 1839, she took him to court, appearing personally to demand his payment. The alcalde agreed with Tules, and the sum was reluctantly paid. Over the course of the year, Kirker and his men, seduced by fandangos and faro—castanets and cards—squandered thousands of pesos, helping make Doña Tules a rich woman.[47]

By happenstance, Matt Field, accompanied by the alcalde of Santa Fe, encountered the Doña on the street in the spring of 1840. A welcome invitation resulted, and Field soon found himself in the señora's home, where Governor Armijo was comfortably resting. No surprise. Field cruelly reported watching the governor's wife, who weighed close to three hundred pounds and "would have fit nicely in a tobacco hogshead," waltz at a fandango "like an elephant dancing 'Nancy Dawson' in the ring of a menagerie." Sizing up Armijo's mistress, Field determined, "Señora Toulous was not handsome, her only pleasant feature being an eye of shrewd intelligence, lit up during our interview with that expression of mischievous brightness which can make any countenance agreeable." However, she possessed a "neat figure," and she moved with "a really elegant ease" across a dance floor—she would have drawn attention at a Washington ball. The reporter referred to her as "the supreme queen of refinement and fashion" and said that her presence at a dance, clad in jewelry and silks, made the affair a true social occasion.[48]

Wise in cards and business, Tules began to accumulate capital from her gambling ventures, prostitution, and mining, as well as investments in trading furs, Mexican mules, and specie from Santa Fe to Missouri. In 1841, a train of more than twenty wagons rolled out of New Mexico carrying upwards of two hundred thousand dollars in gold and silver. James Giddings, who would later marry one of Tules's adopted daughters, Petra Gutierres, served as a guardian of the Doña's financial interests on the expedition. A second train, of forty-two wagons, brought as much as three hundred thousand dollars to Missouri in May 1843. Josiah Gregg claimed that Tules had dispatched ten thousand dollars along the trail that year. Her timing was impeccable, since in August 1843 President Santa Anna moved to shut down the custom houses in the New Mexico area and issued a ban on the export of specie. Could she possibly have been forewarned of the new policy?[49]

As the Mexican-American War threatened Santa Fe in the spring of 1846, an increasingly wealthy and powerful Doña Tules prepared for the "invasion." She was the Mistress of Monte, referring to the game of chance and deception played by all classes of Mexicans. The rules were simple enough: The Spanish deck contained forty cards in four suits—cups, clubs, swords and suns. Four cards were laid out, and the bettor selected one card in the layout. The dealer then turned the deck over, with one card face up. If the card matched the bettor's suit selection, he won; if not, he lost his wager. A three-card variation of monte (mountain) moved the game along without delay, produced a pile of cards, and more rapidly created winnings for the house. The innocent gambler had little chance against an adept dealer with a fast hand. While fees and fines purportedly controlled marginally illegal gaming in Santa Fe, Mary Straw Cook speculates that as many as one hundred monte tables may have operated in the city, funneling payoffs to officials such as Governor Armijo.[50]

When a bettor joined the table of Doña Tules, "a hint of fearful awe" overtook him. She had the uncanny knack of reading the players. One victim claimed that Tules had studied phrenology, the "science" of the shape of the head, to better evaluate male behavior. An American doctor referred to her maneuvers during a game as "amusing." Calm and deliberate, dealing with exacting precision through the night, she might flash a faint smile as her heavily ringed fingers gathered in the gold dust. In 1840, Matt Field observed her at the table; the silence was palpable as an expressionless Tules dealt the cards, her fingers moving as though she "were handling only a knitting needle." Another trader lost his bag of gold coins, vowing to return to equal the score. Richard Smith Elliott similarly reconstructed the gambling milieu, including the bawdy language. He depicted a cool Tules who never shuffled but only dealt, calmly losing hands as she seduced the bettor into throwing yet more money on the table. The invading American soldiers became easy prey.[51]

Once known for "her low morals and her stunning beauty," the years had taken their toll on Gertrudis Barceló. By 1846 Doña Tules appeared far from dazzling. A rare image portrays a woman with penetrating black eyes, shoulder-length dark hair parted in the middle and drawn close to the ears, and rather broad and heavy facial features, drawing on a *cigarrito.* A heavy gold chain and large crucifix dangle above a loose-fitting, widely cut white dress. Spectators remarked that she still retained her curvaceous figure, no doubt a deliberate distraction for the customers, and possessed a grace and ease of movement whether dancing or dealing.

Susan Magoffin was not the only observer to describe Tules, only in her mid-forties, as old; others referred to her as "elderly" or "with a wrinkled countenance." Richard Smith Elliott, who admired Tules and dubbed her "the Princess of Santa Fe," still found her "a little *passee,*" adding that "she had been in her youth, very beautiful and very much admired." Passé, perhaps, but Tules retained an unwavering appeal to younger men. When Manuel Sisneros disappeared from her life in 1841, she promptly adopted other protectors and paramours, including James Giddings, Governor Armijo, and especially a young

Prussian officer, August de Marle, who came to Santa Fe with the US artillery under Colonel Sterling Price. Philip St. George Cooke conjectured, "August de Marle was surely the most educated and brilliant of her lovers."[52]

By the time of the Mexican-American War, Tules had morphed into Señora Doña Gertrudis Barceló, a respected member of the Santa Fe community and a powerful force in the city's economic life. As the years passed, she continued to extract wealth from the locals, as well as visiting traders, trappers, and Americans soldiers. Her monte bank increased, as did her real-estate holdings. Given the enthusiasm for gambling in the Mexican culture, the surprising aspect of her success in the profession was her acceptance as a woman. The army veteran W. W. H. Davis observed that in the 1840s women could take their place at the card tables and lose their doubloons "with a *sang froid* truly masculine."

The situation changed—for the better, Davis contended—when the Anglos impacted societal norms. Within a decade, "the fairer portion of creation" rarely appeared at the tables, and then only at public fairs for amusement purposes. Certainly, few American soldiers or traders had been exposed to a woman with the wealth and influence of Doña Tules. They were likely both astonished and appalled. Women were powerful forces in Mexican family life and certainly held substantial property, but how had this woman of questionable vocation and dubious morality catapulted herself to the forefront of Santa Fe society?[53]

The Mexican-American War brought new economic and social opportunities for Doña Tules Barceló. With the scarcity of specie and reliable currency, both businessmen and the army appealed to the major source of wealth in town. In March 1848, Tules loaned the traders James Hartly and Henry Cunliffe $3,000 at a rather exorbitant rate of 2 percent per month. George Coulter, owner of the United States Hotel, borrowed $500 that same year, stalled his payment, and then offered substitute remuneration through the use of gaming tables at his establishment. The negotiations collapsed amid a shootout in the hotel that had Tules diving for cover under a monte table. Charges and countercharges flew until the case went to court in 1850. The judge finally awarded her $257 of the $500 claim.[54]

Perhaps the most unusual loan made by Doña Tules involved the US Army. In the fall of 1846, the military badly needed one thousand dollars to fund an expedition of the Chihuahua Rangers, commanded by Colonel David Dawson Mitchell. Mitchell contacted Lucius Thruston, a trader, professional gambler, and longtime friend of Doña Tules. Thruston volunteered to assist and set up a meeting with the Doña at her salon. The party smoked *cigarritos,* sipped chocolate, and talked money.

The following day, Tules received an invitation wrapped in pink and blue ribbons to attend a performance of the popular American play *Pizarro,* as well as a minstrel show, at the Palace of the Governors. Her escort would be none other than Colonel Mitchell. The entertainment was generally well received, although few of the ladies in attendance understood a word spoken, and they smoked incessantly throughout the acts. The women laughed in all the wrong places and seemed amused at the "African band" and the males dragged by necessity into playing women's roles. Several Mexican women mentioned that it might be fine for the *hombres* to play women in the *teatro,* but it certainly would not do in the *casa.*

Tules was the star. "Elegantly dressed in silk and jewelry," she entered on the arm of the handsome officer and sat conspicuously in the front row. Wine and cakes appeared at the interval, and Richard Smith Elliott hints at the possibility of a little romance thereafter. The loan soon followed, and the Rangers departed in December, although Mitchell apparently threatened to shoot a St. Louis reporter if he sent an account of the events back to his paper.[55]

Doña Tules not only endeared herself, at least to some, by her loans but kept the influential physically nearby. Her real-estate holdings at Palace Avenue and Burro Alley increased to four properties, and she rented rooms to the likes of the trader Thruston, Lafayette McLaws, a young American officer, and Major John Munroe, the governor of New Mexico. Her influence among the occupation forces never appeared more obvious than when Colonel Price granted her request for a US military escort for a twelve-day round trip between Santa Fe and Manzano. Such a gesture would have been unthinkable in most quarters, but Price had become a good friend of Doña Tules's and frequently gambled at her salon. When an elaborate ball was held by the military at the United States Hotel in December 1847, the Santa Fe newspaper reported that Doña Tules "was there, as young and blooming as we ever saw her, and seemed to enjoy it."[56]

Perhaps a motive other than his proclivity for wagering stirred Colonel Price's kindness toward Doña Tules. In late October, several leading citizens gave credence to the rumor that "Spaniards" intended to create confusion and seize the artillery and magazine in Santa Fe. Mexican women had disclosed the supposed plot, a conspiracy that would have benefited the merchants by compelling the Americans to retain a larger military force in the capital. One month later, Price conversed privately with friends about "attempts to get up a revolt." He apparently gave some credence to the notion and gathered information to determine its legitimacy.

To the north, a rebellion in Taos against American rule had been brewing for some time. The historian David Clary places much of the responsibility for the outbreak at the feet of Charles Bent. Taos, a town of about four thousand, served as a trading hub, and Bent reigned supreme. "Anglos lived very well and warm in fine stone or adobe houses," Clary argues, "while the *peónes* barely survived in rude *jacales,* working at the beck and call of their rich overlords." The wide gap in wealth epitomized the racial and class divisions. Centuries of Spanish rule had been bad enough; American dominance became "insufferable."[57]

Bent allied himself with the legendary Christopher "Kit" Carson. The thirty-six-year-old Kentuckian had come west as a young man and worked for months as a teamster in the Chihuahua copper mines. He wisely departed for the Rockies and a successful career trapping beaver. His wanderings led him to Taos, where he joined Charles Bent in marrying sisters in the prominent Jaramillo family. Carson wed Josefa, while Bent gained María's hand. Such a socially correct move should have aided the enterprising Americans, but Charles's arrogance and disdain for the Mexicans and Indians marginalized any acceptance.

Meanwhile, Kearny had annexed all of New Mexico prior to his departure for California. In this presumptive and sweeping grab of power, the general displaced the locals from authority and named Charles Bent as governor and Sterling Price as commanding officer. The remainder of the territorial officers lacked know-how, and the US district attorney, Francis P. Blair, spoke no Spanish. The acquisition and the appointments troubled many Americans and infuriated Mexicans of all classes. Against his better judgment, Diego Archuleta, the former lieutenant governor under Armijo, had been persuaded not to resist Kearny's earlier occupation of Santa Fe. In return, Archuleta at least expected to share in the patronage that would be dispensed by the Americans. When no post was forthcoming, he found willing coconspirators in the Taos area in mid-December who were eager to launch a rebellion against the invaders.[58]

The conspiracy may well have been temporarily foiled by the spy network of the "Barceló women." Doña Tules's close ties with Mexican officials, including the governor, allowed her access to information that was passed along through a network of women to American officers. Apparently, Tules had family members and prostitutes under her guidance who were interacting with both Mexicans and Americans. One theory contends that an unidentified mulatto girl married to a conspirator leaked the information to Price about the developing Taos Rebellion. Just in time, Bent arrested seven of the conspirators, although Archuleta escaped.[59]

The apprehensions led the Americans into a self-satisfied complacency. Certainly, the grievances against the governor went beyond politics and power to include race and national pride. With a deaf ear to such issues, Bent returned to Taos on January 18, 1847, to discover a mob of drunken residents demanding the release of their friends from jail on arguably fraudulent charges. When Bent refused and dismissively went home, the throng confronted him once again. The second denial resulted in the storming of his house and the governor's scalping, death, and decapitation, as well as assaults on the few foreigners living in the town and the surrounding villages. In short order, the rebels murdered a dozen Americans. The women, including María Bent, sought refuge by digging a hole with a poker and an old iron spoon through the structure's adobe wall into an adjacent building. Violence spread over northern New Mexico in an uprising of more than a thousand Mexicans and Pueblo Indians, who were pursued by Price's force of fewer than five hundred. The ensuing skirmishes lasted almost three weeks before the Americans crushed the insurgents on February 3 at Taos Pueblo, with the loss of forty American and more than one hundred Mexican lives.[60]

Compromised justice was meted out in April to the captured miscreants. Beckwourth remembered, " Señora Bent p'inted out the Purblo what had kilt her Charlie. . . . He didn't show a thing, not one tic, all the way to the gallers. Señora Bent, she'd come to court, Kit Carson's wife along. Now that's a woman to break yer heart! One peep of 'er eye an 'yer life will go direckly up in smoke! Woo-haugh!" Lewis Hector Garrard, also present in the court, concurred. He recalled María Bent's beauty and the courage of the Pueblos facing certain death. Most particularly, Garrard also seemed smitten by Josefa Carson. "Her style of beauty was the haughty, heartbreaking kind—such as would lead a man with the glance of the eye, to risk his life for one smile. I could not but desire her acquaintance." The jury found nine men guilty that day, and more would hang, as heavy-handed Anglo justice now prevailed unchallenged in New Mexico. Doña Tules and the "Barceló women" possibly played a part in attempting to head off the bloodshed, but the Taos uprising and its aftermath left a bitter legacy.[61]

When Doña Gertrudis Barceló quietly passed away on the cold winter day of January 17, 1852, she left her life in order. Her health fading, perhaps from a heart condition, she had made out her will more than a year before. Her son-in-law, James Giddings, clerk of probate, executed the document leaving the estate largely to her children. In the early 1820s in Sonora, Father Francisco Ignacio de Madariaga had attempted to launch a crusade among the women of his flock aimed at saving those flirting with adultery or prostitution. One of his young parishioners had heard but not heeded. Some thirty years later, Archbishop Jean Baptiste Lamy led an elaborate service laying the wayward Doña

Tules to rest in a simple chapel known as La Parroquia in the La Capilla de San Antonio de Padua. A wake followed at her salon, with Doña Tules, dressed in her finery, surrounded in the candlelight by family and friends, who, in the classic tradition, were singing, praying, and eating chilis.[62]

The Magoffins Move South

The death of Doña Tules marked the end of an era in New Mexico and signaled the rise of Anglo domination of the territory. Amazingly, that control, although briefly contested, would be established as early as the summer of 1846, with Kearny's occupation. Distance from Mexico City, a burgeoning philosophy of local control (federalism), commercial realities, and the very real threat of Indian raids made many Mexicans in the northern provinces less adverse, if not welcoming, to the prospect of the greater security and economic prosperity that might result from becoming part of the United States.

The Indian issue was particularly troublesome. As the historian Brian DeLay has chronicled, a number of tribes—the Comanche, the Kiowa, the Navajo, and the Apache—had turned northern Mexico into a virtual wasteland. The "War of a Thousand Deserts" had commenced in the 1830s, not only resulting in widespread death and destruction for thousands of villagers but also stretching their confidence in Mexico City to the breaking point. For many Mexicans, American occupation brought the hope of protection that their own government failed to provide.

Kearny attended to the Indian issue, attempting to persuade the somewhat confused Navajo that they should stop their raids and not make war on a common enemy. The Navajo reluctantly agreed, but the Americans were in no position to enforce the treaty, and it ultimately proved ineffectual in halting the violence. In the short turn, however, the natives were quiet and the Mexicans seemingly docile. Before his departure at the end of September, Kearny attended another fandango held by the merchants at the Palace of the Governors and transferred the governance of the territory to a small band of civilian administrators and several companies of soldiers.[63]

The ensuing tranquility was deafening and misleading. Susan Magoffin bemoaned her dull existence and that "nothing scarcely occurs worth noticing." The troops heartily agreed. As late as October, many soldiers, such as Gibson, had settled into a Santa Fe lifestyle. Gibson observed that after two months the city had become more American than Mexican, and the Yankees found themselves effortlessly encountering old friends on the streets. "We are quite at home," the lieutenant remarked. Within weeks, however, cold weather arrived, accompanied by three inches of snow, and measles claimed so many victims that the men had to break apart wagon bodies for coffins. Ennui set in, resulting in drunkenness and disorder. The soldiers longed for active service or leave for home. Any place would do but Santa Fe.[64]

At the end of September, the bulk of Kearny's command marched out of New Mexico bound for California and the achievement of the primary mission of the Army of the West. The remainder, about five hundred Missouri mounted volunteers under Colonel Alexander Doniphan, soon moved south to rendezvous with other American forces in Chihuahua. George Gibson ecstatically recorded the news of his selection as a quartermaster with Doniphan's forces. "Of course, I shall have some disagreeable duty to perform," he remarked, "but greatly prefer it to life in Santa Fe." When the Magoffin wagons pulled out of Santa Fe on October 5, following the army to El Paso, Susan heaved a sigh of relief, weary of a city that she, like Lieutenant Gibson and most Americans, left with no regrets. Before long, Susan came to rue such sentiments.[65]

While Doniphan's small force headed toward the Rio Grande, the merchants trailed behind. The responsibility for protecting the $1 million in goods from falling into enemy hands weighed heavily on the army. Trading with Mexican villagers and Indians who approached the wagons, Susan Magoffin had her own concerns. Perhaps because she had never had the opportunity to relate to the Indians in their own environment, she kept them at a fearful, emotional distance. "They are a cunning people," Susan observed of the Arapaho in July as they began the trading process on the plains. The interactions became more common, and the Indians seemed more dangerous. Referring to the "savage red man," she expressed an awareness of Apache attacks upon the Mexicans. "The Indian is a wily man," she warned, "and one cannot be too precautious in his territory." Rarely now did she and her maid, Jane, venture far from the wagons to explore for berries or flowers.[66]

On December 28, the Magoffins learned of the initial Taos conspiracy and erroneously recorded that Governor Bent and every American in the town had been murdered. "It is a perfect revolution there," she lamented. Soon thereafter, as their party entered "real Indian country" north of El Paso, the wagons camped on the field at Bracito, where Doniphan had defeated a Mexican army twice as large on Christmas day. Picking up Mexican and American cartridges as souvenirs, Susan recognized that the war was now a closer reality. She confided that she "heartily wished" they were back in Santa Fe at Fort Marcy. Worse still from a family viewpoint, the Magoffins learned that Samuel's brother James had been arrested as a spy while attempting to negotiate a preemptive peace agreement with Chihuahua officials. It took several months and more bribes (including the gift of more than 3,000 bottles of champagne) to enable him to "escape" to El Paso. What a difference four months and three hundred miles had made.[67]

Communication in New Mexico was difficult. Letters were infrequent, and rumors rampant. Fully two months went by before the Magoffins, housed in the village of San Gabriel, learned of Zachary Taylor's September 1846 triumph at Monterrey. Yet as time passed, Susan became increasingly aware of the impact of the Mexican-American War. While attending a September dinner in Santa Fe at which locals were present, she noted the toast by General Kearny: "The U.S. and Mexico—They are now united, may no one ever think of separating." She never reacted to such notions of American destiny with any particular bravado, and rarely did she engage in sharp criticism of the Mexican people, the Catholic Church, or the culture.[68]

Instead, Susan thoughtfully bolstered and embraced those around her. Mexican men, a universal target of Anglo reproach, found a defender in Susan, who wrote in her diary: "They are not to be called cowards. Take them in a mass and they are brave, and if they have the right kind of leader they will stem any tide. Take them one by one and they will not flinch from danger." American women sometimes held this view of Mexican men, often in contrast to the stereotype rendered by their male counterparts. Her own male servants were intelligent enough, but they irked Susan with their gambling and squabbling. She found their greatest virtue in their willingness to work without complaint, their good humor, and their remaining "perfectly submissive."[69]

The Magoffins spent a month in occupied El Paso, where Susan moved smartly among the upper-class women of the town. She also developed a daughterlike relationship with Don Agapita, an old friend of her husband's, and his family. "I can't help loving them," she confided to her diary. More particularly, she talked extensively with the don about the trials and tribulations of her recent travels. He assured her of the value of life events that would have escaped her in Kentucky. Agreeing to the wisdom of his observations, Susan determined, "He is a man not met with every day in any part of the world."

While many American soldiers and reporters attacked the Catholic Church for corruption and blamed the clergy for the general ills of the society, Susan attended Mass. She explained that while she was not an advocate for the faith, "it is not for me to judge; whether it be right or wrong; judgment alone belongs to God." The average Mexican was sincere in his faith, and as for the priests, she knew of no ill-conduct. Calling upon the book of Matthew, she contended,

"I must first remove the beam from mine own eye, and then shall I see clearly to pull the moat out of my brother's eye." Susan was far more upset about her husband's practice of selling goods on Sunday, thus abusing the Sabbath. "It hurts me more than I can tell," she confessed.[70]

As for the culture, by December Susan was engaging in the day-to-day commerce of the San Gabriel market, selling fabric and dresses and driving a hard bargain in the process. The villagers responded to this unusual Anglo woman by sending her tortillas, cheeses, and sweets. Susan vowed that if they were to remain in the region for the winter, she must learn Mexican ways and make serapes and rebozos, as well as tortillas, chili peppers, and chocolate.[71]

Throughout the sojourn, the Magoffins' living accommodations varied, from their tent and the wagons, to forts and, sometimes, much to her relief, established houses in various towns. Her health remained fragile. She survived a fall fever that confined her to bed for three weeks and was finally cured by "Dr. Sappington's Pills," a legendary Missouri remedy that contained a generous dose of quinine. Thus, she especially appreciated the opportunity to sleep in an established dwelling. When that opportunity presented itself in Santa Fe, San Gabriel, El Paso, and Saltillo, Susan seized the moment to learn about the culture and try to develop relationships with the local population. Her failed pregnancy made her particularly susceptible to children. She grew attached to precocious village girls, and the couple bought Francisco, an orphaned boy of nine who had been held captive by the Apache, for seven dollars from an old man.[72]

Chihuahua offered hope of a more "civilized" stay. A large and impressive city, it contained fine buildings, macadamized streets, a magnificent stone church on the public square, and a bullring that resembled a Roman amphitheater. As a major destination for traders, the community housed a number of American citizens, who welcomed the arrival of the army. Disappointingly for the Magoffins, their visit would be of short duration. By the time their wagons arrived on April 4, 1847, Doniphan's troops, who had been in occupation for a month, had apparently done their best to abuse the town. The soldiers' residence of a similar length in El Paso revealed a pattern seen elsewhere with the volunteers. Idleness and boredom bore dissipation and violence. As discipline collapsed, gambling of all types, as well as fandangos, were banned. Even more troubling, Doniphan court-martialed three of his men for raping a Mexican woman.[73]

At least initially, Chihuahua offered the Americans welcome relief in the form of abundant goods, food, alcohol, and companionship. They were enthralled by the city's homes, shops, and cathedral, not to mention its bathing houses, which catered to both sexes. After a paucity of fair skin, George Gibson observed that the women were generally of Castilian descent, "good size, well made, and some very beautiful and fascinating." Gibson emphasized the relationship between color and the existence of a sizeable upper and middle class. Philip Gooch Ferguson offhandedly remarked that the connections with the señoritas were "as might be expected." The women formed passionate attachments, and when the army evacuated in July 1848, the city "was literally bathed in tears." As many as 150 women boarded wagons or walked, trailing their lovers some forty miles before they were forced to return to Chihuahua. "If permitted, they would follow us all the way to the States," claimed Ferguson. The lower classes were also present, reminding George Gibson very much of New Mexico. Perhaps Private John Hughes encountered the latter. He concluded that "a modest, chaste, virtuous, intelligent female" was rare in Chihuahua, but he found solace in their "sprightly" minds, personal beauty, and graceful manners.[74]

Susan Magoffin saw it all differently. She deplored the actions of Missourians who had turned fine houses into stables, made kitchens of the roofs, used the drinking fountains for bathing, destroyed the trees, and engaged in a host of other behaviors unbecoming of American soldiers. A number of troops agreed that the conduct of their comrades could be fairly called "debauched." When Doniphan abandoned the city on April 25 to head east, the wagoners followed closely behind. After three weeks of dusty, bone-jarring travel of twenty to thirty-five miles a day, the party reached Saltillo, near the site of the pivotal Battle of Buena Vista.[75]

The hero of the February contest, Zachary Taylor, had not gone far. His forces remained in occupation of several towns in the area, including Saltillo and Monterrey. Here Susan Magoffin spent the last months of her sojourn. The war had shifted south to focus upon Winfield Scott and his epochal summer march from Veracruz to the capital. The Magoffins spent these weeks reestablishing business ties and socializing with expatriate Europeans and Americans. Susan delighted in visiting, dining, and traveling with the Hewitsons. Dr. Hewitson owned a large cotton factory six miles from Saltillo. The wife of the factory manager, Mrs. Bently, a "plain, good woman from New Jersey," offered them a cup of coffee and buttered bread—a welcome, "truly American" gesture. In Monterrey, Susan found an equally eager reception from the charismatic and affable Mrs. Maria Hunter. With little opportunity to visit with other Anglo women, all the aforementioned were anxious to see and converse for hours in English with "a white woman."[76]

The Magoffins entertained a number of high-ranking officers, including General Caleb Cushing, in August 1847, but the apex of the summer came in several personal encounters with the already legendary Old Rough and Ready. Susan was unsure what to expect, but clearly her image of Taylor did not include much affability or sophistication. Although the general greeted her wearing a somewhat wrinkled uniform, she was later informed that the mere fact that he had donned the outfit was an honor. Mild mannered and with "such regard for the female character," Taylor emerged "very talkative, agreeable and quite polite, tho' plain and entirely unassuming." When she visited him the next day at his camp, some four miles away, he had reverted to his more typical gray sack coat, striped cotton trousers, and blue calico neckerchief. His clothing matched a casual yet continuing gracious and hospitable manner. Extensive conversation, accompanied by cake and champagne, left a somewhat perplexed Susan Magoffin to reconcile her disappointment in the false perception of the uncouth backwoodsman with the reality of the southern gentleman.[77]

Susan Shelby Magoffin finally went home to Kentucky in 1847. The couple soon moved to Sam's extensive holdings in Missouri, where she had her first surviving child, Jane, in 1851. Sadly, following her ordeals and escapades on the trail, Susan died after childbirth in 1855 at age twenty-six.[78] Her story is unique. Few, if any, Anglo women traversed the Santa Fe Trail in this era, and none kept such an insightful, detailed diary. She was obviously a child of privilege; indeed, some of her actions and attitudes reflect her immaturity, age, and station. Often her remarks, while perhaps sympathetic to Mexicans and Indians, reveal prejudices never overcome. Still, Susan Magoffin grew into an extraordinarily intelligent and discerning young woman. Through her eyes we witness not only the evolution of her thoughts about various experiences but also her views of the peoples and cultures she encountered on the trail.

Susan's comments on the Mexican-American War remind us of the gaps in information in the region. The involvement and coordination of the American forces under Kearny and Doniphan with the merchants, as well as Susan's later encounters with Cushing and Taylor, illustrate the importance of American trade to the government as well as to the entrepreneurs themselves. The war may have been about defending the nation's honor, annexing California and New Mexico, and securing the border, but commerce lay at the heart of the matter for thousands of American merchants and farmers.

Susan Magoffin was the first Anglo woman to navigate the Santa Fe Trail all the way to Chihuahua. The city of El Paso commemorated that accomplishment in 2012 with the erection of a statue in Keystone Heritage Park. The two-hundred-thousand-dollar, fourteen-foot-high bronze statue, crafted by the renowned sculptor Ethan Houser, shows Susan sitting on a steamer trunk, with her trusty dog, Ring, standing by her side. The recognition of Magoffin's adventure and adversity should prompt both scholars and the public to a greater appreciation of the courage and sacrifice of those women who shared the ordeal and triumph that accompanied the road west in this era. Her diary is revealing, too, in its depiction of both elite and peasant Mexican women encountered along the way. While Doña Tules is also atypical, her life story informs us about the rise from a hardscrabble existence and the challenges faced and accommodations made by many Mexican women on the frontier. For a price, wealth, power, and place could be had in the provinces, as in Mexico itself.

4

Profiles in Courage

WORKING WOMEN IN MEXICO

Some of the more shadowy stories of the Mexican-American War revolve around the variant roles played by American women who found themselves, either by relationship or in search of opportunity, south of the Rio Grande in 1846. Too often, we know little about them. Passing references or anecdotes, newspaper articles or diary entries offer snippets of information that arouse our curiosity about their backgrounds, their conditions, and ultimately their fate. Frequently, the answers are elusive, but the mere presence of these individuals in significant numbers speaks to the nature of this war and the roles played by women of all classes. Some were considered "respectable"—the wives of ranchers, planters, businessmen, and officers. Others were self-employed single women or factory girls.

Perhaps unjustly, laundresses, cooks, servants, camp followers, sutlers, and tavern keepers struggled to earn both a reputation and a living wage. This chapter touches upon a variety of women and focuses upon two extraordinary individuals, both businesswomen: a fearless prostitute and a daring spy. They form an unlikely duo to be recognized as subjects of profiles in courage. Yet many of the women discussed herein also deserve acknowledgment for their boldness and pluck.

In the summer of 1846, Matamoros was a "hybrid city" with a little of everything, including women of differing backgrounds and classes. As an officer in an army of occupation, Major Samuel Ryan Curtis had the opportunity to interact on a daily basis with the women in the community. In September, after several months in the field, he welcomed the occasion to recover his health and enjoy the luxury of a real bed. A fellow officer obtained a room for him in a modest yet comfortable boardinghouse replete "with a good cot, two soft pillows and fine clean linens," run by Mrs. Kidder. In an effort to remedy his deteriorating condition, Curtis took significant doses of quinine. The major was in good hands;

his landlady provided the needed care and a delicious tamarind drink. Captain Sanforth Kidder and his wife had arrived in Mexico from Connecticut in 1825. She looked after the establishment, while her husband focused on mercantile concerns. Apparently, the Mexican government determined that Captain Kidder smuggled and compelled him to tear down his wharf and warehouses on Punta de Isabel in 1833. The war offered the captain new prospects as an interpreter for the army, while his wife continued to operate the boardinghouse—apparently with her reputation intact.[1]

Curtis spent several months in Matamoros, and the Ohio native marveled at the transformation of the city into an international marketplace. The French assumed a high profile, especially the rapid multiplication of "restorats." In January 1847 the officer complained, "The town is becoming a fragment of New Orleans." On every corner the French appeared with "their smooth hats, cains, and faces." His contempt for the Gallic presence was not universal. He admitted to "one exception": an attractive Parisian woman who owned the best coffeehouse in the city. Curtis marveled at the grit and determination of this remarkable woman, who had come alone to a foreign land in the midst of war. "Women are strange beings," he philosophized, "capable of anything and no doubt this woman has borne fatigues and privation with more fortitude than some of our soldiers."[2]

Curtis's awareness and education regarding the survival skills of the *femme sole* magnified over time. In November, a visit to the Kidders resulted in a chance encounter with Miss Bowen, who promptly became a good friend and functioned as an interpreter for the officer. The New Hampshire native, a teacher, had come to Mexico with an American family involved with manufacturing. Her duties took her from Matamoros to Saltillo and back, traveling hundreds of miles accompanied only by two male servants. Bowen's tale of danger and privation along the route deeply impressed Curtis, who adjudged her as having "all the desire for accumulation and enterprise peculiar to our New England adventurers," combined with "the ambitions, fortitude, and courage of a good soldier." On several occasions during her stay in Mexico, she had attempted to return to the United States, but each time bouts of yellow fever compelled a delay. Weighing the alternatives, as well as her language skills and attachment to the people, she now seemed inclined to stay.

Soon after chatting with Bowen, Curtis made a very different social call on Jane Stryker. Stryker, from New York City, and her husband, John, had purchased a substantial tract of land, the Banco de Santa Rita, on the north bank of the Rio Grande in the early 1830s. When John died, his wife had moved to town with her children, where Curtis located her in December. The officer no doubt pondered the courage of an American widow supporting her family in a foreign country. The records indicate that Jane remarried after the war and remained in Texas.[3]

In March 1848, Curtis's fellow officer Abner Doubleday witnessed parallel acts of gendered independence. Doubleday journeyed one hundred rugged miles on the frontier, from Saltillo to Parras, with a rather elegant woman escorted by a Mexican servant. Assuming that she was Spanish, he addressed her in the native tongue. Much to his surprise, he soon discovered that Mrs. Major hailed from Onondaga, New York, and her husband had managed factories in Durango before the war. The lady's ability to handle the difficulty and danger of stagecoach travel with veteran nonchalance clearly impressed the officer.[4]

Military Wives

Military wives were definitely another matter. Some officers, sometimes too optimistically, presumed the adaptability of their spouses and invited them to move into an often hostile frontier camp environment. Along the Nueces River in 1845, the colorfully named Lieutenant Napoleon Jackson Tecumseh Dana recounted the millions of flies, which infested everything, vying with the cockroaches for space on food and body. The incessant wet weather seemed perfect for insect reproduction.[5]

There was, of course, no privacy. When the wife of Major Hawkins joined her husband in September, Zachary Taylor rapidly made known his opposition to the presence of women in camp. But his objections to army-related wives, not laundresses or cooks, and even children in the field were erratically enforced and often ignored. For weeks, Dana disapprovingly wrote to his wife, Sue, about seeing Mrs. Hawkins out riding with her husband.[6]

The lieutenant also complained about Mrs. Lindsay, his cook and laundress, who had previously miscarried at Fort Pike and now endured yet another troubled pregnancy. She was linked under doctor's care to Mrs. Dorrance, who suffered from a throat ulcer. Dana disdainfully declared them both to be "worthless old hags, not fit for anything, [who] had no business to come along with us." Characteristically insensitive, the young officer did not discriminate based on class. Women in camp were both a danger and a distraction.[7]

By the winter of 1846, the Americans had occupied several towns in northern Mexico, and a number of soldiers' spouses were in residence. In a missive from Camargo, the Tennessean John McClanahan remarked to his sister that an officer's wife had ridden in front of the encampment one evening. "Had she been a wild animal from the shores of Africa or Bengal," he marveled, "she could not have attracted a more riveted gaze from our boys." In a similar vein, W. P. Rogers commented with wonder about the wife of a Georgia officer who relished the role of celebrity. "She is quite a novelty here and excites a good deal of admiration as she dashes by on her mustang pony neatly dressed with sash, belt, and pistols. She is a ladylike woman—full of spirit and fun." Such displays were dealt a sobering blow just before Christmas, when news arrived of an imminent clash of the armies. "Women cried, their husbands exulted, and we resolved to thrash Santa Anna," one officer proclaimed. When the rumor proved untrue, "all were disgusted."[8]

While the absence of combat disappointed many, the eventual realization that disease, Indian raids, guerrillas, and an inhospitable climate supplemented the dangers to middle-class officers' wives compelled their exclusion from the war zones. Exceptions remained, however, and the tale of two such women reveals the unpredictable nature of their perceived roles and missions. The winter of 1846 heralded the arrival in Saltillo of undoubtedly the most colorful, most prominent, and most persevering wife in the Army of Chihuahua. Maria Indiana Kinzies had married David Hunter in 1829, when the young West Point graduate was stationed at Fort Dearborn. The match was perfect. The twenty-year-old Kinzies was the daughter of a wealthy fur trader who also happened to be a founder of the city of Chicago. Hunter, whose grandfather was a signer of the Declaration of Independence, traced his roots back to the prestigious Stockton family of New Jersey. He rose to the rank of major and the post of paymaster in Taylor's army. The couple spent the war in northern Mexico, finally departing with the withdrawal of US forces in the summer of 1848.[9]

For more than twenty months, commencing in San Antonio, Maria Hunter marched with the army. She suffered, as Josiah Gregg admiringly affirmed, "innumerable sacrifices, privations, and dangers." In the process, her travails, combined with rather forthright behavior and an aggressive personality, earned her a reputation as a heroine in the popular press. Gregg, who referred to Maria as "Mrs. Paymaster Hunter," deemed her "the only respectable female in the army" and "a very amiable, meritorious, and remarkable lady." Some critics found her presence problematic and pointed out that she could lay claim to no particular deeds of bravery. An undeterred Gregg defended her courage and dedication to her husband and dubbed Maria "truly the heroine of General Wool's campaign."[10]

Helen Chapman, whose husband, William, was also a West Point alumnus and served as quartermaster, met Maria in January 1848 in Matamoros. Born into an upper-middle-class Massachusetts family, Helen had received a boarding-school education in Philadelphia. The two swiftly bonded, and Maria became Helen's mentor. They were also polar opposites. Chapman, dark-haired and ten years younger than Maria, stood about five feet tall and barely weighed one hundred pounds. Helen's classically Victorian appearance and language evoked a sense of modesty and unassuming comportment. Yet she clearly brought a New Englander's reformist zeal and the power of female moral suasion to Matamoros.

Helen embraced the population and sympathized with their poverty, referring to them as an "abused, downtrodden race." Seeing promise where others did not, she championed Mexican-American equality, came to the relief of orphaned children, and urged the creation of schools and charitable institutions. Debauchery and decadence consumed the constitutions and reputations of too many young soldiers, Helen claimed, and she pushed for the establishment of a Protestant church and concerted efforts at temperance. No supporter of the war, she bemoaned the cost in money and lives and "the wide-spread ruin of promising young men for territory which is not worth possessing."[11]

Maria Hunter was a legend in northern Mexico, although Helen Chapman acknowledged that she did not possess "the marked characteristics for a heroine." Still, she exuded an undeniable energy and physical presence. Helen described her new friend as tall and slender with dark brown hair and a "stiff" figure. While emphasizing a strong chin and mouth, Helen unflatteringly noted Maria's large hands ("unaccustomed to labor entirely"), "sallow complexion," and "common grey eyes." With some envy, Chapman pointed out that with a family fortune and no children, Maria could indulge in the fashionable life in New Orleans, New York, and Philadelphia. While accustomed to elegance, she enjoyed riding, shooting, and hunting and was simply too high spirited to be a "fine lady." Helen realized that Maria "loves attention and loves to give advice." Wisely deferential, Chapman noted that she had no intention of becoming a rival and was open to taking sage counsel. After some deliberation, Helen concluded, "She is very agreeable to me."[12]

Chapman's diary depicts the months following the peace treaty signed in February 1848 as filled with a leisurely, indeed comfortable lifestyle for the women, who devoted their time to horseback riding, walking the town, observing and commenting upon Mexican habits and customs, and short-distance travel. Concurrently, Helen's social conscience began to evolve along with her recognition of the plight of the Mexican people. She also came to realize that Maria did not particularly share her values. Mrs. Hunter focused her rather controlling persona on promoting her own social and political connections. Maria favored Taylor for the presidency but found the Democratic senator Lewis Cass, of Michigan, an old family friend, also perfectly acceptable.

When Old Rough and Ready sailed from Mexico in November 1847, Maria seriously considered accompanying him and his party to New Orleans. At the last minute she changed her mind, deciding to remain with her husband in Matamoros. When the Hunters reached Louisiana in June 1848, however, Maria went straightaway to Baton Rouge and spent two weeks with the general. Although the Hunters had encouraged the Chapmans to join them in a new gold-rush adventure in California, Helen now fully expected that their friends would find themselves traveling to Washington for Taylor's inauguration. In September 1848, Helen pronounced in retrospection and with a hint of disillusionment, "Mrs. Hunter was selfish and her sympathies exclusively given to her relatives."[13]

The presence of a Maria Hunter or Helen Chapman became increasingly rare as the war progressed. There were good reasons why soldiers' wives should not be resident in Mexico. Their irregular and situational appearance—and disappearance—as time passed can be contrasted with the more defensible presence of women in camp as laundresses and cooks. Each regular army company, not volunteers, was entitled to four laundresses, who received one ration a day (meat, bread, and whiskey), plus shelter and medical care. Officers generally negotiated their salaries. In the aforementioned case of Mrs. Lindsay, each officer agreed to pay her six dollars a month to *both* cook and launder.

Not surprisingly, these women were often the wives or sweethearts of the enlisted men. Many were foreign born—Irish or German. Their work enabled them to earn income and stay, perhaps with their children, in proximity to their husbands. Some were prostitutes, who used the laundress label as a cover for a profitable second career. Regardless of motive, the soldiers valued their services but concurrently made serious efforts to confine them to areas of conquest. Zachary Taylor made that view clear in the spring of 1846, when the rapid occupation of northern Mexico allowed for the presence of officers' wives and camp women in comparative safety. The paradigm shifted as the campaign for Monterrey took shape and the danger increased. An annoyed Napoleon Dana informed his wife, "All our women go back from here (Reynosa) as we cannot provide for them any longer. They are a great pest in the field anyhow. I hope we will not see any of them again so long as we are campaigning."[14]

Individual officers could also hire a servant, and the government reimbursed the monthly costs of the servant's salary of $7.00 to $8.00 and clothing at $2.50, plus an allowance for rations. Many soldiers took advantage of this perquisite and hired African Americans, Mexicans, and the occasional Irishman for the job. The historian Robert May observes that "a sprinkling" of black women, free and slave, served as cooks, laundresses, and nurses. For example, Lieutenant P. P. Peel, of the Second Indiana Volunteers, employed Blanche, a mulatto. Most noncommissioned volunteers, however, could not afford the assistance of a servant, nor were they entitled to one by law. This compelled them to either do their own cooking and washing or hire a Mexican girl. Many of the soldiers sent what little money available back home, so they came to appreciate the drudgery of "women's work."[15]

A female presence in camp persisted throughout the war, in spite of the grumbling and periodic mandates to send all women back to the United States in times of danger or deprivation. Even for the rule-oriented General Winfield Scott, issuing an order was one thing, enforcing it quite another. Old Fuss and Feathers encountered resistance when he attempted to prohibit American camp women from embarking on a grueling march, a common occurrence for Mexican *soldaderas,* from Veracruz to Mexico City. Complaints were raised, often unfairly, about the morality of the American women. Most were not prostitutes, although it would be naive to assume that sexual license was not taken. Patrick Duffee, a member of the Massachusetts regiment, whose wife accompanied him on the campaign, discovered that she had been familiar with a number of the officers and men of his outfit. He attempted to kill her on several occasions, and in May 1848, in a drunken rage, he succeeded. Duffee was arrested for murder.[16]

Factory Women

Most American women in Mexico during the conflict were associated with the army in difficult routines that involved hard labor in an often adverse climate. A significant number, however, arrived from the United States before the war and engaged in various activities largely within the textile sector. Cotton factories formed part of the young Mexican republic's effort to join the industrial revolution.

Beginning in the 1830s, patriotic entrepreneurs spent millions of pesos to buy equipment and erect factories from Puebla and Queretaro in the central region to Saltillo in the North. The looms were purchased in the northeastern United States, where a decade earlier Francis Lowell and his contemporaries had constructed their mills. With the opening of the New England factories arose new opportunities in the public sphere for village and farm girls to garner income and observe the world beyond small-town Vermont. But the Panic of 1837 struck, wages declined, and Irish immigrants rapidly poured into the region to replace the legendary "Lowell mill girls."

The English had penetrated Mexico with their capital and their presence in both mining and textiles. They carried with them a lifestyle that many Americans would not find "foreign." For example, Mineral Del Monte, a rugged mining community of ten thousand souls, reminded Lieutenant D. H. Hill of "an English town with English houses, English manners and customs." Francis Rule, the director of mines, had spent more than twenty years in Mexico, spoke Spanish fluently, and had acquired immense wealth and power, more than any "English Nabob had on his Indian estates," Hill supposed.[17]

Another American soldier met an old Scotsman in Jalapa who had been in Mexico forty years and "made lots of money" managing a textile factory. His boss, named Hall, had come from Georgia and brought his wife with him. The British generally did not take women across the Atlantic—either workers or wives—and most married or adopted Mexican women as their mistresses. Both the English and the Mexicans needed the practical know-how of individuals who had actually shored up a tunnel or worked a loom. They unearthed the former in Cornish miners and the latter in Yankee women who could both labor themselves and instruct others. For an ambitious young New Englander, the disintegrating environment at home might be replaced by relocation to Mexico, where her talents would be more highly valued. The present conflict, however, often placed these women in a precarious situation and presented difficult choices.[18]

In November 1846, D. H. Hill happened upon several women on a road near Saltillo. They had labored in a cotton mill "a great while" and were delighted to see an American. One woman, from New Jersey, offered a somewhat confusing explanation: "I have seen but one white man in eight years, a negro from New Orleans." A week later, the lieutenant, escorted by a few comrades, visited a small cotton factory employing thirty people. The officers noted that the building had been largely constructed by Americans, who had supervised the installation of the machinery, manufactured in Patterson, New Jersey. After completing their instruction in the use of the equipment, the men had departed the country, turning the management of the Mexican-owned factory over to two Irishmen.[19]

The Irish also operated a second mill, the property of an Englishman, by using looms from the Etteawan Company of New York. Among the seventy employees, overwhelmingly women, were several Americans, three with their families. The war had made their situation virtually untenable. A New Yorker named Steele told Hill that the Mexicans had been "so insolent and overbearing" that the Americans, fearing for their safety, had fortified themselves in their houses and prepared for a fight. Taylor's triumph at the Battle of Monterrey in late September and the ensuing occupation of the area barely modified Mexican attitudes. The Americans all voiced their dissatisfaction and their desire to return to the United States. Hill, who always had an eye for the women, pronounced the factory workforce "good-looking and one of them I thought was beautiful." An unmarried American woman caught Hill's attention. He mentioned that she had been in Mexico for seven years and spoke with particular bitterness about the people.[20]

Not all women had a negative experience in Saltillo. When General William Worth's command approached the city in January 1847, they came upon four young women clad in American dress standing by the roadside. The curious soldiers engaged them in conversation and learned that they had come from New Jersey and supervised the operatives in a factory making cotton and woolen goods. They were probably among the same women D. H. Hill had happened upon several months earlier. The troopers took great pleasure in seeing and saluting American girls, while the homesick women encouraged them to sing *Yankee Doodle.* Interestingly, Hill, who evidenced no condescension in dealing with these unknown factory women, later commented when he met the wife and sister of a sutler that they were "third class women." He did reluctantly concede that they were the "nearest approach to ladies I have seen since leaving Old Point. I mean among American women."[21]

Hill had not contended with the femme fatale Caroline Porter, perhaps the most well known and most celebrated of the recent immigrant women. In 1844, Miss Porter, who hailed from Lowell, and two women compatriots had been persuaded to move to Mexico to share the expertise they had acquired in Massachusetts's celebrated mills. Apparently, the local priests deemed such factories objectionable, and they shortly failed. Porter's comrades returned to the United States, but she remained and rose rapidly to become a manager in the Arispe cotton factory, owned by the powerful General Mariano Arista.

The white-walled building five miles from Saltillo, surrounded by cacti and roses, was described as a "floral retreat." Caroline rapidly emerged as its "presiding goddess." Samuel Chamberlain described her as "freckled, snubbed nosed, and red haired." She had not been in Saltillo many months before captivating the heart of the army commander General José Vicente Miñon. The Spanish-born Miñon, a veteran of the Alamo campaign, had earned the nickname "the Lion of Mexico."[22]

With the commencement of the war with the United States, the Lion had been given a field command, and in late February 1847 was ordered by Santa

Anna to surround Old Rough and Ready's forces near Buena Vista. From this point in the story, the waters of the myth and reality become muddy. An assault on Taylor's rear by Miñon's three thousand lancers may well have changed the course of the campaign. However, as his troops passed the Arista mills, Miñon saw the familiar figure of Caroline Porter on the balcony, waving her handkerchief. Unable to resist her charms, he abandoned his troops for several hours to enjoy the company of his former mistress. Apparently, his officers finally had to enter the house and persuade him to resume the march. Too late, the Mexicans lost the advantage, and the attacks were repulsed. Miñon was called back to the capital in disgrace. Meanwhile, Porter argued, and some Americans agreed, that her delaying tactics might well have saved Taylor's command. Chamberlain, whose tale of the Miñon-Porter rendezvous may indeed have been fabricated, claimed to have later bumped into the self-assured "Yankee Delilah" in Saltillo. He reported with some satisfaction that while she did not receive a government pension for the general's dalliance, Porter rewarded herself by marrying an American dragoon.[23]

Sarah Bowman

By the summer of 1846 the Heroine of Fort Brown had already become somewhat of a legend. Sarah Bowman could not be missed when she appeared in an American army camp as a laundress several months earlier. About age thirty, standing six foot two and weighing two hundred pounds, and with flaming red hair, she commanded attention. While Sarah drew men to her because of her attractiveness, observers also repeatedly acknowledged her muscled arms and the ability to lift men and equipment off the ground with equal ease.

Almost a decade earlier, in April 1838, the largest, most powerful, and most elegant vessel afloat had belched coal smoke from twin four-hundred-horsepower engines as she steamed into New York harbor. The black, oak-hulled ship had made the voyage from England in an amazing two weeks. The *Great Western* had arrived, and the era of regular steam travel across the Atlantic began. Many men in Zachary Taylor's army were similarly impressed with Sarah Bowman.[24]

Bowman's background remains murky, with sources indicating her birth in 1812 or 1813 on the Tennessee or the Missouri frontier. She spent her youth in the West and seems never to have become literate, although her business acumen and her mastery of the Spanish language indicate a level of intelligence that melded with a rather forceful personality. When John Langwell, the first of her several husbands, enlisted in the military in 1840 at Jefferson Barracks,

Missouri, Sarah signed on as a laundress in order to be with him. As previously noted, the regular army allowed its officers the luxury of employing women to wash, cook, and generally care for them. Part of her legend also indicates that Sarah traveled to Florida with Langwell to take part in the final phases of the Seminole conflict—and there she would first meet Zachary Taylor.

When the Mexican-American War commenced in the spring of 1846, however, Sarah (who gave her name as Bourjette in 1850) separated from her husband. She joined Taylor's force of four thousand men as they moved south from Corpus Christi to build a camp across the Rio Grande from the Mexican town of Matamoros. Newspaper reports indicate that Sarah, undeterred by heat, lack of water, and terrain, drove a mule cart loaded with supplies for her officers along the punishing march.[25]

When they neared the Little Colorado River, a demonstration and threatening gestures by Mexican soldiers on the opposite bank agitated Sarah, who approached Taylor with the offer to traverse the river "and whip every scoundrel that dared show himself." The general wisely declined. US soldiers forded the stream, and the Mexicans retreated, but Sarah again made her presence known. Lewis Leonidas Allen, who scribbled and made sketches that he later published as *Pencillings of Scenes along the Rio Grande* (1848), in 1846 became one of the few writers to actually speak with Sarah and record her story. He detailed a hair-raising tale of what followed as the American troops attempted to negotiate the river. "There was great danger in crossing, she rendered great assistance; and, in one instance saved the lives of a number of soldiers who were crossing in a flatboat, which sunk while she and her children were in it." Sarah's courage matched her bravado and made her the toast of the ranks.[26]

The image of Sarah appearing in camp out of a morning mist, as very ably described by Brian Sandwich, creates an Amazonian vision. Contemplating her dimensions and form, an awestruck trooper aptly compared her to the mighty *Great Western,* and Sarah promptly inherited the name. The legend, however, was based on courage, as well as strength and size. Her loyalty to Zachary Taylor was unfailing, and her willingness to take on the Mexicans single-handedly was only a portent of events to come.[27]

In late April, hostilities commenced when Mexican troops crossed the Rio Grande and surprised a party of Americans, killing or wounding seventeen and capturing almost fifty others. President James K. Polk, unaware of the assault when he called a cabinet meeting on May 8, had already decided that war was an appropriate remedy to longstanding grievances with Mexico, including issues of debt and the Texas border. Polk's desire for California and the Southwest was much less transparent. The attack, however, gave the president a more legitimate cause for conflict; after all, American troops had been killed on American soil.

Taylor had not been lax in preparing for the eventuality, if not the inevitability, of war. Soon after his arrival opposite Matamoros, he ordered the construction of a rather formidable defensive position. Dubbed "Fort Texas," the imposing structure had nine-foot walls, parapets, and a moat but offered little shelter or protection to those within. In early May the general knew, if Polk did not, that war had unofficially begun, and he responded speedily to rumors that his supply center at Port Isabel was threatened. Taylor marched most of his army to the defense of the base, leaving Major Jacob Brown and five hundred men to guard Fort Texas.[28]

On May 4, the Mexicans bombarded the fort, which housed not only soldiers but also support personnel such as Sarah Bowman. Major Brown dispatched the women and the sick to small shelters, but Sarah brewed coffee and cooked in her tent, then darted about the walls bringing a much-needed morning beverage to the besieged soldiers. She apparently did draw the line, however, when some requested she deliver meals as well. Lewis Allen reported her indignation at the request for chow: "After she had run such great risks, and periled her life, to demand her to expose her life still more in carrying food from her tent to them was asking a little too much, and she begged to be excused, and upbraided them in very severe terms for their want of courage." The danger was real. A bullet pierced her bonnet, and another hit a bread tray. By one o'clock, the tired and hungry troopers noticed Sarah still ignoring the danger and preparing bowls of bean soup.[29]

Throughout seven days of shelling, she cooked and served meals to the men, tended the wounded, and requested (and was given) a musket in case the Mexican forces attempt to storm the barricades. The enemy closed round the fort, but the beleaguered garrison hung on until Taylor could fight his way through from Port Isabel on May 9 to relieve them. Three days before that, Major Brown became, unfortunately, one of only two fatalities during the week-long assault. A shell struck his right leg, inflicting a mortal wound. In his honor, the fort was renamed after him, and the surrounding town evolved into Brownsville.[30]

A booklet entitled *Incidents and Sufferings in the Mexican War,* written by "A Volunteer Returned from the War" (Lieutenant George N. Allen) and published in Boston and New York in 1847, depicts Sarah on the cover above the label "The Heroine of Fort Brown." She is shown amid smoke, a fallen soldier at her feet, dispensing coffee from a bucket to two appreciative troopers, one of whom, oddly, has his gun resting on his shoulder. In this composition, Sarah's size is not emphasized; in fact, one of the soldiers appears larger than her. The anonymous author of *Incidents and Sufferings* echoed Lewis Allen and numerous officers who toasted Sarah's courage and compassion. Lewis Allen strangely remarked, "For woman never appears more lovely than when engaged in her respective sphere, and which is more particularly her province, in bending over the couch of the sick and dying." Sarah did considerably more that fell outside her "respective sphere."[31]

There were skeptics. Major John Corey Henshaw recalled that it would take a considerable amount of time and many pages "to record the imaginary feats of courage said by some would-be literati to have been perpetuated by a woman bearing the Cognomen of the 'Great Western,' who instead of being a modern Lucretia, as this writer would have the public suppose, is and has been for years a Camp woman, who is notorious for her frailties, which are only equaled by her giant size."[32]

The critics were swept aside. Braxton Bragg, a young lieutenant drinking with a group of Louisianans, offered his praise for Sarah's heroism. A later Fourth of July toast by an officer, "The Great Western—one of the bravest and most patriotic soldiers at the siege of Fort Brown," was welcomed with enthusiastic applause. The Great Western, well known in Taylor's army, had also become the Heroine of Fort Brown, a nationally recognized figure representing the bravery and resiliency of American womanhood.[33]

Sarah Bowman was not the only American earning a reputation in May 1846. A much larger Mexican force challenged Zachary Taylor as he attempted to come to the aid of Fort Texas. The resultant battles of Palo Alto and Resaca de la Palma (May 8–9), the first major engagements of the war, left the Mexican military humiliated and Old Rough and Ready victorious. The Mexicans withdrew, and the American Army of Occupation moved in, seizing Matamoros without a shot. Sarah's husband seems to have vanished, so she likely continued her duties as a laundress with Taylor's army.

Sarah's biographer Brian Sandwich logically supposes that she may also have opened her first restaurant or hotel in Matamoros to supplement her meager wages. She certainly had the drive, the personality, and the skills to create such an enterprise, and she did so again on numerous occasions. Apparently, Sarah was content to remain in Matamoros through the summer as Taylor's army moved west along the Rio Grande.

She departed the city in late August, joining up with the US column as it then headed south. Sarah was spotted several weeks later driving a light wagon with two Mexican ponies and carrying all the equipment for her mess, which now counted a dozen young officers of the Fifth Infantry, along with numerous women and young children. There is no indication that she was involved on the field at the bloody American victory that followed at Monterrey. Records do show, however, that she soon launched a full-service hotel, the American House, "the headquarters for everyone," which provided food and women.[34]

As the army moved, so did Sarah. She accompanied Taylor's forces in December as they marched sixty miles southwest to occupy the town of Saltillo. By January she had opened the third and most successful American House. Sarah had barely had time to embark on her latest enterprise when Taylor and his five thousand troops were challenged by a force of almost twenty thousand led by the resilient Antonio López de Santa Anna. Santa Anna eschewed the opportunity to bring relief to the walled city of Veracruz on the Gulf of Mexico, presently besieged by an American army commanded by Winfield Scott. Instead, the Mexican general chose to use his numerical superiority to crush Taylor's inferior force. The Battle of Buena Vista (February 22–23, 1847) took place only seven miles from Saltillo. Taylor refused Santa Anna's demand to surrender and stood his ground through a bloody two-day struggle. The outcome determined Old Rough and Ready's stature in American military history.

Taylor already held an exalted place with Sarah. The Texan George Trahern recalled the scene when a group of panicked deserters fled the fray and tried to take refuge in the American House. A frightened Indiana volunteer loudly proclaimed that "Gen. Taylor was whipped and the army was all cut to pieces." The Mexicans were headed for Saltillo! Trahern, the wonder clear in his words, declared that Sarah "just drew off and hit him between the eyes and knocked him sprawling: says, 'You damned son of a bitch, there ain't Mexicans enough in Mexico to whip Old Taylor. You just spread that report and I'll beat you to death.'"[35]

The thoroughly humiliated and intimidated soldiers scurried back to the field. And so did Sarah. Assuming her not unfamiliar role as nurse and cook, she delivered coffee to the well and care to the wounded. Reports state that she actually gathered the injured from the battlefield and carried them to Dr. Charles M. Hitchcock for treatment. Devastation overtook her, however, when she learned that Captain George Lincoln, who had recruited her at Jefferson Barracks in 1840, had been killed. "We have lived together," a distraught Sarah wept, "that is he has eat at my table all the time since." Sarah searched the area for his corpse, fearing that it would be stripped during the night by "them rascally greasers." After securing Captain Lincoln's remains and ensuring a proper burial, she proceeded to rescue the officer's magnificent white horse. Bidding

$250 at auction, Sarah made certain that the animal was taken back to Massachusetts and presented to Lincoln's family as a symbol of the captain's sacrifice, as well as her appreciation.[36]

The Americans remained in Saltillo, and Sarah built a growing clientele. Many of the army officers stayed at the American House, where the combination of a real bed, decent food, and young Mexican women earned her a small fortune. Abner Doubleday entered the town and realized that he was among officers of all grades in "a kind of tavern kept by a gigantic camp woman." In April 1847, Samuel Curtis desperately tried to escape the Mexican sun and sought a comfortable room and bed at the hotel. There he came upon Sarah—"Mrs. Bourgette." "She is nearly six feet high and well proportioned," Curtis observed. "She has several servants, Negro and Mexican, and she knocks them around like children. While I am writing she is watering her horse."[37]

Major William Chapman informed his wife that he was unimpressed with Sarah's appearance. "She is a large, coarse, six feet high woman without a single attraction, except her great kindness of heart." Nevertheless, Chapman noted that Sarah was a "remarkable personage" who remembered all the army officers she had met and greeted them with either hugs or kisses. "She is really a privileged character and a great favorite," he understated. Indeed. She owned the most elegant carriage in Saltillo, dined with General John Wool, and traveled to Monterrey to sup with Zachary Taylor. Wool returned the favor several days later, riding into town to socialize with the Great Western at her hotel.[38]

No doubt the army more than tolerated Sarah. Her early dedication and heroism endeared her to all ranks. When she added the role of madam to that of laundress and cook, the generals gave a wink and a nod to the morale boost provided by the creature comforts of her establishments. Sarah supplemented her income as a prostitute, and apparently a quite good one, before focusing her attention on management.[39]

Samuel Chamberlain offers us one of the few images of Sarah in his rather dramatic painting of a scene at the American House. At one end of the bar, several US soldiers sit and stand, drinking, perhaps playing cards. At the opposite end, a trooper converses with an attractive young Mexican woman. She ignores him. Behind the soldier, two women talk with each other. In the center, in front of the bar and a large mirror, stands the formidable Great Western in a bright red dress. Chamberlain focused on her size, depicting her larger than anyone else, with muscular arms and a broad face highlighted by her long dark hair, parted down the middle, and bushy eyebrows. In her hand, close to her waist, she holds a pistol. Sarah confronts a smaller Mexican man, perhaps a *vaquero,* whose hat

Sarah Bowman—"The Great Western"—US Army cook, hotel owner, and madam at her bar. Pencil and watercolor by Samuel Chamberlain, 1846.

in hand and bent knee, with the other hand on his chest, imply a position of request, perhaps supplication.[40]

There is no doubt who dominates the painting, the scene, and the hotel. Samuel Curtis wrote that he paid $2.50 "for my entertainment at the boarding house of the Great Western." Soldiers frequently complained about the price of a dozen eggs or a chicken (each cost half a dollar), but few objected to the charges for rooms and services at the American House. Sarah became a very capable businesswoman, as evidenced by her carriage, her clothing, and, by 1848, the claim to have $15,000 in cash, a huge sum for the day.[41]

The vices of the army were many, especially among the volunteers, and officers struggled to maintain discipline and sobriety. In the weeks, even months, between battles, the men engaged in endless drills and chasing guerrillas who had murdered their comrades. Boredom blended with a racial vengeance to turn the men not only against the Mexicans but also against one another and their officers. The potential for violence placed the well-run American House under scrutiny. In June 1847, Sarah's good friend General Wool issued Special Order #517, which forbade the presence or sale of liquor at the hotel and restricted the flow of traffic only to those officers who resided there. The building would be closed at sundown, and the only women allowed were those servants to "Mrs. Bouget." A sentry would be posted outside the front door to enforce the mandate. Sarah remained. The impact of the order and its observance is unclear, but it probably cut into her thriving business.[42]

The war ended by treaty in February 1848, and by midsummer the Americans had departed Mexico. The volunteers headed home, and the regulars were often dispatched to new duties in the West. Zachary Taylor seemed destined for the White House, but Sarah Bourgette saw her future with the military in the newly annexed territories. In mid-July she rode a horse, together with three wagons, into an army camp near Arista Mills, Texas. Sarah wanted to join their march toward California, but a recent order prohibited civilians from joining the column. Sarah responded, "All right, Major. I'll marry the whole Squadron and you thrown in but what I go along." She thereupon trotted in front of the ranks demanding, "Who wants a wife with $15,000, and the biggest leg in Mexico! Come my beauties, don't speak at once—who is the lucky man?"[43]

Eventually, a soldier, apparently David Davis of the First Dragoons, overcome by either the size of Sarah or her purse, agreed to the nuptials. They were hastily married, and she promised her new husband, "Bring your blanket to my tent tonight and I will learn you to tie a knot that will satisfy you, I reckon." Her affections and the marriage lasted only a few months. In southern New Mexico, Sarah came upon a large man ("a Hercules") bathing and "conceived a violent passion for his gigantic proportions." The ensuing affair, though evidently somewhat brief, impelled the demise of her sham marriage to Davis.[44]

Sarah moved on to El Paso in 1849, once again opening a "hotel." Restlessness drove her to Socorro, New Mexico, and an exchange of vows in 1850 with yet another dragoon, twenty-four-year-old Alfred J. Bowman. Bowman, attended by his new bride, was transferred several times before receiving his discharge from the military in November 1852. Sarah continued to impress Albert's command, one awestruck soldier remarking that she was "modest and womanly notwithstanding her great size." She wore a red velvet waistcoat, a riding skirt, and a gold laced cap. Seeing her thus attired, and carrying a pistol and a rifle, the trooper wryly observed, "She reminds me of Joan of Arc and the days of chivalry."[45]

The couple moved to Fort Yuma, Arizona, where Sarah resumed her seemingly lifelong domestic duties for the officers' mess, while Albert prospected for gold. Her "boarders" included the post commander, Major Samuel Heintzelman, with whom she developed a personal and business relationship that allowed her to set up a house across the Colorado River on Mexican soil in 1854. Like so many other soldiers before him, Heintzelman fell victim to Sarah's charms. She could not, perhaps did not try, to escape her past. The scar on her cheek from a Mexican saber at Matamoros revealed a woman familiar with danger. A pioneering and relentless entrepreneur, she and Albert opened a string of projects, including a hotel. Impatience consumed Sarah, and when the military moved on to build Fort Buchanan in the Sonoita Valley, she soon followed in 1856.[46]

Launching yet another house for gambling, dancing, and drinking outside the fort, she plied her trade very successfully until the advent of the Civil War prompted the abandonment of the post. Sarah dispatched her girls back to Mexico and returned to Fort Yuma in the summer of 1861, wryly observing that "there was just one thin sheet of sandpaper between Yuma and hell." Divorced from Albert and now a legend in the West, she fell back into her familiar role as cook, laundress, and mother of adopted Mexican children. Sarah, a survivor of so many precarious situations, succumbed to the bite of a tarantula on December 22, 1866. Reflective of her status, she was buried at Fort Yuma with full military honors and then exhumed and reinterred at the Presidio in San Francisco in 1890.

Sarah Bowman's unique role and contributions in the Mexican-American War were celebrated by many who not only refused to condemn but actively endorsed and supported her notorious lifestyle. Colorful and outrageous, tough and unflinching, Sarah certainly failed the Victorian test of a "true woman." Yet her acts of courage and compassion in the fort and on the field won the undying devotion of thousands of soldiers and yielded her a special place on the American frontier. She gained broader and deserved recognition within the popular culture in 1998, when Lucia St. Clair Robson penned a romanticized novel of her life appropriately titled *Fearless.*[47]

Ann Chase

Within the context of twenty-first-century US history, the label "Heroine of Tampico" weighs in somewhere between meaningless and mystifying. In her lifetime, however, Americans celebrated Ann Chase with poems and patriotic gifts for one particular incident of courage and sacrifice during the Mexican-American War. Born Ann McClarmonde in northern Ireland in 1809, she lost her father at age eleven. Ann, her mother, and two brothers saved enough money to make their way to New York in 1824 to begin a new life. Tragically, her mother died, obliging Ann to join her brother James, a businessman in Philadelphia. Sharing an adventurous and entrepreneurial spirit, the siblings agreed to sell their mercantile business in 1834 and seek their fortune in New Orleans.

Ann Chase, merchant and spy in Tampico. (Photo courtesy Dallas Historical Society. Used by permission.)

This notion quickly yielded to the opportunities available on the east coast of Mexico at the modest (5,000 residents) but thriving port of Tampico. The town, described by one American officer as "beautiful," was situated on the Panuco River, six miles from the Gulf of Mexico. A fine natural harbor enhanced the import-export trade, valued at about five hundred thousand dollars a year. The one-story, flat-roofed stone houses and paved streets, once the site of an ancient Aztec village, gave the community an aura of permanence. Some might argue that the relentless heat and humidity, along with malaria, dysentery, and cholera, compromised this tropical haven.[48]

Other foreigners preceded Ann and James, including the US consul, Franklin Chase, who had started his own mercantile firm. The Maine-born Chase joined the Columbian Navy in his teens, refined his Spanish, and became a prosperous trader. Ann, now 27, and Franklin discovered they had much in common and married in 1836. A photograph of Ann reveals a proper Victorian lady, her long dark hair in ringlets, pulled back from her forehead, with broad features and a wide mouth. Her demure voluminous dark silk dress evoked the perfect wife for a merchant-diplomat. For the next decade, she combined her role as social hostess and business partner with a variety of intellectual endeavors.[49]

Arguably Ann's most amazing accomplishment was a remarkable history of Mexico. The lengthy manuscript reflected detailed research into religion, politics, and society, thoughtful analysis, and a readable writing style. Her study of the rise and fall of Agustin de Iturbide in 1819–24 is a prime example. Iturbide fought for Mexican independence from Spain, but his antirepublican sentiments led him to a major role in the ensuing civil war and a meteoric rise to emperor. Exile and execution followed thereafter in what became a blueprint for the nineteenth-century struggle between republicans and royalists in Mexico. Chase keenly observed that Iturbide desired to become "the immortal Washington, the liberator of his country," but instead appeared as "the Mexican Washington without the moral virtues." Iturbide concurrently envisioned himself as "the great Napoleon, to be placed upon a throne and swing the scepter." The two contrary goals became impossible to achieve.

Chase relished the arrival of the Mexican Republic. She warmly praised the Constitution of 1824, which paralleled the US model. Surely, her scrutiny of the document in terms of form, powers, and rights would have delighted James Madison. Additional calculated thoughts poured forth on topics as varied as the rebellion in Yucatán (the locals were more industrious and better educated than their fellow countrymen) and the condition of the Mexican Navy ("very dilapidated").[50]

Chase was particularly analytical and carefully respectful in her views about Mexico and the possibility of invasion. Her journal reads like a manual that might be distributed at West Point. She evaluated a variety of issues facing an invader, from the condition of the army to strategic landing problems (sand bars) and the positioning of the Mexican forts. Chastising the Europeans for their mistaken notions about the bravery of the individual soldier, Chase contended, "They will follow their leaders to the last moment and only cease to follow when the artillery of death arrests their footsteps." Hungry, tired, and poorly supplied, their usual nourishment being water, herbs, and wild plants, they would still remain loyal. Family and force compelled the Mexican soldier to "meekly submit to his ill-starved destiny."

Geography should also give an invading force reason to pause. The shoreline offered few points where troops could comfortably disembark, and once they landed, a largely roadless interior added to the challenge. Where would the invaders obtain supplies, and how could they survive the deadly climate? Chase predicted that "destruction and death would be inevitable" for any European or American army attempting conquest in the summer months. She carefully scrutinized the French naval assault of 1838 and concluded that Veracruz was a viable landing option. Ironically, Winfield Scott took a similar path, but he defied her logic with his brilliant summer campaign from Veracruz to Mexico City a year later.[51]

A clearly frustrated Chase lashed out at those self-serving forces who kept a resource-rich Mexico backward, poverty ridden, and divided. With an even-handed resentment, she argued, "Mexico would as a state have been better under the dominion of Spain. If she is free it is only in name, for she is still under the iron rod of oppression. The state has many masters, but no head—power is the motto, and self-interest the object of pursuit, and this motto and object dissolves every tie of blood and friendship—whilst the country which is so highly favored by the god of nations is left without cultivation and the minds of the natives like the bleak barren waste by which they are surrounded."

Chase waded into the shadowy waters of church-state politics, deftly exploring the efforts of the Spanish government to maintain power in the hands of Old Spain clerics at the expense of the native-born priests. Madrid and a carefully chosen clergy emerged as the champions of intolerance and major obstacles to progress and enlightenment. In time, native-born priests became alienated, and many emerged in the forefront of the anti-Spanish insurgency. Stimulating the "lower orders," when they opposed "the tyranny of the mother country," the "poor benighted Mexicans" followed.[52]

Chase identified a comparable situation of intolerance and oppression in a "disturbed" Ireland, where turmoil bubbled up in an atmosphere of dissension and disunion. She breathed a sigh of relief. Fortunately, those days had passed, and "liberty of law and religion has again united the people under the happiest monarchy on the habitable earth." Surely, many on the Emerald Isle would have disagreed. "Happy England," Chase exulted, "long may she as a limited monarchy retain her power—that power which is the envy of the world but which is administered with equity and justice to her subjects." Chase, the product of a working-class Protestant background in northern Ireland, remained firm and consistent in her suspicion of papal intrigue but became rather schizophrenic in her British identity.[53]

The Chases had survived the years of tension between Mexico and the Lone Star Republic, but the commencement of the war along the Rio Grande and the accompanying US blockade of Tampico raised a new set of problems. On May 12, the axe fell, as the Mexican government issued an order demanding that American citizens immediately leave the country or, alternatively, withdraw about twenty-five miles into the interior. The US commodore G. W. Saunders, stationed offshore, advised Franklin to leave Mexico.

The couple anguished over their decision. Finally, they agreed that thirty-seven-year-old Ann, who retained her English citizenship, would remain. Franklin had transferred his stock of eighty thousand dollars' worth of goods to her name, and she now took the title "acting consul." On June 7, he embarked for Veracruz on the USS *St. Mary's,* planning to continue on to Havana. Unfortunately, for more than a month he was unable to book passage on any vessel bound for Cuba. Franklin corresponded with Ann but was obliged to remain aboard an American ship off the Mexican coast until a British mail packet took him to his destination in July.[54]

In her passionate and detailed journal of more than two hundred pages, we get a real sense of Ann's heightened outrage blended with a cool deliberative streak. Beginning in June and extending into December, she arose with the dawn and continued scribbling into the evening hours, complemented by the often relentless pounding of drums and blaring of bugles on the plaza. She recorded in painful comprehension the trials and tribulations of a marginalized woman in a city hostile to her and her husband. Isolation energized and enervated her; religion offered solace and salvation. When the government expelled Franklin in early June, a broken-hearted Ann found succor in the comforting visits of old friends in the European community. As time passed, however, pressure mounted on foreigners to refrain from any contact with her lest they suffer repercussions from provincial officials. "Few friends to console and none to cheer—alas! In the hours of adversity how few stand the Test," she somberly observed. Increasingly, Ann realized that she was alone with her thoughts, her faith, and a few household companions.[55]

Whether Mexican officials pushed Ann Chase too far seems uncontestable. She lived in an elegant house on the same plaza as the army barracks and possibly overheard conversations and pronouncements that could be of value to the Americans. By mid-July 1846, the thoroughly angered woman began sending information regarding community developments and troop movements, as well as maps of the Tampico harbor and area, to both her husband and Commodore David Conner, the commander of the US Home Squadron, which was blocking the Gulf coast. As a subject of Queen Victoria, she developed contacts in the British embassy and consulate, as well as the Royal Navy. James William Glass, the British consul in Tampico, and Francis Gifford in Veracruz were likely among those Ann relied upon for information.

Gifford, now a seasoned diplomat, had first been appointed vice-consul in 1833 and had a keen sense of his environment. His timely reports in the spring of 1846 kept Lord Palmerston and the Foreign Office apprised of the events transpiring along the coast. Gifford included the number and identity of the American warships patrolling the harbor, as well as noting the cooperation of their officers in allowing free access to mail packets and freighters bearing materials critical to British mining and mercantile interests. While the Royal Navy ferried his London correspondence in safety, beginning in June 1846 the crafty consul, out of fear of the officials or guerrillas, halted any updates of his situation with the British embassy in Mexico City until March 1848—after a treaty had been signed ending the war. Since Mexican authorities carefully scrutinized her letters and messages, Ann passed information along surreptitiously to the Americans offshore in the ties of British sailors.[56]

While her burdens drove Ann into a downward spiral of depression, she viewed her situation as an opportunity to be seized. Perceptive observations came fast and furious. Some were reconsidered after months of conflict, but most stayed unchanged. She was well aware that civil war among the various states combined with the American invasion to throw Mexico into chaos. Trying to assess the power games played by the generals and politicians proved a unique and ongoing challenge. Her balcony offered an eagle's perch from which to monitor the arrival and departure of troops, their size, point of origin, discipline, and morale. She could never escape the images of poverty and oppression. Among her more telling emotions, sympathy for the Mexican people permeated the pages of her journal. Repeated references remark on the courage, bravery, and self-sacrifice exhibited by the soldiers and their *soldadera* spouses in defense of the nation. Their feckless and self-absorbed leaders proved unworthy of such dedication.[57]

Although Tampico was spared bloodshed, early, overblown enthusiasm for chastising the cowardly Yankee invaders gave way to skepticism and doubt covered by a patina of military ardor. Awaiting further news from Franklin, who remained offshore aboard the *St. Mary's,* Chase watched the scene unfold. When an English officer on the royal steamer *Vesuvian* passed along a letter to Ann from her husband but appeared to vacillate in taking a note back in return, she exploded. Would John Bull callously ignore the request of his own countrywoman, a "helpless supplicant" who was only trying to reach out to her "beloved husband"? What "heartless indifference," she sniffed. Ann blamed the attitude on her Irish heritage, asking God to never let her become an English "supplicant, kneel at the shrine of St. George's cross, or crouch to his Lion." Ultimately, her missive was delivered when a later conversation revealed that both she and the officer had been born in "the green fields of Erin" and he took pity on her situation.[58]

Ann Chase's cynicism regarding England ran proportionate to a flowering American chauvinism. Praising the Union, blessed with equality, liberty, and opportunity, she enthused, "May she soon spread her Eagle wings over the whole western hemisphere, may the whole of those ill-fated republics yield to her wise counsels." As for Mexico proper, "she must change language, customs, morals and government—and change all her present system."[59]

The noose tightened around Ann's neck. She was deprived of her husband's companionship and abandoned by friends and countrymen, and the Mexican authorities applied what they believed would be the final pressure. On June 25, they commanded Ann to close the shop; her privileges were revoked and the property confiscated. A swift rebuttal began a spirited exchange between her and Mexican officials. She claimed to be not only the store's designated agent but also a British subject with natural rights. Her sarcasm was underscored by instructing the judge's messenger to bear her kind regards "to his *learned* judgeship and to please inform himself better in the British Law—and in the Laws of Nations—and fit himself for judge before he gave such rapid decisions against an unprotected female with only God for her counselor and faith to uphold her."[60]

Mexican officials were doubtless perplexed, but they were not amused by the attitude of such a strident woman. They rejected her plea, citing Spanish law, under which men were the heads of households, and denied her claim to special concessions. Judges also denied the notion of British citizenship, maintaining that she was indeed an American. She confided to her journal, "I myself am the only American in the place *in my feelings and sentiments.*" Days later, her home and warehouse were robbed, but Ann refused to leave Mexico. "What is property without security—," she later pondered, "when your goods can be so easily robbed, and many who bore the name of friends from selfish motives desert you the day of trouble."[61]

The summer passed, and Ann Chase remained isolated and alone in her faith. "I enjoy solitude and love self-communion," she rationalized, comparing herself to the female characters in James Fenimore Cooper's *Red Rover* who were cut adrift and left "helpless and lonely amongst those semi-barbarians." Depression reoccurred, monotony remained. She took solace in the Bible, the familiar streets of Tampico, and the occasional visit of a royal mail steamer. News from the Mexican capital placed a layer of patriotic bluster and bravado over a rot of factionalism, selfishness, and discord "eating deeper into the vitals of the nation." Ann pronounced that "Mexico, like the cruel crockadile [*sic*] of her coast, . . . devours her own offspring who are now without means and no resource left but discord and an unsupportable pride."[62]

Repeated reports of civil war, revolution in the northern provinces, and the drive to form a new republic did little to cloud that view. Ann, who possessed knowledge and insight into the labyrinth of national politics, concluded that many Mexicans appeared to desire the return of General Santa Anna. She marveled that in spite of "his atrocious acts," they felt he offered the best hope for unity and leadership. Only the erudite Mrs. Chase, who had a penchant for quoting Shakespeare, would muse about the English novelist Edward Bulwer-Lytton's *Renzi, The Last of the Roman Tribunes* and the ideal qualities needed for leadership of a vast and diverse empire. As the politicians and generals jostled for power and the title of "greatest patriot," the masses remained "without a voice, a mere cypher." Ann recognized that the infernal drumbeats and drilling on the plaza outside her home did not reflect military preparedness to confront either a domestic uprising or a foreign foe.[63]

July dragged on with few ripples in Ann's life. Business continued to languish, and her "painful mental distress" weighed heavily. She commented on the inhumane ambush and death of a dozen American sailors seeking fresh water ashore and on her sad separation from her husband on their anniversary. The martial music on the plaza seemed endless. Ann did not rest well. "Grief and sleep are in general bad friends," she opined. Consequently, her reverie was barely disturbed by a noise in the wee hours indicating a late-night attempt to enter the store. "Miss Amelia," Ann's young female companion, and a Mexican servant girl were also in the house at the time. Amelia had become "like a staff in the hand of an invalid to lean upon and to console." In this situation, however, Ann seemed more than up to the challenge. Seizing her husband's sword, she headed downstairs to confront the intruder. Fortunately, no one had broken in, but the women found evidence of an effort to force the iron bolt locks, and that same night a neighbor was robbed. Ann rejoiced in their good fortune and relished the bonds of friendship strengthened by the rather traumatic incident.[64]

Little that occurred in Tampico escaped Chase's keen eye. She calculated the number of troops parading (500), their height (4′11–5′2), and their ethnicity, writing, "Their lineaments resembling the ancient Moors much more than the Indians." The smaller women, with their tiny hands and feet, drew her attention. The handsomest women she had ever seen came from Jalapa and Puebla, although Ann could only guess that the temperate climate and high elevation of the towns were reasons for their beauty. She compassionately recalled a conversation with a young woman from Puebla, a *soldadera,* who had come into the store. Her tale of poverty and starvation following her husband, a member of the Sixth Regiment from Veracruz, was heartbreaking. Ann described in sympathetic detail the fragile, delicate infant the woman carried in her arms, whom the mother was "doomed to support," possibly without the aid of her spouse. Mother and son had endured a life of "squalid poverty," and they scarcely had clothing to protect them from the torrential rain. The woman spoke about her birth in Puebla and their encampment in Tampico for the past three months. She wore her only clothes and many days went without food. "We had not much," she explained, but she thanked God for the good fortune to avoid death. Ann could only listen, marvel at her fortitude, and ponder the lack of courage and leadership of the Mexican generals.[65]

Fortunately, Ann had contacts in Mexico City who kept her abreast of the swirling military and political situation, including the return of Santa Anna at Veracruz, the celebrated clashes at Palo Alto and Resaca de la Palma, and the naval activities on the California coast. Despite Mexican euphoria, Ann had no use for Santa Anna. She mockingly called him "Saint Anna" and derided him as "the subverter of liberty and the great enemy of freedom." In contrast, Taylor made her almost giddy. She received reports on his victories from British Consul Gifford. Ann recorded at great length the details of these battles in her journal and heaped praise upon the heroic Old Rough and Ready, who had previously shown his mettle against "the crafty and cruel Seminoles" in Florida. She lauded his "liberality," reflected in his returning captured baggage to the Mexicans and honoring their bravery in combat.[66]

In the Pacific, Commodore John D. Sloat bore watching. His "prompt and decisive conduct" in that theater augured well for the future of American Manifest Destiny. Occasionally, Chase obtained erroneous information, such as the August news of the wreck of the brig USS *Somers* while in pursuit of a blockade runner. "My heart bleeds," she confessed, "for the fifty crew members and six officers who sought refuge on shore and were quickly captured and imprisoned." The *Somers* was indeed involved in enforcing the blockade along the Gulf coast but managed to survive until enveloped by a squall and sunk in December 1846.

Foreign vessels nearby saved half the crew, but the misfortune of the *Somers* and eight sister ships since the outset of war attested to the danger of the blockade.[67]

The season brightened in mid-August when a British mail steamer bound for Havana arrived off Tampico bearing the news of Santa Anna's homecoming and, more importantly, a surprise visit from her husband. Ann, prepared with her "rights as a neutral" argument, expressed amazement when officials raised no obstacles to her visiting the ship. She overcame her sea-sickness and the on-board rendezvous lasted several days, time enough to allow a renewal of her affections of the heart and to provide Franklin and American naval officers with additional intelligence regarding the port's troops and fortifications. An appreciative Commander William J. McCluney, of the *John Adams,* took the time to write Ann a note of thanks for the "valuable information."[68]

The Navy Department, now under the leadership of the Virginian John Y. Mason, had already contemplated the seizure of Veracruz and Tampico, separated by two hundred miles, as Gulf coast depots for US provisions and stores, a vital component of any plan for invading Mexico City. Mason informed Commodore Conner on September 22 that a move by Zachary Taylor's forces into northern Mexico was imminent and said that the capture of Tampico by the US Navy would "be of the utmost importance" to the ultimate success of the operation.[69]

On September 25, Monterrey fell to the Americans. The news that reached Tampico five days later intimated otherwise: Taylor had been soundly defeated, with the loss of a thousand dead and half as many wounded. A celebration swept the town, the mob chanting, "Death to the Americans!" A son of the collector of the port taunted Ann, telling her not to shed any tears for the loss of any "American tyrants." Steaming with anger, she felt the impulse to harshly respond to the insult by "the poor little aborigine—the abortion that nature in one of her fanciful freaks had brought forth." A cooler head, and her Christianity, prevailed: "I said, Father forgive them, for they know not what they do." Later that evening, rockets, which could have ignited her house, were fired onto her balcony. Worse still, the next night thieves broke into the store, plundering some of its most valuable goods and leaving behind a putrid-smelling corpse. Ann's situation had become precarious.[70]

Ann Chase was many things, including a politically astute and shrewd businesswoman. She immediately recognized both the financial extent of her loss and the likelihood that the military was involved. Her home was attached to the Customs House, an official building guarded continuously after hours by four sentinels. Demanding safety due a British citizen, she registered her complaint with the town's commander, General Anastasio Parrodi. Parrodi denied any responsibility for the protection of private property but promised that he would look into the situation. She recognized the hollowness of his pledge but played along, while receiving advice and comfort from British Consul Charles Whitehead and security from a resident Irish-born friend.[71]

Ann's situation did not improve when news arrived on October 4 of the reality of the Mexican defeat at Monterrey. Fingers pointed at Ann Chase. Tampico authorities suspected that she had provided information to the Americans, and consequently they changed her household staff, placing spies to act as servants. Ann, well aware of such subterfuge, confided outrageous estimates of the number of US troops she expected to momentarily invade the country, specifically Tampico. When this knowledge was relayed to the officials, the captain of the port hauled Ann into his office and demanded to know whether her husband had informed her about the twenty-five to thirty thousand American troops about to strike the city. With her credibility on the rise, Ann quietly mentioned to the father-in-law of General Parrodi that "an early retreat" might be the wisest course of action. On October 20, she simultaneously relayed her bluff to Commodore Conner.[72]

Parrodi had gotten himself into a bind. The forty-one-year-old Cuban-born commander and Santa Anna loyalist had earlier been ordered by the government to reconstruct and improve the battlements around Tampico. The port had a natural defensive position. By October 1846 the general had his fortifications in place and three thousand soldiers, 120 artillery pieces, and three war vessels at his disposal. The preparations were impressive, but if Ann Chase's intelligence was accurate, Tampico could not resist the onslaught of twenty-five thousand Americans. He wisely sought the counsel of his commanding officer, Santa Anna, in San Luis Potosí.[73] The Napoleon of Mexico faced his own problems. Fearful that Taylor or a second American army would move against him in strength, Santa Anna wanted to ensure that Parrodi's troops, convoying valuable war materials cached in Tampico, united with his forces. He instructed Parrodi to prepare for the Americans. However, should his men face probable defeat, he had permission to withdraw. Concurrently, the national government, the provincial governor Nunes Ponce, the Tampico citizenry, and the soldiers sought to hold the city as long as possible. Although the Americans had not yet appeared, an increasingly concerned Santa Anna ordered Parrodi to abandon the city on October 27 and march his forces inland to Tula.

The frustrated officer and the townsfolk grumbled and resisted; too much had been invested, and too much would be lost if the port fell to the invaders.

Santa Anna reaffirmed his orders. General Francisco Garay took command of Tampico, and Parrodi complied with the demand to evacuate, albeit too late to save his position. General José Urrea relieved him on October 29, arriving with the men in Tula on November 16. A small army had been saved, but they had left behind a significant amount of public property and war material. Ann stated with resignation, "At last in Mexico, so many incongruities, so much character, and so little principle."[74]

With both apprehension and hope, Ann Chase watched the flurry of activity, civilians desperately fleeing Tampico with their money and goods in hand, and then the quiet. On October 29, she observed, "Our deserted city seems to repose in its listless silence." Apparently, her strategy had worked. But where was the American navy? Should a mob appear, her goods could easily fall into their hands. The spotting of an English ship and the cross of St. George helped relieve her anxieties. "Far from being an unpleasant sight," she confessed, "the sturdy sons of Neptune" proffered a welcome safeguard. "The nation with all her faults looks well after her interest at home and does not neglect it abroad."[75]

Finally, reports arrived on November 7 of an impending American landing, and a week later the US squadron appeared in the harbor. Ann recognized the irony in the crush of foreigners seeking sanctuary. The following day, she jotted in her journal that "it is really astonishing the effect of yesterday's news. Relative to the expedition coming here, members are flocking to my house in order to solicit my protection on the arrival of the Americans, amongst whom are some who at the outset tried to bruise the broken seed. I do not pretend to any influence—as power with the party now said to be coming in, although I stood as them in name, and as a nation, when alone in peril and danger—I was like a swallow in the house top."

Foreign consuls scrambled to hoist their flags in an effort to save their goods and property from American bombardment or violation. On the morning of the November 14, Amelia rushed into Ann's chamber announcing the presence of seven American vessels off the mouth of the river. Ann climbed to the rooftop of her house and with the help of two friends raised the Stars and Stripes. Having proudly "defied the whole town of Tampico," she said, sharply, "I sent for some Americans, but no one possessed the courage or national spirit enough to lend a hand."[76]

The resultant exchange between Mrs. Chase and the city council, which Ann recorded in her journal, bordered on comic opera. Just minutes after she hoisted the flag, several local officials arrived to demand that she take it down. Ann responded that she flew the banner for protection. After all, other consuls raised their flags. If the US banner had gone up "a little too soon," she conceded, "it was of but little consequence." Caught off guard by Ann's cavalier defiance, the embarrassed councilmen softened their approach. What would they say in Mexico City, one pleaded, if the government found out that the enemy's flag was flying in the main plaza of Tampico and had not been raised by the Americans? "The expressions on their faces, I shall never forget," Ann mused. Obliquely referring to an impending American landing in the town, she pointed out that her doors were open and the flag was intended to protect Mexicans as well as foreigners in danger. Tempers quieted. The councilmen apologized for "molesting" her, and Ann assured them that she had "not been disturbed in the least." They departed with a "friendly salute," and she hurried to the rooftop, where the Stars and Stripes still proudly waved in the air. The legend evolved, and her bravery grew. One version had her defiantly gripping a revolver.

Such self-sacrifice proved unnecessary. The arrival of Conner's squadron, followed by the landing of 450 sailors and marines on November 22, induced a flag of truce from the council and the surrender of the town without bloodshed or a shot fired. Ann's journal becomes sketchy during the American military occupation in December and ends with the pessimistic observation that the community of foreigners and the Mexicans looked upon the Americans as "usurping their rights" and had little sympathy for their cause.[77]

On November 30, Secretary Mason effusively thanked and praised Conner and his command for their triumph at Tampico. Mason confided the difficulty of estimating "the important consequences" of the operation for the future of the war. Conner no doubt reveled in the honors, while Ann Chase was never mentioned. The historian Justin Smith asserts that Conner informed his wife on November 17 that he was "surprised to find the city evacuated." Conner mused, "Why Mrs. Chase did not give notice of the evacuation cannot be explained."

The commodore's silence in acknowledging Ann's contribution is understandable. After struggling along the Gulf coast in several operations, meriting the scorn of his subordinates and the press, he had finally secured a victory. Yet, as the scholar K. Jack Bauer emphasized, the feat was "bloodless and lacked public appeal." The Navy Department followed up the commendation three months later with orders replacing Conner with Matthew C. Perry. Conner, an old salt, had done his best with limited resources and was not prepared to share credit for his achievement at Tampico, especially with a female civilian.[78]

Attempts to marginalize Ann Chase's role had some impact. When Lieutenant Theodore Laidley arrived in Tampico in March 1847, he was well aware of "the romance that the papers had thrown around her name for her heroic conduct in the war." Inquiring about Ann, Laidley was swiftly "dispelled" of any notions of her contribution by the description given him. Seeking to confirm his information, he visited her shop on the plaza and witnessed a "great strapping Irish woman" selling tape and common articles. Laidley departed unimpressed.[79]

Ann sought to set the record straight and ensure that her deeds would not go unrecognized. In December 1846, she sent a lengthy, detailed account of her actions over the summer to a Louisiana friend, B. M. Norman, who dispatched the letter to the *New Orleans Evening Mercury.* The editor went on at length about her bravery, stating, "Much less praise, we think, has been bestowed on the noble conduct of this courageous and patriotic lady than she deserves." He added that the government should "unhesitatingly reward her with enduring honors." Newspapers in the Northeast, including the *Philadelphia Ledger* and the influential *Niles' National Register,* widely reprinted the correspondence.[80]

Clearly, the campaign for recognition bore fruit and translated into more than modest acknowledgment. Maryland's senator Reverdy Johnson read of her sacrifice and immediately volunteered legal assistance with claims against the government. In March 1847, the citizens of New Orleans gave her two solid silver pitchers with an octagon pattern and a "magnificent" silver tray, all crafted in New York by Wood & Hughes. "The fair and gallant" crowded Hyde and Goodrich's store on Chartres Street to get a glimpse of the "valuable and nobly-earned tribute, which is to be presented to one of the most deserving and chivalrous of her sex." The ladies of Cincinnati likewise recognized her bravery, appropriately presenting her with an American flag. The editor of the *New York Sun* solicited her for columns on Tampico and the region. The military granted its kudos speedily by naming a large battery of artillery defending Tampico "Fort Ann." She modestly responded, saying that the "complement to myself is an honor I really did not anticipate."[81]

Not to be outdone, a Tennessee ship captain, H. H. Harrison, built the USS *Ann Chase,* which was commissioned by the Quartermaster Department to transport troops and supplies back and forth to Mexico. In the summer of 1847 a boiler on the ship suddenly exploded off Galveston, resulting in several men killed and a number wounded. Six months later, Ann solicited and got letters from Commander Josiah Tatnall and Lieutenant Samuel Chase Barney acknowledging her role in communicating with Conner that the city was easy prey, stripped of cannon, and abandoned by the military. Upon receipt of this news, Conner had moved with dispatch upon Tampico.[82]

Ann likely appreciated her newly found fame but focused instead upon obtaining compensation from the government for the losses her business sustained during the war. In the summer of 1847 she departed Tampico for Washington to contend with Congress. Within six months she filed petitions with the Senate Committee on Foreign Relations for indemnity based on the 1832 Treaty with Mexico. On April 11, 1848, the committee favorably reported out her petition, but there is no indication that payment was ever made. Franklin Chase resumed his consular duties in January 1847, also holding the post of city treasurer and joining the chamber of commerce. Ann lobbied on Capitol Hill, traveled to Europe, composed poetry, and completed her nine-volume "History of Mexico," covering the years through 1848. Her subsequent research and writing carried the study into the 1860s and the crisis involving Maximilian and the French occupation.[83]

One scholar referred to Ann Chase as "fearless and patriotic," while virtually all who commented on her career conceded her contributions in providing valuable information to the US Navy. Although an underdeveloped road system prevented Tampico from becoming the launching point for the invasion of Mexico City, its capture nonetheless proved important to the war effort. Ann herself surely engaged in self-promotion, and in 1847 she attained a level of celebrity among the American public.

In an era of rising feminism, Chase's cunning and bravado generated both praise and concern. Sarah Josepha Hale, editor of the very popular *Godey's Magazine and Lady's Book,* agreed that Ann merited the applause and honors extended for her "daring exploits." In her "Progress of the World" column, Hale admitted that "the civilization of the world is to be the work of woman." However, after citing numerous global incidents of the rise of female power, including suffrage, she expressed a fear of "a petticoat ascendancy." Heroes were increasingly overshadowed by heroines, and women had forgotten their proper domestic roles. They should not be engaged in "man's work, such as managing a ship in a storm or a fire engine in a conflagration." Hale admonished her readers, "Casa mia, casa mia!, Per piccina che tu sia, Tu mi pari Una Badia!"

While this view resonated with many subscribers to *Godey's,* some years later an anonymous poet named simply "Clara" offered a much different tribute titled "To Mrs. Chase: the Heroine of Tampico."

Oh! May some nobler lyre than mine,
Sing paeans to thy name,
Emblazoned with a nation's pride
Upon the scrolls of flame,
That where so ere our banner waves

At home, or on the sea
The Heroine of Tampico
May loved and honored be.[84]

Ann's name faded from public view in the 1850s, and her deeds were not emblazoned "upon the scrolls of flame." Intelligent, articulate, and forceful, she lived her life with aggressive purpose. K. Jack Bauer calls her "indomitable." Unfortunately, Franklin became caught up in the infamous Whiskey Ring scandal, which enveloped the Ulysses S. Grant administration in 1869. Ann rushed to Washington, where she dedicated months to defending Franklin's reputation. In May 1870, she reported to her husband that the cabinet was against them and that the president was "in the hands of grafters." By the summer, Grant had appointed a new consul at Tampico, and a disillusioned Franklin suggested that they relocate to Ireland.

Instead, the couple departed Mexico in August 1871 to retire to a home in Brooklyn. On the voyage to New York, however, Ann engaged in one final heroic act. A young boy fell down the hatchway of their ship. She rushed to rescue him but in the process sustained an injury to her breast. The seriousness of the wound was ignored, and a cancer took hold that required extensive surgery in the spring of 1874. Ann refused anesthesia and suffered "unflinching" through a prolonged operation. All efforts to save her failed, and she died at age sixty-five in December. Her legacy rested south of the Rio Grande. She prophetically commented in 1846, "The picture is incomplete, and the reality left far behind."[85]

An American woman needed a certain kind of audacity, stamina, and savvy to survive in Mexico during the war years. Caroline Porter seems to have possessed those qualities; Sarah Bowman and Ann Chase definitely did. The reasons for their presence in very difficult times varied as dramatically as their backgrounds and socioeconomic status. Some came south of the Rio Grande before the war to work in factories and businesses, perhaps marry, or travel as entertainers with the theater or circus. Others were associated with the military, as officers' wives or as suppliers or supporters of the army, perhaps as camp followers, washing clothes or cooking for the troops. Some were naive; many were brave and struggled, often alone. While most American women debated the conflict in the relative safety, if not comfort, of their homes and farms, many experienced firsthand the threat of danger, disease, and death.

5

Women Editors Report the War

A combination of the heated political climate and technology allowed Americans to stay abreast of a foreign conflict for the first time. Whigs, especially in the North, opposed "Mr. Polk's War" from the outset and quickly took control of the House of Representatives. Young Hickory's narrow victory in 1844, the provocative nature of the flashpoint along the Rio Grande, and the president's partisan style of leadership did little to build a national consensus in support of the imbroglio. Both parties used whatever tools of propaganda they had at hand to advance their cause, and both came to rely heavily on cheap daily newspapers—"the penny press." Technology moved almost in rhythm with the intensifying political environment. Railroads ran east-west to connect the Atlantic Seaboard with the Mississippi, while steamboats plied the Big Muddy, Missouri, and Ohio Rivers carrying goods, people, and information from north to south.

On this side of the Atlantic, Samuel F. B. Morse emerged as the pioneer in developing a long-distance electronic telegraph. In 1844, the words "What hath God wrought" reached Baltimore from Washington, DC, and lines formed a web linking cities throughout the East. Soon thereafter, in 1847, Richard March Hoe patented his lithographic rotary press, a revolutionary invention that allowed the *Philadelphia Public Ledger* to print eight thousand papers an hour. This combination of transport, telegraph, and press enabled Americans to receive communications in record time.

Big city editors, such as the New Yorkers James Gordon Bennett, Horace Greeley, and Moses Beach, took advantage of the politics and the technology to excite, inform, and increase their readership. Although the Mexican-American War spurred patriotism, national consciousness, and a sense of adventure, it also sparked serious opposition. The press epitomized the polarizing nature of the conflict, with arguably most of the papers, especially in the larger cities (Boston, Baltimore, New York, and Philadelphia), supportive of the war and a minority (Chicago, Louisville, Pittsburgh) opposed. Very few took a neutral stance. By the end of the fighting, many editors had wisely formed a consortium in which they pooled their resources to facilitate daily delivery of the news and reprinted stories from other papers.

Since New Orleans became the drop-off point for men and material headed for Mexico, the delta city emerged as the place of origin for war reports sent back to New York and beyond. Rather than wait for intelligence to be leaked or conveyed by government sources, editors dispatched their own correspondents, again for the first time, to cover the front lines. George Wilkins Kendall, of the *New Orleans Picayune,* became the most renowned of this first generation of reporters, although as many as a dozen were embedded with Scott's and Taylor's armies. Others operated as freelance columnists, sharing their views in hometown papers.[1]

Men plainly dominated the fourth estate, yet numerous women reported their perspective on the war and expansion. Anne Royall, Jane Swisshelm, and Jane Cazneau were among those women who left their mark on journalism at midcentury both in support of and in opposition to the Mexican-American War. While other women labored almost exclusively in the vineyard of reforms such as temperance or antislavery, Royall, Swisshelm, and Cazneau also dedicated extensive time and ink to the political turmoil of the period. All three edited their own newspapers. Royall, the resident capital curmudgeon, was of simple southern birth and became a Washington insider. Swisshelm, the humanitarian reformer, emerged from an equally deprived situation in western Pennsylvania to editorialize and campaign against the war. The colorful Cazneau, raised in a privileged environment in New York, championed labor and women's rights while concurrently hurling herself into the cause of American expansion in the Caribbean. None of these women was typical of the era, yet their backgrounds reflect the commonality of struggle and a quest for place and recognition.

Anne Royall

Anne Newport Royall, a pioneer in print, was undoubtedly the most notorious of the three. For almost a quarter century she fired off incendiary volleys about religion (she advocated separation of church and state and reserved special venom for Presbyterians), reform, and politics. Born in Baltimore in 1769, Anne survived a poverty-stricken childhood in western Virginia to enjoy a comfortable lifestyle married to the wealthy, elderly William Royall. His death in 1812 and the resultant loss of their estate in the courts to his family left her virtually homeless and penniless.

Anne Royall had friends, however, especially among the Freemasons, so the entrepreneurial and adventuresome widow spent the next decade traveling extensively in the South and New England. In 1826, she published her impressions of America and Americans. Arrested and fined numerous times for her opinions and actions in Washington, DC, she and her friend Sally Stack embarked on the founding of a newspaper, *Paul Pry.* The nettlesome Mrs. Royall was beloved by her many supporters, who considered her an uncompromising freethinker, beholden to no faction, party, or faith. Enemies threatened her and scorned her outspokenness, and brutal editorials branded her "a common scold."[2]

By 1836, Anne had settled on Capitol Hill and abandoned *Paul Pry* for a new venture, the *Huntress.* The weekly cost her subscribers $2.50 a year, and they got their money's worth. In April 1845, soon after the debates over Texas annexation concluded, Royall printed a letter from a gentleman in Veracruz defending John Tyler and blasting warmongering Democrats, especially the Missouri senator Thomas Hart Benton and the administration's *Washington Globe.* The writer speculated, "This Mexican War, should there be one, is too far off for the gentlemen's purpose which is mainly revenge." One year later, hostilities had begun, and Royall shared the views of many Americans that blame should rest with Mexico. When asked in May 1846 whether the war was just, Royall deflected the question. However, she did have it on "good authority of their [Mexican] barbarity to our friends and others," and she added that "we would not be sorry to see them beaten and drove from the city of Mexico, every soul of them, if they have any." Two months later, her temper was aroused: "Somebody ought to give her [Mexico] a good licking, and no people can do it neater than our boys. Let her behave herself and pay up the indemnities she owes us. The vile murders: think of the Alamo!"[3]

Royall's passion grew as the war progressed. In April 1847, she exploded in a column, "Barbarous savages. The vengeance of heaven has at length overtaken them for their inhuman massacres, their insolence, and their frauds." She dismissed General Santa Anna as "a cruel and unwavering tyrant." Instead of allowing his return to Mexico from Cuba, which the Polk administration had done, "our people ought to have taken the monster and have kept him in close confinement until the war was over."[4]

Royall made her opinions about politics, the military, and expansion quite clear. Political parties aggravated her. They served their own self-interest, not the good of the nation. Sadly, their presidential candidates, once elected, fell under the spell of private interests, who held dictatorial sway in considerations of the public good. Candor reigned. Secretary of War William Marcy "ought to go home and mend his pants." She blasted the New Yorker, who displayed "the tardiness of an old woman," his department, and especially the party that had given him such responsibilities for their poor planning, as well as for the insufficient beds, blankets, and tents for the soldiers. "Though at one time a man of much cleverness, he is a hard case now," Anne determined. Royall exulted when she heard the ill-founded rumor in April 1847 that her old friend the Democratic general William Butler would replace Marcy. She despised Senator Benton as bitter and ambitious. Secretary of State James Buchanan seemed "a man of ability, a patriot, steady, meek, cool and dispassionate. He is always a friend to humanity." General Winfield Scott should "go home, too, where he can take his time to sup his soup!" In fairness, this judgment was made before the Veracruz–to–Mexico City campaign.[5]

Royall saved her real affection for one individual—Zachary Taylor. Old Rough and Ready, the soldier above party, caught her eye early in the war. "He is a brave and good man," she told her readers in the summer of 1846, "and a skillful General." By October his victories ranked "amongst the first military achievements of ancient or modern history." This "extraordinary man" possessed "the bravery of Caesar without his ambition; the prudence and policy of Washington, and the unflinching coolness and skill of General Jackson—as a great General he has few equals in the art of war, or in the grandeur of his mind."[6]

Royall saw in Taylor many of the qualities necessary for a good president as well as for a good general—modesty, humanity, and generosity—but was not beyond criticizing her nascent hero. She severely chastised him for agreeing to an armistice with General Ampudia after the Battle of Monterrey that allowed the Mexicans to withdraw from the city with their weapons. Royall believed a harsh punitive policy would swiftly end the war; Taylor had only prolonged the conflict. She became concerned, however, when the administration moved in January 1847 to pass a bill creating a new lieutenant-general position, seemingly bypassing her frequent favorite. She demanded, "Where will they find a more skillful commander than General Taylor?" Perhaps it would be "our big gun" Secretary Marcy, Royall mused, her tongue planted firmly in her cheek. "He and General Scott are about a tie." Ironically, Scott received the command to lead the assault on Mexico City, but the promotion to lieutenant general eluded him until 1855.[7]

Geographic expansion troubled Royall. Not only did it create a sectional irritant but the republic was simply becoming too large, too unmanageable. During the debate over Oregon in 1846, Royall expressed her reservations about the great distance to the Pacific Coast and the high costs to defend and maintain "the colony or whatever it be called." How, too, would territories in the Southwest or Oregon be governed? "Only think of it!" she later cautioned, "from ocean to ocean, and from Canada to—we forget where. Can this vast domain be held subordinate to our government? We have our fears!"[8]

The high-spirited editor remained in the vortex of politics, even as she shied away from the discussion. When she was visited by a group of mechanics from Troy, New York, the conversation soon turned to the upcoming presidential election. The workingmen asked Royall whom her choice was in the contest. They threw out the names of various Democrats; Governor Lewis Cass, General Sam Houston, and Vice President George Mifflin Dallas. A bemused Royall responded with a list of Whigs, including Daniel Webster, Henry Clay, John McLean, and John J. Crittenden. Refusing to identify a preference, she pondered why men should ask her the most important question they would consider as citizens of the republic. Royall remarked with no apparent sense of contradiction that "women had no business with politics, and besides being no judge of the subject, we were no partisans." In fact, the editor and her paper were very much involved with politics, relentlessly commenting on issues and intrigue, plots and schemes, officeholders and aspirants.[9]

While shying away from an open embrace of Whiggery, as early as May 1847 Royall noted with some pleasure "the prospect of a Whig President." She repeatedly denounced the Free Soilers as the "Church and State" party, seeking to annihilate the constitution and destroy freedom in the country. She heaped similar scorn on the anti-immigrant Native American Party, which she said was "worse than the evil it proposes to remedy." Through it all, Royall never forgot Zachary Taylor. Noting almost with pride that the general had never voted, she mocked the Whigs who denounced an "infamous" war, yet seemed comfortable discussing her hero for the nomination. Taylor somehow survived against overwhelming odds at Buena Vista, and his legend grew. Royall became increasingly defensive regarding the purported assaults on his reputation. His fame was undeniable. "They might as well try to stop the Niagara Falls with a feather as to check the popularity of General Taylor. His hold on the hearts of the people is too strong." Most certainly, he held hers.[10]

Anne Royall had not attended an inaugural since Andrew Jackson's in 1829, but she "wrapped up warm" to witness the oath of her champion in March 1849. She must have been disappointed. Given the crowds, she could not see much of Old Rough and Ready that day. Redemption came in November, however, when Taylor invited her to a levee. Royall's biographer Bessie James notes that Anne "closed down the *Huntress* and spent a week getting her clothes in order" for the grand affair. She arrived at the White House early, and when Taylor made his entrance, her faith in the new president was reaffirmed. Royall shook his hand, chatted, and was charmed by the simplicity of his dress and manner. To Anne, such qualities were "inseparable from all men of sense." A devoted fan, she made it a point to visit Old Whitey, Taylor's famed horse, and pay her respects to the mount that had carried her idol through many a battle.[11]

As US troops evacuated Mexico City in the summer of 1848, Anne Royall celebrated her eightieth birthday. Through war and peace, she unyieldingly offered her viewpoints on matters large and small but often returned to the right of the individual to express independence of thought and action. She championed reform in government, separation of church and state, and rights for Indians, women, and, broadly speaking, humanity. In July 1847, under the headline "Outrageous in Mexico," she decried the murders and rapes of Mexican women by US volunteers. Indicting units from Massachusetts ("this shows how they convert the heathen"), Indiana, Arkansas, and Pennsylvania, she demanded that the regulations be enforced and the perpetrators of the crimes prosecuted. "What has become of the law?" she insisted. "Will the people of the United States stand with arms folded awaiting the issue?"[12]

Almost concurrently, she reacted to a letter condemning women who flocked to the galleries of Congress instead of staying home to attend to their more appropriate domestic tasks—washing, cleaning, cooking, and mending their husbands' clothes. An exasperated Royall responded, "We do not agree, women have rights as well as men, nor is it any business to any one with the exception of their parents, guardians, or husbands. Women has [*sic*] a hard time of it in this world, at the least therefore, let them make the most of it, and if it affords them any amusement to sit in the galleries let them do so, it hurts no one—This is a free country."

While this was hardly a resounding statement endorsing the feminism of Seneca Falls, Royall demonstrated an awareness of women's evolving place within the society and their right to engage in the public sphere. At the time of her death in 1854, the world around her seemed barely recognizable to this pioneering, if not arguably the first, woman political journalist in the United States. Present for the Revolution, the Constitution, and the trying and triumphant years of the expansive early republic, Royall now witnessed her beloved Union crumbling under the weight of the slavery issue. Anne Royall's death removed one of the few editors who voiced an independent stand on the politics and conduct of the Mexican-American War and championed a successful presidential candidate.[13]

Jane Swisshelm

Several hundred miles and a much greater intellectual distance away in western Pennsylvania, another strong-minded, independent woman made her mark in opposition to the Mexican-American War. Jane Grey Cannon was only 8 when her father died, leaving her mother and her in dire poverty. Industrial Pittsburgh began to materialize, and the hardworking young woman labored tirelessly as a lace maker to help provide for the family. A few year later, she taught school, and in 1836, at the age of twenty-one, she married a local farmer, James Swisshelm. The couple soon moved to Louisville, Kentucky, where Jane's intelligence, resolute nature, and commitment to reform were immediately manifested. Her biographer Sylvia Hoffert contends that the doctrines of the Covenanter Church pushed her into politics and journalism. Jane believed "that it was up to her to follow the example of her female forebears and martyr herself in an effort to remedy all the evils she could identify."[14]

Indeed, Swisshelm identified numerous evils. Over the next decade, she made her views known in support of abolition and women's rights, as well as her opposition to capital punishment. Kentucky did not suit her, and Jane soon moved back to Pennsylvania, becoming increasingly committed to the antislavery cause. Her husband joined her there in 1841. The exuberant reformer noted in her memoir, "I organized a society at which we read, had refreshments and danced—yea, broke church rules and practiced promiscuous dancing minus promiscuous kissing. Of course this was wicked."[15]

The abolitionist cause had splintered by 1840 over the issue of women in politics. Those men who, led by William Lloyd Garrison, envisioned a role for women in the public sphere and avowed a course of moral suasion in abolition had formed the American Anti-Slavery Society. In contrast, those who embraced politics as a reasonable and proper way to address the slave issue but saw no place for women in the traditional political rituals had splintered to form the American and Foreign Anti-Slavery Society. The latter organization endorsed the editor James G. Birney for the presidency on the Liberty Party ticket in both 1840 and 1844.

Swisshelm knew the obstacles she faced. "Abolitionists were men of sharp angles," she thoughtfully observed. "Organizing them was like binding crooked sticks in a bundle." She wanted to engage in antislavery political activities, and she knew that gender models at best allowed her to participate in rallies or host events but not to take part in the nuts and bolts of candidate selection and election. Swisshelm compromised by writing letters to Pittsburgh's *Spirit of Liberty,*

Jane Swisshelm, antiwar editor and reformer.
Photo by Eugene Hill, ca. 1850.

urging that they be published using only her initials because she "had a dread of publicity and the fear of embarrassing the Liberty party with the sex question."[16]

Swisshelm's letters did not, of course, prevent the triumph of the forces of Manifest Destiny. Whigs and Liberty men feared that James K. Polk's victory would mean conflict and the extension of slavery, but when war came in 1846, she witnessed both parties crying, "Our Country, right or wrong." In Swisshelm's view, the country demonstrated "military madness," and "the slave went to the wall." The *Spirit of Liberty* ceased publication, leaving the antislavery cause in Pittsburgh without a voice. She felt that something must be done. Her husband, James, and the reformer Abby Kelley urged her to consider public lecturing as an option. The Covenanters, however, disparaged such a role for women. So while she was liberated by church theology, she was confined by church practice. Editorials or a newspaper might be the answer. Yet Jane fatalistically feared the worst, relishing the martyr's role. The experiment would be "dreadful," but she must throw herself into "the great political maelstrom, and would of course be swallowed up like a fishing boat." Shame and disgrace would be heaped upon her; she would never again be able to hold her head up in the community. Swisshelm rationalized her fate. "But what matter," she reflected. Jane had no children; and only one person who had ever loved her remained alive, and "she *no longer needed me*" (italics added). She could risk everything.[17]

Swisshelm began sending letters to the prominent Whig *Daily Commercial Journal* attacking slavery and the Mexican-American War. There were no abstractions in her language; she had seen the brutal lashings and separation of mothers from their children in Kentucky. As for the war, a great nation "engaged in the pusillanimous work of beating poor little Mexico—a giant whipping a cripple." She indicted every man who served in the conflict as a coconspirator to the crime of slavery. By design, Swisshelm wrote with "reckless abandon" and in an admittedly crude, country style that delighted her readers. She used sarcasm, ridicule, and denunciation with such effectiveness that the editor, Robert Riddle, began to receive mail threatening libel suits and denouncing him for publishing "such unpatriotic and incendiary rant." Swisshelm thrived on the controversy and the regional debate over the identity of the anonymous provocateur—a man, of course, some wags even speculating a county judge. In her memoir, she proudly noted that no woman in western Pennsylvania "had ever broken out of woman's sphere."[18]

Swisshelm's scrutiny overflowed the banks of the Ohio. Gabriel Adams, who was an old family friend, an elder in her church, and the mayor of Pittsburgh, affronted Jane by ordering the illumination of the city even on the Sabbath in honor of the victory at Buena Vista. She blasted his hypocrisy as a Christian who had announced that his faith was incompatible with slavery. Adams later apologized, telling Jane, "You were right." She similarly criticized Samuel Black, the son of her pastor, who also rushed off to Mexico and returned a colonel. Black's family confided to Jane that they approved of her salvos, but Jane never forgave Samuel. Some years after the war, he was engaged in conversation with several friends when she passed him on the street without recognition. He stood in her path and extended his hand, which she refused to take. As Swisshelm recalled, the following exchange took place:

> I drew back, and he said:
>
> "Is it possible that you will not take my hand?"
>
> I looked at it, then into his manly, handsome face, and answered:
>
> "There is blood on it; the blood of women and children slain at their own altars, on their own hearthstones, that you might spread the glorious American institution of woman-whipping and baby-stealing."

"Oh," he exclaimed, "This is too bad! I swear to you I never killed a woman or a child."

"Then you did not fight in Mexico, did not help to bombard Buena Vista."

Samuel's friends exerted considerable effort to persuade Jane of his goodness, and finally she allowed him to take her hand. Jane said nothing and hurried away. She later noted that Samuel Black had been killed in the Civil War at the Battle of Fair Oaks in 1862, fighting for "that freedom he had betrayed in Mexico." Beneath her columns, Jane's name appeared as "Jane G. Swisshelm," and the editor noted effusively that the "new contributor" to the *Commercial Journal* "dips her pen in liquid gold, and sands her paper with the down from butterflies' wings." Moreover, the social ostracism that she had expected never materialized.[19]

In 1848, however, Swisshelm decided to separate from the *Journal* and launch her own weekly. The local abolitionist paper, the *Albatross,* had folded. She had enough start-up capital from her own estate, her husband supported the venture, and a sympathetic Riddle allowed her to use the materials and facilities of his paper to publish the *Pittsburgh Saturday Visiter.* The first edition of the four-page sheet appeared on January 20, 1848, and sold for five cents a copy. Swisshelm wisely marketed her paper as more than an antislavery oracle, including a variety of news, commentary, and market and literary items. Local businessmen promptly bought advertising space. Hoffert explains that a sense of insecurity also accompanied this initial success. Swisshelm had not edited and published a paper, nor did she have experience in politics. She knew that there had been few women in journalism, especially political journalism, and that she would be roundly criticized for disrupting the gender boundaries of true womanhood.[20]

Indeed, both Democrats and Whigs nodded in agreement about this violation of the sanctity of the fourth estate. When the Louisville editor George Prentiss labeled Swisshelm "a man all but the pantaloons," she felt compelled to respond. Challenging Prentiss's morality and manhood in a single short poem, she silenced her critics:

Perhaps you have been busy
Horsewhipping Sal or Lizzie,
Stealing some poor man's baby,
Selling its mother maybe.
You say—and you are witty—
That I—and tis a pity—

Of manhood lack but dress;
But you lack manliness,
A body clean and new,
A soul within it, too.
Nature must change her plan
Ere you can be a man.

Again, modesty and ego collided as Swisshelm reveled in the widely publicized clash between herself and the rival press. She notes with pride in her memoirs that the *Visiter* was welcomed by Horace Greeley's *New York Tribune,* the *Saturday Evening Post, Godey's Lady's Book,* and the *Home Journal.* She pointed out with some amusement the exchange of "saucy notes" between herself and the Cincinnati editor John Smith, of the *Great West.* They "pelted" each other with editorials before Smith revealed in a private letter that "he" was really Celia Burleigh.[21]

Burleigh herself had already become engaged with reform, speaking out against slavery and the Mexican-American War. In one defining moment, as the twenty-year-old toured Tioga County, in northern Pennsylvania, in the spring of 1847, the sheriff closed the county courthouse to her lecture, forcing the event to be held at a local school. Nevertheless, a crowd filled the building and heard her denounce the conflict as "infamous." Even that term she felt too mild. When men in the audience challenged her patriotism, Burleigh responded that she could not silently witness "this crowning crime of my country's sins—the invasion of the feeble country of Mexico." The language became so heated that the assemblage decided to continue the conversation again the next afternoon. The prowar men arrived the next day with a calmer demeanor and a better-prepared argument. They attacked Burleigh as a Hartford Convention Federalist and an abolitionist disunionist, charges she dismissed with both logic and humor. In a column for the *Pennsylvania Freeman,* she recalled with considerable magnanimity holding nothing but friendly feelings for those men "who came to defend what I deem a great wrong." Undeterred, Burleigh continued her tour, speaking at Methodist churches in several counties in western Pennsylvania. She returned to Ohio, where her tenure with the *Great West* lasted just a year, until 1850. Unemployed and soon divorced, Burleigh moved to New York, but her ongoing friendship with Jane Swisshelm ended only with her death in 1875.[22]

Both Burleigh and Swisshelm appeared to take their causes, if not themselves, too seriously. Prentiss and pantaloons aside, Jane patently had little use for the affectations of femininity. In 1851, Jane's good friend James Riddle made the mistake of asking her about the "hideous caps" she wore each day. He said that his wife and her friends had opined that Jane had "good hair" and wondered "why do you make yourself such a fright?" They implied, of course, that improving her personal appearance might help the paper. Swisshelm patiently explained that she had health issues and the cap helped to protect her tonsils. She confided in her memoirs that she had no interest in male or female admiration. "Any attempt to aid business by any feminine attractions was to my mind revolting in the extreme, and certain to bring final defeat." "When a woman starts out in the world on a mission," Jane contended, "she should leave her feminine charms at home."[23]

In 1848 the war ended, and Swisshelm switched her editorial focus to electing an antislavery candidate as president. She again endorsed James G. Birney and the Liberty Party and then switched her support to the fledgling amalgam with the Free Soil Party and Martin Van Buren. The Red Fox fared reasonably well at the polls, garnering 10 percent of the popular vote, for which Swisshelm took some credit. Over the course of the next several years, the paper gained as many as six thousand subscribers, yet it struggled to achieve financial stability.

Swisshelm tried a variety of strategies to maximize her involvement in antislavery politics and salvage the paper, including turning the editorship over to friends for periods of time. The *Visiter* could not be saved, but Swisshelm labored on in the abolitionist cause, writing for Greeley's *Tribune* at five dollars a column. Perhaps the most defining moment at this point in her career came in April 1850, when she was issued a pass to sit in the Senate press gallery—the first woman to be granted a permit—as the great debate over the compromise raged.[24]

Later in the decade, Swisshelm divorced after a lengthy and unhappy marriage, moved to Minnesota, and began a memorable and controversial stint as an antislavery editor in St. Cloud. During the Civil War she served as a nurse and thereafter edited another newspaper, the predictably anti–Andrew Johnson *Reconstructionist* in Washington, DC. Her death in 1884 in Pittsburgh marked the last stroke of a pen that demonstrated amazing courage and steadfastness in the promotion of various causes, especially opposition to slavery and to the Mexican-American War. Swisshelm operated as an isolate; she belonged to no organization, and much of her overt support often seems to have come from men. She did not become the martyr that she envisioned becoming when she began writing her editorials in the early 1840s. However, her career is a tribute to her sense of female self-identity, persistent energy, and uncompromising purpose.[25]

Jane Storm Cazneau

While Jane Swisshelm battled her demons in Pittsburgh, half a continent away another Jane accepted an even more daring set of challenges. By the age of forty, Jane Maria Eliza McManus had lived a full and certainly controversial life. Beautiful, cerebral, outspoken, and ambitious, she had traveled to Texas as an entrepreneur, been accused of adultery with Aaron Burr, spied for the Polk administration, and reported on the Mexican-American War for the *New York Sun.* It is no wonder that she has become one of the most recognized and celebrated women of her era—"the Mistress of Manifest Destiny," her biographer Linda Hudson calls her. Born in upstate New York in 1807, Jane was a child of wealth. Her father, William, a successful lawyer and congressman, sent her to the finest local school, Emma Willard's Troy Female Seminary. Raised by her aunt in Brookfield, Connecticut, at 18 she married Allen Storm, had a son, and was divorced by 1831. Family financial problems prompted William to join Aaron Burr and other investors in a speculative venture called the Galveston Bay and Texas Land Company.[26]

In 1832, Jane and her brother journeyed to Texas to secure the land title. The following year, they visited again with their father, joined by a party of German immigrants, to promote settlement on the McManus property. Unfortunately, Indians and unsettled relations between Stephen F. Austin's colony and the Mexican government prompted the Germans to withdraw from the arrangement. Matters became worse in 1834, when Burr's wife of only one year, Eliza Jumel, filed for divorce and named Jane McManus as a corespondent. The wealthy Jumel, who had a checkered past, accused her seventy-seven-year-old husband of having the affair with the twenty-six-year-old Storm at his house in New Jersey in August 1833. The court granted Jumel the divorce in 1836, only days before Burr died. Enveloped by scandal and economic difficulties, Jane surrendered her land title to pay off her debts. She moved to Matagorda, Texas, witnessed the emergence of the Lone Star Republic, refined her Spanish, and became fascinated by the politics of the new nation.[27]

Returning to New York in 1839, Jane reclaimed the name Storm and composed articles for some of the city's major newspapers, such as the *Herald,* the *Sun,* and the *Tribune,* which willingly paid for her thoughts on government and foreign affairs. Well written and informative, the pieces portended a lengthy career in journalism and an important boost to her income. The scholar Thomas Reilly describes her writing style as "fluid and forceful, heavily laced with opinions, insights, predictions, and on occasion biting sarcasm." Robert May remarks that she "felt her way into diplomacy through the back door of journalism." Of course, social constrictions obliged her to disguise her gender and use a partial name, initials, or often the pseudonym Cora Montgomery or Montgomery.

Given her prior relationship with Texas and Texans, her editorial support of annexation in 1844 was predictable. During her sojourn there in the 1830s, Storm had developed both personal contacts and a philosophical commitment to expansion. A friend of Presidents Mirabeau B. Lamar and Sam Houston, she wrote a series of biographical sketches about them, Anson Jones, and David Burnet entitled "The Presidents of Texas" for John L. O'Sullivan's *U.S. Magazine and Democratic Review.* The articles were insightful, balanced studies reflecting her intimate knowledge—some might argue too intimate in the case of Lamar—of her subjects.[28]

The timing of the publication, March 1845, intersected nicely with the passage of the joint resolution of Congress annexing Texas in the twilight of the Tyler presidency. In May, Storm followed her sympathetic piece on Lone Star leadership with a sharp critique of the failed Mexican political state, which had legitimatized the Texas Revolution. Gaining literary steam, she crafted a column on annexation for the summer 1845 issue of *U.S. Magazine* that defied those nations whose goal was "thwarting our policy and hampering our power, and limiting our greatness." While not ignoring the subject of slavery, Storm expressed no great moral outrage and believed that annexation would promote the "diffusion," and perhaps the demise, of the institution in the Southwest. Providence, she maintained, had set aside the continent "for the free development of our yearly multiplying millions." Such was our "manifest destiny."[29]

The multifaceted Storm embraced more than the Texas crusade. In the spring of 1845, she became particularly active in championing the cause of working women. She spoke at the Hall of Science, wrote features in the *Sun,* sponsored benefits and rallies, and helped organize the Female Industrial Association, a group dedicated to women in the dress- and book-making trades. Storm urged self-improvement, education, and entry into higher-paid male professions as the avenue to advancement. The association boycotted New York stores, prompting several to hire young women as clerks. Realizing the importance of changing the laws, Storm penned a piece for *U.S. Magazine* titled "The Legal Wrongs of Women," which urged special protection under the law for women regarding their property, earnings, and children.[30]

Hudson describes the splintering of literary women in the early 1840s in New York as between the Whig feminists of Margaret Fuller, compelled to act by a sense of noblesse oblige, and the Democrats of Jane Storm, driven to urge "self-reliance and concrete solutions for women." Hudson sees Fuller as "elitist, racist, and ethnocentric," while Storm advocated "racial tolerance, and believed that other races and ethnic groups were capable of republican government." Fuller wrote for the *New York Tribune,* Storm for *U.S. Magazine* and the *Workingman's Advocate.* Storm unabashedly championed the annexation of Texas, while Fuller stridently opposed it, largely on the grounds of slavery. Mary Cheney Greeley, the *Tribune* editor's wife, held teas to which she invited members of the rival sets, prompting lively and stinging discussions. Their competition, sometimes bitter and certainly personal, abated when Fuller sailed to Europe and an Italian revolution and Storm sailed to Mexico and her own date with destiny.[31]

Storm's talents and voice could not be obscured or controlled. She outgrew *U.S. Magazine* and rejected an offer from the administration's organ, the *Washington Union,* before accepting a post in the fall of 1845 as a full-time regular columnist for Moses Beach's *New York Sun.* The paper's circulation skyrocketed to more than fifty thousand during the war, its commentaries reprinted throughout the nation. Jane Storm had established her expansionist credentials several years before the first shot was fired along the Rio Grande, and her articles, under the byline Montgomery, did not disappoint. Between December 1845 and May 1846, she kept her readers informed regarding the intrigues and manipulations of the governments in Washington and Mexico City as they attempted to quiet tensions and resolve the issues of the Texas border and the acquisition of California.[32]

Storm continued to support American "destiny" and the Polk administration but hoped US goals would be achieved through patient negotiations. Fluent in Spanish and a Catholic, Storm had faith in the future of a Mexican republic and understood the difficulties that any government would have in conceding additional territory to the United States. As the nations drifted toward war in the spring of 1846, she fatalistically observed the political shifts in both capitals. Increasingly upset with the president's tactics, Storm denounced Polk as "a base, narrow-souled man" who "would sell his mother's grave to buy up a Senator." She feared the increased power of the White House and believed that the president had placed the United States on a course for conflict. With amazing astuteness and accuracy, Storm predicted the amount that Polk was prepared to pay for California and the Southwest and the failure of the diplomatically inexperienced John Slidell to resolve the outstanding issues in Mexico City in January 1846.[33]

Throughout the year, Storm traveled back and forth between New York and Washington, visiting and communicating with men of power and influence, including John Hughes, the New York bishop; the State Department clerk

Nicholas Trist; Secretary of War William Marcy; and Secretary of the Navy George Bancroft. Men were often charmed or threatened by Jane Storm. Hudson contends that the dark-complexioned, five-foot-three-inch Storm "could be termed a coquette, if not a *femme fatale.*" Unlike Jane Swisshelm, Jane Storm had no qualms about using her femininity to best advantage. When queried about Storm's identity, Marcy, an old family friend, replied, "*She* is an outrageously smooth and keen writer for the newspapers in New York."[34]

Not lacking in self-confidence, Storm wrote to Bancroft at the beginning of the war audaciously suggesting naval reforms and strategies. Men often flirted with her, more than one considered marriage, and she undoubtedly used her looks and brains to gain access to the seats of power in Washington. Robert May asserts that Storm employed her mind and her political skills more than her physical allure. He emphasizes that in a male world Storm "stressed the utility of power and those who failed to see the logic of her arguments." The terminology used to describe Storm is both unusual and fascinating. Aaron Burr dubbed her "a woman of business," while Thomas Hart Benton claimed that she had "a masculine stomach for war and politics." Few journalists, let alone a woman, could claim having access to Polk and the cabinet secretaries Buchanan, Bancroft, and Marcy, as well as members of Congress.[35]

Storm's anger toward the president and the war continued unabated through 1846, and the administration reciprocated. She informed her old comrade Mirabeau Lamar, "I am as you may judge, not in favor." As Zachary Taylor's army moved from Matamoros to Monterrey in the summer, Storm bemoaned the money, blood, and goodwill wasted unnecessarily. She continued to embrace an improbable vision of a separate Republic of the Rio Grande comprising the states of northern Mexico. While this dream failed to resonate with the administration, Polk was, however, willing to work toward a negotiated settlement. A scheme that failed miserably allowed General Santa Anna to return from exile in Cuba by slipping through the American blockade. He promptly and predictably reneged on a proposed peace treaty. Another stratagem involved the State Department's dispatch of the *New York Sun* editor Moses Beach, his 26-year old daughter, Drusilla, and Storm to Mexico City to discuss an end to the war.[36]

After witnessing the summer military debacles suffered by the Mexican Army, a coalition of clerics and aristocrats offered a plan for peace, conveyed through Taylor's lines. The plan would cede the Southwest and California to the United States—for $3 million. The proposal found its way to Beach and perhaps the New York bishop, John Hughes. Beach volunteered to lead a secret mission to negotiate a settlement. The plan involved Beach, Drusilla, and Storm posing as an English family on a business trip. Ostensibly, they represented private interests seeking to establish a national bank. Beach's official goal, however, was to resolve the Texas and California issues. Secretary Buchanan agreed that they might add a transit route across the Isthmus of Tehuantepec, for which the Mexicans would receive $15 million in compensation. The payoff for Beach and Storm would be the granting to them and their partners of the right to construct a road, a railroad, or a canal. After obtaining California, an easier passage to the West Coast would be imperative. Her language skills and understanding of Mexican culture made Storm a critical part of the plan.[37]

In fact, the scholar Anna Kasten Nelson argues that it is "not unreasonable" to assume that the entire scheme was conjured up by Storm. Nelson believes that Beach the businessman was understandably interested in the banking and canal profits Mexico might offer. However, Storm had the political contacts, the audacity, and the imagination to craft and gain official Washington's endorsement of a secret mission. The rather conventional Polk appeared somewhat skeptical of their success, but that doubt did not prevent him from giving his conditional endorsement. Beach could gather information, but he would not negotiate a treaty. The president invited Storm to a reception at the White House in November 1846, before the group's departure. The respect for her intellect and broader role was reflected in a letter from the diplomatic agent Nicholas Trist discussing the importance of the Tehuantepec transit. Storm's credibility was further enhanced by her close relationship with Trist's sister-in-law, Cornelia J. Randolph, who also happened to be Thomas Jefferson's granddaughter.[38]

The mission found its way to Mexico in part because of the cooperation of the British, who had a vested interest in the payment of Mexican debts to the Crown, as well as a quick end to the war, which would minimize US territorial gains in the region. The British embassy in Havana facilitated passports and transport to Veracruz in January 1847. For the four months between December 1846 and March 1847, Storm felt obliged to continue her role as a *Sun* columnist, regularly informing its readers of her sojourns in "Tropical Sketches" from Cuba and Mexico. The initial eleven letters from Havana reveal an early interest in Cuba and the annexation of the island. Linda Hudson notes that Storm wrote at least thirty-eight signed columns on Cuba between 1846 and 1853 for papers in New York, including the *Sun,* the *Herald,* and the *Tribune.*[39]

The ambitious advocate managed to juggle her aspirations for American interests in both Mexico and Cuba. She filled her columns with comments calculated to both inform and provoke. Writing from Charleston, South Carolina, she sharply criticized the treatment of American sailors at the hands of their captains and took some parting shots at old enemies. Referencing the reform energies of Lydia Maria Child, Storm wrote: "I only wish that good lady would spare some of her loving sympathy she passes out on the colored race for the slaves of the ocean. They are not black, to be sure, but they have some claim on us. . . . Of all the blessings Madames Child and Fuller contemplated, I am least grateful for their darling scheme of 'universal god-like amalgamation.' I am not selfish and ask none of it for me or mine." Storm returned to this theme of sailor mistreatment in later columns, arguing that the sea was "the last refuge of despotic cruelty in our nation." If only sailors were black, she maintained, there would be societies crusading to arouse the nation and right the wrong. Storm noted with considerable bitterness that since they are "but white men they must wait until Africa is civilized and Asia converted."[40]

Arriving in Havana in December, Storm described in her "sketches" during her month-long visit various facets of the Cuban character and daily life in detail. She pulled no rhetorical punches, disparaging the government for an absence of imagination and energy in fostering internal improvements and an efficient steamer service. No wonder, Storm supposed, "the proud, self-conceited character of the people has not yet acquired the malleability, the power of fusion and adaptation." Frustrated by the commercial potential of the island in the hands of the indolent and indifferent Spanish merchant classes, Storm struggled to find a beam of hope.

The people offered little recourse. "The mass is nothing," she concluded. "They have no aspirations beyond the animal wants of the day." They were not only powerless but "poor, apathetic, and devoid of enterprise," certainly not a populace on which to build a free and thriving democracy. Liberty and privacy proved elusive; everything, she charged, "down to that poor old woman's pig and chicken," is "under legal censorship and restriction. Nobody seems lord of himself, his tongue, or of his faith." Referring to Cuba as "an infant Hercules," Storm predicted that the combination of government restrictions and economic mismanagement would eventually spark the Creoles to independence. She balanced that observation with the view that the politically savvy and careful Creoles might also support an invading force that would offer them "independence and a liberal constitution." Regardless of the means, separation from Spain seemed their future.[41]

Nothing seemed off-limits for Storm. The Spaniards had no functioning banking system, and they had a "strange passion" for destroying trees, more so than the Americans. She even turned her sharp wit and keen eye to a column comparing English boxing, American bear-baiting, and Cuban bullfighting.

Given the brutality and violence of their "sports," the Anglos were hardly in a position to criticize "El teatro de los Toros"—where at least the matador demonstrated grace, refinement, and chivalry. She paid the women of the Creole gentry backhanded compliments for their grace and form while riding in their carriages, prompting a metaphor for personal independence. Delicately reclining in their luxurious cushions for self-support, Cuban women fittingly reared "courtly gentlemen and loyal subjects." American women, in turn, assumed a more rigid posture of "self-sustaining equipoise." Such women would raise hardy republican men "who would rather rule senates, conquer continents and tame lightning than shine at royal festivals or be first lord in waiting to a queen's baby."[42]

After a month of Cuban travel and cutting social, economic, and political commentary in the press, Storm joined Moses Beach in January for the voyage to Veracruz. The British aided their passage, but an American blockade and a suspicious welcome delayed their journey. Letters had found their way from Havana exposing the mission. Some writers indicted the party as "American agents," while others saw them as a welcome path to peace. Storm simply took the opportunity to survey the scene and blast the US Navy for brutality, "deplorable inefficiency," and a failure to build the steamers necessary to fight the war. After several days of interrogation, the "family" persuaded the Mexican authorities of their legitimacy and were allowed to travel on, reaching the capital on January 24, 1847. They planned to speak with congressional moderates and sympathetic church officials about peace terms and an exit strategy. The scheme involved the Americans occupying Veracruz, followed by a staged "crisis" that would compel General Santa Anna to urge talks, allowing both nations to end the war with their honor intact.[43]

With American compliance, Santa Anna had indeed returned to Mexico and was soon elected president. But as the talks inched along in February, a perfect storm of military and political events doomed the mission. Instead of following through on a maneuver to seek peace, the general took command of an army and marched into northern Mexico, challenging Taylor at Buena Vista on February 22. After a bloody engagement, Santa Anna claimed a dubious victory, then hurried to Mexico City, where five National Guard regiments (referred to as *los polkos* for their love of the dance) were launching their own revolt against the state and in defense of clerical power. Vice President Valentín Gómez Farías had moved aggressively in January to tax, seize, or sell up to 15 million pesos of Catholic Church property. One-third would be taken from the clergy within the archbishopric. The purpose was to provide desperately needed funds for the war, but, understandably, the church leaders resisted this attack on their wealth and power.

On February 26, ten days of street fighting erupted in Mexico City as *los polkos* demanded the repeal of the offensive laws and the removal of Gómez Farías. While the rebellion collapsed, they succeeded in their goals. Santa Anna arrived in March to denounce the rebels and arrange a "compromise" that provided for the departure of Gómez Farías and the naming of Pedro María de Anaya as "substitute president." The offensive tax laws were repealed, and Santa Anna received a loan from the Church to help continue the conflict. Some contemporaries insisted that "the Church should provide Santa Anna with fewer prayers and more aid." Ultimately, as the historian Pedro Santoni emphasizes, the Church protected its own assets against its domestic enemies, failed to adequately support the war effort, and contributed to the national unrest.[44]

Storm accurately perceived the fragility of the political state, wondering how Mexico might fend off two American armies while engaged in a fratricidal internal struggle seemingly devoid of principle. She described the chaos in a letter to her *Sun* readers from the capital in March 1847: "Was ever a nation so determined on suicide? The treasury is the god of these military adventurers and they have no creed, doctrine or party beyond the simple belief and practice that the people were created to be plundered. . . . The city could be reduced to terms in a week. Mexico is not true to herself, and even at this hour, she is doing more for the generals of the United States than they can do for themselves. [Mexico] would be more than ready to receive an American government."

She particularly detested Santa Anna and the officers who had betrayed their country and sapped the resistance and spirit of Mexicans by turning their attention to civil war. Storm, however, who genuinely liked the people, continued to hope that somehow military tyranny would end and a truly republican solution emerge. By the end of March, too late to affect the negotiations, Veracruz fell to Scott's forces. The moderates, discredited, headed into hiding or exile. Beach had meddled in the civil war, providing forty thousand dollars to the pro-Catholic rebels. Soon thereafter, Santa Anna offered to meet with Beach, who wisely feared the stability of the shifting political sands and fled for his life to US-held Tampico and then Veracruz on the Gulf of Mexico.[45]

Jane Storm missed the high drama in the capital. In mid-March she had traveled two hundred miles by stagecoach to Veracruz to report to Scott on the mission's progress and witness the anticipated revolution in the city, its fall to American forces, and the ensuing peace arrangements. Before her arrival in the port, US Consul John Black, in Mexico City, dispatched a critical letter to Scott warning him of Storm's impending visit and her influence within Washington's inner circles. Black thought little of Beach and Storm, sarcastically noting that the administration considered them "wonderful" and "real hopers." "La Storm" knew powerful people within the Catholic clergy in the United States and planned to use those ties to influence the church hierarchy in Mexico to end the war. With the conflict concluded, the United States could press ahead with its annexation of all Mexico, and she could advance her dream of a transit route across the isthmus. Black detailed how and why the Beach mission had imploded and said that Scott should be wary.[46]

General Scott replied with his thanks for the sage counsel. "I found her outrageously smooth," he acknowledged. Storm was a "pusher" who pummeled him with her ideas of Manifest Destiny and the complete integration of Mexico into the United States. Scott grumbled about the difficulty not only of winning the war but also of occupying a country the size of Mexico with only twenty thousand men. "I heard her out and sent her on her way," Scott added, thoroughly annoyed by her "meddling" and "wrong notions." Openly resentful of Storm's involvement in the process, he told Black to advise both Polk and Buchanan "that they are not to send more worthless messages to this command by way of a plenipotentiary in petticoats."

Storm's status quickly became clear: she was not to be given a place on a US ship. Instead, standing at the rail of an English naval vessel, she reported on the unrelenting bombardment of Veracruz into submission, accompanied by numbing casualties among the civilian population. Angered at Scott's assault on women and children and his unwillingness to consider her suggestions for cooperation with the Mexican peace factions, Storm became alienated from the unctuous Old Fuss and Feathers. The frustrated columnist explained to her readers in May that there was another way to pursue the war: "Gen. Scott can have the people with him—or at least passive—while he exterminates their old oppressors; he can march to Mexico [City] without the loss of a single man in battle, if he will pursue the wise, explanatory, protecting system of [General] Kearney [*sic*]; but if, like brave Old Taylor, he will use no argument but the sword, it will cost many lives, much treasure and still more precious time to conquer the peace."[47]

Storm continued to monitor events and report thoughtfully in more than a dozen letters to her *Sun* readers, particularly regarding the wisdom of allying with Mexican republican forces. While agreeing with the Beach plan that provided for California, a Texas border, and the Tehuantepec project, she also suggested that in order to provide financial and physical stability, the United States should control Mexican ports and collect enough tariff duties to pay claims against the government. The lightly guarded border areas, which had suffered for decades from Comanche raids, should be protected by American troops. Recognizing the serious divisions within the country, she continued to press for the creation of three separate Mexican republics, with their focus along the Rio Grande, in Veracruz, and in Yucatán.

Storm presciently cautioned in May 1847 that if Polk did not endorse and promote the "three republic" option, the United States would find itself either annexing the entirety or leaving "the rest for some European prince." Some seventeen years later, Mexico found itself in the midst of a civil war and confronted with French intervention. The Austrian archduke Maximilian, under the aegis of Napoleon III, arrived in 1864 to establish a short-lived empire and confirm the accuracy of her prediction.[48]

Storm's vision of an independent, prospering Mexico yielded to the reality of the impact of the war and the chaos that appeared around her in Mexico City and Veracruz. This transformation was not born exclusively of cultural sensitivity and altruism. In 1846 she became engaged to William Cazneau, a freewheeling Texas politician and merchant and an ally of Mirabeau Lamar's. Storm had met Cazneau in Matagorda in 1832, and he had once managed her Texas properties. Congressman Robert Dale Owen, a friend and correspondent of Storm's, indicated to Nicholas Trist that the relationship was at its heart more practical than romantic. While Storm respected Cazneau's skills and talents, she suspected his commitment and their mutual compatibility. They did not marry until 1849. The couple did, however, share the dream of independent Mexican republics that would be friendly to the commercial interests of them and their friends. Storm owned vital watering holes in northern Mexico, and both had boldly invested in a company slated to be given access across the Isthmus of Tehuantepec, which would allow them to build a road or a railroad and perhaps later a canal. The extent to which financial considerations dictated her opinions in the *Sun* remains open to speculation, although she vehemently denied the dominance of self-interest.[49]

The Beach mission had collapsed, and with relief and joy the editor and his daughter sailed for New York in mid-April 1847, leaving Jane behind and leaving the next chapter in secret diplomacy to Generals Scott and Santa Anna. In May, Polk dispatched Nicholas Trist to join Scott and added a layer of presidential authority to any negotiations. Soon thereafter, Scott began his heralded campaign from Veracruz to Mexico City, culminating in the fall of the capital in September.

Jane Storm no doubt felt deeply the failure of both her personal and her diplomatic goals. The canal route was not part of Washington's peace initiative. Perhaps more importantly, her letters, lectures, and harangues on the wisdom of supporting Mexican republicanism had fallen on deaf ears. Certainly, neither Taylor, Scott, nor, apparently, the State Department seemed unwilling to embrace her vision or comprehend the consequences. Beach himself alerted his readers to the wisdom of the "All Mexico" movement, an aggressive strategy adopted by many expansionists to annex the entire country. Returning to New York in May, Storm immediately traveled to Washington and met with the president and Secretary Buchanan. Polk's hour-long private conversation with Storm on May 12 yielded little from his point of view. She was an intelligent woman, he acknowledged, but "I did not feel that I was enlightened by any information which she had given me." No doubt. The president had met the previous day with Beach and engaged in a lengthy discussion in which the agent "gave me valuable information." Storm found herself in the awkward position of reiterating what the White House already knew.[50]

The war had not yet ended, but Storm's responsibilities to both Beach and the administration had been fulfilled. Undoubtedly frustrated with their views and attitudes, she decided that the time had arrived for her to move on. The separation came with some difficulty. She continued to counsel Buchanan, Marcy, and Bancroft on tactics to end the war, appointments, Mexican politics, and US special interests, frequently offering more objective and accurate advice than they likely would have received elsewhere. She unremittingly pounded the drum for the Tehuantepec route, but by April her rejection of All Mexico had softened. Buchanan, in turn, tried to lure her back into service by asking if she would return to Mexico in the summer. Storm demurred, already courted by and committed to the cause of Cuban independence.

In the fall, Storm launched a column titled "Letters from Cuba," published in the *Sun,* and she encouraged Polk to meet with the leaders of the junta. Whether a "free" Cuba would result in independence or annexation to the United States remained unclear, although Storm's sentiment for incorporation was apparent. In both September and October she wrote from Havana, and Linda Hudson suggests that she may well have traveled to Mexico City for Buchanan in an effort to move the stalled peace talks along.[51]

Storm continued to juggle her concerns over the fate of Mexico with her promotion of Cuban revolution into 1848. In conjunction with Cuban exiles in New York, she established *La Verdad* (The Truth), with herself as editor, in January and lobbied both Polk and Buchanan. While the mission of the bilingual paper was to promote republicanism and liberty literally throughout the Western Hemisphere, Storm did not hesitate to weigh in on the Treaty of Guadalupe, which Hidalgo presented to the Senate for ratification in late February. The agreement, negotiated by Trist, settled the border along the Rio Grande and surrendered California and the Southwest to the United States. It was not All Mexico, but the once proud Mexican eagle had surely been plucked.

Storm opposed the pact largely based on selfish motives. The goals of her republican friends along the Rio Grande had been ignored, and her own financial situation had been compromised by the absence of a transit and trade route across Tehuantepec. Storm admonished Polk on the wisdom of the treaty, now warning that a rising tide of public opinion demanded even *more* Mexican territory. New commercial, mining, and manufacturing enterprises, launched under Anglo-Saxon guidance, would better the lives of the Mexicans and implicitly enrich Americans.

When the Senate approved the agreement on March 10 and the president added his assent, a disappointed Storm blamed the vote on alcohol and the secret sessions of Congress:

> Following the war, she bitterly assessed the situation and the immoral payouts in the treaty. "We need not go to Asia to find suffering heathen; we have five millions at our very door, and what is written in black letters against us—loud-voiced self-praisers that we are—is that we have just taken eighteen millions from the industry of our own honest toilers to supply their tyrants with more scourges and stronger chains. We knew when we were paying all these millions to the Mexican generals that every dollar would be expended to the hurt of the oppressed workingmen of Mexico, yet we had the audacity to demand that all the world should sing paeans to our magnanimity. In this our hypocrisy was yet more superlative than our absurdity.[52]

By the summer of 1848, Storm was fully engaged in the cause of Cuban independence and ultimate annexation. Lying ahead was a new chapter in her life: an attempted purchase of Cuba by the administration, repeated filibustering efforts launched from the United States to liberate the island from Spanish rule—and her marriage to William Cazneau. With heightened sensitivity to the slave issue in the North, Storm contended that incorporating Cuba would draw the institution from the West and into the Caribbean. She thereafter championed extensive US commercial involvement with Nicaragua and then the Dominican Republic, where the Cazneaus had substantial investments, in the ensuing decades. In December 1878, on her return to the Caribbean from New York, the *Emily B. Souder,* with Jane Cazneau aboard, was lost at sea off Cape Hatteras, North Carolina.[53]

While Storm embraced another cause and another country, her contributions to the Mexican-American War should be remembered. Her knowledge of the region, the culture, the language, the people, and the politics, she believed, gave her insight few other Anglos possessed. Equipped with a vision, she boldly shared her wisdom with policy makers in Washington as well as the American people. Not only did her columns for both the *U.S. Magazine* and the *Sun* provoke and inform but they revealed an intellectual content that surely could not have emanated from a woman. In 1847, by the time people suspected that Montgomery was a woman, her readership was already assured.

Storm somehow seemed to sort out the chaos of Mexican politics, and she tried to offer solutions to grievances with the United States short of war. She believed in American expansion and perhaps coined the term *manifest destiny.* While Polk's objectives in Oregon, Mexico, or Cuba were on target, his execution suffered. Storm placed the blame for the conflict squarely on the shoulders of the administration and was unhesitatingly critical of the military for its excesses and outrages. Taylor and Scott garnered her wrath by their overeagerness to use force and their reluctance to cooperate with Mexican patriots to fashion a workable peace. "The sword is not the implement of republicanism," she lectured. Her apparent abandonment of Mexican independence and increased promotion of territorial annexation by 1847 reveals perhaps not only certain political realities in the United States but also the advancement of her financial interests and the collapse of her ideals about the future of Mexico.[54]

Tom Reilly argues that Storm was a strong, independent voice in Mexico, reporting the war as she saw it unravel. Critical of both the American and the Mexican political and military establishments, through her uncensored voice and incisive commentary she provided more than news, and she differed sharply from her male compatriots in the press, who rarely uttered a discouraging word. She recognized and exposed the moral shortcomings of the soldiers, as well as the flawed policies of their commanders. In truth, Storm failed as part of the Beach mission and in her diplomatic goals, but she evidenced an almost unparalleled brand of brashness, self-confidence, and courage both in her attitude and in her presence in correspondence and discussions with the leaders in Mexico City and Washington.

The impact of her views and columns upon those politicos and her readers will never be known. A stridently independent individual who championed the cause of working women, she preferred to lobby the power brokers in the capital rather than advocate for rights at Seneca Falls. In addition to her editing career, the prolific Storm crafted one hundred newspaper columns, twenty journal articles, and fifteen books and pamphlets. Harry Watterson, editor of the *Louisville Courier-Journal,* opined that "a braver, more intellectual woman never lived"; he admired her talents as "a born *insurrecto* and a terror with a pen." Whether she is considered a success or a failure, Jane Storm's role as a reporter, lobbyist, and diplomat during the Mexican-American War—and as a woman in those capacities—appears remarkable.[55]

If length of time at one newspaper, either as a columnist or an editor, serves as the measure for women and the press, then many women in the era appear at best modestly successful. Conversely, if the marker is time spent in journalism with a variety of papers and in several cities, then numerous women, including Royall, Swisshelm, and Storm, enjoyed extraordinary careers. The Mexican-American War was only one part of their extensive and celebrated lives. As independent thinkers, sometimes obliged to disguise their identity or use a nom de plume, they found a way to convey their diverse views about various aspects of the war to Americans often hesitant to accept the opinions of women regarding the public sphere. Their achievements joined with the literary feats and reform-minded handiwork of other women of this generation to increase the volume of their collective voice.

6

The Señorita as Fantasy

THE FAN, THE FEET, AND THE REBOZO

In November 1845, fully five months before the first shots were fired along the Rio Grande, Lieutenant Napoleon Dana wrote to his wife about a supply train headed for San Antonio, Texas. Dana pointed out that among the inducements for the officers to make the trip was the understanding that the town "is said to have many pretty girls." In January 1848, at the conclusion of the conflict, a columnist for the *John-Donkey* penned an article entitled "The Conjugation of Mexico." The author recommended that the generals simply withdraw from the country and leave the "gallant and vigorous young privates to arrange a settlement of all the difficulties with the Mexicans." Since women run nations, it would only be a matter of time before the señoritas capitulated to Yankee charm and the whole of Mexico was "conjugated."

Prior to, during, and even after the Mexican-American War, US soldiers and the broader public reckoned with the notion of exactly *who* was a Mexican maid, how she might be approached, and whether relationships between soldiers and señoritas had any future. Tragically, illusion and courtship too often disintegrated into abuse and violence. Far too many American soldiers yielded to the forces of revenge or power to commit atrocities that would strike fear among the Mexicans and stain their reputations at home.[1]

The lure and fantasy of the Latin woman was very much alive in the 1840s. Many volunteers eagerly signed their papers and headed off to the land of Montezuma with the hope that at war's end their dream of a payout, a homestead, and a Mexican damsel would usher in a new life in the West. Even those with less traditional ideas about farm and family relished the perception that physically and intellectually stronger Anglo men, "valiant knights," would be welcomed by fair women, and rewarding liaisons would result. Nancy Isenberg points to the sexual politics that pervaded this thinking and how Mexican women were too often considered "trophies of war." The cavalier racism and gender superiority of most soldiers sometimes led to tragic cruelty and devastating offenses against the civilian population. James McCaffrey accurately explains the double standard, widely embraced by the Americans, that vilified Mexican men and extolled the beauty of the women. Not surprisingly, the longer the men remained absent from the home front, the more attractive the local women became.

The historian David J. Weber evaluated the situation as follows: "American males allowed their hormones to overcome their ethnocentrism." Understanding that hormonal rush and fantasies of youthful soldiers is critical to understanding this chapter. Base motives, violence, and anger provided a sinister backdrop to the actions of many men. Their voices will be heard, and their language used. While frequently smacking of racism and sexism offensive in the twenty-first century, their words most accurately convey the prevalent raw emotions, feelings, and desires.[2]

Race, Dress, and Behavior

Over the course of the war, the soldiers debated and disagreed about a variety of subjects, not limited to female elegance, dress, modesty, morality, and accessibility. Most troops encountered Mexican women of various classes and had some opinion on these issues but may well have tempered their remarks if writing to a wife or female family member. Race inevitably played the major role in their judgment of beauty. Images of lovely, light-skinned, dark-eyed Castilian ingénues flickered in their imagination, while the reality was in many ways much darker. Tracing its racial heritage to the pre-Columbian era of the Aztecs and the Mayans, Mexico was in large part an Indian nation. Power shifted in the sixteenth century to the Spanish, who imported Africans from the Caribbean to meet labor needs. The resultant Castilian domination of politics, society, and economics placed a minority in charge of a racially mixed country comprising fair-complexioned Spaniards (Creoles), Indians, blacks, mestizos, and mulattoes.

Some Americans had previously read William Prescott's *History of Mexico* (1843) or cared enough to acquire knowledge of the geography and people of the nation they invaded. In 1847, the Marylander John Kenly offered a rather interesting if naive analysis of the status of the Indians, who arguably made up the majority of the population. Kenly contended approvingly that Mexican Indians were inherently mild and docile, the gentlest creatures made by God. Guns and whiskey ruined the American Indians and contributed to their resistance to white advancement. In contrast, the Mexican Indian had the good sense to yield. Kenly's experiences in central Mexico allowed him to confuse pragmatism with cultural makeup. He remained seemingly unaware of the ongoing and successful rebellion of Indians in Yucatán.

Lieutenant Dana shared a brief thought upon entering a village near Monterrey in the summer of 1846: "The people here are whiter than in the other towns we have visited and much better looking." Marcellus Ball Edwards, a nineteen-year-old Virginian marching with Kearny's Army of the West, was taken with a dusky maid wearing white stockings and carrying an earthen pitcher. She was the first woman he had seen in two months. Captivated by her charm and appearance, Edwards confessed, "If I had never seen a woman before, I might have considered this one handsome, notwithstanding her complexion." Lieutenant John Lowe, of Ohio, perhaps summed up the racial arrogance of many Anglos in October 1847 when he defined the distinctions between "the haughty Castilians in whose veins flowed the pure blood of Cortes, the yellow Aztec, the stupid Indian and the decrepid negro."[3]

Largely unaware of these divisions, the eager troops of Zachary Taylor's army who entered northern Mexico in the spring of 1846 received a rude awakening. Fearful of their fate and virtue at the hands of the conquering Yankees, "respectable" women hid behind locked doors and shutters or abandoned Matamoros and Monterrey for the countryside, leaving the lower classes behind. In May, Dana found Matamoros "a mean, dirty-looking place" full of fleas and dirt. He noted the departure of the "better class of people and all the decent women." Those in residence looked "as dark as mulattoes and dirtier and more filthy than Indian squaws." Dana told his wife, Sue, that "our ugliest camp woman is better looking than any Mexican woman I have seen yet." Several months later, he reinforced the view. Taking the brown Mexican women as a race, he assured Sue, "They are without exception the most revolting, forbidding, disgusting creatures in the world, not even excepting our own Indians."

Major John Corey Henshaw seemingly agreed, determining that the women of the "lower order" were indeed unattractive. He confirmed this perspective several months later in Tampico, when he wrote, "The ladies of the place are exceedingly ordinary in their appearance and in the United States would all be called ugly." Henshaw admitted, however, that what once had seemed repulsive over time would be compromised. William Henry found Monterrey deserted in December, watching as the "delicate, genteel females" hurried off with their children to a rancho in the countryside. He grumbled that "I have yet to see a pretty girl," while at every corner there seemed to be an old woman with wrinkles who had an "intimate acquaintance with the last century." Henry hoped the better classes would return when they were confident that their rights and persons would be protected.[4]

Fortunately for a number of young officers, by June 1846 an element of trust had been restored in northern Mexico, so the "decent" women could venture out of their homes or return from the country. Lieutenant Rankin Dilworth was smitten by the "handsomest female" he had seen since parting with his Emily. "She was very beautiful," he admitted. "She was dressed in a loose white dress and walked like a queen." When one of Dilworth's shirt buttons came off, she sewed it back on. As the lady completed the task, she drew the lieutenant's arm toward her mouth. Quite flustered, Dilworth resisted, although "I saw a pair of lips that could not be surpassed approaching my hand." Disappointment soon took hold as he realized she was only going to bite off the thread. The officer, who was later rescued from a scorpion bite by a quick-thinking señorita, enjoyed a two-month encampment in Reynosa, on the Rio Grande. He danced until 3:00 a.m. and found that a number of the women "looked very well." When his unit marched out of town in early August, Dilworth bid farewell to the young ladies, as the community lined the streets in a friendly send-off.[5]

Down the Rio Grande in Matamoros, Lieutenant John James Peck saw promise when his first glimpse revealed that the "ladies are dark, but surpass ours in symmetry of form, smallness of their delicate hands, and their elegant rebozos worn so gracefully." Peck's equivocation was apparent. "After all," he affirmed, "no ladies compare to those of the North. A clear white skin is preferable to these brown ones, although under the influence of sparkling black eyes, more brilliant than diamonds." Much to his delight, Peck encountered the "pretty, elegant forms" of the Castilian women in Saltillo in December. George B. McClellan, a consummate elitist, expressed his relief upon arriving at Jalapa in the spring of 1847 in meeting genuine ladies and gentlemen—"or at least they dressed and appeared as such." He mused, "The white faces of the ladies struck us as being exceedingly beautiful—they formed so pleasing a contrast to the black and brown complexions of the Indians and Negroes who had for so long been the only human beings to greet our sight."[6]

Perhaps no one act struck Victorian American men as more shocking or culturally baffling than public swimming in the nude. After careful observation, the columnist George W. Kendall believed that there were only four things that Mexican women could not do gracefully: chop wood, throw brickbats, chase turkeys, and *swim.* No matter. For Americans excited by the glimpse of a bare ankle in Boston, the sight of Mexican women "going swimming in the river quite naked and in full view" drew extensive and varied commentary. In the North, where the Rio Grande and San Juan Rivers offered respite from the dust and heat, it was common for groups of women of various ages to gather to seek relief. The Americans, depending upon their modesty, would spend hours on the riverbank, apparently overcoming their racial prejudices. Others doffed their clothes and jumped into the river only to find the tables turned and the women on the bank looking at or joining them. Abner Doubleday stumbled upon a stream in Cerralvo where a number of señoritas were swimming "in the costume of Mother Eve." He added with some amusement that none of them seemed at all abashed, save one who tried unsuccessfully to hide behind a small tree.[7]

Napoleon Dana made the mistake of telling his wife about this cultural disconnect. After graphically describing the women's nudity, he backpedaled furiously. Struggling to assert his own innocence, Dana reassured Sue and her envious uncle that "everybody looked at them," but he would only view the women "as so many wild beasts, orangutans." He certainly would not kiss them. "These are only the lower classes who are so in public. They are quite dark and most excellently ugly."

Perhaps a skeptical Sue believed him. Feeling the need to maintain her own femininity and submissiveness to her "dear, dear husband," however, she described learning to sing and play the guitar and said that she welcomed his return so he could help correct her faults. As for the Mexican women, the leering of Dana's compatriots, possibly combined with more aggressive conduct that was unrecorded, prompted an adjustment in their behavior. Several months later, Daniel Harvey Hill took a bath in a familiar stream near Cerralvo on a very hot day in January. Not surprisingly, a woman joined him in the water, but he saw that now all the female bathers wore gowns.[8]

The state of dress of Mexican women was an ongoing subject of fascination to foreigners, especially in light of the American "cult of true womanhood" and prevailing standards of modesty. In the 1840s, the German engineer and artist Carl Nebel traveled the country sketching the native populations with a keen eye toward their appearance. Nebel drew men and women, and the accompanying annotation, while candid, lacked the racial prejudice so often present in American diaries or letters. From a decade that predated photography in Mexico, his renderings are important for their cultural depictions. For example, Nebel crafted flattering portraits of Sierra Indian women clad in intricately woven handcrafted cottons that reflected their bond between man and nature. "The finest dress, the greatest variety in form and color, always are found in the mountain peoples." His more sophisticated portrayals of upper-class women showed the long dark dress, *mantilla,* and fan. All "Mexican" women, he observed, referring to the upper classes, wore the *mantilla* in the morning, but at night covered their heads with a rebozo. The soldiers universally pointed to the importance of the garment as an essential element of dress and when describing

Upper-class Mexican women wearing *mantillas. La Mantilla,* hand-colored lithograph by Carl Nebel, 1836.

the elites attached the terms *elegant* and *graceful.* The appealing employment of the rebozo made the wearing of hats in the European fashion unnecessary.[9]

Shoes were a very important component of the wardrobe, since they affected the grace and manner with which a young woman walked. Low-heeled sandaled footwear was thus preferable. American men who had little interest in such things prior to their arrival in Mexico frequently mentioned the feet of the women. Lieutenant Peck watched as young señoritas of twelve or fourteen moved more gracefully than Yankee girls. "Their walk is natural and beautiful. Their feet are so small you fancy they scarcely touch this nether world." An officer in Monterrey conjectured that the Mexican woman, regardless of class, "bestowed all of her choicest sympathy upon her feet." Beauty, bright eyes, virtue, intelligence—all were for naught if a woman lacked small feet. Consequently, when walking, sitting, or at Mass, women made a special effort to assure that their satin pointed slippers commanded everyone's attention. Peck referred to the behavior as "an intellectuality about their extremities truly remarkable to behold."[10]

Mexican women did dress differently from the women back home. Helen

Chapman, the wife of the army quartermaster at Matamoros, described the attire of the common folk as a petticoat and a chemise, "with the neck and sleeves fitted into a binding and a shirt of calico very often frilled around the bottom." "It is so loose," she noted, "that the breast is very much exposed and, indeed, some of the servants seem to have nothing over the bosom." Chapman scribbled these thoughts in her diary without judgment or criticism, emphasizing that women used their rebozos in a manner that "completely conceals these deficiencies of costume." She watched Mexican women endure the cold of winter, washing clothes by a riverbank, thinly clad, "leaving the chest and bosom entirely bare." Rather than chiding the women for a lack of modesty, she expressed her sympathy for their poverty and the hardship of their lives.

Lieutenant Peck was equally eager to critique female clothing soon after he marched into Matamoros in late June 1846. He duly considered, and reported favorably upon, the ubiquitous rebozo, which was stylishly worn "wrapped around their waists after passing over the heads." Below on the body, a waistcloth was tied around the waist and loins as a separate garment from the skirt. Peck pointed out that skirts were worn only in the heat of the day. He labeled the dresses "rich and gaudy," noting that the women had a fondness for laces and muslins. In contrast, the "common people" wore very little, many "nothing save a skirt of some cheap but gaudy goods." A month later, the lieutenant described the women much as Nebel had, as clad in "neat white linen or cotton" and with a preference for "highly colored patterns." Other correspondents confirmed Chapman's and Peck's impressions of the women of the region: the common dress was a loosely tied white muslin skirt with only a short-sleeved chemise that exposed the neck and bosom down to the waist. A stunned officer marveled that Mexican women made no more effort to conceal their breasts than an American lady would of hiding her hand. To add to the horror, they wore no stockings except at Mass. Pride of dress clearly gave way to the extreme of comfort and ease. Decency had been compromised.[11]

A correspondent for the *New Orleans Bee* was equivocal. Mexican women might be beautiful, but the vast majority appeared indolent, slovenly, "and destitute of that female delicacy which characterizes our own women." Ralph Kirkham, stationed in Puebla, largely shared this view. He rarely saw the "better classes" in the streets, for they emerged from their homes only to go to Mass or ride to the public gardens on Sunday. Kirkham admitted that when he did encounter them, they were dressed in "considerable taste" and were more graceful than American women. However, any report of the women being handsome or pretty "is all a mistake. Nine-tenths of the people resemble the Cherokee Indians as much as possible." The masses were poor, ignorant, superstitious be-

Mexican women with rebozo and *cigarillo*. Drawing by Brantz Mayer from *Mexico as it is and was,* 1844.

ings, Kirkham reckoned. The women, barefooted and bareheaded, smiled and worked hard, while their lazy husbands seemed to idle away their time.[12]

De Lancey Floyd-Jones, also bivouacked in Puebla and anxious to meet the señoritas, graciously conceded, "It is the only town where I thought there was any gentility." Floyd-Jones shared his long-range fantasy with his sister Cate. As early as January 1847, he dreamed about settling down after the war on a plantation with "a nice little wife." Floyd-Jones prodded Cate, only half teasingly, about whether she would like a "black-eyed señorita" as a sister and would prefer to winter in Mexico, rather than on Long Island. He promised Cate a pony to ride each morning, a flower garden for her amusement, and rooms on his hacienda of three thousand acres, where the peons would do her bidding. He waxed eloquently about the delicate nature of the Mexican woman and her magical fingers plying the needle or playing the keys of a piano.

Of course, Mexican men did not appreciate the talents or company of their women, who cried out for understanding companions. As the year passed, Floyd-Jones became increasingly convinced that Mexicans were incapable of self-government and would quickly be consumed by endless revolution. They needed—and many wanted—the protection of the Stars and Stripes. Eventually, the United States would be obliged to occupy the country permanently. "The sooner the better for in my opinion it must come," Floyd-Jones firmly declared. The perceived political reality only reinforced his postwar domestic vision. He acknowledged in December that Cate might be saying, "Lan is full of his nonsense," but, he told her, "I would advise you to keep a bright lookout in this direction."[13]

John Kenly used some of the same language as Kirkham and Floyd-Jones to describe the women of Tampico; however, he did not share the latter's fantasy of a Mexican future. Kenly was astonished at the crowded streets, filled with women fashionably dressed in the European style, their black hair accented by a flower, and the rebozo falling "gracefully" (the term always used) over the shoulder. When watching their "inimitable carriage, the birthright of a Spaniard," one could never doubt that the blood of Castile or Aragon coursed through their veins. "They were Mexicans, yet they were women," Kenly concluded with marked approbation. The soldiers consistently mentioned the Spanish Castilian appearance of their fantasy woman. The Kentuckian Daniel Runyon fell in love repeatedly, although he spoke no Spanish and could not adequately express his affection. He admitted this failing to his sister, worrying that unless the war continued longer, he would be unable to present the family with "a Spanish Beauty as my bride." Runyon playfully cautioned that he did not want a word spoken "about my being in love with the beautiful Castilians of the 'Sunny South.'"[14]

Even with the opportunity to meet fashionable and respectable women limited by custom, culture, and circumstance, hope nevertheless sprang eternal among the troops. Visits to private homes and dances were much-anticipated occasions. Auspiciously, American soldiers, regardless of class or ethnicity, loved music. Whether played on the farmer's fiddle or on the urban pianoforte, popular music had become a widespread means of entertainment in the theater and home in the antebellum era. Music for the masses took many forms, from the sentimental ballad to the minstrel show. Stephen Foster composed and Edwin Christy's troupe performed uniquely American tunes that were touching, spirited, and memorable.

When the volunteers and regulars traveled south of the Rio Grande, they were pleased to discover that the Mexicans shared that affection for song and dance. Guitars and violins seemed ever present, with instruments snatched from the wall with rapidity and spontaneity, much to the delight of the American visitor who found himself in a Mexican home. Numerous diarists were perplexed at the widespread embrace of *tabacos* (cigars) by entire families at such occasions. A memorable scene transpired when a young officer observed a ranchero rolling his own from Havana and sharing the result with his kinfolk and guest. When his fetching daughter offered the Yankee a half-smoked end, "reduced to a pulp between her luscious lips," he was most agreeable to the gesture. Conversely, when her equally hospitable grandmother did so, the soldier strained to continue the smoke.[15]

While family dinners and accompanying individual performances helped forge bonds between the two cultures, most soldiers sought the pleasures awarded by the fandango. The affairs were held regularly in public spaces and private homes and sponsored by various classes and races. Anglos first received their introduction to the sensual nature of women participating in the dance in New Mexico and Texas. For many puritanical spectators, here was the true sign of Mexican moral depravity. *Lewd, lascivious,* and *erotic* seemed to describe how many offended, yet intrigued onlookers viewed the motions and gestures. Only the custom of open-air bathing rivaled the fandango as confirmation of the perversity of what passed for Latin culture. Accompanied by liberal amounts of alcohol and gambling, usually four-card monte, the fandango often lasted well into the morning hours.

Since the society limited the places to meet a young lady either publicly or privately, the soldiers sought out the fandango for conversation and a dance. Certainly, the social opportunity also greatly stimulated their interest in learning and practicing the Spanish language. Their frustration at being unable to communicate with a lovely señorita is mentioned repeatedly in their diaries. Daniel Harvey Hill attended his first dance in the summer of 1846 and was duly impressed that both sexes were talented, well dressed, and "behaved with great propriety." While some American officers promptly joined in, Hill, with a heightened libido and sense of isolation, quickly saw the merits of learning the native tongue.[16]

Samuel Curtis appeared at a rather unpretentious fandango in a one-story brick house with a dirt floor in a remote part of town. Surprised to learn that he was the only American present, he remained about an hour, receiving the "distinguished attention" of the thirty to forty people there. To his credit, Curtis attempted to waltz but found his step out of time. While a combination of factors undoubtedly contributed to the officer's early departure, he mentioned that the party came from the "medium class" of the city and "displayed the darkest outline of Indian features"—unlike the "great many very pretty señioras [*sic*]" he found in Matamoros. Seeking Castilian beauty, instead he discovered that "the women were generally dark and none of them pretty."[17]

Fandangos could also be dangerous. An American soldier who rode to an event had to pay off a sentinel for protection or risk having his horse stolen. Even worse, Abner Doubleday recounted how he and his friends went to a regular affair staged for the officers in a dangerous and largely deserted Matamoros: "Of course," Doubleday declared, "it was not attended by the better class of females." The soldiers removed their swords to dance only to see that the weapons were being examined by the Mexican men and passed to the rear of the room. Fearing an assassination attempt, the Americans unholstered their pistols, seized the swords, and hurriedly exited the building.[18]

Many fandangos failed to meet the expectations of the young officers. Napoleon Dana dedicated a significant segment of his correspondence with his wife, Sue, to convincing her that he would never look at, dance with, or even touch a Mexican woman. He dutifully reported from Reynosa that many of his comrades frequented the fandangos "and cut all kinds of capers among the girls. From what I hear of them I should suppose they were very rowdy things." Not seeking to panic her, Dana assured his wife that his comrades danced, joked, drank punch, "and had all sorts of a frolic." "All appear to enjoy the fun," he concluded from afar. After he yielded to temptation several days later, Dana explained that about forty Americans had shown up at what was purported to be a "high-flung" fandango with the promise of beauty and fine dresses. After two minutes, they believed there must be a mistake. The twenty Spanish girls disappointed, with Dana claiming that he felt like he had fleas on him thereafter. He crudely scrutinized the event: "They [fandangos] are vulgar disgusting places, and I believe I would rather go to a nigger breakdown."[19]

The Virginian Philip Gooch Ferguson believed that the fandango presented the Mexican woman at her best advantage. "For once," he bitingly stated, "she has an exterior appearance of cleanliness and refinement." Franklin Smith provided the most detailed description of a dance held in the yard of a Mexican express rider named Silvester. Smith, a careful eyewitness to the affair, emphasized that the women, dressed in silk and gold beads, waltzed tirelessly "with great ease and grace" and put on quite a show for the volunteers. At another soiree in Mier, Smith marveled at two to three dozen women "well dressed after the American fashion." With their hair clubbed and adorned with artificial flowers, the ladies, who he determined were a "sort of Aristocracy," waltzed beautifully and executed a dance called the *lanceros,* in which they effected the motions of the cavalry.

Smith also echoed the viewpoint held by many that the young, single girls were generally chaste and inaccessible. Among the "lower orders," however, incest was a common sin, and married women welcomed the opportunity to cuckold their husbands. The woman sought attention from other men, which she, and everyone else, recognized not as an insult but as a compliment to her charms. Smith shared these views in his diary without condemnation but in contending that the character of the Mexican people was quite different from his own. Affirming the notion that Mexico was "a nation of thieves and strumpets," he came to the conclusion that "there is and must be in every country any ways civilized a class that has pride of character—the men honourable—the women virtuous but in Mexico this class must be smaller than in any other country called civilized." Accordingly, Smith proffered a cautionary reality regarding the dangers of courting Mexican women.[20]

When the fortress of Chapultepec, guarding Mexico City, fell in September 1847, Winfield Scott's ten thousand troops moved in for a prolonged period of occupation. English schools were quickly established, and columns in English were published in Mexican newspapers. Conversely, a self-proclaimed Harvard graduate opened a Spanish and French institute for those officers who wished to familiarize themselves with the native tongue. Dances and balls, for which a two-dollar ticket would admit a gentleman and *two* ladies, supplemented the theater, music, and the circus to entertain people of all classes. A homesick soldier could purchase eggnog and mince pies and consume the advertised "Mash and Milk at All Hours." The Eagle Coffee House served the finest wines, liquors, chops, and cigars and had two billiard tables.[21]

As a modicum of tranquility enveloped the city and the social pace accelerated, the relationships between the American soldiers and Mexican women similarly were energized. The officers, billeted about the town, sought the acquaintance of señoritas in the streets and in the theater. The attention of the soldiers sometimes proved unwanted, prompting a petition published in a Mexican paper. The women rejected the flattery of the Yankees as an insult to their patriotism. Predictably, the negative reputation of the invaders had preceded them, and the officers struggled to gain the attention and respect particularly of the upper classes. As Theodore Laidley poignantly discerned, "The higher classes receive us as kindly as they dare."

The *American Star,* published in the capital, tried to assure Mexican families that the virtue of their daughters was safe. Nowhere in the world was the female character more highly regarded than in the United States, the editor exalted. The free mingling of the society allowed young people of both sexes to exchange their thoughts openly. Indeed, "no mother in Mexico need covet any higher distinction for her daughter than an alliance with an accomplished American gentleman." By mid-October 1847 the paper could report that Mexico City had become safer, quieter, more welcoming. Importantly, the women "ceased to flash the fire of indignant scorn from their beautiful eyes," stood on their balconies, and walked the streets. The city had indeed changed.[22]

Such was not always the case. Some liaisons were serious, and the extrication from the physical and emotional bonds became quite painful. Many were temporary matters of convenience, pleasure, and economics. The Hotel Bella Union typified this subculture in which young women, called "Margaritas," entertained the American soldiers. The Mexican scholar Antonio García Cubas deridingly referred to them as "harlots of the lowest class." The first floor of the building housed the gambling hall; the second, the saloon and dancing; and the third, the rooms for prostitution. Crowds would gather to cheer and applaud the "coarse and immoral acts" often performed on the balconies of the hotel. The audience would serenade the couples with a mocking ballad entitled "La Pasadita," one stanza of which was worded,

> All the Margaritas speak English now,
> you say: do you love me and they answer:
> jes, I onderstand de money ees very good,
> and on to La Pasadita.

García Cubas, who attended several of the balls, sarcastically described the efforts of the US volunteers to engage in folk dancing with their Margaritas. The *jarabe* often involved a good measure of foot stomping, which the Americans did awkwardly in their heavy boots, tripping and stumbling about the floor. The ensuing conversation was also limited to pidgin English and Spanish accompanied by gestures and contortions. Dancing, discussion, and "orgies which never had been seen before in Mexico" lasted until three in the morning. Critical Mexican observers bemoaned the abundance of girls willing to engage in such activity. They blamed the behavior on base wickedness but also expressed their sorrow that honor would be sacrificed for a simple piece of bread.[23]

In several instances, casual relations evolved into true affection, or perhaps economic opportunity. Some Yankees sought the fantasy of the young Castilian beauty, while others sought that of the wealthy older widow. When bonds between a Mexican woman and an American soldier became complicated in nature, however, both sides were likely to step in to prevent a marriage. D. H. Hill reported the rumored nuptial of a fellow officer and a resident woman and the accompanying efforts of her friends to halt the wedding. "So much for the feeling of the fair sex of Mexico towards the Barbarians of the North," Hill ruminated. Another soldier criticized a member of his unit who had apparently gone off and married the daughter of the alcalde. This tale proved untrue, and the Pennsylvanian speculated with an audible sigh of relief, "Don't know how he got it into his head." The young man's mates welcomed him back to the company by getting him "royally tight."[24]

The fantasies the soldiers brought from Indiana or Maryland were very real, and a number of them played out in their diaries or letters. John Corey Henshaw, recovering from an intestinal malady in Puebla in the summer of 1847, found himself in a quandary with "the beautiful Carmelita García." Carmelita and her cousin, Guadalupe, lived nearby and sent Henshaw "a most exquisite dish" along with some fruit. The appreciative major, who spoke no Spanish and had seen Carmelita but twice from his balcony, was uncertain about the proper response to their kindness. "One thing is certain," he avowed. "They are both very beautiful and if I were single I should long since have been deeply smitten." The meals, brought by Carmelita's servant, continued for some time as the perplexed Henshaw tried to chart a course of action that would avoid hurt feelings. Even when the women removed to their country house, they planned on conveying dinner to his lodging.

Henshaw's brother officers chided him good-naturedly about being "the biggest ninny they ever saw" and not meeting Carmelita halfway. Finally, he wrote Guadalupe a letter of thanks for their generosity, while regretting that his diet prohibited the ingestion of the sumptuous fare sent his way. Henshaw, who was amazingly candid with his wife about what he labeled "a romantic adventure," did eventually speak with Carmelita, and the brief daydream ended.[25]

By the summer of 1846, the twenty-five-year-old D. H. Hill admitted that like many of his peers, "I am more and more captive to Mexican charms." His world improved when he was transferred in August to Cerralvo, a community of four thousand that he initially found cleaner and neater, its people "fairer and more intelligent" than other towns. More importantly, as an officer of the plaza guard, he had the opportunity to chat with Señora Garcia and her lovely daughter Manuela. Hill discovered that the bright eyes of the señorita dramatically improved his understanding of Spanish. Thereafter, he would sit for long periods staring at the front of her house. Hill expressed clear disappointment about bidding her farewell as she departed for her home in Camargo. Six months later, he mentioned rather laconically, "I learned that my little favorite Manuela Garcia, was pregnant and I would not go to see her."

In October, Hill eased his discontent in Monterrey as part of Taylor's army of occupation. He enjoyed the bed and board of a señora at seventy-five cents a day and reflected wistfully, "Next to my own friends I *love* the family of Mrs. Tato." Unfortunately, Hill was destined to spend the new year in Saltillo, a rough-and-tumble city in which he had few opportunities to dine with, let alone court, a woman of the upper class. In nearby Parras the ladies rode out in their carriages to greet the American officers at their camp, while the gentlemen hosted the ensuing dinner parties. In Saltillo, "the streets are crowded tonight with strumpets," and "lower class women who had male protectors with them" abounded on the streets. Hill might be invited to visit a middle-class home, but the mothers had warned their daughters about the avaricious appetites of the Yankee heretics. Hill contented himself with ice cream at six pence a dish.

Hill's life entered a new, brief, and exciting phase in December, when Mariana Ramos, the daughter of the alcalde, seized his heart. He spied her in church—"the most lovely little thing I ever saw"—and walked past her house some forty times (by his count) without further success. They exchanged glances at Mass, and Hill fantasized that some act of fortune might throw them together. His ardor spiked, as he confessed to his diary that she intruded on his thoughts during the day and his dreams at night. Disappointed at the absence of an invitation to the home of his "little bonita," Hill queried several women and learned that Mariana was engaged to a Mexican officer. To no avail, he befriended a male cousin in the hope of finagling a way into the household. At least he could enjoy seeing her from a distance sitting in the window of the cousin's home.

Hill was informed that the more reliable route to Mariana was through the female servants—whom he must either make love to or bribe. He apparently rejected both approaches and decided instead to improve his Spanish. On a daily basis, his diary recorded whether he had seen his "little bonita" in the street or at church. In January, Hill's unit was ordered to Monterrey. The disillusioned lieutenant wanted desperately to tell his "little angel" farewell. "So ends this farce," he wrote with resignation. "I have seldom been so much in love with anyone as with her." Hill emotionally added, "It seems to me that her presence alone has kept this cursed town from sinking into perdition." Notably, this chimera, conducted with no spoken or written words to the young woman, enabled the young officer to survive.[26]

Henshaw and Hill suffered the torment of a month-long fantasy with no meaningful contact with the objects of their affection and yet relished it. The situation confronting Grayson Prevost appears more problematic, and troubling, since it represented a cultural adjustment facing many young American officers in Mexico. Prevost embodied the essence of Anglo-American manhood.

The handsome young Philadelphian graduated from a summer-long medical program and worked his way into the service as an assistant surgeon in 1845. With Taylor's army during the early months of the war, he found himself stationed at field hospitals. In the summer of 1846 he formed some of his first impressions of Mexicans, whom he found attractive, mendacious, and totally immodest. Desperate for combat experience, Prevost had an opportunity to distinguish himself at Buena Vista.

By June 1847, he was back behind the lines in Saltillo, although residing in a house owned by the governor of the province. Prevost's early letters to his sisters discuss the comfort of his quarters and a lifestyle that included fine furniture and chocolates. As for women, he confided that previous experience had convinced him that the Mexicans were best admired at a distance. With little humility, Prevost admitted that he was "fairly canonized" in Mier but tired of the game of trying to gauge the level of affection between himself and any particular woman.[27]

The doctor's abstinence was short-lived. A visit to the family across the street led to a relationship that lasted five months and would no doubt leave contemporary psychologists scratching their heads. Prevost was befriended by Doña Jesusita Peres and her children. A daughter of eleven or twelve, Pomposita, drew his attention; Prevost contented himself with patting her on the head rather than taking her upon his knee. Very quickly, the doctor justified that Pomposita was really a young woman, rather than a child, and that marriages and pregnancies were quite common in Mexico at her age. The girl, clearly drawn to the good-looking officer, gave him a small ring and revealed both her affection and her jealousy. Prevost claimed that early in the relationship he attempted to explain to her the difference between friendship and love. As an aside, however, he mentioned that Mexican women were fickle and that another man's flattery could easily carry them away. There was nothing special in the attachment of a Mexican woman to a foreigner, he expanded, especially given the weakness—which the women recognized—of their own men.

Prevost boasted that Pomposita was "famed for her beauty throughout the camp" and that he was the only officer with access to the house. Other officers wished to be introduced to her, however, and he determined that it would best for her if he did not do so. She was a mere child, he now rationalized, attracted by the epaulette and brass button, and thus he should protect her from those who would not respect her virtue. Within a month, the twenty-three-year-old lieutenant jested that because of Pomposita's youth, he doubted his sisters would consent to his marrying her. He would be considered a "Mahomedan" back in

Philadelphia. Yet Prevost assured them that she had "all the warm and chaste feelings of an American girl of 16 yrs."[28]

Prevost's confessions of vulnerability to the young girl's charms may reflect an adolescent innocent rather than a predatory ogre. Prevost understood that his appeal rested in large part upon his status and healing role as a doctor—he was perhaps the most feted and esteemed man in the community. By the fall of 1847 he had become a long-term (nine-month) resident and engaged in part-time private practice. The gifts of quince marmalade, fruit, chicken, even a pet lamb, came in unrelenting streams, although Prevost tried to graciously decline them. While the doctor developed affection for some of the citizens of Saltillo, he still referred to the general population as "greasers." He continued to succumb, however, to the "kisses and eatables" of "my sweet little cherub." Apparently, Prevost's sister cautioned him about Pomposita, prompting Grayson to reassure his father that he would never form an attachment "of any strength" with a Mexican girl.[29]

Prevost continued to spend money (twenty dollars) on gifts for Pomposita, visiting at her window, flirting, and being entertained by her song. It was never enough. He grumbled that he might feel "tolerably happy" for just an hour alone to talk with his "little sweetheart," but the manners of the country prohibited such privacy. Prevost's tenure in Saltillo approached an end in the fall of 1847, and a transfer to Monterrey seemed imminent. Pomposita sent a message and gifts to his sister, which no doubt created an uncomfortable situation for Prevost, who acknowledged to his sister that she might now receive Pomposita's attentions "with the more unalloyed pleasure, as our acquaintance is about to terminate forever and your doubts as to the result are at an end." He reaffirmed his feelings in a particularly candid letter, tinged with a bit of anger, to his sister in mid-October. Defending Pomposita and fervently expressing his interest and tenderness, he clarified his feelings: "Were she of a different blood and a Protestant, and no objection existed to my marriage, this sentiment would soon ripen into love." It already had, but such a scenario was unlikely ever to occur.[30]

Prevost's mother also weighed in regarding yielding to temptation, and the dutiful son responded with thanks for her counsel and confidence in his strength of character. Vice was ever present, he admitted, especially gambling, and Mexico had a recognized deleterious effect on the morals of his comrades. Prevost explained his relationship with Pomposita rather differently to his mother. In very analytical terms, he discussed how their conversations had been of benefit to her and, in a country of "universally depraved" men, exposed her to virtue and "perfect moral principle." Yet, Prevost realized that Pomposita was confused about his intentions and unable to separate love from friendship. Family mattered more than his infatuation. Prevost pledged never to act in any manner that would displease his parents or dishonor his family. He also managed to convince himself, as did many of his comrades, that Mexican women lacked enduring virtue and could be easily led astray. As a result, Prevost engaged in painful and tear-filled visits with Pomposita and her mother, discussing the impractical nature of marriage and moving any ties with the family to a level of cordiality. He informed his sister with undisguised bitterness, "Here ends for the present this chapter of a sad and singular love tale."

The war changed the lives of many men, including Grayson Prevost. The separation from his family and their reactions to his experiences contributed to a palpable shift in attitude. He came to embrace Mexico and its people. Resigning from the army in spring of 1848, he traveled to Philadelphia to reconnect briefly with family and then returned to Mexico to practice medicine. Helen Chapman, the wife of the army quartermaster in Matamoros, was clearly taken with Prevost, whom she categorized as someone women read about in romances. She described him as a young man of "extreme and delicate physical beauty," not effeminate, and "undeniably intellectual." Chapman waxed at length about his moral and physical courage and the extent of the admiration for him within the community.

In 1850, Prevost met a woman ("Anita") in Parras, but they could find no priest to marry them. Consequently, the couple traveled to Brownsville, where a Presbyterian clergyman performed the vows in the parlor of the Chapmans' home. More than 150 witnesses remained for "a very merry and pleasant" dinner. Two years later, when the Prevosts returned to Brownsville, Helen noticed that Anita was "very much Americanized in appearance and improved." The couple soon moved to Zacatecas, living there until Grayson's death in 1896. Apparently, the esteem of his kin and his perception of the fidelity of Mexican women had undergone a transformation. While very few soldiers brought their Pompositas home, a number of Americans remained in Mexico to realize their personal and professional dreams.[31]

Fraternizing with the enemy occurred from the commencement of hostilities and could objectively be considered harmless. Many "common" women, curious and seeking a profit, sold their produce, fruits, and notions on board the riverboats or in the market squares. D. H. Hill took particular delight in the clarified squash, which was sugared and sold as candy. Women also provided services; they cooked, cleaned, laundered, or nursed the sick and wounded to enhance their income. Upper-class women entertained officers in their homes, well aware of the sympathetic treatment they might receive from the occupiers or the earnings that might accrue from the sale of a ranchero's goods to the army.[32]

Any and all encounters could also prompt ugly reactions as the Americans withdrew from various towns in the countryside, such as Cuernavaca and San Angel and, in the summer of 1848, the capital. The women left behind—the "Yankedos"—suffered shorn hair, homes sacked, and often the letters "U.S." branded on their cheek. Samuel Chamberlain related worse, including Mexican soldiers violating the women. In Saltillo, during a drunken celebration at the end of the war, Padre Olitze, a Dominican priest, virulently denounced the sympathizers before the townsfolk. In a frenzy, they dragged the women from their homes, raped them, cut off their ears and then cut their throats. Chamberlain claimed that in one night twenty-three collaborators were killed without interference from the military or civilian officials. A *New Orleans Crescent* reporter explained the panic as the Americans departed Mexico City. Women with "particular friends" in the army begged the teamsters to take them along in their wagons bound for the United States.[33]

Even before the withdrawal occurred, those Mexicans who demonstrated hospitality to or sympathy for the invaders paid a heavy price. American papers protested that women friendly to the Yankees were "mercilessly maltreated." An alcalde in Puebla welcomed American officers into his home and encouraged his daughters to play and sing for their guests. Word of treason quickly spread, the alcalde defamed with charges of aiding the Yankee cause and selling his daughters. As a result, the family was obliged to leave the city, fearful that their home would be burned.[34]

In distant California, Felipa Osuna enjoyed position and privilege in the San Diego community. Her father had been a political force, and her husband, Juan María Marrón, was named administrator of the struggling mission of San Luis Rey, as well as alcalde of San Diego in 1846. The couple divided their time between town living and their farm, Rancho Agua Hedionda. When the American troops arrived in the winter of 1846–47, the population was caught in a crossfire between the Yankees and the Californios. Felipa recalled her impression of the invaders: "I was very afraid of the Americans because they were undisciplined troops." "Some of Fremont's men were mercenaries," she insisted, "and one day they robbed our home." Felipa's brother, Leandro, had been involved in the Battle of San Pasqual and had the blood of an American officer on his lance.

Still, many Californios suspected Felipa and Juan María of aiding and abetting the occupiers. "The accusations that Marrón and I were allied with the Americans did not cease. My husband was upset that his countrymen would treat him this way and that they were making off with all his possessions." Indeed, Felipa feared that Juan María would be killed by the Californios, who seized more than a hundred head of their cattle. As the fighting ended in early 1847, the Marróns decided to profit from the power shift. They sold about one thousand sheep, cattle, and other supplies brought in from the rancho to Commodore Robert Stockton. Felipa crowed with satisfaction, "He paid for everything in cash."[35]

Perhaps the most tragic tale, if it is to be believed, was detailed by Chamberlain in his aptly titled *My Confession: Recollections of a Rogue.* His memoirs, which he penned in Boston several years after the war, included numerous supposed encounters with attractive women. A boyish teenage sergeant who made no apologies for his weakness for the opposite sex, he found himself posted in San Nicolas, where he rescued a naked girl about to be whipped by her much older husband, who was known as a cutthroat and a scoundrel. Carmeleita Veigho, unsurprisingly "a girl as fair as any Anglo Saxon lady," was the progeny of an Irishman and a full-blooded Spanish woman.

Chamberlain contended that "a platonic attachment between a wild dragoon not yet out of his teens, and a young, passionate daughter of Mexico was an impossibility." The girl was thirteen and "as voluptuous and graceful in shape as the Venus de Medici." He rationalized that he had saved her from the cruel fate of a forced marriage, and "this was in Mexico, where mothers at twelve are not uncommon." A sympathetic officer allowed him to rent a room in Monterrey with Carmeleita, and good fortune at gambling put several thousand dollars in his pocket, enough to clothe his love in silk and buy her a horse and side saddle. A new commander ordered the young soldier back to camp but allowed him to take his Mexican "wife" with him.

Their idyllic existence lasted three months, until the provost guard appeared with Carmeleita's husband demanding her immediate return. Troopers restrained Chamberlain while the miserable girl was given up to "El Tuerto." To no avail, the frustrated American scoured the countryside in an effort to locate her. A conversation with a parish priest soon thereafter revealed her awful destiny: Carmeleita had been turned over to a band of guerrillas to be raped and then cut to pieces. Chamberlain bewailed her fate and even considered remaining in Mexico after the war to hunt down El Tuerto and avenge her murder. Instead, the adventurous soldier mustered out of the army in 1848, took up with Ellen Ramsey, an eighteen-year-old, six-foot-tall Scottish immigrant, and headed for California.[36]

Philip Gooch Ferguson recorded an equally troubling situation while serving with the Army of the West in New Mexico. Benjamin Talbot, his lieutenant, was keeping a thirteen-year-old Mexican girl "of great beauty" in his quarters. Ferguson viewed her manner and appearance as those of a child and lamented that someone her age should be "so deeply engulfed in sin and vice." The men of the company were likewise outraged. By living publicly with his "Mexican whore," the lieutenant had disgraced the unit. Seventy-two men signed a petition demanding that the officer be broken of his commission. Talbot retaliated, ordering Ferguson's arrest and threatening the guardhouse for all the petitioners. Ferguson did not back down, and the plea against Talbot was presented to Colonel Ralls, although with the words "he has rendered himself unworthy of the title of a gentleman" stricken.

The colonel determined that while he did not approve of Talbot's conduct, the charges were not sufficient to remove him from rank. Instead, Ralls settled for verbal castigation. While no doubt disappointing to the company, the rebuke did prompt Talbot to "discard" the girl. Sadly, she was placed in the care of a comrade, Lieutenant Hepburn, an equally dissolute fellow. Hepburn had been arrested by Ralls for beating a French merchant and using abusive language to the colonel. Several months later, following the Battle of Santa Cruz de Rosales, Ferguson, without any emotion, reported that "the body of Lieutenant Hepburn had been found completely stripped of clothing." While the fate of the young girl remained unknown, Ferguson objected angrily to the indecency and "moral depravity" of many officers keeping two or three mistresses at the same time. "Is there no virtue extant?" he implored.[37]

The relationships that existed between American soldiers and Mexican women, imagined and real, were both simple and complex. The physical attractiveness, particularly of light-skinned Spanish women, drew untold numbers of Yankee soldiers into fantasies unlikely to culminate in any meaningful bond. Most Americans initially believed that the absence of upper-class women from newly occupied towns had been prompted exclusively by the fear of physical violence. The more perceptive men came to realize that even when these women returned to their homes, Mexican customs, highlighted by barred windows and the presence of a *dueña,* augured badly in terms of extensive contact.

The Alabama captain Tennent Lomax was stationed in Orizaba, a charming valley city of twenty thousand inhabitants, in 1848. Most of the population, he allowed, were the "color of mulattos." There were exceptions, however, and Lomax found one—a "delicate little creature" with rosy cheeks, fair skin, and coal dark eyes and hair. He deliberately passed by her window, where she stood dressed in black, six to eight times a day. "She gave me no token of recognition except occasionally to throw her burning eyes upon me, I invariably touched my hat to her as I passed and looked as love struck as possible." A month later, Lomax confirmed the beauty of the women in the town and their skill in playing the harp but complained that "they seem to shun intercourse with us." Clearly, the dream collided with reality. The captain told his sister that he might well bring one of the "perfectly lovely señoritas home with me "if she would consent." The prospect seemed highly unlikely. Moreover, while officers saw an invitation to a Mexican home as a positive sign of acceptance and accommodation to the realities of war, many locals viewed such activity as collaboration and a betrayal of the nation. D. H. Hill encountered and bowed to his "little bonita," the daughter of a prominent official betrothed to an army officer, but never spoke to her.[38]

Equally hopeless, but for different reasons, Grayson Prevost represented those Americans who tried to come to grips with a society that permitted coquettish young women to flirt and tease and indeed marry. But how could Prevost possibly introduce Pomposita into his Quaker City family? While many Americans certainly had physical relations with more "common" women of color, few soldiers envisioned leaving Mexico with a dark-skinned bride. Caught in a situation in which they could have women they did not desire to marry but could not have women they truly wanted, most American soldiers departed the country somewhat wiser about the culture, but with their fantasies unfulfilled.

Military Madness

The most devastating facet of the American occupation related to the acts of physical mistreatment, wanton murder, and deliberate destruction leveled against property and people, especially women. When the war began, the US Army numbered fewer than nine thousand men, largely scattered about the frontier. To meet the demands of conquest at a great distance, Congress and the Polk administration felt compelled to call up fifty thousand volunteers. At least initially, the conflict proved to be resoundingly popular in most areas of the country, and enlistments came fast and furious. Young men, caught up in a patriotic rush, seeking adventure in an exotic foreign land, or just pursuing the opportunity for employment, crowded recruiting offices. As many as 40 percent of the enlistees were recent immigrants, often Irish and illiterate. The lower-class roots of the volunteers did not necessarily separate them from their comrades in the ranks of the regulars. However, the attitude of the new enlistees toward professionalism, obedience, and army life most certainly did so—and the resentment was palpable. Lieutenant De Lancey Floyd-Jones cynically claimed that the volunteers "work when they please and get drunk when they can." He assured his brother that "a long and dusty days march is a sure antidote for patriotism."[39]

Notions of glory and treasure quickly faded amid the pervasive killer diseases, stifling heat, and relentless fleas, mosquitoes, and scorpions. Many men merely wasted away with typhoid or dysentery, dying without honor or recognition, save a brief inscription in a mate's diary. Should they survive, the soldiers endured a monotonous diet of salt meats and hard bread, improper wool uniforms, and uncomfortable tent housing. A hostile reception from the citizenry made matters worse. While not expecting to be received as liberators, the soldiers hoped that the occupation of a town would mean better food, more comfortable quarters, and an enhanced social life. Indeed, in some instances they found relief from their privations, but more often they experienced closed doors or a throat slit in a narrow dark street.

Reporters attempted to explain how decent, generous Christian men could leave their homes with noble intent and somehow become transformed into thieves, plunderers, and murderers. The harsh treatment, they rationalized, drove the soldiers to a level of selfishness and sordid behavior that the men never would have contemplated before crossing the Rio Grande. Others cited their conduct as revenge for brutal Mexican assaults on a hapless US soldier drunk in a café or riding alone to deliver a dispatch. Still others were aware of the differences in religion and culture that made the term *greaser* easy for many Americans to utter and made it even easier for soldiers to take or abuse the Mexicans' land, property, or person.

Yankees measured a "civilized" people by the honor of the men and the virtue of the women. Many found the Mexicans wanting, since the men seemed thieves and rascals and the women flirts and prostitutes. George McClellan sneered that they were content "to roll in the mud, eat their horrible beef and tortillas, and dance all night at their fandangos." This contempt helped many Americans allay any urge they might have had to treat virtually any Mexican with decency.[40]

The army compounded the problem by sometimes enrolling less desirable elements of society and training them poorly. The resultant license for bad behavior manifested itself along the route to Mexico, especially in New Orleans. In February 1847, three volunteers invaded the home of Lavinia Mitchell and attempted to force her into an antechamber. She had hidden a pistol in the room and shot one reprobate soldier in the neck, obliging the others to flee. Several months later, a company of seventy armed Pennsylvania volunteers barged their way into a public ballroom, where a confrontation with the residents, who were equipped with bowie knives and pistols, was barely avoided. Fights, drunkenness, gambling, rowdiness, insubordination, and desertion became all too commonplace as the officers sometimes futilely attempted to maneuver their men into the war zone.[41]

Occupation of a town frequently provided little relief, as the residents of northern Mexico discovered in the summer of 1846. Virtually no American had experienced Mexican food, and while some appreciated the beans and tortillas, liberally sprinkled with ever-present red peppers, many considered the diet too spicy for their taste. Far better, they found, to invade the farms, fields, gardens, and orchards of the Mexicans to supplement their meager fare with fresh fruits, vegetables, and the occasional cow or chicken. Such seizures were rarely compensated. Tensions understandably grew when aggressive Texas volunteers shot Mexican cattle, horses, and mules for amusement in Camargo. The Texans proved particularly problematic. When General William J. Worth relaxed the control of his troops in Monterrey in September, murder, rape, and robbery resulted.[42]

D. H. Hill, who referred to the Texans as "fiends," estimated that more than one hundred civilians were killed in cold blood and said that the city would have been burned had most of the buildings not been fireproof. The volunteers did succeed, however, in torching the thatched huts of the peasantry before being discharged and sent back across the Rio Grande. Hill remarked several months later with some pride that "in spite of the beastly depravity and gross outrages" of the Texans, the people of Monterrey had treated the soldiers of the *regular* army "with civility if not friendship." A distraught Theodore Laidley understood why the Mexicans would have a low opinion of those Americans who apparently had left their consciences behind and committed acts of degeneracy that they would not have considered at home. "A long, long time will it be before we get over the ill consequences of this war," he sagely predicted.[43]

Barbarities occurred both in cities and in small towns. Embedded reporters, often hesitant to register such events, did not want to demean the character of the troops or cast a shadow over the patriotism and purpose of the war effort. Witnessing the results of guerrilla attacks, the reporters understood and even sympathized with reprisals against a civilian population they deemed inferior. Christopher Haile, of the *New Orleans Picayune,* and Jane Storm, of the *New York Sun,* expressed the courage and moral indignation absent in most of their colleagues, pointing out the repeated invasion of homes and assaults on the female inhabitants. Haile called for immediate redress of misdeeds in the area around Monterrey: hang the soldiers involved and dismiss the officers who sanctioned such conduct.

The atrocities began as early as the summer of 1846 in Matamoros. The antiwar *Albion,* of New York, joined the chorus, "the semi-civilized Mexican looked with horror and disgust upon such scenes of beastly depravity and awful wickedness never before enacted in this barbarous land." Boston's *Liberator* demanded a cessation of "the brutal outrages upon their females" and a halt to "this infamous and piratical war." However, American officers seemed either unable or unwilling to effectively control their men.[44]

Generals Taylor, Scott, and Wool were among those of high rank who vehemently complained to Washington in explicit terms about the lawlessness of the volunteers but struggled to effect ongoing changes in their behavior. At a time when disease ran rampant and healthy troops were needed, officers were reluctant to chasten entire units, which might result in animosity and insubordination. Taylor tried hard to thwart the miscreants, arresting and jailing dozens. He had problems with the Kentuckians, especially the Louisville Legion, who committed a series of murders. A band of twenty-five soldiers regularly sought out Mexicans to kill in retaliation for one of their drunken comrades being dispatched by a group of locals. The parents of a victim, a small boy, brought his body to Taylor's tent. He determined that the murderer was a Kentuckian, but no one in the regiment would cooperate, so the general sent the entire unit to the rear in disgrace. Another report identified a group of volunteers who entered the home of a "respectable family," forced the husband out of the room, and held a pistol to the head of the wife while she was ravaged. As the scholar Amy Greenberg sums up the American attitude toward such transgressions, "Vengeance, in their eyes, was justice." Napoleon Dana perceived that word of the abuse of women spread quickly and many families departed towns in advance of the American armies. Those who could not leave locked their doors and windows and prayed.[45]

The volunteers bore the brunt of the criticism, and diaries and reports by the regulars reflected their indignation and embarrassment at the conduct of their comrades. Yet the volunteers had their defenders as well. In January 1847, Samuel Curtis reported the raids on several ranchos near Matamoros by a party of regular dragoons. The soldiers had robbed the men and attempted to defile the women, including tearing all the clothes from a young girl. An incensed Curtis claimed that "such villainous outrages, if they had been committed by volunteers would be heralded all over the country—We would never hear the last of it." In the interest of goodwill with the alcaldes, Curtis was given seven troopers and ordered to investigate the incidents. The resulting interviews revealed the robbery of everything from jewelry to chickens. One woman exhibited her chemise, which had been torn to shreds in a brutal attack "in an attempt to violate her chastity."

Curtis sent his report to General Worth, demanding that the regulars be reprimanded. No such wrongdoing, Curtis said, had been committed by his men. He hectored that the regulars should be cautious before denouncing the volunteers for their behavior and added that to expect perfection among men from all classes in a lawless environment was unrealistic. Curtis agreed that the regulars were better disciplined but said that responsibility for crimes against civilians should be broadly shared.[46]

The Bombardment of Veracruz

That shared accountability involved not only individual random acts of violence but Winfield Scott's well-planned and celebrated assault and bombardment of Veracruz in the spring of 1847. Veracruz, a critical port on the Gulf coast, contained sixty-five hundred inhabitants and was protected by a fifteen-foot-high stone wall with sturdy forts at each end and by the imposing San Juan de Ulúa, 136 guns strong, guarding the harbor, a half mile outside of town. The army, less than impressive in quality and quantity, numbered about 4,500 soldiers. On March 8, Scott's army of 12,000, aided by the US Navy, made a bold and successful landing outside the city. Fearing the high casualties resultant from storming the citadel, the general commenced a siege—a strategy that continued for less than two weeks.

The Mexican commander refused to surrender, and as the impending yellow-fever season loomed, Old Fuss and Feathers advanced his timetable. He began a relentless bombardment that lasted almost a week. Heavy naval guns ashore launched as many as seven thousand shells, some weighing sixty-two pounds, against a vulnerable city. The damage was horrific. Adobe structures were no match for ten-inch projectiles. The Mexicans had no place to hide as buildings disintegrated around and over them, and starvation began to take its toll.[47]

The missives of British Consul Francis Gifford over a month-long period offer an intimate look at the crisis as it unfolded. As early as February 28, Gifford accurately predicted an American attack on Veracruz with "disastrous consequences." Although Scott reassured the Mexicans and the foreign community on March 11 that he had no intention of bombarding the city, the consul had no faith in these guarantees. Gifford shrewdly analyzed the situation: Scott must be well aware of the dangers that climate and disease fostered and the impact a protracted siege would impose on his army. Moving on without seizing Veracruz offered the unrealistic alternative of hostile forces at the rear "and would almost insure its [the army's] destruction." On March 22, the anticipated assault began, and a number of foreigners sought sanctuary on ships in the harbor, "fearing the excesses to be dreaded from an army composed as is that of General Scott."[48]

When Veracruz fell, a furious Gifford berated the Americans for an unrelenting three and a half days of shelling—not of the fort but of the city itself. Imitating Andrew Jackson's tactics at New Orleans, where the Americans hid behind bales of cotton, Scott's men entrenched themselves. They "preferred destroying a fine city unnecessarily," Gifford sneered, to fighting. They neither spared nor respected hospitals or consular headquarters. Miraculously, the women and children at the British, French, and Spanish offices were unhurt, but many foreigners who had not sheltered there had been killed. Scott's rejection of several appeals to evacuate the neutrals appalled Gifford, who could not comprehend the shelling of Mexican civilians—"wretched occupiers." This "unscrupulous use of superior force" by "ruthless assailants" only halted when its victims surrendered.[49]

Gifford wanted the Foreign Office to understand the seriousness of his charges. On April 6, a follow-up report accused Scott of lying. In a meeting with the consuls, Scott claimed that he had been candid about his strategy. Not so, maintained Gifford. Both the general and Commodore Conner had stated that they would fire at the fort exclusively, and thus there had seemed to be no need to evacuate families. And should there be any doubt, Gifford held a letter from Scott to the consuls dated March 25 rejecting a truce to allow neutrals to leave the city.[50]

Gifford was not a lone voice. American journalists, as well as US soldiers, joined in the condemnation of the day and night attack on churches, chapels, convents, hospitals, and homes. The dramatic events, as recorded by a Mexican witness, were published in papers in both countries. He too accused the Americans of cowardice for hiding in their trenches behind cannon while they blasted the innocent. By March 28, more than half the city had been destroyed, millions of dollars in damage inflicted, and as many as a thousand Mexicans killed. US losses amounted to thirteen men killed. A stunned Napoleon Dana described houses with their doors, windows, and furniture blown to pieces. Splendid churches that had contained costly oil paintings, cut-glass chandeliers, and alabaster ornaments now were just "one confused mass of fragments." Staring at the decaying bodies, Dana sighed, "The poor Mexicans."[51]

The Alabaman S. F. Nunnelee praised Scott's efficiency but remembered, "It was a most pitiful scene. I heard the screams of men and women." Lieutenant De Lancey Floyd-Jones walked through the torn-up streets, observing the naked walls that had once been houses and smelling the stench from the decaying bodies. "The destruction of life must have been immense," he concluded. Captain

Robert E. Lee mourned, "My heart bled for the inhabitants." Most present would agree that the impact on the civilians was unacceptable, but who was to blame? Lieutenant John Peck grieved for the "hundreds of poor women and children [who] have been killed or injured for the maintenance of Mexican honor." Meanwhile, cowardly Mexican soldiers hid in bomb-proof shelters or near the wall for protection. Not everyone agreed with his conclusion.[52]

The luster of Scott's triumph rapidly tarnished as word of the civilian casualties spread by letter and newspapers. Upright and noble Americans did not bomb defenseless women and children, yet clearly this had happened. Rather than joining in celebration, the antiwar press called the assault "inhuman butchery" and expressed their sympathy for "the injured and outraged Mexicans." "How could we rejoice," the *Pennsylvania Freeman* declared, "or even seem to look on with any pleasure upon these manifestations of her triumphant enemy?" "How long," the editors pleaded, "must we see pictures like the torn and broken city of Vera Cruz, with its seven hundred bleeding and mangled daughters? How long, O Lord, how long?" As Amy Greenberg points out, Veracruz was the most widely and most negatively covered battle of the Mexican-American War. The sight of the corpses and the blood of dead women and children affected those who attempted to occupy the ruined city. Reporters from New Orleans to Philadelphia decried the carnage, and readers who had cheered Taylor's victories at Monterrey and Buena Vista gave Scott's approach a more somber evaluation.[53]

Scholars hold divergent views. K. Jack Bauer defends the general, pointing out that the bombing tactic worked—"the morale of both inhabitants and defenders was on the verge of shattering"—and at a minimal cost (100 civilians and 80 soldiers) in Mexican lives. Recent biographers of Scott are similarly defensive. Timothy Johnson argues that he was intellectually superior to the officers in his command and, in spite of their desire for heroics, opted for "brain over brawn." His approach resulted in very few American fatalities, and perhaps as many as 400 Mexican civilians killed and 250 injured, along with the 350 Mexican soldiers who died. While papers back home branded the attack as "cruel and unnecessary," his men appreciated not wasting their lives in a likely fruitless charge against the walls. Allan Peskin determined that "the cost was surprisingly low" and that, unjustly, "this impressive achievement was lost on Scott's countrymen." John S. D. Eisenhower does not address the issue of civilian deaths but provides a Mexican account recognizing that "the bombardment was highly effective" and "the devastation was severe." Bauer, Johnson, Peskin, and Eisenhower are largely uncritical and write glowingly of Scott's efforts thereafter to restore order and control to the city and win the support of the Mexican people.[54]

Conversely, Greenberg suggests that the general opted for "civilian deaths over U.S. casualties or any delay in his plans." After all, she reminds us, this is the same Scott who supervised the Cherokee debacle of the "Trail of Tears" in 1838. David Clary caustically refers to the result as "the slaughter of innocents," emphasizing the impact such an attack had on the mind-set of the Mexican people. Scott himself remembered the siege many years later in his memoirs. He had called his staff together and laid out the options. An attack on the city would have resulted in "immense slaughter" on both sides, including two to three thousand of his best soldiers, as well as Mexican men, women, and children. He had found the "horrors of such slaughter . . . most revolting."

Scott had earlier proposed an evacuation of noncombatants and neutrals in Veracruz, an offer the Mexicans and foreigners rejected. Once the seriousness of the shelling manifested itself, the consuls had a change of heart. The general refused their request for safe conduct. He speculated that the delay to the operation and the advent of the *vomito* (yellow fever), plus the approach of Mexican forces, might well have led to the loss of his army, a risk he could not take.

Ultimately, he believed his tactics had been vindicated, particularly since the enemy's loss was "not considerable" and among the civilians "not three were slain—all being in stone houses" where most inhabitants took refuge in the basements. No mention was made of the destruction to the city. The *Emancipator* sarcastically reported Scott's shamelessness in attending Catholic Mass in the shattered cathedral several days after the surrender, saying that he had appeared "very solemnly holding a long wax candle, as if doing penance for the desecration of the church and the massacre of female devotes."[55]

Nothing restores the shine to a military career like victory, and Scott rebounded from whatever damage might have been inflicted with his brilliant capture of Mexico City in September 1847. In 1852, the Whigs nominated him for an ill-fated run for the presidency. He bounced back to command the entire US Army on the eve of the Civil War. Even so, one is left with the assurance given by an officer in March 1847 to an aged ranchero living several miles outside of Veracruz: "The Americans will take your city, Senor; they will commit no outrage—they are Christians—you will return to your house in the city;—do not fear to return—you will have ample protection from our general."[56]

The March to Mexico City

Tragically, the abuse of people and property continued on the road to Mexico City and beyond. Too often, volunteers bore the responsibility for the misdeeds. The assertion of their masculinity spiraled out of control as they engaged in

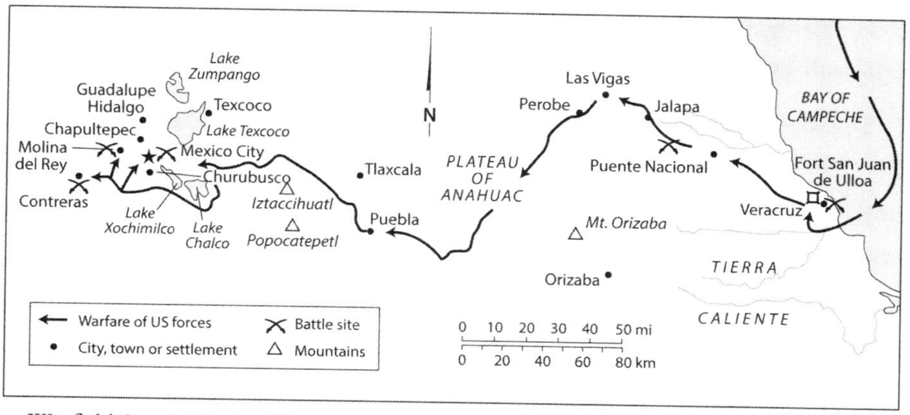

Winfield Scott's Mexico City campaign. (Map by Bill Nelson)

binges of drinking, gambling, and violence. Soon after the fall of Veracruz, American soldiers and sailors looted and burned the nearby village of Boca del Rio and raped the women. Scott tried to restore order by closing the liquor stores and whipping several of the culprits. One soldier was executed. An African American camp follower insulted a Mexican woman and was hanged for his behavior. The antislavery press railed against the racism of Scott and the army for seeking to salve the wounds of war by making an example of the hapless fellow. A month later in Jalapa, a Prussian officer serving with Scott, Carl Von Grone, wrote to his brother that the volunteers "committed the most shameless acts of depravity on a daily basis." Such deeds included robbing churches and women on the street.[57]

D. H. Hill recorded his view of the Mexican landscape as he marched with Scott in August 1847. Passing through the village of San Gregorio, he noted that the volunteers had been there the night before and committed "the most shameful depredations." The population of the ancient town of Xochimilco had been reduced from two thousand to two hundred people by the time Hill arrived. They fled to escape "these savages." Traveling several hours down the road, the officer reached San Augustine, where "the vile volunteers had committed the usual excesses and the lovely town was in good part deserted." Theodore Laidley, in Puebla, likewise sharply criticized the volunteers: "They rob houses, steal, sack churches, ruin families, plunder and pillage. The outrages they have committed, here, will never be known by the people of the U.S. They would not believe it if they did hear of it."[58]

When Scott reached Mexico City, he resumed the bombing tactic used at Veracruz, neutralizing blocks of houses and killing an unknown number of civilians. The surrender of the city on September 14 failed to halt the violence. Rioting continued for the next three days, with the urban poor hurling paving stones from rooftops onto unsuspecting soldiers. Patriots and criminals haunted the alleys, and many a drunken or disoriented Yankee lost his life on a dark night. Individual acts of resistance and mayhem occurred at every turn, and Scott's soldiers resorted to Draconian means in an effort to suppress the snipers, rock-throwers, and knife-wielding bandits. Rapes and murders took place for weeks thereafter. Private homes were vandalized, and a convent was torn up for firewood.

Certainly, Mexican retaliation for violations committed by the US troops, both regulars and volunteers, sparked some of the hostility. Hill referred to the debauchery as "a disgrace to humanity." Soldiers of all ranks engaged in gambling, drunken bouts—"sprees"—and general hell-raising with regularity, especially around payday. Hill contended that the Texans alone murdered two hundred residents of Mexico City in three months of occupation, and added, "It seems impossible to punish a volunteer for anything." To his credit, Scott established military courts to discipline soldiers guilty of offenses against Mexican civilians. Apparently, the administration of the whip and a hanging helped to restore order.

While many in Mexico City continued to engage in acts of defiance, others acceded to the ongoing American presence with varying degrees of compliance. The upper classes were particularly desirous of ending the violence and restoring order. The notion of the underclasses waging war against the Yankees on the streets of Mexico City, destroying property and challenging authority, deeply troubled the gentry. Better to cooperate with the Americans and end civil disobedience. The difference between cooperation and collaboration, however, mattered, and those who crossed the line could well pay the price.

The New Orleans reporter G.W. Kendall related a story in October 1847 that may be true. Vincente García Torres wrote a piece for *El Monitor Republicano* intended as a warning to women who might choose to fraternize too closely with the enemy. The article declared that a certain unnamed "good singer" had become "familiar" with an American officer and would soon be "annexed, like Texas." García Torres was obliged to retract his words two days later, but the damage had been done. A lieutenant, perhaps the gentleman in question, took it upon himself to administer a "terrible cowhiding" to the journalist. Mexican patriots kept an eye on citizens, from politicians to prostitutes, to monitor behavior. Of course, it was much easier to exact "justice" against the latter than against the former when the Americans departed the capital. In January 1848, the *American Star* reported that at least twenty-three hundred women were attached to the US Army, "cooking, washing, tending the sick, and loving the survivors." Their fate would be problematic.[59]

In the North, Samuel Chamberlain and George W. Kendall recounted Indiana and Ohio volunteers' raping and pillaging their way through the states of Nuevo León and Tamaulipas. An assault on a wagon train in March 1847 left twelve teamsters dead. The retribution against the inhabitants included twenty-four Mexicans massacred, excessive taxes placed on the populace, and "their wives and daughters outraged and carried off." The misconduct infuriated Zachary Taylor, who in the absence of witnesses willing to testify could chastise no one.[60]

Fantasy and reality did not meld, but too often collided, for American soldiers in Mexico. Their vision of romancing and perhaps wedding a Castilian beauty became an unfulfilled dream. Instead, they found themselves sharing a bed with a girl in her mid-teens with little promise of a future relationship or engaged with prostitutes, who satisfied their needs temporarily and for a price. The high rate of venereal disease, especially syphilis and gonorrhea, in Saltillo and Mexico City had a predictably demoralizing effect on the army. While many of the troopers rationalized behaviors unacceptable to their families or friends in Baltimore or Boston, the assaults on women are much more troubling and difficult to explain.

Both contemporaries and historians contend that the base nature of many lower-class recruits, devoid of a firm moral center, allowed them to act without conscience. Others say that they did recognize the difference between right and wrong, yet revenge drove them to move both deliberately and impulsively to inflict pain and suffering upon a people who had murdered or disfigured their comrades. While those who exploited or committed crimes against Mexican women are likely in the minority, the behavior of too many American soldiers and the inability of their commanders to alter or halt that behavior demands the severest censure.[61]

7

Sensational Literature

MARITAL BLISS, DOOMED RELATIONSHIPS, AND MALE REDEMPTION

Lieutenant Rainford led his dragoons into a trap. In the summer of 1846, he rode hard to corral and capture the elusive guerrilla leader Don Pedro and his band of fifty renegades near Matamoros. Now the officer found himself the prisoner of the young ranchero—"a ghost, a devil"—who had defied and mystified the US cavalry for weeks. The brave but inexperienced Rainford, a tall, striking fellow "with fire in his hazel eyes," had been defeated and held captive in a hacienda cell in a remote valley. What would be his fate, he wondered, at the hands of these brigands?

As the lieutenant considered the unpleasant possibilities, he heard the lilting song of a young woman outside his quarters and soon discovered that beauty accompanied the voice. Doña María, the wife of the bandit, wished to learn English, and much to his relief, Rainford could ease his incarceration by providing the lessons. Instantly smitten, he recognized his dilemma. The señora retreated to her bedroom, musing that her prisoner was handsome and educated and then fatefully projected, "I fear that I shall love him!" Their emotions scripted, the outcome seemed unclear in a racially charged conflict. Thousands of readers awaited the next edition of the paper, anxious to learn whether the couple were to be star-crossed lovers or life mates.[1]

The saga of Rainford and Doña María, authored by Newton Curtis and published in 1847, was typical of sensational Mexican-American War literature. With tales of adventure, daring, courage, and sensuality, the genre compelled Americans' attention. Sexuality may also have been implicit in the language. Heterosexuality and homosexuality, cross-dressing, and ideologies of womanhood all played major roles in the scholarly deconstruction of the literature. A number of experts in literary studies, led by Shelley Streeby and Jaime Javier Rodriguez, have persuasively argued for a more complex debate in which the nations of the United States and Mexico assume masculine and feminine identities. Empire in Central America, the Caribbean, and the Pacific materialized at the vortex of the discussion over the interplay between gender, race, and foreign policy.

Facing the perplexing dilemma of writing about a war for empire, yet denying any predisposed interest in exploiting another country, mid-nineteenth-century writers avoided the larger theme of territorial annexation and focused instead on the possibilities and limits of racial amalgamation. Promulgating the fantasy of "annexing a señorita," a favorite ploy of expansionist Democrats, army recruiters, and ambitious editors, played well among the laboring classes and those who believed in America's divine mission.[2]

Amy Greenberg expands on the significant confluence of women, domesticity, and expansion in the nineteenth century. Growth and progress were intimately linked, but as that progression took on a more violent tone, female domesticity emerged as a benevolent cover for the fierce nature of a spreading empire. Moreover, the era of Manifest Destiny offered men more than one avenue for asserting their gender: *restrained manhood,* which found its expression in the hardworking, moral, religious, family-based men, who rejected temptations of the flesh and welcomed the moral compass of a good woman; and *martial manhood,* in which violence, sin, and alcohol served as hard-living physical manifestations of a "real man."

Greenberg explains how the struggle between these two versions played out in the Mexican-American War. Restrained men generally opposed the hostilities, while the martial man seized the moment to demonstrate his masculinity. Supported by their female ideal, an attractive woman who asked no moral questions, martial men believed they could dominate a continent. Boosters reiterated the liturgy of fantasy. The sensuous Latina would make herself available to a brave American man eager for adventure and the creation of a robust civilization and advancing Anglo race.[3]

Such thinking fit perfectly into the imagination of a carpenter in Pittsburgh or a clockmaker in Newburyport. For most American readers of what would be considered "pulp fiction," the works' analyses of plot and characters offered a rather predictable, less analytical course. Print technology, literacy, immigration, urbanization, and a healthy two-party system resulted in a working and a middle class that devoured provocative, entertaining, and, importantly, cheap literature. The publishers, housed largely in Boston, New York, and Philadelphia, employed agents in Baltimore, Detroit, St. Louis, and Louisville. The Williams Brothers' *Flag of the Free,* Frederick Gleason and Maturin Murray Ballou's *Flag of Our Union,* and Justin Jones's *Star Spangled Banner* were weekly tabloids that serialized stories and sold them for pennies. Referred to as "dime novels," an entire volume might cost twelve to twenty-five cents. Profit and patriotism trumped politics or class conflict. The editors huckstered romance, melodrama, and empire.

The writers, mostly men, but occasionally a woman, met the demand with a florid flourish. Charles E. Averill, Harry Halyard, Ned Buntline, Joseph Ingraham, Harry Hazel, George Lippard, and Eliza Allen joined Curtis in keeping readers on the edge of their seats. Their saccharine style and chivalric content would not be confused with Edgar Allan Poe, Herman Melville, or Nathaniel Hawthorne, but they rewarded their publishers with a generous payday and their audience with a glorious tale. More accomplished writers swallowed hard at the compromise.[4]

Perhaps the most telling self-revelation of how literature had quickly shifted in theme and audience was recounted by the popular antiwar poet and social activist Sara Jane Clarke, who wrote under the pseudonym Grace Greenwood. Clarke, while traveling on a train in the summer of 1849, observed the reading habits of a female companion in her compartment. The woman put down a contemporary classic to pick up "a miserable Mexican War story, with diabolical wood cuts" and an outrageous title. Horrified that the woman was reading "for the sake of the story alone," Clarke pondered that "some people seem to have a sort of love for the beautiful, existing with the propensities for the commonplace and the low; as cattle devour roses and cabbages with the same course relish." Clarke only momentarily rejected the future of popular literature: within a year Grace Greenwood had written her own potboiler.[5]

The authors' timing was risky. When many of the novels were penned, Mexico City had not yet fallen, nor had the treaty of Guadalupe Hidalgo been negotiated to determine the diplomatic outcome of the war. Consequently, the action often occurred in and around Monterrey in 1846 or Veracruz in early 1847. While the Yankee characters exuded confidence of ultimate victory, obvious ruts existed on the road to the Halls of Montezuma. What to do with the nettlesome immigrants, particularly the Irish Catholics? Millions poured into the United States to supplement the labor force, and thousands joined the army, but their loyalty to the nation and their effect on the culture were widely questioned.

The historians Jenny Franchot and John C. Pinheiro document a virtual paranoia about Rome and how those long-standing Protestant fears played out both along the Atlantic Seaboard and in the heart of the beast, Catholic Mexico. Franchot explains how Americans sought to cleanse themselves from the pollution of Europe and Catholicism. The New World offered separation by water—the

Atlantic Ocean—and an opportunity to start afresh in "Nature's nation," free from the sin and corruption of the city, reborn on the frontier. History itself was defined within a Protestant context, as a contest "between European contamination and American purity." Should the pope, his priests, and his minions be feared or pitied? Many Protestants agreed that the Catholic Church deceived its followers with tall tales, myths, and miracles, and therein rested its danger. Rome looked backward, not forward.[6]

Attacks on the Church increased exponentially with the flow of immigrants in the 1830s and 1840s. The nativist Samuel F. B. Morse, the inventor of the telegraph, railed in the press against potential papal conspiracies, while the public devoured copies of salacious tales of Catholic immorality. Rebecca Reed's *Six Months in a Convent* and María Monk's *Awful Disclosures of the Hotel Dieu Nunnery* revealed the salacious and devious core of Catholicism. Reed and Monk claimed to have firsthand knowledge of the illicit notions planted in the minds of innocent young women by depraved clerics and the sexual liaisons—and children—that resulted. Thousands of God-fearing Protestants needed no more information.[7]

For the more intellectually curious, William H. Prescott's *History of the Conquest of Mexico* became a blockbuster bestseller. Prescott, a conservative Boston Whig, took concerns about Catholicism to a new level. Amid mounting anxiety about the Irish in the Northeast, should the United States really contemplate adding Hispanic Catholics in the Southwest? Prescott's account of Hernán Cortés's march from Veracruz to Mexico City in 1519 not only foreshadowed the march of Winfield Scott in 1847 but also explored the racial and cultural dynamic of a Mexico forming an amalgam of Aztec and Spanish. The resultant fusion offered territory-minded Americans an unsavory blend of mixed races and superstitious religion. As Prescott cautioned his sister, "The Spanish blood will not mix well with the Yankee."[8]

Several years later, US soldiers tested Prescott's hypothesis and explored the legitimacy of nativist fears. Pinheiro demonstrates how the synthesis suggested by Lyman Beecher's *A Plea for the West* (1835) laid the interpretive foundation for many Americans', including soldiers', understanding of Mexicans. The tract linked republican liberty, Protestant religion, and social, economic, and political progress. Mexico offered fertile ground for assessing preconceived prejudices about the antirepublican, idolatrous nature of the "Catholic race." For Anglo-Americans, Mexico would confirm their impressions of Latin inferiority, which they believed was the result not only of race but also of religion. Their experiences south of the border "provided fresh evidence of Catholic debauchery, economic stagnation, and political tyranny." Soldiers decried the priesthood as corrupt and attacked the system of peonage as worse than slavery. The large Indian population only made the redemption of the country more difficult. Republican Protestantism might save Mexico, but the struggle would be difficult, and the Catholic Church would have to be crushed.[9]

The soldiers were often emotionally torn. They admired the churches, spoke with friars, attended Mass, and particularly enjoyed observing attractive Mexican women at prayer. Conversely, the splendor of an edifice such as the three-hundred-year-old Puebla cathedral or the pomp and perplexing ritual of the Mass seemed overpowering, off-putting, and inconsistent with the poverty and ignorance the men found in Mexico. The conduct of a number of priests—smoking, drinking, gambling, and womanizing—left the Americans angry and distraught. Sadly, the lack of respect for the faith spilled over into atrocious behavior on the part of soldiers, who physically attacked clerics and vandalized and looted churches and convents.[10]

For many Americans, their prejudices had come full circle. Attitudes held about Catholics before the war were confirmed in Mexico and melded conveniently with evolving views of the Irish. Skepticism about immigrant soldiers had increased when Irish Americans began deserting the US Army before Congress declared war in May 1846. Although thousands of Irishmen volunteered and served loyally and bravely, attention then and now has focused on the small number who joined the Saint Patrick's Battalion. Heralded and mythologized in popular culture, including a motion picture, were the San Patricios traitors or freedom fighters? More than seventy of these men, elements of the battalion who fought valiantly in the defense of Mexico City and were captured and severely punished, prompted many writers and the general public to grant the Irish a dubious place in the literature. Both Harry Halyard's *The Chieftain of Churubusco* and Charles Averill's *The Mexican Ranchero* depicted the desertion theme. The Irish may have been white, but in an era troubled by a rising nativist sentiment, their patriotism and trustworthiness remained under suspicion.[11]

Race became an increasingly significant theme. Indians made up a large percentage of the Mexican population, and their place and role could not be ignored. The novelists generally dealt with this issue by casting mestizos and Indians as loyal servants who frequently died defending their Castilian mistresses. More problematically, how would the editors and writers handle the matter of interracial courtship and marriage within the context of the Mexican-American War? Such relationships—invariably involving a dashing young American officer from Kentucky and a young (late teens), fair señorita—needed a delicate touch.

The historical record suggests that while a number of ambitious Americans married Mexican women in the borderlands of New Mexico, Texas, and California, the vast majority of Americans had no knowledge of those relationships. Would they have approved the nuptials of a son of the Bluegrass to a Castilian beauty? Perhaps. The writers of the serialized saga varied in their solutions to the dilemma of racial romance on the basis not only of skin color but of class and ethnicity as well.

What, then, was the fate of Lieutenant Rainford and Doña María? Their budding romance intertwined with Mexican avarice and infidelity, two common themes in the literature. Doña María Guadalupe had escaped a convent and a promised union with the conniving Chevalier Rijon by choosing to live as the reported mistress of the bandit chief Don Pedro. The Chevalier, "an unprincipled villain," had an affair with Zulia, the ambitious and avaricious young wife of Doña María's father, a clear sign of the unworthiness of both Zulia and Rijon.[12]

The unlucky Rainford had escaped the bandits but was captured by the Mexican Army and turned over to the governor in Monterrey to be hanged as a spy. Don Pedro fared no better, with a thousand pieces of gold placed on his head as a traitor. When the Americans attacked the city, Don Pedro, with the assistance of several of Rainford's Kentucky mates, took advantage of the confusion to free the lieutenant from prison. In the process, Don Pedro confronted the Chevalier and dispatched him with a sword blow. The ranchero chief hurried Rainford back to the camp, where Don Pedro revealed himself to be . . . Doña María! Monterrey soon fell to Taylor's forces, and Doña María, who retired her weapon, wed Rainford. Since they planned on residing at her father's sumptuous estate, his compatriots expressed their envy at his good fortune—beauty *and* wealth. Exactly how the American officer would juxtapose the ongoing war with his new life of leisure and marital bliss remained unclear.[13]

Newton Curtis, a small-town New York teacher, left his audience with a warm glow, but perhaps no American writer was better suited to telling the tale of doomed relations than the irrepressible Edward Judson. Born into a middle-class Yankee family in 1821, the rebellious and peripatetic Judson served as a midshipman in the US Navy and a newspaperman in the West before the Mexican-American War. Judson possessed a fondness for drink and women. When a dalliance in Nashville resulted in a duel and the death of the betrayed husband, unhappy relatives attempted to lynch Judson, who survived and reinvented himself in New York under the name Ned Buntline.

Buntline seized the moment. In several bestselling works, he escorted his readers over familiar battlefields, commencing with Monterrey and culminating

Journalist and novelist Ned Buntline (Edward Judson). From *The Life and Times of Ned Buntline,* 1919.

with the bloodletting at Buena Vista, always keeping his audience guessing by varying his conclusions. The tale *Magdalena* signifies that somewhat darker turn. Charley Brackett, half Castilian, half American, and all Texas Ranger, is "a true man." Dark-skinned, fluent in Spanish, and with a knowledge of weaponry, in the early months of 1847 Brackett seems the perfect choice for Zachary Taylor to send into Mexico as a spy. His mission takes him on the road to Saltillo and the hacienda of Don Ignatius Valdez and his daughters Magdalena and Ximena. The striking seventeen-year-old Magdalena, known as the Maiden of Buena Vista, has captured the hearts of many a cavalier, but especially the gallant and brutal Colonel Gustave Alfrede.[14]

Readers learn that the colonel in an earlier raid into Texas had raped and murdered Brackett's mother and sister. Alfrede succeeds in capturing Charley only to have him escape, aided and abetted by the lovestruck Magdalena. Such defiance prompts Alfrede to confiscate the hacienda and demand his immediate marriage to Magdalena, or he will use his power to force the entire family into peonage. Brackett's attempt to rescue Magdalena fails, he is captured (again), and the Valdez family faces a horrible fate until the Rangers break into the estate, freeing the family and allowing the spontaneous vows of Charley and Magdalena. American resistance quickly collapses, however, the Rangers are driven off, and Charley is captured (for a third time) by Colonel Alfrede. Magdalena promptly demonstrates her cunning, charm, and courage by freeing Charley from San Luis Potosí prison. While the plot goes awry, and Alfrede kills Magdalena's faithful Indian servant, Zalupah, Brackett escapes to Taylor's lines at Buena Vista and is soon reunited with Magdalena, Ximena, and Don Ignatius.[15]

Any hopes for a happy ending are quickly dashed, as the loyal Charley rushes to the side of Old Rough and Ready. Meanwhile, Magdalena tells her father, "We are not Mexicans. Spain alone has a right to our allegiance." As for her true devotion, she confides, "When I wedded him, I became an American." Magdalena waits, but Charley fails to return from the front lines, a scene of undeniable bravery but terrible casualties. Wandering through the bloodbath, she discovers, side by side, the dead bodies of her beloved and Alfrede. The scene prompts the disconsolate Magdalena, in stark imitation of Romeo and Juliet, to kill herself with a dagger hung about her neck. Buntline's tale concludes with the gloomy but morally satisfying observation, "The virgin bride sleeps by the side of her husband." In fact, Charley himself was compromised by his dark skin and mixed blood. Although he shared vows with the Castilian Magdalena, she denied her Mexican heritage, and the reader senses there might well have been no place for them in a postwar world.[16]

Buntline lightens the mood in *The Volunteer: or, The Maid of Monterey.* The hero, George Blakey, is a "dashing, true-hearted" lad of 21, the only son of respectable mercantile parents in Logan County, on the Kentucky frontier. While loved and admired, George fits a typical mold: astute and bright, he "had never been inside of a school house." Duty overpowers the tears of his mother, as "Captain Blakey" organizes a company of local boys to respond to the call. Importantly, we are assured that George left no *one* sweetheart behind—all the fair maidens of the county lamented his departure.[17]

The Kentuckians see almost immediate action in September 1846 at Monterey, where the chivalric captain saves the life of a stricken Mexican cavalry officer. Once again, cross-dressing plays a major role, as we discover that the officer is Edwina Canales, the sister of a local guerrilla leader. The gallant Blakey not only frees Edwina but sends her on her way on his horse. We have a foreshadowing

$100 PRIZE TALE!

THE VOLUNTEER:

OR,

THE MAID OF MONTEREY.

A Tale of the Mexican War.

The Heroine of Monterey cheering her companions on to battle.

BY NED BUNTLINE.

F. GLEASON'S PUBLISHING HALL,
CORNER OF TREMONT AND COURT STREETS, BOSTON.
S. FRENCH, 293 Broadway, New York. A. WINCH, 116 Chestnut Street, Philadelphia
STRATTON & BARNARD, 121 Main Street, Cincinnati. T. S. HAWKS,
Post Office Building, Buffalo. J. A. ROYS, 37 Woodward Avenue,
Detroit. WM. TAYLOR, North Street, Baltimore. FLETCH-
ER & SELLERS, Rue Champs Elysees, New Orleans.

Cover illustration from *The Volunteer: or, The Maid of Monterey. A Tale of the Mexican War,* by Ned Buntline, 1847. (Courtesy of the Bancroft Library, University of California–Berkeley.)

of their destiny when George murmurs, "Beautiful as she is brave" as he watches her "noble figure" depart.[18]

As the plot progresses, Buntline reveals that "Edwina" is really Helen Vicars, the daughter of prominent Texas parents, an Anglo father and Mexican mother, who recently had been killed. Her father's ethnicity offers the reader hope that the relationship may well have a future. Midway through the novel, the smitten Blakey falls desperately in love. Edwina confesses, much to his chagrin, that she cannot reciprocate, since he has invaded and destroyed her country. This response only heightens George's affection.[19]

The villain of the story, Gorin, is the very Texas Ranger who fruitlessly sought Edwina's hand, murdered her parents, and presently was fighting with Taylor's forces. Blakey saves Edwina from Gorin's clutches, then is captured and facing a firing squad, whereupon she saves his life. Edwina only reveals her passion when she realizes that George's patriotism rivals her own and he would not abandon his men or duty—even for her. "Now I love you," she confesses. "You are indeed a soldier and a man." The tale revolves around the repeated captures, near-fatal experiences, and timely rescues of both the hero and heroine, as they clash with rival armies, the evil Gorin, and each other.[20]

Gorin meets his fate at the hands of Mexican lancers, but miraculously, both Edwina and George survive the awful carnage at Buena Vista. His enlistment over, George persuades Edwina to leave her brothers and accompany him back to Logan County. A letter to his parents advising them of his marriage prompts a predictable discussion. Uncle Ned and Aunt Letty grouse that "blue eyes are prettier than black ones any day" and speculate that George could have found a perfectly suitable girl in the neighborhood. Uncle Ned allows, however, that George fought hard for his nation and says that if he wants to bring back "some curiosity of the country," he probably deserves the reward. After due deliberation, Ned and Letty agree that they will accept "a real Mexican gal" as their own. The barbeque in the village of Rural Choice attracts more than a thousand cheering Kentuckians to welcome their returning heroes and the Maid of Monterey.[21]

Buntline draws the reader in with the ideal couple, the handsome, courageous, and principled George Blakey and the beautiful, high-spirited, and equally dedicated Edwina Canales. She shines as the cross-dressing cavalry officer, relentlessly swinging her sword as the cowardly Mexican soldiers around her flee. When Edwina dons female attire, she is the classic señorita, radiating her feminine side and making her yet more attractive to the lovestruck George. Their survival, wedding, and return to Kentucky, however, are all made possible by her Creole status. "Helen Vicars" can be embraced by the residents of Rural

Choice. If she had been an Indian or a mestiza, her reception as the Maid of Monterey would perhaps have been much different—if it had taken place at all.

Charles Averill crafted two very popular novelettes with cumbersome titles and familiar themes, *The Mexican Ranchero; or, The Maid of the Chaparral: A Romance of the Mexican War* (1847) and *The Secret Service Ship; or, The Fall of San Juan D'Ulloa: A Thrilling Tale of the Mexican War* (1848). The ranchero, General Raphael Rejon, and the maiden, his sister Buena, join forces with Captain Herbert Harold and his sister Alfredine. The Mexicans are quickly validated by our knowledge that they are half American. This novel can end well, at least for the heroes. The villain, an Irish deserter based upon the San Patricio leader John Riley, is hanged, while the legendary cross-dressing guerrilla Buena Rejon kills his dark-skinned henchman and chops off his head. Raphael is a renegade chief sworn to vengeance against the invader. Yet, he is a patriot, brave, honest, and true. He soon renounces violence against the Americans, then weds Alfredine, and remains in Mexico. Buena has a sensitive side; she marries Harold, and they move to his plantation in Virginia.[22]

In the *Secret Service Ship,* Isora La Vega disguises herself as the head of a group of banditti and fights heroically for the Mexican Army. On several occasions, Isora saves her love, the naval officer William Rogers, from captivity with her physical prowess and courage. He in turn rescues her. They become engaged, but both realize that their commitment to their own nations prohibits a union as long as the war continues. Torn between despair and respect, Rogers exults, "You are indeed a noble girl, Mexico's maidens are the noblest gem and the most beauteous flower of her fair land."[23]

The novels' outcomes become predictable, but they generally hold brighter prospects if the woman is Anglo. Henry Halyard's *The Heroine of Tampico* gives us Avaline Allerton, the Boston-educated daughter of a bankrupt American merchant. To salvage his business and replenish his coffers, the unscrupulous George Allerton conspires with his mistress to marry Avaline to the rich Don Vincenzio. Avaline thwarts his plan temporarily by feigning her death and then escaping to a nunnery. While in New England, Avaline had met the intrepid Marine lieutenant Charles Wallingford, the son of a successful trader.[24]

As the war comes to Tampico, Wallingford appears to rescue Avaline from her plight and then finds himself imprisoned for attacking Don Vincenzio. In the dramatic conclusion, Wallingford and a party of American soldiers are caught in open country by a larger company of Mexicans. Wounded, and facing certain death at the hands of the evil Don, Wallingford sees Avaline in front of him with a pistol in one hand and the Stars and Stripes in the other. She defiantly stands her ground against all odds and shoots the Don, prompting his awestruck men to retreat. Fortunately, her remorseful father kills himself, clearing the marital pathway and allowing the celebrated "Heroine of Tampico" to be whisked off to New York, where she and Charles marry and presumably live thereafter in comfort and happiness.[25]

In sharp contrast to the stories by their male counterparts, those crafted by female authors often conveyed a redemptive touch, perhaps none more so than the account of Eliza Allen, who claimed that her travels and tribulations were indeed factual. Surely, the Brontë sisters could not have composed a more compelling saga of ill-fated romance. William Billings, the son of poor but respectable Canadian parents, courts the lovely twenty-year-old Eliza Allen, the daughter of one of the first families of Eastport, Maine. Because of their class difference, the relationship is kept secret from Eliza's parents and two protective brothers. Love flowers, however, and the couple pledge their undying devotion. The young swain gives his Eliza a ring, a token of little intrinsic value but deep meaning, with his name engraved upon it. She offers him a miniature of herself.[26]

When Eliza admits to her parents their intent to marry, they of course upbraid her and forbid her to see William under threat of disinheritance and expulsion from the family. Eliza weighs duty against devotion—not an easy choice. She is rescued from her dilemma by a letter from William saying that he cannot put her through such an emotional crucible and has decided to join the volunteers heading off for Mexico. Vowing his eternal love, he promises that should he "fall pierced by the lance of a fierce and bloody Mexican" and be left exposed to die, his last thoughts will be of her. Shocked and bereft, Eliza quickly determines to follow William and share "every danger which he might be called upon to encounter." So begins the Mexican-American War tale of *The Female Volunteer; or the Life, and Wonderful Adventures of Miss Eliza Allen.*[27]

Although a somewhat transparent Victorian romance, Eliza's story has some credibility within the context of her society. However, what follows has been understandably subjected to criticism in terms of its legitimacy. Slim of body, she dramatically cuts her long hair and acquires a male outfit. Thus reconfigured, Eliza travels to Portland unrecognized, takes the name George Mead, and joins a volunteer regiment headed for the Rio Grande. Only several weeks distanced from her comfortable home in Eastport, she finds herself advancing with Taylor's army on the walls at Monterrey. Eliza details the campaign and "the murderous slaughter" from which she somehow emerges unscathed. Her enlistment expires and, not having located William, she joins up with General Scott, who is on his way to Mexico City.[28]

THE FEMALE VOLUNTEER;

OR THE

LIFE, AND WONDERFUL ADVENTURES OF

MISS ELIZA ALLEN,

A YOUNG LADY OF EASTPORT, MAINE.

ELIZA ALLEN

Being a truthful and well-authenticated narrative of her parentage, birth and early life—her love for one whom her parents disapproved—his departure for Mexico—her determination to follow him at all hazards—her flight in man's attire—enlistment—terriffic battles of Mexico—her wounds—voyage to California—the shipwreck and loss of her companions—her miraculous escape—return to her native land—meeting of the lovers—reconciliation of her parents—marriage, and happy termination of all her trials and sorrows.

Cover illustration from *The Female Volunteer; or the Life, and Wonderful Adventures of Miss Eliza Allen, a Young Lady of Eastport, Maine*, by Eliza Allen, 1851. (Courtesy of the Indiana University Libraries, http://purl.dlib.indiana.edu/iudl/wright/VAC6427.)

Tanned, blistered, and more muscular, Eliza contends that her own mother would not recognize her. Her left arm cut by a saber at Cerro Gordo, she fears that the visiting surgeon might reveal her gender. She escapes this dire prospect, and better news followed. As fate would have it, William, with a wound to his hip, lies only a few feet distant. He does not recognize her then, nor does he recognize her when they are convalescing in a private home in Mexico City. Perhaps just as troubling, the don of the estate becomes fond of "George" and encourages him to remain in Mexico, manage his properties, and marry one of his daughters. Demurring, George instead tests William's fidelity by suggesting that *he* have a liaison with one of the daughters. William proves worthy, rejecting the overture and confiding to George that he loves another far away.[29]

As the war ends, George and William have become friends. After a year of harrowing episodes, including disastrous exposure to both shipwrecks and card sharps, a morally weakened William yields to the temptations of fickle friends, alcohol, and gambling. A much wiser George refrains from such vices and squirrels away a share of the fruits of their labor—a total of thirteen thousand dollars in California gold. Upon their return to Boston, Eliza transforms herself into her female form and then arranges a rendezvous with William to confess her faux identity. Producing the earlier tokens of their affection, they reaffirmed their love and decided to wed. Eliza's distraught but now relieved and repentant parents gave the ceremony their approbation. The story ends happily with their tearful reunion in Maine, the vows exchanged in the Allen family home.[30]

Eliza Allen's narrative, published in Eastport in 1851, quite possibly sold well in its day. The subject matter, including the transgendered identity claimed by the heroine, strays only somewhat from conventional sexual norms of the era. Eliza makes no great claim to strength, bravery, or glorious deeds in combat. Her tale is one of survival and bonding with her mates. It is a story of an emotional quest and unfulfilled love. George carefully fails to name any military unit or officer, other than Taylor and Scott, and offers no clues or details as to precise locations or dates. Her descriptions of the fighting include general summaries of the horrors of war: whizzing bullets, exploding shells, falling comrades, and glorious victory. Eliza demonstrates both compassion for the Mexicans and an appropriate amount of patriotism toward the flag and the sacrifice of her brethren.

Ultimately, however, this is a love story filled with adventure. Tucked away in the tranquility of their parlors, many Victorian women likely found the fantasy of donning the uniform and acting out exploits on the battlefields and gold fields appealing. Eliza also redeems her man, showing him financial discipline, planning, and restraint when he gives way to temptation. Her nest egg, not his, emerges from their adventure to give them a new start in life. While the tale is satisfying to the imagination, Eliza Allen probably never fought in the Mexican-American War. However, the publication of *The Female Volunteer* is evidence of the interest in the conflict on the part of both men and women of that generation, perhaps even in antiwar New England.

In 1850, Grace Greenwood constructed a tale of a romance apparently doomed by a formidable and principled woman who challenged her ambitious and determined beau. The story "The Volunteer" begins with a troubling conversation in "a handsome house in a western city" between Margaret Neale and her fiancé, Herbert Moore. With some parallels to the saga of Eliza Allen and William Billings, Moore, a boy of poor and obscure origins, has been taken under the wing of Margaret's father, a successful Scottish merchant. Young Herbert, a generous fellow of warm heart and modest education, rises to the post of chief clerk in the Neale firm. Though he earns a fine salary and supports his widowed mother, Herbert realizes that his success has been built on the outreach and blessing of his patron. What to do, then, when he falls in love with the beauteous Margaret? Waves of inadequacy sweep over Moore, the "penniless protégé," who would be viewed by society as little more than a merciless schemer if he married Margaret. Success in his own right would provide for equality in the relationship and in the eyes of the townspeople. The answer, of course, rests in achieving fame and glory in the Mexican-American War.[31]

Herbert urges Margaret to utilize her influence, and that of her family, to help him obtain a commission as an officer in a newly formed company. Rather than assisting him, the outraged woman admits her shock and amazement. How could Herbert sacrifice his principles and enlist in "this most unrighteous war—a war without one just cause, or one noble object; but waged against an unoffending people, in the rapacity of conquest, and for the extension and perpetuation of human slavery?" The author confides that Herbert clearly does not understand the complexity of Margaret's persona and intellect. He observes her "devoted love and clinging tenderness," while neglecting to appreciate her "vigorous mind, clear judgment, and hearty independence."[32]

Upon her father's death, Margaret, who is well respected throughout the community, inherits his considerable fortune. Greenwood assures the reader that Margaret is "a strong, impressive, decidedly, though delightful, individual." An angry Margaret accepts Herbert's condemnation of the war and its purposes, but she is confounded by his actions taken out of stubborn pride. He is no longer the man to whom she gave her heart, devotion, and faith. Sadly, the lovers reached an impasse, and the engagement is shattered.[33]

A defiant Herbert enlists as a private and fights valorously throughout the conflict. He eventually becomes disenchanted, however, as the "coarse and vicious" men of his regiment betray any nobility in pursuing the war. As Herbert, wounded and ill, makes his way home, his memory is shrouded in disillusionment rather than glory. Margaret was right. Alone, delirious, and close to death, he finds comfort in the Neale home. She, of course, has not abandoned him, but emerges as his healing angel. Thoroughly repentant and humiliated, Herbert is determined to speak out for codes of justice and freedom. He pens a farewell letter to Margaret, confessing that he "has been taught a deeper reverence for woman, a higher estimate, a more adoring worship of love." She intercepts his departure, assures him of her undying love and, most importantly, that she "gloried in his victory over self, in your regeneration."[34]

The economic, intellectual, and, in particular, moral superiority of Margaret Neale hallmarks the story. Crafted several years after the Seneca Falls gathering, Greenwood's tale of a consistently confident, resilient, and unyieldingly principled woman resonated with a New England constituency that largely rejected both slavery and the Mexican-American War. The somewhat hapless but caring Herbert paid a heavy price for his misplaced ideals of American empire and a myopic view of women. Fortunately, Margaret melded compassion and understanding with her affection in accepting Herbert's confession and redemption. Without her, his rebirth would have been impossible.

A half century later, in the 1890s, several American writers found an impetus to recapture the romance and intrigue of the Mexican-American War as the nation embarked on a second wave of imperial ventures. As with Greenwood, the conflict remained a slave owners' conspiracy, and the relationship between the Spanish maid—no matter how light-skinned and elevated in class—and the American officer might still be doomed. The writer John Roy Musick emphasized in the introduction to his 1893 antiwar novel *Humbled Pride,* "Mexicans were not so far advanced in civilization as Americans." Yet, the war itself was "of a doubtful quality," and the United States had little to be proud of in its victory. The armies on both sides, however, did retain an air of nobility, as Mexican bandits and guerrillas emerged as the villains in the piece.[35]

More than a story of a dubious conflict, *Humbled Pride* is the saga of two proud families, the Stevenses and Estevans. They actually share common roots in Havana in 1561, but fate, and a few rearranged letters, separated them. By 1840, Fernando Stevens, the firm and kindly patron of his clan, has purchased a thousand acres of prime Kentucky land, which is farmed by his numerous slaves. His son, Arthur, volunteers early in the war and finds himself an officer with Taylor's forces moving against Monterrey in September 1846.

General Estevan owns an extensive hacienda outside Puebla and takes great pride in his son, Captain Felipe, and his celebrated daughter, Madelina. Felipe has already engaged in action against the Americans and saved Arthur from certain death, amazingly, by a Comanche spear. The young lancer then dashes to the city to help prepare for the defense of the town and rescue his sister. Madelina, long the object of many suitors, has been proclaimed the Belle of Monterrey. Musick reminds the reader of the grace of Mexican women on the dance floor, their cheerful voice in song, and their small hands and feet. However, "generally they are too dark to be beautiful," he maintains, except for the purely Spanish women, who are "exceedingly" lovely. Madelina, "of the bluest blood of Old Castile," captivates any gathering with her many charms.[36]

The young maiden rightfully fears for her country. The "northern barbarians" take advantage of Mexico's political weakness and internal divisions to press Monterrey on every side. Felipe, desperate to get his sister out of the city, seeks safe passage through the American lines. The solution emerges in the form of the captain from Kentucky, who gratefully promises to guide and protect Madelina. He is struck by her beauty; she perceives that he is "handsome, gallant, and no doubt brave." Danger persists. Arthur saves Felipe's life at Buena Vista, and Felipe then rescues Arthur and Madelina from bandits. As the bond between the two men strengthens in spite of their loyalties, Arthur falls in love with Madelina.[37]

Significantly, their conversations prompt Arthur to question the war and why he is fighting the Mexicans. What cause has he to quarrel with them? They have never invaded American soil. Arthur comes to believe that the war is "a giant swindle to rob Mexico of a large part of her territory." Veracruz and Mexico City fall, and Arthur leads his company in ferreting out guerrillas near Puebla. He discovers that Felipe has been wounded and is recovering at the family hacienda. Seeking to comfort Felipe, as well as to court his sister, Arthur fails miserably in trying to persuade Madelina of his innocence in the death and destruction brought upon her people. "You have humbled the pride of Mexico, señor," she cries, "and I cannot wed you." A second discussion strikes a similar note: "You are an American, and that as such you humbled our flag and slew women and children." Duly chastened and disconsolate, "Arthur went home a conqueror, yet sad, broken hearted and humbled."[38]

This ill-fated romance once again engages the lustrous, affluent belle parrying with an audacious and lovestruck American officer. His sixteenth-century Spanish roots and the end of the war suggest some promise of a happy outcome, but her staunch sense of national pride and the bloody sacrifice of the Mexican people are simply too great to overcome. After cutting through the patina of class and race, the author offers an interesting and even-handed portrayal of the Mexican perspective of the war, set in the context of their culture, food, habits, and relationships. Through the course of the conflict, Arthur questions, evolves, and matures. Madelina weeps, but grows more dedicated to her people and more self-confident. Arthur predicts that she will seek the solace of a convent within six months. Perhaps so, but only one woman is on the stage in this novel, and she is not be trifled with.

A young Princeton playwright latched onto a similar theme and scripted a period piece simply titled *Mexico.* Reworked and given the more commanding moniker *Captain Impudence,* the play became a smash hit in New York in 1897 and was rapidly adapted into a novel by Arthur D. Hall. The narrative chronicles the adventures of Captain Will Shields of Kentucky, predictably handsome and fearless, as he fights his way from Monterrey to Mexico City. The reader is rewarded not only by tales of Shields's bravado but also by sifting out his ongoing relationships with Jovita Talamanca and Lucretia Bugg. A charming, flirtatious, moody, dark-eyed, dark-tressed maiden, Jovita "was as brilliant as she was beautiful," an heiress and the only child of a well-to-do father in Monterrey.

In contrast, Lucretia appears to be the eighteen-year-old picture of "coquettish innocence, dainty maidenhood, and perfect proportion." Her delicate complexion is accented by auburn hair, blue eyes, and "a gown of pale blue muslin with one crimson rose in her bosom." She is the daughter of the company commander. Although the story was written a half century after the war, the outcome seems inevitable. Shields survives the conflict, often aided by information provided by the daring Jovita, who compromises her patriotism for the man she loves. Lucretia, though spirited, remains within the proper sphere of the Victorian woman and wins the captain's heart. The need for a choice, however, is resolved when Jovita throws herself in front of a bullet intended for Shields. While the reader is assured of Jovita's Spanish heritage, loveliness, intelligence, wealth, and courage, Lucretia's major asset appears to be that she is "exceedingly pretty"—and Anglo.

When the play premiered on Broadway, Edward Dunham, of the *New York Times,* praised the work as "brisk, lively, entertaining drama, mirth provoking and thrilling by turns." The author himself carried the lead as Captain Shields, while his wife, Selina Fetter, assumed "the least grateful" of the major roles, Jovita Talamanca. Jovita's divided loyalties and foreseeable fate seem to have been lost upon Dunham, who characterized her as "the vengeful, emotional Mexican woman, and, perhaps, the least understandable." At least Selina acted the part "with zeal and is always picturesque." Shields's ultimate selection of the virginal

Lucretia confirms the continuity of American racial and gender attitudes. Given a choice, Shields could not prefer a Latina over an Anglo woman.[39]

The dime novel of the nineteenth century moved American literature to another level. Although pulp fiction of dubious literary quality, the stylized and sensational images created by the writers ushered in a new wave of popular culture that took advantage of advances in printing and distribution. In an increasingly literate nation, these stories catered to the fascination and taste of urban middle-class as well as rural and working-class Americans. The authors took literary risks that pushed their readers into the realm of feelings, sentimentality, emotion, shock, and sympathy. Love was often lost, gained, and lost again, all within a hundred pages. The plots laid out issues of gender, race, ethnicity, and class and sometimes teased with the resolution. The wary novelist played cautiously with the conventions of the early Victorian woman, "the cult of true womanhood," in stretching the boundaries of the characters.

The male heroes generally were young, courageous officers of undetermined class, some economic means, and Anglo ancestry. The author sent a signal if the hero, such as the ill-fated Charley Brackett, was himself of mixed blood. Almost invariably the protagonist came from Kentucky, pioneered by Daniel Boone and populated by the sons of Virginia gentry and common folk alike. The state epitomized the vision of the Protestant agrarian republic with a blended sectional identity and filled with hope and opportunity. By the 1840s, the frontier mighty have moved on, but Americans still romanticized about the Bluegrass ideal of manliness, family, and nation.

Both Eliza Allen and Grace Greenwood flirted with the boundaries of their redemptive, upright, and knowledgeable women, who also seemed independent and empowered. The heroines in most novels constructed by men similarly flouted social norms; they were upper-class American or Castilian belles who defied their parents' wishes, cross-dressed in male garb, romanced the enemy, and demonstrated courage and bravado alien to the behavior of a respectable lady of their era. Aided by loyal and respectful men or women of mixed race or lower class, they were comfortable in the convent and in combat. The outcomes were conventional and within the framework of the "cult"—often marriage, sometimes death.[40]

Female writers also constructed stories of gloom and doom. Mrs. H. Marion Ward penned the heartbreaking Mexican tale of "Lolah Montana" in an 1847 short story for the Charleston, South Carolina, *Southern Patriot.* A wounded American officer takes healing refuge in the cottage of Lolah's father. As he recovers, passion blooms. Ward remarks in an aside, "To me, there is more pure, holy, beautiful religion in this love acknowledged, yet not acknowledged, than the cold practical theorist ever dreamed of." They marry, and for several weeks they steal away to meet in the moonlight under a tree on the chaparral near the American camp. One evening, Lolah discovers her lover lying in the agony of death, shot by a ranchero. Unable to go on, she returns to the spot of their rendezvous and dies of a broken heart. Ward's tale of ill-fated romance is significant for several reasons. Short stories, as well as novels and poems, could detail love in wartime. A female writer removed violence and patriotism from the narrative and rendered everyone else, including the American soldier, nameless. Ward penned a yarn about the honest pursuit of the heart against the uneven field of war and family opposition. Importantly, this is Lolah's story, and no doubt the tragic ending brought a tear to the eye of her readers.[41]

Death seemed a cheerless but suitable solution to many a couple's dilemma. Rarely, such as in the case of the patriotic Madelina, who rejected Arthur's pleadings for understanding and forgiveness, would a gender standoff result. Identity, disguised and revealed, served as an important part of the female role. Cultural convention generally dictated that gender remain obscure while women bravely went about the task of rescuing their imperiled paramours. When ultimately exposed, women accepted their traditional place and eschewed the adventuresome "other life." Devotion to country might remain a valid passion and an impediment to marriage, but abandonment of their masculine trappings was an imperative.

Scholars such as Streeby and Rodriguez tend to view most of these women as real or potential trophy wives. Though accepting of their gender status, few Hispanic women in the novels, like their real-life counterparts at the end of the Mexican-American War, found their way to the United States. One Alabama officer did take his Mexican bride "of pure Castilian blood" home to Montgomery when his regiment mustered out, prompting a volunteer to speculate that there would have been more instances if the army had provided transportation for the women. Perhaps George Blakey succeeded because his new wife was really Helen Vicars, and the environment a small community in rural Kentucky. Love would generally find its way in these novels. Still, Americans continued to equivocate about the nature and place of a Latin woman in their literature and culture.[42]

8

More Voices of Popular Culture

MUSIC, POETRY, AND THEATER

In August 1846, only four months after the war commenced, George Wilkins Kendall, a correspondent for the *New Orleans Daily Picayune,* made a desperate inquiry: "Do you know anything about 'The Rose of Alabama' in New Orleans? Here among the regulars and volunteers, they appear to think, and especially to sing, about nothing else save the 'Rose of Alabama'. . . . Seriously, the song is in everyone's mouth in the army." The lyrics rejected the belles of Spain and Liza Jane, countering, "Your charms will all be put to shame [by the Rose]." Kendall offered a bound edition of the popular *Western Songster* to anyone who could provide information on the lady and her creator.

He did not have to venture too far. The tune, composed by the multitalented Alabama jurist Alexander Beaufort Meek, paid homage to the beauty of "brown Rosie, a sweet tobacco posey." The white man in the Mexican-American War warbled his affections and, with banjo in tow, pursued Rosey across the river—"like a young coon out so sly"—to steal the love of his intended. "We hugged how long I cannot tell," the triumphant Romeo crowed. The similarities to Confederate soldiers lamenting their absence from the "Yellow Rose of Texas" some fifteen years later seem striking.[1]

Music, poetry, and theater played a vital role in the popular culture of American soldiers in the field, as well as in the lives of the families back home. The Mexican-American War extended a unique opportunity for the broader populace to embrace, or occasionally reject, the conflict through the arts. The sound and the images were inescapable on farms, in small towns, and in large cities. The clarion call to repel the invader and rally round the flag gave Americans a needed shot of patriotic adrenalin as they sought to define themselves more clearly as a nation and a people. A half century removed from independence, Americans remained culturally and politically defined by the tree of Anglo identity. Perhaps the most popular sentimental ballad of the era, "Home,

Sweet, Home" ("Be it ever so humble, there's no place like home") was an Anglo-American composition of the 1820s. Seeking to sever those roots, congressmen "twisted the lion's tail" in stump speeches. They railed against British imperialism, drawing cheers and clenched fists from the crowds. Meanwhile, a new generation of authors scratched pen on paper separating themselves from their English predecessors, and American actors attempted to bring their unique form and style to the stage, even when performing Shakespeare.

Music, poems, and the stage also furnished Americans the opportunity to stand up for their aggrieved nation. The Mexican-American War was neither the inglorious War of 1812 nor the recent unpopular struggle against the Seminoles in Florida. Both working and middling classes could afford tickets for the performances of numerous talented artists singing airs both rousing and melancholy. The progress of print technology allowed for the widespread and inexpensive distribution of sheet music, so that a pianoforte in a middle-class home or a fiddle on a farm might repeat a familiar refrain. The war presented a unique opportunity for the popular culture to express itself, and the response proved overwhelming.

The Revolution and the War of 1812 had contributed their own musical memories, providing a patina of patriotism through songs emphasizing freedom and liberty. The creative minds of William Billings ("Chester") and Francis Scott Key ("The Star-Spangled Banner") created an inspiring legacy, but arguably one difficult to sing in a tavern or town hall, except perhaps for "Yankee Doodle," which held a special, persistent place in the public mind. The ballads of the Mexican-American War empowered Americans, propounding not only views of the destiny and role of the United States in North America but also whimsical takes on race, ethnicity, gender, love, and loyalty. Pro- and antiwar advocates imaginatively expressed their attitudes, and the appreciation of their work, at least in part, could be found at the box office or the cash counter.

South of the Rio Grande, music was a critical part of the soldiers' world. Amazingly, for purposes of both inspiration and entertainment, full brass bands accompanied both American and Mexican armies. Spirits soared when a city fell, the Stars and Stripes was raised, and the band struck up "Hail Columbia!," the nation's de facto national anthem through the nineteenth century. In the town square, common choruses reassured and eased both tension and boredom. More casually, soldiers folded away tattered copies of *The Rough and Ready Songster* so they could readily join in a capella or perhaps pull out a fife to accompany any number of popular favorites. Not surprisingly, the music was often aggressively patriotic or tragically sentimental. Very often women were involved. Mothers, wives, and sweethearts left behind wept and prayed while their young men faced a hail of Mexican bullets and the equally dangerous off-the-shoulder charms of the señoritas.[2]

Not only the allure of the tobacco-colored Rosie but also, for soldiers fighting their first foreign war, the anticipation of bonding with a Latina maiden sent pulses racing. An unwavering sense of Anglo-Saxon superiority almost demanded an image of a Mexican flower, unappreciated by her lazy male counterpart, her beauty cherished by a noble Yankee. The writers trumpeted the fantasy of Anglicized salvation of Mexico through a worthy blending of bloodlines. Those loud in song could determine for themselves whether territorial expansion would coincide with the passion and amalgamation propounded in the melodies. Composers allowed that there might have been some apprehension on the part of the women to such an encounter but that American soldiers were gentlemen who valued a true woman. All turned out well in "Yankee Doodle in Mexico":

The gentle señoritas feared
Till Yankee Doodle smiled, sir
And they laughed quite heartily,
And us Amigos styled, sir.

A poem with a similar message, "They Wait for Us," appeared in a Boston paper in June 1846:

The Spanish maid, with eye of fire,
At balmy evening turns her lyre
And, looking to the Eastern sky,
Awaits our Yankee chivalry
Whose purer blood and valiant arms,
Are fit to clasp her budding charms.
The man, her mate is sunk in sloth—
To love, his senseless heart is loth;
The pipe and glass and tinkling lute;
A sofa, and a dish of fruit;
A nap, some dozen times a day;
Somber and sad and never gay.[3]

This challenge to American womanhood did not go unnoticed. Would the belles of Dixie or the flaxen-haired beauties of Ohio be replaced by a Latin fantasy in the heart of a true man? Never. A defensive J. Wakefield reminded readers of the superior attributes of "Yankee Girls":

> I'm angry when a freeman sings
> Of foreign maids, whose shallow aria
> Are spent in winning lords and kings
> Instead of their hearts
> But there's a fair and lovely band,
> Decked with no pearl or costly gem—
> The daughters of my native land—
> I bow to them![4]

Professional performers rarely missed an opportunity to lend their talents to the war effort. When the legendary Hutchinson family, of New Hampshire, began their musical tour of England in 1845, similar groups merged to fill the void in the United States. The most prominent were the Alleghanians, a talented male trio who launched their public career in 1846, playing both romantic and patriotic songs to receptive audiences in the Northeast. While their audiences grew in number, they realized that the ballads of the era often required a high, sweet female voice. By the summer, the band had settled upon a brunette teenage contralto, a German immigrant named Caroline Hiffert. Unlike the Hutchinsons, who had laid down the gauntlet by espousing a variety of reforms from temperance to antislavery, the Alleghanians eschewed abolition, allowing them to travel from Canada to New Orleans earning plaudits in theaters throughout the land. The war was widely popular, at least outside New England, and the group sang about love and loss.

Separation from wives and mothers prompted a variety of songs, some whimsical, others rather fatalistic. In the lyrics of one particular tune, Hiffert observed, "Despondency is all the rage and moping all the go, / Our husbands, sweethearts, all gone away to Mexico!" The wives who had quarrelsome relationships with their husbands now sobbed and moaned and wished to join them. Such a course of action would be a mistake, she insisted. Hiffert spoke as a maid whose beau had joined the volunteers. "I'm true to him—yet love to flirt—/ And have a youth in tow, / Who'd do as well, were poor Charles hurt, / Away in Mexico." She consoled, "So ladies, dry your weeping eyes, / Nor let their currents flow, / We've chaps on hand as good as those, / Away in Mexico." Finally, Ms. Hiffert encouraged her peers to continue to write letters to "gull our swains" but to also remember the old proverb, "Whilst shines the sun, Your hay you'd better mow." These somewhat insensitively opportunistic sentiments echoed in this Broadway melody likely did little to alleviate any anxieties felt by soldiers on the march to Mexico City.[5]

The serious nature of separation, love lost, and perhaps death was captured before the war by the composer Thomas Haynes Bayley:

Oh, no! We never mention her, her name is never heard
My lips are now forbid to speak that once familiar word
From sport to sport they hurry me, to banish my regret
And when they win a smile from me, they think that I forget.

The substitution of *him* for *her* in the lyrics made the tune applicable to the departed soldier.

By the 1840s, minstrel songs had gained widespread national appeal. The masses embraced numbers such as "Old Dan Tucker," accustomed strains like "Lucy Neal," or the ubiquitous "Yankee Doodle." Lyricists shamelessly pirated these melodies and substituted words appropriate to the Mexican-American War era. Imperialism, honor, and Anglo-Saxon superiority made for a heady brew in numerous tunes. "Uncle Sam in Mexico" promised in black dialect,

Dey're kicken up gunpowderation,
About de Texas annexation,
Since Mexico makes sich ado,
We'll flog her and annex her too.
Den march away.[6]

Interestingly, there seemed little guilt in some quarters about recruiting new immigrants to this noble cause. Germans and especially the widely reviled Irish, many escaping the ravages of the potato famine, found themselves drawn to enlist in volunteer units for a cash bounty and the promise of land. "By a Lady" played on the themes of loyalty and masculinity in suggesting that both native-born and immigrant patriots would join together to defend the nation:

Come rally true Americans,
And show your skill in war,
Your bravery and your talents
For fighting none's at par.
Your own adopted brethren
From Erin's fertile isle,
With trusty hearts will by you stand

And never you beguile.
The iron band of friendship
Will bind our Union strong.[7]

Texas appeared repeatedly in feminine form in songs of the period, such as the aforementioned "Uncle Sam and Mexico" and "The Texian Camp Song." "Uncle Sam's Song to Miss Texas" woos the Lone Star Republic: "Walk in my tall haired Indian gal / Your hand, my star-eyed Texas." "The Female Volunteer for Texas" regrets the restrictions of her gender but reflects both her courage and her goals:

Oh, had I a beau, Who for Texas would go,
Do you think I'd say no,
No, no not I; When his rifle I saw,
Not a sigh would I draw,
But give him *éclat* for his bravery.
If a band of young patriots should come in my way,
A volunteer for Texas I'd march away.[8]

In spite of the bravado, however, the dangers of war were ever-present in music and verse. Numerous songs attempted to reflect feelings for family and sweethearts, especially as the young man drew his last breath. In "Song of the Memphis Volunteers," the soldier reminds the belles:

Now ladies will you remember
If we fall as soldiers should
To shed for us a secret tear
A tear of gratitude.[9]

Significantly, mothers, but rarely fathers, were never far from the soldiers' thoughts. "Be Kind to the Loved Ones at Home" admonishes the absent son to

Remember thy mother for thee will she pray,
As long as God giveth her breath;
With accents of kindness then cheer her long way,
E'en to the dark valley of death.

With the smoke of battle still rising in the distance and his comrades charging the enemy, a young man lies prostate on a blanket, with a comrade kneeling beside him, placing a hand on his shoulder for comfort. This evocative lithographic image accompanied the music to "The Dying Soldier of Buena Vista." The young soldier's thoughts turn to his mother, who will soon hear the heartbreaking news of his death:

> Speak not to her in hurried words
> The blighting news you bear;
> The cords of life might snap too soon—
> So, comrade have a care.
> I am her only cherish'd child;
> But tell her that I died
> Rejoicing that she taught me young
> To take my country's side.

Beyond reassuring his mother of his patriotism, the soldier also had a few wistful words for a sweetheart about memories and unfulfilled dreams. He admonished his comrade to

> Tell her, when death was on my brow,
> Her voice, her form, her parting words,
> And life receding fast,
> Were with me in the last.
> On Buena Vista's bloody field,
> Tell her I dying lay,
> And that I knew she thought of me,
> Some thousand miles away.

Clearly the officer who wrote the words to the song wanted to reassure any soldier who doubted the fidelity of his love at home. "The Rio Grande" relates similar thoughts, as the young man sees himself: "He is sitting now, her darling boy, beside his mother's knee / the Wild fawn 'mid the free blue hills not happier than he." In his fading vision, he also glimpses

> A bright-eyed girl, more beautiful than morn's first rosy beam
> His fond enraptured spirit stirs with love's enchanting dream
> She chides his warm caresses not—he clasps her gentle hand—
> Ah! Thrill'd with pain he wakes again, beside the Rio Grande.[10]

Perhaps the New Hampshire–born Marion Dix Sullivan, the sister of the reformer Dorothea Dix, composed the most powerful songs of this genre. In

1844, Sullivan had written an early popular hit, a love ballad about American Indians along a river in eastern Pennsylvania entitled "The Blue Juniata." Three years later, she turned her talents to the Mexican-American War and composed "The Field of Monterey." While Caroline Hiffert received a warm response when she sang the mournful "The Soldier's Bride," the audience was moved to tears by "Monterey," the tale of a young woman, "the May queen," who recalls, "and the noblest and manliest was by my side that day / Who now in death is sleeping on the field of Monterey." The lyrics could be interpreted as equivocal regarding the war. As the church bells pealed and the populace rejoiced over the resounding victory, "bitter tears are gushing for the gallant and the gay" and "lonely hearts are bleeding upon the glorious day / For the loved in death are sleeping in the field of Monterey." It is difficult to know whether the Alleghanians sang one of their several tributes to Zachary Taylor ("Old Rough and Ready") before or after "Monterey," the site of one of his great victories.[11]

Mexicans crafted their songs and poetry to uplift and energize a people invaded. The course of the war, however, revealed the internal division and cynicism that helped spark Mexican defeat. Women played a vital role here too. The scholars Christopher Conway and Gustavo Pellón emphasize that Latin American tradition and cultural barriers restricted women within the domestic sphere; rarely would they engage in oral or written public discourse. Conway has studied the culture of Mexican female poets both before and during the war, as well as the nuanced nature of their work. He portrays a group of well-connected middle- and upper-class women who sought to push the bounds of domesticity, engaging in discussion of the proper role for women, particularly the need for education.

The creation of several women's magazines in the 1840s, including the conservative *Semanario de las Señoritas Mejicanas* and the more candid *Panorama de las Señoritas Mejicanas,* advanced a platform for dialogue about how far women might wander from the image of the *angel del hogar* (angel of the hearth). As in the United States, the debate remained unresolved prior to 1846, but evidently Mexican women felt constrained to articulate their poetic views about the war in a conventional manner. Conway notes that the emergence of an educated female elite coincided with romanticism and the rise of print culture to pave the way for an audience, a venue for female expression, and the evolution of a supportive literary sisterhood bound by family and class.

The war also gave these women an opportunity to channel their energies in a structured manner with the formation of charitable societies and organizations such as the Junta Patriótica de Beneficencia in Zacatecas. In harmony with their

American counterparts, the women engaged in traditional activities, gathering supplies for hospitals and sewing clothes, sheets, and bandages. Concurrently, they might also script a poem or compose a song to arouse the departing soldiers. Such actions fell within the approved women's sphere. Writing often collectively or without attribution, they authored poems to incite Mexican men, exhorting patriotism and demanding that they stand up to the Yankee barbarians and defend their vulnerable mothers and virginal sisters.

Guadalupe Calderón, Josefa Teran, and Josefa Letechipia de González were in the forefront of these literary activists, publicly reading their poetry in support of the war. In the fall of 1846, the three collaborated on two powerful poems intended to both warn and motivate, "La tempestad" ("The Storm") and "A la patria" ("To the Motherland"), for the newspaper *El Republicano.* The pieces discussed invasion, failed masculinity, fragile women, and disintegrating national unity, but the former presented the menace metaphorically through the use of rain, bulls, and birds.

> Already the black storm clouds
> Darken the horizon, and the terrible echoes
> Of the deafening thunderbolt, that intimidate
> Criminal and cowardly breasts,
> Inspire awe in the silent woods,
> Resounding in the vast hollows
> Of the deep ravines, and seem to
> Move the earth to its foundations.[12]

The poets hoped to arouse resistance in their brethren by intimating that internal weakness from the beginning of the war had compromised the country and jeopardized its women. Victories were few, however, and the poets pleaded for unity against the common foe in "To the Motherland":

> The fratricidal hand takes up the steel,
> In deranged delirium, tearing your bosom
> Those who swore to avenge your injuries
> Oh, motherland! Bring poison to your lips indelible insult,
> The ravenous rapine of the fierce savage on you stamps its shame
> Your virgin countryside the Yankee profanes
> Mexican blood tinted the grass
> Defenseless motherland, what lies in store for you?[13]

Conway praises these female poets for developing their own style of sentimental nationalistic verse. "Their poetry was a poetry of negotiation, challenge and plural voice;" he argues, "it was a form of discourse that was fully self-aware of its precarious authority in the arena of national debate, and as such, more nuanced and conditional in its expression."[14]

With minor variations, their expressions seem inexorably consistent throughout the conflict. Poems such as "When the Women Oppose the Cowardly Men" represented a brutal dare to the *machismo* of their kin:

> Taylor is mistaken
> If he thinks he can rule here;
> He will rule over the men, yes,
> But the women . . . Never!

The nine stanzas, hard-hitting and relentless, put down Mexican men as slaves and fools who can be humiliated, while extolling the valor of the women. If the men chose not to fight, then they should leave their guns to devoted, clever, free, brave women, who never conceded to oppression.

> They should tell us if they are afraid,
> If they have exhausted their courage,
> And Taylor we will conquer
> Defending our land, we will die fighting;
> The men will falter,
> But the women . . . Never![15]

In an August 1846 article in *El Republicano,* the writer María de la Salud García posed the same challenge. If Mexican men were not up to the task of defending their homeland against the invaders, she contended, then women, admittedly the weaker sex, would pick up the cudgel and assume the role of daring Greek women prepared to fight to the death. The theme of warrior women as an assault on masculinity touched a nerve, empowered women, and almost guaranteed a male response.[16]

The fate of Old Rough and Ready also awaited Old Fuss and Feathers in "An Old Woman Calls for the Death of General Scott." This paean to patriotism warned the general that a united people would stand against his invasion, and "a beating you will receive by an Old Mexican Woman." Independence and peace would be at hand, but only after "Death at last to the traitors / death to Scott, death to his people, / long live brave Mexico / with all its defenders." And with them would be an "old Mexican Woman."[17]

If Mexican men were not yet affronted, "The Prayer that Yankees Recite to Shame the Mexicans" assured an angry reaction from any red-blooded Latino man. The American invocation acknowledged the Mexican trinity that by right belongs to the conquerors: gold, beautiful girls ("who will be at our disposal and our every whim"), and fertile and boundless lands. Marriage would be abolished, and Mexican women would serve the Americans, "just like a shirt or a pair of shoes to wear and do with as we please." No real obstacle existed to this end result, since "there are no men in Mexico." Some still might wear pants, but out of habit. Many men wore women's clothes and sought to deceive, "but we already know what they are: sissies in dresses, and the proof is that they are completely submissive."

The market women of San Luis Potosí leveled a similar "pants" challenge—to stand up and act like a man—to Mexican men as early as 1846, demanding that they take up arms to demonstrate their honor:

> If you no longer have pants
> Vile and Cowardly men
> Abandon the muskets
> The mortars and the cannons
> We will take them up
> Let's see if we can use them
> And if by chance we do not triumph
> At least we won't run away.

Both the United States and Mexico began the war with small professional armies. The rank and file in both countries often comprised men of low class and status. In Mexico, however, the soldiers were largely conscripted into service, while in the United States they volunteered, often out of patriotism or economic desperation. The longer and wider war and extended campaigns led to the need for additional forces. The scholar Peter Guardino emphasizes the pressures society placed on the average male citizen to meet the needs of his country. Whereas armies of the seventeenth and early eighteenth centuries gleaned troops from the top and bottom rungs of the social ladder, by the nineteenth century the patriotic man was obliged to rise up and fight to protect both the nation and defenseless women.

The female role was to represent the integrity of the home and to produce soldiers willing to sacrifice themselves for family and country. Men were to prove their honor and masculinity through their behavior. The United States more than met these needs, especially in 1846, with thousands of enthusiastic fixed-term volunteers. The Mexicans created National Guard units formed specifically to hurl back the American aggressors. Women in both nations used honor and embarrassment to promote courage among men who were not trained professional soldiers. In the United States, women emphasized the "Spartan ideal" to spur their men to undertake acts of bravery that would redound to the honor of the family and the community.[18]

In Mexico, women used poetry, among other cultural vehicles, to bolster the confidence and commitment of men not prepared for combat. Broadsides and songs featured parallel refrains. Were they penned by women, or were they the work of increasingly desperate male loyalists who understood that a shameless gendered appeal to Mexican manhood and patriotism might help unite the nation? While a definitive answer is elusive, certainly the barrages prompted a response from "a concerned soldier to his comrades-in-arms": The country was in disarray, he despaired. Regional loyalties splintered the republic, and in 1847 the Caste War, led by disaffected Mayan Indians, erupted in Yucatán. The power of the central government wilted under the sometimes subtle, sometimes overt provincial lack of cooperation. In his piece, titled "Federation or Death," the "concerned soldier" exhorted his countrymen to rally around their religion, their flag, and their nation to preserve their independence against "the evil conqueror." Calling up familiar themes of rape and pillage, the soldier said to his comrades, "We have wives, will we watch them brutally dishonored? We have daughters, will they be fodder for their [the Americans] lasciviousness?" "Do not look away," the soldier demanded, "fix your eyes even if just for a moment on the picture of your wives and daughters dishonored in your presence."[19]

Mexico City fell to the Americans in September 1847, the nightmare realized by its residents, who endured an occupation that lasted into the next summer. Perhaps the most poignant and cynical of Mexican songs, "La Pasadita," a dramatically altered version of an old favorite, appeared soon after the capital was subjugated.

Hear my friends a story all the world should know—
How Yankee glory spread thro Mexico!
To the ball advancing, all in bright array,
The Yankees had the dancing, but for the music made us pay!
When the ladies listened to their martial air,

How their dark eyes glistened in the whirl to share!
But in vain their glancing, beauty had no sway,
The Yankees had the dancing, but for the music made us pay!
All the men most bravely vowed they'd have a turn,
But they gave up gravely, steps they could not learn,
Champions of the nation—Guards! Why were ye not
True to your vocation paying off the Scott? Hah!
Ye were enhancing shame upon the day!
The Yankees had the dancing, but for the music made us pay![20]

American music and poetry advanced analogous yet markedly different themes. The enduringly patriotic, rousing or sentimental ballads focused upon the parting of young men from their mothers, wives, sweethearts, and sisters and were layered with heroism, self-sacrifice, and death. Poetry, often epic and delivered in numerous cantos, described comparable emotions. While poetry traditionally appealed to a more exclusive clientele, wartime poetry propounded a powerful statement of battlefield masculinity that could be captured in verse and published in a variety of newspapers and magazines for a broader readership. Tales of Mexicans' treachery rapidly mixed with those of their cruelty and abuse of the wounded. Together with the mounting casualties from combat and disease, these tales created a sharp dichotomy between the evil Latins and their honorable neighbor. A sense of the righteousness of the cause enveloped many Americans, who sensed that the blame for Mr. Polk's War should really be placed at the threshold of Mexico.

Amateur poets abounded, including William Faulkner's great-grandfather W. C. Faulkner, who served ingloriously in the occupation of Monterrey. He felt compelled after the war to write a four-thousand-line saga entitled *The Siege of Monterey,* which included an intriguing love story between a courageous Mexican girl and her Mexican soldier lover. The poem sold poorly, so Faulkner tried his hand at fiction, crafting *The Spanish Heroine; a Tale of Love and War.* The novel, wrapped around the Battle of Buena Vista, told a more traditional romantic tale of an American soldier and his Mexican love.[21]

Accomplished and aspiring poets were joined by lawyers and doctors, soldiers and pacifists, men and women of varied backgrounds who gave voice to their pride and frustration by writing verse. Their lines delivered the message of morality, heroism, conquest, and culture, reflecting the divisions that existed over the purpose and conduct of the war. In this milieu, the antiwar reformers and intellectuals put forward a particularly dismal view. The historian Robert

Johannsen speculates that while the works of celebrated poets such as James Russell Lowell and John Greenleaf Whittier remain powerful critical statements, Lowell's *Bigelow Papers* "had little influence on Americans' perception of the conflict."[22]

The midcentury also produced female poets, such as Caroline M. Sawyer and Frances J. "Fanny" Crosby, who had large followings, especially among Protestant church members. Death dominated their Mexican-American War poetry, as they often removed themselves from the motives for the hostilities to reflect on the painful outcome. The cultured Massachusetts-born Sawyer wed a Presbyterian minister and devoted decades to drafting verse, especially for juveniles, intended to impact their morality and their perception of war, while affording rather maudlin comfort to the late soldier's loved ones:

Warrior, rest! Our star is vanish'd
That to victory led the way;
And from, our lone heart is banish'd
All that cheer'd life's weary day!
There thy young bride weeps in sorrow
That no more she hears thy tread;
That the night which knows no morrow
Darkly veils thy laurell'd head![23]

Fanny Crosby, blinded in infancy, became perhaps the most well known and most prolific composer of Methodist gospel hymns in the nineteenth century. The amazing Crosby devoted additional time to fashioning dozens of poems. A committed Whig, she wrote glowingly of Winfield Scott and Henry Clay, but especially of Zachary Taylor. Old Rough and Ready's untimely death in 1850 prompted an outpouring from her heart, mourning his loss and fearing for the nation. Crosby's most memorable poem, however, is the fifteen-page canto entitled simply "Monterey." While many of her creations tender unbridled praise for the courage and dedication of American officers in battle and a defense of "the flag of the free," "Monterey" is a beautifully written, restrained tale of tragedy. Young Edward hears Columbia's call to defend the nation, and against the wishes of his mother, sister, and fiancée, Lucy, he enlists in Taylor's army. A mortal blow cuts him down on the field at Monterrey, but, sadly, both his mother and Lucy have also died, so only his sister remains to mourn his passing. Clearly lacking in the patriotic bombast of her earlier efforts, "Monterey" gives the reader a more tempered view of war:

The faithful son of Mexico
That fell beneath Columbia's blow
Lies pale beside his dreaded foe
Their glazing eyes malignant met
Ere the last ray of life had let
They hated till their feeble breath
Was stifled by the hand of death[24]

By the mid-1840s, Lydia Jane Pierson had won acclaim as the Forest Minstrel. Born in Middleton, Connecticut, she moved to the wilderness of northern Pennsylvania with her farmer husband. Fully five miles from the closest neighbor, Pierson challenged the loneliness and isolation through the revelations of nature and wildlife in her poetry about violets and bluebirds. During the war, she dedicated her skills to exploring the causes of the confrontation in a poem with the cumbersome title "On the proposition to surrender to Mexican barbarity and tyranny, the land between the Nueces and the Rio Grande—the battle-field of Palo Alto and Resaca de la Palma." Published in *Literary World* and widely circulated in various newspapers, Pierson's work answered the question with a stirring tribute to the valor and sacrifice of Major Samuel Ringgold, killed at Palo Alto, and Zachary Taylor, the engagement's victorious commander. Could Americans withdraw or yield after such bravery and in defiance of her destiny?

It may not be! Forbid it God!
Forbid it, all that patriots prize
This land has tasted freemen's blood;
Their dust within its bosom lies.
. . . .
No! By our country and by our God;
We will not yield that dear-bought soil!
On! To the rescue! Hearts of steel!
On! To the rescue! Souls of Fire![25]

After the raucous, flag-waving rhetoric, Pierson turned her attention to the war in two rather somber poems, "The Dying Soldier" and "The Battlefield." The first, a paean to courage and patriotism, seemingly validates the war and allowed the reader to hear the confession of a man whose heart would be forever entwined with that of his beloved, Geraldine. As for his sacrifice,

Yet I shall live forever in the light of my proud country's glory!
And my grave shall be a holy altar
Where the free shall celebrate the worship of the brave
And this is death in glory!
With the wreath of victory's laurel fresh upon my head
Oh, ardently I sought for such a death.

"The Battlefield" presents a brutally realistic and more confusing portrayal of the aftermath. Dismemberment abounds—a head here, a leg and arm there. Amid blood that is everywhere, a soldier gazes skyward, a still hand clutching a miniature to his breast. Its language markedly different from that of "The Dying Soldier" in tone and content, "The Battlefield" describes young men dead, from "butchery slain" upon a "polluted plain."

While thousands fall upon the field of blood
And pour life out at once in sanguine flood
Thousands are slain who linger on for years
And waste life, day by day, in bitter tears.[26]

Frances Dana Gage, the sprightly and talented poet lovingly nicknamed Aunt Fanny for her cheery domestic advice to farm and small-town women in the *Ohio Cultivator,* became a leading advocate of women's rights and antislavery in the Midwest in the 1840s. Married to an abolitionist lawyer, Gage evolved in her stridency on issues related to war, slavery, and the Whig Party. An antiwar advocate of passive resistance, in her poem "Woman's Warfare" she challenged the notion of chivalry in combat, questioning how the killing of women could be rationalized, especially if they defended their homes and families. As the historian Nancy Isenberg commented, "Men could not honorably protect and murder women." Gage also blasted the equivocation of the war hero and 1852 presidential nominee, the Virginian Winfield Scott, in a poem sarcastically concluding:

Up then Whigs do your duty
Bow beneath the Southern rod
Save the Union, save the party—
Leave the slave alone with God[27]

Gage earlier witnessed the impact the furor over the gold rush had upon the young men of Ohio. She opposed the expansion and the abandonment of personal responsibility and family attendant with gold and greed, and she urged the boys to stay true to the field and plow in "Don't Go to California":

> There's a world of wealth, gold cannot buy,
> In the homes you leave behind!
> There's wealth in the maiden's trusting love;
> There's wealth in the wife's fond fears,
> There's wealth in the sister's tenderness,
> There's wealth in the mother's tears,
> Enjoy it while you may; For the gold in California,
> Don't barters life's loves away![28]

The stage presented yet another way for Americans to demonstrate their patriotism and support for the war. The democratization of the theater allowed all social classes to partake of representations of high and low culture, from opera to minstrel shows, comedy, and drama. Theater was reasonably priced and became a part of the conscious and concerted effort to develop a national culture separate from that of Great Britain. The scholar Sam Haynes thoughtfully analyzes this evolution, which manifested itself in ways both creative and violent, the latter represented most poignantly by the Astor Place riot of May 1849. The confrontation had deep roots in Anglo-American rivalry and class issues, but the spark was struck over the dispute about whether the accomplished Englishman William Macready or the vaunted American Edwin Forrest was the better Shakespearean actor. The resulting disturbance inside and outside the theater prompted authorities to call in the militia and left a score dead and more than a hundred wounded.

During the Mexican-American War, plays of marginal quality or dubious accuracy, but high in action and heroics, were rushed into production for eager audiences. Invariably focusing upon US military success, the dramas provided an opportunity for Americans to see their warriors up close and to validate their national pride and triumphs at Matamoros, Buena Vista, and Mexico City. In Joseph C. Foster's *The Siege of Monterey, or The Triumph of Rough and Ready,* Americans could witness military spectacle and pageantry. The play, with a cast of thirty, drew thousands, as audiences jammed theaters in Philadelphia and New York.[29]

Not surprisingly, such action-laden dramas allowed little room for women. They did, of course, grace the American stage, particularly in European operas, in which the female voice was frequently an essential element. While the military melodrama drew widespread attention from the theatergoing public between from 1846 to 1848, American soldiers in Mexico had the opportunity to attend variations of often well-known plays in cities that they occupied or in cities nearby.

Stationed in Tampico in February 1847, Napoleon Dana exulted that he and his mates had gone on a spree, attending the theater and staying out until one o'clock in the morning. The theater itself had been improvised, "a miserable place," but the actors, who had performed previously for the army at Corpus Christi and Matamoros, had been quite good. The pattern was established, as troupes of professional American actors followed the army and produced plays in spaces ranging from the jury-rigged to classically impressive, well-built, spacious theaters.[30]

In Puebla, the entrepreneurs Hart and Wells commandeered a theater on the western side of town and earned handsome profits by presenting Edward Bulwer-Lytton's romantic melodrama *Lady of Lyons.* The play, first performed in New York in 1838, featured a Miss Christian, a young woman in her mid-teens, who in the lead role of Pauline could "outdance MacBeth's witches." A South Carolinian observed that she "was universally admired as a beauty." Hart and Wells also wisely employed Mrs. Morrison, "a fine actress and a splendid looking lady," who possessed an exceptional singing voice. Both women played to packed houses each night. The American Company charged fifty cents a seat, while the Spanish Company, occupying a second theater across town, asked only twelve cents. Arguably presenting equal if not superior productions in terms of talent and costuming, the Spanish troupe was at a disadvantage because of the linguistic barrier, which challenged many soldiers.[31]

Language, of course, mattered far less to the more sophisticated or culturally curious American who was fascinated by the extravagance of the theaters in Mexico City and the talent of the actors. The oil-lit Gran Teatro Nacional, the largest venue, seated three thousand in its gallery, series of circles, and five tiers of boxes. Superbly decorated, its reputation for magnificence was surpassed only by that of the San Carlos Theater in Naples, Italy. In the occupied capital in the fall of 1847, a soldier had numerous choices for entertainment, including the persevering American Company, which had followed the army from the Rio Grande. Such commitment drew little respect from George B. McClellan, who smugly wrote that the productions of the company "were rather too bad to be endured." The better choices, he submitted, would be the Spanish Company's staging of *The Magician of Seville* and the Italian Opera Troupe's dramatizations of Vincenzo Bellini's *La Somnambula* and Gaetano Donizetti's *Daughter of the*

Regiment. The highly regarded plays gave the soldiers, teamsters, and camp followers the opportunity to hear great music in impressive settings. Shocked that the Americans allowed such lower sorts to occupy the private boxes of the aristocracy, many Mexicans felt the theater had been desecrated.[32]

The star of *La Somnambula,* the legendary, "unsurpassed" María Cañete, quickly became a favorite with the Americans. Before the war, the Spanish actress had packed large halls, including the Teatro de Santa Anna. In December 1844, she dazzled the audience, including the general himself, with her performance as Doña Inés in *Don Juan Tenorio.* Clearly, she had not lost her magic. Lieutenant John James Peck stood in awe, remarking that while she was "quite advanced in years," acting remained for her "nature" rather than an effort or habit. De Lancey Floyd-Jones, a New York soldier familiar with the theater, agreed. "Everybody is in love with her," he enthused. "Although neither young nor handsome, her intelligent, sprightly appearance was the delight of all." The elitist McClellan conceded that Cañete and the Italian troupe "did very well," though not as well as Anne Childe Seguin, whom he had heard several years before in Philadelphia.[33]

Over a long career, Cañete had amassed a considerable fortune while enchanting crowds in Mexico City, Havana, and Madrid. In February 1843, her sold-out show at the Teatro de Nuevo Mexico became the center of political violence. When the presidential aspirant Gabriel Valencia, a rival of Santa Anna's, was unable to procure tickets, soldiers sympathetic to Valencia's cause twice disrupted the performance. The Americans challenged Cañete's love for the profession when they asked her to entertain the soldiers in occupation of the capital. A committee of officers determined that she and another actress who focused upon tragedy were the principal stars of the Mexican stage. The tragedian refused the US request, reasonably contending that her reputation would suffer by association with the Americans and she would pay a fearful price once they departed the country.[34]

Cañete, however, adopted a markedly different posture. She declared that Americans' money was good, and "their judgment, she was sure, was better." Her employment would benefit not only herself, she rationalized, but the large company of thirty to forty who were also engaged in the plays. Besides, as a professional, she cared little whether the audience was Mexican or American. The Yankees certainly valued her rather practical viewpoint, rewarding her with dollars and full houses. One Mexican commentator remarked with thinly disguised resentment, "Cañete was the fascination and idol of the American chiefs."[35]

Cañete later fled the country for Havana, but Mexicans soon forgave her any patriotic missteps. When Manuel Eduardo de Gorostiza died in 1851, the nation lost not only a distinguished diplomat and politician but also a talented dramatist. In his honor, the Gran Teatro Nacional presented a solemn tribute followed by one of his comedies, *Indulgencia para todos,* with María Cañete playing the lead. A decade after the war, she could be found performing at the capital's beautiful new Teatro de Iturbide. A reviewer in *El Omnibus* rhapsodized, "She is every bit as powerful on the stage today as she was in 1843. She deserves the public acclamation she always receives." Juan Mateos, writing for *El Monitor,* remarked on the individual style of the "congenial" Señora Cañete, "who has achieved so many triumphs on our stage, continues in her dominant style, sets the pace for the epoch, and her dramatic talent does not let her down, nor will it even to the end of her days in the theater." Among its many offerings, her company put on *Uncle Tom's Cabin.* There is no indication that she had a role.[36]

The rejuvenation of María Cañete's career in the 1850s rested upon the memory of the Mexican people and their willingness to pardon her for temporary transgressions. Mexico and the United States shared a divisiveness that echoed within the popular culture. Although both nations were dominated by prowar elements, a significant minority in the United States opposed the fighting on moral grounds, while in Mexico many demonstrated a halfhearted enthusiasm for the combat and for the central government. Both Washington and Mexico City struggled to maintain the level of intensity among the masses necessary for a prolonged confrontation.

Popular support for any war ebbs and flows depending upon the causes, intensity, length, and cost in lives and treasure. In modern society, governments play a role in stimulating or maintaining excitement by strategically embedding reporters with the military, channeling news items through well-disposed television networks, or, more creatively, utilizing social media. In the nineteenth century, the Polk administration had sympathetic journalists who communicated their views by telegraph and steamboat. Americans read newspapers, and their stories were widely reprinted across the nation for a citizenry thirsting for information. As early as November 1846, the military funneled updates from the front or campsite through telegraph lines on the East Coast.

The partisan nature of the Mexican-American War created an environment in which Democratic papers delighted in describing the ongoing conflict, while the Whig press often focused upon the moral bankruptcy, death, and destruction of a war to extend slavery. The posture of outrage was frequently toned down when dealing with the courage of Americans under fire or the accomplishments of the potential Whig presidential contenders Zachary Taylor and Winfield Scott.

While the center for intense political discourse has shifted from the nineteenth-century tavern and newspaper to the twenty-first-century coffee house and social media, most Americans then and now have wanted to believe in the rightness of the cause and to embrace the president's justifications for war. Contemporary culture manifests its patriotism in myriad fashions, through music (often country-western), television, film, and athletic events. While not rising to the level of the contentiousness surrounding the Vietnam War, contradictory views about the US role in the Middle East play out in dueling soundtracks and a half dozen admired or award-winning films.

Antebellum Americans utilized similar, if less sophisticated, outlets. The popular culture responded positively to songs, poems, and plays that raised the patriotic spirit or engendered an emotional response with the reality of sacrifice and loss. Some simply entertained, and to good purpose, in boosting the morale of civilians and soldiers. The war enhanced both pro- and antiwar artists and intellectuals, enlarging the images of women such as Fanny Crosby, Lydia Jane Pierson, and Caroline Hiffert.

The antiwar minority registered its attitude with arguably greater effect as the skirmishing, guerrilla activities, and civilian violence dragged on into 1848. In contrast to public expectations, the battleground successes were not bloodless, and disease claimed thousands of young American lives. The conquest of vast expanses of territory became a reality, but Americans impatiently began to demand resolution for a war that had gone on too long. Politicians pushing for an end to Mr. Polk's War were on increasingly solid ground. South of the Rio Grande, Mexican women could only support the war publicly, which they did by encouraging flag-waving unity of purpose or, more negatively, belittling their male counterparts for lack of courage. Nothing resonated in Latin society quite like an attack on masculinity. The culture was uncertain what to do with the words or behavior of Guadalupe Calderón, Josefa Teran, or María Cañete.

Both Mexican and American women played vital roles in voicing their support and criticism within the popular culture. Whether writing or performing, American women expanded the opportunities to advocate for their respective positions and heighten their profile. There would be no retreat, as hearts and minds turned to new causes and issues after the war. Mexican women, however, found themselves confronted by far greater obstacles and would meet with more limited success.[37]

Conclusion

The termination of the Mexican-American War resolved a number of issues and created many others. Both countries found themselves in a political quandary, debating the honesty, wisdom, and moral uprightness of their old leaders and pondering selection of the new. The loss or addition of territory and the implications for each republic raised questions of blame and recognition. Certainly, the nations had been transformed, but how would the conflict, and particularly the role of women within it, be remembered?

Mexico and Memory

Discussions of individual transgressions, ambition, and incompetence dominated the stage of Mexican popular culture following the "War of North American Intervention." An understandably angry and bitter people sought to learn from the disaster and to indict those who had failed the nation. As a result, poets, painters, and scholars commemorated their fallen heroes and blasted the politicians and generals whose self-serving behavior had opened the door to the Yankee aggressors. The ensuing debate brought no closure on the major matters and ended with the return to power of the resilient Santa Anna in 1853. Predictably, and with some justification, Mexican writers attributed the war to long-standing American territorial greed. Taylor's "invasion" of land north of the Rio Grande in 1846 had been not only provocative but a sign of overall US duplicitousness, treachery, and unethical behavior. The seizure of half the Mexican republic in the Treaty of Guadalupe Hidalgo confirmed their view.[1]

It served no purpose to impeach the honor and integrity of the average soldier, so journalists struggled to find excuses for defeat. Inferior weaponry and ordnance were frequent culprits. Mexicans, perhaps rightly, claimed victory at the Battle of Buena Vista and dramatized the courage of the defenders of Chapultepec, especially the heroic *niños.* US accounts reinforced the legend. In one version, told by an officer, a young man, in classic Spartan manner, is instructed by his mother to die by his cannon rather than return to her disgraced and without honor. While fulfilling his duties, he is captured and brought to the United States to complete his education, thus providing a happy ending to the American, if not the Mexican, rendering of the story.[2]

While writers composed scant commemorative music, lithographers and engravers did their best to demonstrate the bravery of Mexican soldiers in battle. The government took the leading role in directing public memory. Memorials and monuments, especially to those who had fallen in defense of the capital, were erected. President José Joaquín de Herrera labored to elevate the image of the National Guard in the public mind, and funerals were held honoring citizen-soldiers, as well as the officers of the regular army. By the late 1850s, however, all these efforts to control historical memory were being destabilized as the country sank into civil war.[3]

The United States and Memory

Americans had a markedly different, and very divided, approach to memory of the war. As in Mexico, politics became a factor as early as 1848 with the victorious campaign of Zachary Taylor prompting Americans to re-examine the causes of the quarrel. The Whigs found themselves in the awkward position of long-standing opposition to the war in principle, while supporting Old Rough and Ready. The Democrats delighted in pointing out this inconsistency, and accused the Mexicans of instigating hostilities after Polk had tried to resolve the issues through diplomacy. War heroes still had cachet in 1852. The Whigs turned once again to a major commander with no political experience, Winfield Scott. The Democrats chose a lesser known general in New Hampshire's Franklin Pierce, dubbed "Young Hickory of the Granite Hills." Pierce's success did not signal the end of the appeal of combat veterans. John C. Fremont, "the Pathfinder," a key figure in the California campaign, captured the first Republican Party presidential nomination in 1856.[4]

While the parties exploited the war's outcome by offering heroes of varying magnitude as candidates, the country continued its debate over matters of morality. Had the conflict been an immoral effort to spread slavery, or had Manifest Destiny been a legitimate exercise of God's will? Dueling literary genres filled shelves as authors competed for the hearts and minds of the public. Racism and religion rooted in Anglo-Saxon Protestant superiority offered a plausible defense for American conduct and a rationale for victory. Lithographs, novels, paintings, sheet music, and histories of the war—overwhelmingly patriotic—sold well for several years following the peace treaty. By the early 1850s, other subjects, from westward expansion and the gold rush to political compromise and sectionalism, pushed the topic into the background.[5]

Even so, Americans remained highly aware of the sacrifice. They visited battlefields, collecting relics, including Santa Anna's prosthetic leg and weaponry, built museums, and named towns and streets after major US victories. Public ceremonies were commonplace, as the townsfolk saluted the returning soldiers with medals and swords for their valor. Those officers less fortunate were brought home for reburial, and served as a new jolt to the collective memory of the war. While the focus of these funerals frequently was to honor the dead and promote nationalism, they also became a touchstone for political controversy and the divisive nature of slavery and territorial acquisition. Mexico and the United States made concerted efforts to commemorate, if not celebrate, the recent war. By placing heroic figures and victorious battles at the vortex of the popular culture, both societies attempted to glean the positive from a clash that had caused doubt in triumph and defeat.[6]

The emphasis was invariably upon the sacrifice and courage of men. Were women at all recognized for their contributions? If so, what form did that recognition take? The city of El Paso acknowledged the achievements of the courageous traveler Susan Shelby Magoffin by erecting a statue to her (and her dog) in the town center. But what of Sarah Bowman, Doña Tules, and Ann Chase? Should the good people of Brownsville, Santa Fe, and Brooklyn cast bronze memorials marking the service and accomplishments of these women?

Likely, the less than romantic nature of their occupations—hotel owner, gambler, and merchant—plays a role in their marginalization. So, too, does the obscure context of the Mexican-American War. One of the most important confrontations in US history is barely recognized today among the American people. Though it was a war of relative brevity compared with the Vietnam War or the wars in Afghanistan and Iraq, more than twelve thousand soldiers lost their lives in the Mexican-American War. Mexico suffered similar casualties, and thousands of civilians also perished.

Was the war inevitable? K. Jack Bauer uses the term *unavoidable,* especially given the rigid mind-sets of the two sides and their lack of mutual understanding. While not absolving Polk of errors in judgment or misunderstanding of Mexican culture, Bauer argues, "Mexico's leaders bear a large share of the responsibility for the conflict." They promoted and took advantage of popular resentment of gringo belligerence to advance their own political careers. When events spun out of control, they "found themselves captive of that propaganda."

Young Hickory must also be held accountable. He was relentless in his desire to expand the American republic. Pledged to one term in office, Polk publicly targeted Oregon and the Southwest for annexation. California, however, was not part of the campaign framework in 1844 and was spoken of quietly in the White House. The president hoped to get the entire package pacifically, but Mexico refused to receive John Slidell. Both time and options had expired, leaving Polk with no other choice save war. The two nations seemed to welcome a violent and controversial confrontation that appears to have been unavoidable, if not inevitable. The transformative results, the fulfillment of US Manifest Destiny in reaching the Pacific Ocean and the stripping of Mexico of her empire, not only afforded Americans tremendous opportunity but also exacerbated the issue of slavery, which had plagued the nation since its inception.[7]

American Women

Women played a critical role in all aspects of the war. From the outset of hostilities in April 1846 to the evacuation of Mexico City in July 1848, women chose sides, supporting the conflict or rallying against it. Operating within the domestic sphere, patriotic women across the country contributed their skills and talents to what they considered a noble cause. Certainly, the American Revolution and the War of 1812, largely fought within the new United States, generated the assistance of thousands of women, who performed traditional tasks, raising funds, knitting garments, and serving with the army. In that regard, the Mexican-American War shared similarities yet proved markedly different. For the first time in the nation's history, thousands of Columbia's soldiers sailed off to a truly distant, foreign land. Often, their bodies rested in shallow graves across the Rio Grande.

For many women, despair and disillusionment with the war, and particularly the leadership in Washington, soon scuffed the initial varnish of enthusiasm. Concurrently, equally patriotic women gathered in 1846 to reinforce their set opinions about this "wicked war." Divided on whether to cheer on their young men or damn them as dissolute racists, female reformers held steadfast to their belief in the immoral extension of the republic and the accompanying institution of slavery. They crafted poems and songs and performed and spoke against the war. The impact of their efforts on the outcome remains debatable. Some historians contend that they contributed to the rising antiwar tide, which muted the territorial ambitions of the power brokers in Washington, while others argue that Polk's intended goals were accomplished. Regardless, the war brought thousands of women into the public sphere, whether participating in celebratory ceremonies or, by word or action, protesting the hostilities.

Female editors boldly trod on the sacred ground of the fourth estate, criticizing the war, the president, and the military. Some, understandably, felt obliged to covertly mask their gender, all the better to lure unsuspecting readers into perusing perceptive columns discussing matters more appropriate for men in public print. The contributions of these writers and editors, whether "an old Washington hand" such as Anne Royall or the rather brazen Jane Swisshelm, were unconventional and innovative. The other Jane—Cazneau—antagonized still more traditionalists. These women pioneered wartime journalism, and Cazneau's presence in Cuba and Mexico, along with her Washington contacts, reinforced the image of a woman with courage and credentials.

While Cazneau darted in and out of Mexico on her "secret mission," perhaps hundreds of American women labored south of the border in a variety of capacities. We know too little about the lives of those who sought opportunity in the cotton mills, taverns, or shops. Like Caroline Porter or Ann Chase, they commonly arrived in Mexico before the war commenced and were obliged to make difficult choices regarding loyalty and engagement with the Yankee interlopers. Others, like Sarah Bowman, drifted into Mexico with the action and found themselves in complex and shifting roles. Both Chase and Bowman emerged as heroes, though their activities and occupations defied the traditions of the Victorian woman. Sarah, bawdy and presumptuous, became a legend, beloved by the army. Ann, more introspective but just as headstrong, should be remembered as much for her acumen and survival skills in a city hostile to her interests as for her efforts to relay timely intelligence to the Americans.

Voices sang loudly within the broader popular culture. In New York, a small party of the new urban middle class gathered in the parlor, accompanied by a pianoforte, and extolled the virtues of the "old" commanders, Rough and Ready and Fuss and Feathers. Outside Nashville, a farm family in a log cabin, inspired by a fiddle, warbled the same tune. Actors and poets weighed in, widely praising the virtue of American arms and the brave soldiers who bore them. Surely, the dissenters had their day, but the masses who could afford sheet music or a theater ticket echoed their approbation for a war that was about a United States that was confronted by a dastardly foe and rose to assert itself as a force for democratic republican principle.

Mexican Women

Scholarly attention has focused on the social extremes—upper-class poets and peasant *soldaderas.* Mexican women of both extremes had fewer alternatives in terms of their role and support of the war than their Anglo counterparts. Also, in many ways, Latin society shared conventional values with the United States, at least regarding women of a higher class. The duty of the woman was to rally support for her country. For a number of educated women, inspired nationalistic prose became a preferred avenue of expression—although that expression could turn brutally biting and sarcastic. Most women who participated in the war functioned as *soldaderas,* providing invaluable sustenance and care to Mexican armies in desperate need. Some were opportunistic and self-serving. The majority of these women, however, dedicated their labor, and in some cases their lives, to a nation rent by internal unrest. The brave and tragic plight of the *soldaderas* continued unchanged. They suffered and died along with their men in the impending civil war and the French occupation of the 1860s.

There were exceptions to the extremes. Gertrude "Tules" Barceló bridged the divide as an irresistibly romantic figure. The subject of two novels, Anna Burr's *The Golden Quicksand* (1936) and Ruth Laughlin's *The Wind Leaves No Shadow* (1948), Tules, powerful and compassionate, seductive and virtuous, was far more than the Mistress of Monte. Laughlin's book entered a fourth printing, but one ponders the marketing strategy that placed a blonde, Anglo woman on the cover of the book.

In literature, Mexican women served as objects of male American fantasy. Novels, short stories, and poems depicted brave Latina belles. These dedicated women, frequently frustrated with the poor performance of their countrymen, took the defense of their nation into their own hands. They encountered, of course, young American officers—"real men"—who matched them in courage and commitment. The novels, devoured by the broader US populace, fed the American soldier's dream of acquiring a hacienda in Mexico or bringing a beautiful woman home.

Few soldiers fulfilled that dream. Dozens of contemporary accounts reflect how the war heightened the awareness of those who hoped to exercise their libido in courting an irresistible señorita. Their vision of a Mexican woman emphasized the delicate features and light complexion of an ethnically Spanish woman of a certain class. The shock and disappointment the troopers experienced when they beheld a multitude of poor Indian or mestiza women is expressed in dozens of diaries and letters. For some, the racial obstacle was eventually overcome.

The literature and the courtships, portraying real and imagined scenarios, fed and salved the American conscience by showing that "our brave boys" had advanced a mission that went beyond adding land to a burgeoning empire. The assumed attraction of Mexican women to Yankee men simply reinforced notions of Anglo manhood. The theme of amalgamation meant more than territory, although the Mexican-American War likely produced fewer war brides than any other foreign conflict fought by the United States. The religious and racial divide that caused concern within Congress and thwarted the movement to annex all of Mexico contributed as well to the reluctance to create interethnic families. While marriage seemed an infrequent option, thousands of soldiers abandoned their morality by the banks of the Rio Grande in the search for female companionship. While some Mexican women profited as prostitutes, they were recurrently victims of exploitation and sexual violence. The behavior of many American soldiers in Mexico remains a permanent stain on the reputation of the military.

Evolution

The Mexican-American War temporarily altered the lives of thousands of women on both sides of the Rio Grande by offering opportunities for different roles and the exercise of unique talents. Since a majority of Mexican and American men promulgated a nineteenth-century standard of relationships, they reluctantly endorsed even a temporary shift in women's status or role. In the course of the war, men frequently equivocated over when and whether to credit women for their bravery and sacrifice. The Angel of Monterrey, martyred in her traditional role of bringing water and comfort to dying soldiers, was widely recognized, whereas the nontraditional independence and involvement of spy-in-residence Ann Chase was met in some quarters with denial and disbelief. Laundresses, cooks, and *soldaderas* remained largely nameless and faceless, their contributions too frequently mocked, marginalized, or unappreciated by their own people.

The war did not generate a significant change in the way gender roles were viewed within the societies. The transformation was evolutionary, not revolutionary. Clearly, for the first time, many women were provided the opportunity and place to exercise voice and power. The movement appeared more like a series of tremors than an earthquake. A rising female consciousness and the parallel demand for rights manifested themselves in the era. Prior issues of social and moral justice now reached out to include Abigail Adams's call during the Revolutionary era to "remember the ladies." From Boston to Baltimore, women arose with a powerful impetus for reform that not only engaged and enraged the citizenry of numerous states over the issues of divorce, property rights, and the suffrage but extended into the fashion arena—should women wear trousers, he infamous "Bloomer costume"?

Latin women faced far more difficult challenges than did their American sisters. In Mexico City, social custom and culture muted truly open discussion. While the doors of state-sponsored public education began to open wide for women in the United States, including the opportunity to attend colleges such as Mount Holyoke and Oberlin, women in Mexico City struggled merely to attain literacy. A majority of the capital's population were women, often single and from the countryside. Elementary-level schooling was available to a small number, and the intent persisted to make the girls "good daughters, excellent mothers, and the best and most solid support of the goals of society." Women who acquired a high level of learning or took up more difficult subjects, such as the sciences or history, were regularly ridiculed. By the mid-1850s, however, some gains had been made. A small cadre of Mexican women who possessed both education and a voice pressed the government to establish a secondary school for girls, although no reformers advocated educational equality.[8]

Similarly, the legal status of Mexican women changed only slightly. The historian Silvia Marina Arrom contends that while a subtle movement pressed for increased freedom and authority for women, "this trend, though discernible, was weak and discriminated among women of different marital statuses." Widows and single adult women benefited, while wives and daughters lived under the careful scrutiny of the man in the household. Mexicans might grudgingly recognize the competence and intelligence of women, but the Catholic Church, social cohesion, and public order dictated the subordination of married women. Within the decade, divorce became more accepted, and the laws more lenient, and women began to pursue legal separation from their husbands more aggressively. Still, the reform law of 1859 prohibited couples from parting on the grounds of incompatibility.[9]

The hostilities had a tremendous impact on a backward Mexican economy that lacked a transportation network, capital, and industry. Fighting ravaged the towns and countryside and increased an already burdensome national debt. It is difficult to gauge the longer-term impact on the masses of Mexican women. Among the lower classes, generally young and Indian, women labored in poverty as domestic servants, seamstresses, and sellers of food on the street or from their homes. A very small number, usually European, opened their own businesses offering women's fashions. Politically, no groundswell materialized for the suffrage, and the influence of women in politics remained largely confined to the private rather than the public sphere.[10]

Mexico experienced a critical upheaval in 1846 that further shook the unstable foundation of the republic. As the historian Timothy Henderson notes, "Mexico went to war with the United States not in spite of its weakness, but *because* of its weakness." Even the provincials, who rejected the strong hand of Mexico City, felt the humiliation. The capital had been occupied for months by Yankee troops, and the proud Mexican eagle stripped of its territorial feathers. The nation-state was further threatened by caste and class discord, economic devastation, and political chaos. In the midst of this turmoil, ruling-class men, the *hombres de bien,* desperately sought a peace with the United States—at a high price—that would allow them to remain in power and minimize the risk of revolution on the part of the masses. Members of the elite found place and comfort in the stability of the family and a freshly minted role for women.[11]

By the 1850s, the major change for Mexican women, Arrom and other scholars argue, came with the rise of the Latin equivalent—*marianismo*—of the American "cult of domesticity" or "true womanhood." The increased significance and reverence for motherhood coincided with the notion that women were different from men, rather than inferior. Just as in the United States, the assignment of women to a role in this vital yet separate sphere in the home recognized their competence, intelligence, and moral superiority but limited the options of utilizing their education, particularly in politics or the workplace. While many middle-class American women soon rejected elements of this construct, engaging in reform and pushing for domestic and political rights, elite Mexican women adjusted to the new paradigm with little dissent.

Importantly, the acceptance of *marianismo* distanced the upper classes from their peasant sisters, who continued to struggle in crowded living conditions performing low-wage jobs. Indeed, the privileged in the capital city did make gains following the war, but as Arrom emphasizes, "Despite the significance of gender, female solidarity did not come to outweigh class identification in Mexico."[12]

The Mexican-American War should be incorporated in our consciousness as an incremental step toward advancing greater gender awareness and promoting female involvement within the Mexican and American societies. By the middle of the nineteenth century, the struggle for social, economic, and political justice and equality for women remained a work in progress. Tragically, the bloodshed on both sides of the Rio Grande abated only temporarily. A decade later, the two countries would find themselves in brutal civil wars that lasted years, exacerbated by the Mexican-American War and related to issues of race, culture, and the power of the national government. These subsequent conflicts would demand of their women much greater involvement and more painful sacrifice.

NOTES

Introduction

1. Jack Larkin, *The Reshaping of Everyday Life, 1790–1840* (New York: Harper & Row, 1988), 6–9. Both Lola Sanchez and Nancy Conner are composite images representing women on both sides of the Rio Grande.

2. Harvey Mansfield and Debra Winthrop, eds., *Democracy in America* (Chicago: University of Chicago Press, 2000), 512.

3. Harry Watson, *Liberty and Power: The Politics of Jacksonian America* (New York: Noonday, 1990), 231–53.

4. David Meyer, "The Roots of American Industrialization, 1790–1860," eh.net /encyclopedia/the-roots-of-american-industrialization-1790-1860/.

5. Larkin, *Reshaping of Everyday Life,* 211–28.

6. Christine Stansell, *City of Women: Sex and Class in New York, 1789–1860* (Urbana: University of Illinois Press, 1987), 89–101, 131–49. New York Police Chief George Matsell estimated that there were approximately five thousand prostitutes in the city in the mid-1850s. Ibid., 171–92.

7. Thomas Dublin, *Women at Work: The Transformation of Work and Community in Lowell, Massachusetts, 1826–1860* (New York: Columbia University Press, 1979), 86–131.

8. Keith Melder, "Aspects of the Changing Status of New England Women, 1790–1840," teachushistory.org/detocqueville-visit-united-states/articles/aspects-changing-status -new-england-women. Melder emphasizes the role of sentimentality in giving women their elevated moral role and status, especially within the home. Sentimentality also implied their physical and intellectual weakness.

9. Nancy Cott, *The Bonds of Womanhood: Woman's Sphere in New England, 1780–1835* (New Haven, CT: Yale University Press, 1977), 63–100.

10. Melder, "Changing Status of New England Women," 8–11.

11. Timothy J. Henderson, *A Glorious Defeat: Mexico and Its War with the United States* (New York: Hill & Wang, 2007), 25–30.

12. Dennis E. Berge, trans. and ed., *Considerations on the Political and Social Situation of the Mexican Republic, 1847* (El Paso: Texas Western Press, 1975), 16–18, 26–27. Numerous scholars argue that the author of this tract was the Mexican moderate politician Mariano Otero.

13. Ibid., 20–23; Mark Wasserman, *Everyday Life and Politics in Nineteenth Century Mexico: Men, Women, and War* (Albuquerque: University of New Mexico Press, 2000), 63–65.

14. Ana Maria Alonso, *Thread of Blood: Colonialism, Revolution, and Gender on Mexico's Northern Frontier* (Tucson: University of Arizona Press, 1995), 131–37, 154–56.

15. Berge, *Mexican Republic,* 26–27.

16. Wasserman, *Everyday Life and Politics,* 41–43.

17. Silvia Marina Arrom, *The Women of Mexico City, 1790–1857* (Stanford, CA: Stanford University Press, 1985), 92–95.

18. Berge, *Mexican Republic,* 45.

19. Paul Bergeron, *The Presidency of James K. Polk* (Lawrence: University Press of Kansas, 1987), 15–21.

20. Ibid., 113–35.

21. Ibid., 63–72.

22. Ibid., 74–76; K. Jack Bauer, *The Mexican War, 1846–1848* (1974; reprint with an introduction by Robert W. Johannsen, Lincoln: University of Nebraska Press, 1992), 66–70.

23. Bauer, *Mexican War,* 164–96.

24. Ibid., 127–38.

25. Ibid., 81–102, 205–18.

26. Ibid., 238–53.

27. Ibid., 287–323; Henderson, *Glorious Defeat,* 163–72.

28. Henderson, *Glorious Defeat,* 172–78.

1. Women, Reform, and the US Home Front

1. Steve Abolt, "Militia Flags," in *The United States and Mexico at War: Nineteenth-Century Expansionism and Conflict,* ed. Donald Frazier (New York: MacMillan Reference Books USA, 1998), 159; *Indiana State Journal,* June 24, 1846. The Missouri lieutenant George Gibson vividly remembered the day of departure—the silk flag woven by the women of his community, the parade, the crowded streets, the fervent applause, the last farewells. George R. Gibson, *George R. Gibson: Journal of a Soldier under Kearny and Doniphan, 1846–1847,* ed. Ralph Bieber (Glendale, CA: Arthur H. Clark, 1935), 35.

2. S. F. Nunnelee, "Alabama and the Mexican War," *Alabama Historical Quarterly* 19 (Fall/Winter 1957): 415–17. Nunnelee penned his memoir in 1906.

3. R. M. Edwards, *Down the Tennessee: The Mexican War Reminiscences of an East Tennessee Volunteer (R. M. Edwards),* ed. Stewart Lillard (1895; Charlotte, NC: Loftin, 1997), 5–6, 81n14.

4. Teri Klassen, "Polk's Fancy: Quiltmaking, Patriotism, and Gender in the Mexican War Era," *Uncoverings* 27 (2006): 10.

5. Peggy M. Cashion, "Women and the Mexican War, 1846–1848" (MA thesis, University of Texas at Arlington, 1990), 89–101. Cashion offers a detailed and skeptical discussion of the extent to which American women embraced the Spartan mother ideal. Handing him his shield, the Spartan mother had admonished her son, "Either this or upon this." See Plutarch, "Lacaenarum Apophthegmata, 16," in *Moralia,* ed. Frank Cole Babbitt, Loeb Classical Library 265 (Cambridge, MA: Harvard University Press, 1961),

464–65. John Blount Robertson, *Reminiscences of a Campaign in Mexico* (Nashville: J. York, 1849), 64–66.

6. Edwards, *Down the Tennessee,* 21, 85n35; Cashion, "Women and the Mexican War," 46.

7. Amy Kaplan, "Manifest Domesticity," *American Literature* 70 (March 1998): 581–91. Kaplan also considers the work of Sara Josepha Hale, an early and strong advocate of a national day of thanksgiving. Hale, the editor of *Godey's Magazine and Lady's Book,* prompted a reconsideration of race and the contradiction of how an imperial United States might even consider amalgamation or annexation of people of different colors and ethnic backgrounds. See Linda S. Hudson, *Mistress of Manifest Destiny: A Biography of Jane McManus Storm Cazneau* (Austin: Texas State Historical Association, 2001), 60–62.

8. Mary W. Gibson to Thomas Ware Gibson, April 5, 1847, in R. B. Weber, ed., "The Mexican War: Some Personal Correspondence," *Indiana Magazine of History* 65 (June 1969): 138–39.

9. Cashion, "Women and the Mexican War," 92; Journal of Marcellus Ball Edwards, in Abraham Robinson Johnston, Marcellus Ball Edwards, and Philip Gooch Ferguson, *Marching with the Army of the West, 1846–1848: Journal of A. R. Johnston, 1846, Journal of M. B. Edwards, 1846–47, Diary of P. G. Ferguson, 1847–48,* ed. Ralph Bieber (Glendale, CA: Arthur H. Clark, 1936), January 17, 1847, 242–43.

10. D. W. Bartlett, "Woman and War," *Advocate of Peace and Universal Brotherhood* (Boston), November 1846; Jane Grey Swisshelm, *Half a Century* (Chicago: Jansen, McClurg, 1880), 95–96. Swisshelm's painful conversation with Black is recounted in detail in chapter 5 below.

11. Caroline Healey Dall, *Selected Journals of Caroline Healey Dall, 1838–1855,* ed. Helen Deese (Boston: Massachusetts Historical Society, 2006), xv–xvii; Dall, *Daughter of Boston: The Extraordinary Life of a Nineteenth-Century Woman, Caroline Healey Dall,* ed. Helen Deese (Boston: Beacon, 2005), xii–xv; Spencer Lavan and Peter Hughes, "Caroline Healey Dall," *Dictionary of Unitarian and Universalist Biography,* March 12, 2004, uudb.org/articles/carolinedall.html.

12. Dall, *Selected Journals of Caroline Healey Dall,* August 2, 1847, 249. Dall commented blandly, "Read my own article on War—fewer misprints than usual." *Boston Daily Chronotype,* July 22, 1847, in Dall, *Daughter of Boston,* 98.

13. Caroline Healey Dall, "Thoughts on War," *Monthly Religious Magazine* (Boston), August 1847.

14. Klassen, "Polk's Fancy," 11.

15. Cashion, "Women and the Mexican War," 47; Klassen, "Polk's Fancy," 3–13; DeLancey Floyd-Jones to his sister Sarah, May 20, 1848, DeLancey Floyd-Jones Letters, Special Collections, University of Texas at Austin.

16. *Pittsfield (MA) Sun,* March 9, 1848.

17. Ernest M. Lander, *Reluctant Imperialists: Calhoun, the South Carolinians, and the Mexican War* (Baton Rouge: Louisiana State University Press, 1980), 42–43, 149.

18. John M. Belohlavek, *Broken Glass: Caleb Cushing and the Shattering of the Union* (Kent, OH: Kent State University Press, 2005), 193–96.

19. "Women on the War Field," *Emancipator* (New York), April 28, 1847.

20. Amy S. Greenberg, *A Wicked War: Polk, Clay, Lincoln, and the 1846 U.S. Invasion of Mexico* (New York: Alfred A. Knopf, 2012), 159; Maggie MacLean, "Caroline Kirkland," *History of American Women* (blog), May 2, 2013, www.womenhistoryblog.com/2013/05/caroline-kirkland.html; "Caroline Kirkland," www.scribblingwomen.org/ckbio.htm.

21. *Union Magazine of Literature and Art* (New York), July 1847, 44, 48, October 1847, 188–89.

22. Ibid., January 1848, 21.

23. Cashion, "Women and the Mexican War," 83–89.

24. Greenberg, *Wicked War,* 129; Belohlavek, *Broken Glass,* 210–11; Bartlett, "Woman and War." Women were also involved in the National Association of Mexican War Veterans. Mrs. Moore Murdock assumed the secretaryship in 1897 and pressured Congress to increase pensions to twelve dollars a month. She also founded the Dames of 1846, the women's auxiliary, in 1901. Steven A. Butler, "Veterans' Organizations," in Frazier, *United States and Mexico at War,* 462; Nunnelee, "Alabama and the Mexican War," 432.

25. Elizabeth R. Varon, *We Mean to Be Counted: White Women and Politics in Antebellum Virginia* (Chapel Hill: University of North Carolina Press, 1998), 88–90.

26. Ibid., 91–93.

27. Ronald J. Zboray and Mary S. Zboray, *Voices without Votes: Women and Politics in Antebellum New England* (Hanover, NH: University Press of New England, 2010), 151–53.

28. Greenberg, *Wicked War,* 193; *Ohio Statesman* (Columbus), September 16, 1847.

29. Zboray and Zboray, *Voices without Votes,* 153–56.

30. Ibid., 158–62.

31. Varon, *We Mean to Be Counted,* 94–97; Zboray and Zboray, *Voices without Votes,* 157–62.

32. Nancy Isenberg, *Sex and Citizenship in Antebellum America* (Chapel Hill: University of North Carolina Press, 1998), 105.

33. Burritt espoused a philosophy of nonresistance, a distinctly minority viewpoint within the peace movement. Valarie H. Ziegler, *The Advocates of Peace in Antebellum America* (Bloomington: Indiana University Press, 1992), 107–8; Isenberg, *Sex and Citizenship,* 69, 139–40; *Pennsylvania Freeman* (Philadelphia), June 25, 1846; Ernesto Chavez, *The U.S. War with Mexico: A Brief History with Documents* (New York: Bedford/St. Martin's, 2008), 88–90. For a somewhat different emphasis that utilizes strongly religious language, see *Cincinnati Weekly Herald and Philanthropist,* June 24, 1846. This letter laments that men might deem it honorable to make war, while "nothing so becomes

a woman as to make peace." The women hoped to use their Christian influence to avert a conflict, but also to bind up the nation's wounds should war occur.

34. Chavez, *U.S. War with Mexico,* 90; Isenberg, *Sex and Citizenship*, 69.

35. Parker Pillsbury, Salem, OH, to William Lloyd Garrison, June 22, 1846, *Liberator* (Boston), July 3, 1846.

36. Linda L. Geary, *Balanced in the Wind: A Biography of Betsey Mix Cowles* (Lewisburg, PA: Bucknell University Press, 1989), 52–56; Stacey Robertson, *Betsey Mix Cowles: Champion of Equality* (Boulder, CO: Westview, 2014).

37. Geary, *Balanced in the Wind,* 57–66; Isenberg, *Sex and Citizenship,* 142–44.

38. Sarah to Joel McMillan, Lamoil, Bureau County, Illinois, October 10, 1847, Alice McMillan Papers, collection 591, box 1, Ohio Historical Society, Columbus; *Anti-Slavery Bugle* (New Lisbon, OH), September 17, 1847.

39. Henry County Female Anti-Slavery Society Papers, Indiana Division, Manuscripts Collection, Indiana State Library, Indianapolis; *Western Citizen* (Peoria, IL), July 27, 1847, January 25, 1848; Greenberg, *Wicked War,* 197.

40. Ziegler, *Advocates of Peace,* 109–15.

41. *Pennsylvania Freeman,* July 2, 1846, September 23, 1847; Lydia Chevalier, McKean Co., PA, to *Pennsylvania Freeman,* September 23, 1847; Greenberg, *Wicked War,* 196–97; Rebecca Gratz, Philadelphia, to Ann Gratz, July 22, 1847, in Rebecca Gratz, *Letters of Rebecca Gratz,* ed. David Philipson (Philadelphia: Jewish Publication Society of America, 1929), 341–42.

42. John H. Schroeder, *Mr. Polk's War: American Opposition and Dissent, 1846–1848* (Madison: University of Wisconsin Press, 1973), 116; Margaret Fuller, *Margaret Fuller: Critic,* ed. Judith M. Bean and Joel Myerson (New York: Columbia University Press, 2000), 424, 465.

43. Margaret Fuller, *The Writings of Margaret Fuller,* ed. Mason Wade (New York: Viking, 1941), letter 18, December 1847, 427, letter 24, Rome, April 19, 1848, 470; Cashion, "Women and the Mexican War," 80–83.

44. Cashion, "Women and the Mexican War," 5–6, 44–45. Cashion is particularly critical of several of Robert Johannsen's assumptions in *To the Halls of Montezuma: The Mexican War in the American Imagination* (New York: Oxford University Press, 1985), 136–41.

45. Frances Butler, Dunboyne, to E. G. W. Butler, June 18, July 8, 15, 26, 1847, and Isabelle Butler, Belmont, to E. G. W. Butler, September 25, December 11, 1847, Butler Family Papers, Historic New Orleans Collection, Williams Research Center, New Orleans.

46. Frances Butler to E. G. W. Butler, September 16, 30, 1847, ibid.

47. Frances Butler, Dunboyne to E. G. W. Butler, October 27, 1847, ibid.

48. Frances Butler, Dunboyne, to E. G. W. Butler, November 4, December 2, 9, 27, 1847, January 1, 3, 27, February 15, 21, 1848, ibid.

49. Frances Butler to E. G. W. Butler, April 10, May 1, June 15, 1848 , ibid. The politically driven inquiry into Scott's conduct and command lasted from March through June 1848. The site of the hearings shifted from Mexico to Frederick, Maryland, where Scott was embarrassed and his enemies exonerated. See John D. Eisenhower, *Agent of Destiny: The Life and Times of General Winfield Scott* (New York: Free Press, 1997), 309–21.

50. Robert A. Hunter, New Orleans, to Sarah Hunter, February 28, April 21, 1846, and Sarah Hunter, Red River, to Robert A. Hunter, March 3, May 18, 1846, Hunter Letters, Louisiana State University, Baton Rouge.

51. Robert A. Hunter, Matamoros, June 21, 1846, to Sarah Hunter, March 3, May 18, 1846, and Sarah Hunter, Pine Wood, LA, to R. A. Hunter, July 12, 1846, ibid.

52. Sarah Hunter, Red River, to R. A. Hunter, New Orleans, January 27, March 9, 1847, ibid.; Alcee Fortier, ed., *Louisiana: Comprising Sketches of Parishes, Towns, Events, Institutions, and Persons,* vol. 3 (Madison, WI: Century Historical Association, 1914), 215–16. Apparently, only five of Sarah's twelve children lived to maturity.

53. Cashion, "Women and the Mexican War," 52–56; Thomas Ware Gibson to Mary Goodwin Gibson, March 4, 1847, in Weber, "Mexican War," 132–36.

54. Cashion, "Women and the Mexican War," 49–51, 57.

55. Cornelia Howard (CH), Baltimore, to John E. Howard (JH), February 24, April 1, 1848, Howard Family Papers, Maryland Historical Society, Baltimore. Cornelia thought little of Louis Philippe, who was "not the rightful King," but she opined, "I do not suppose the French are prepared for self-government."

56. CH to JH, April 15,l 24, May 22, 29, June 15, 9, 21, 1847, ibid.

57. CH to JH, May 22, June 15, September 23, 1847, February 24, 1848, ibid.

58. CH to JH, April 15, May 29, June 8, 11, 1847, ibid.

59. CH to JH, June 11, 1847, January 1, April 1, 1848, ibid. Henri de la Tour d'Auvergne (1611–1675), a Protestant, was one of France's finest generals, serving in the Thirty Years' War and beyond. Cornelia admonished her son to emulate the Frenchman and make the morale of his men a priority. She demurred on buying the railroad stock, determining that it would have been better "if a pushy Yankee were at the head of the company." CH to JH, February 4, April 1, 1848, ibid.

60. CH to JH, April 10, 15, May 22, 29, 1847, ibid.

61. CH to JH, April 24, June 11, 15, 24, 1847, ibid.

62. CH to JH, May 7, 1847, January 1, 14, February 11, April 1, 1848, ibid.; R. McKim Marriott to JH, Baltimore, January 6, 1848, ibid. Cornelia wrote twenty letters to her son in 1847 and received only a handful in return, a source of constant complaint and irritation to an anxiety-ridden mother. John owned a farm which an Irishman named Mulvey managed efficiently for him during the war. CH to JH, February 4, 1848, ibid.

63. CH to JH, April 24, May 7, 22, October 25, 1847, February 4, 1848, ibid. Polonius was the meddlesome and ill-fated counselor to the king in *Hamlet.*

64. CH to JH, June 30, July 9, 1847, January 14, February 4, 5, 1848, ibid.

65. Cashion, "Women and the Mexican War," 47–48, 18–20, 61.

66. Ibid., 21, 30–31.

67. Gibson, *George R. Gibson,* August 21, 1846, 217n355, August 30, 1846, 227n361; Cashion, "Women and the Mexican War," 22–26.

2. *Soldaderas*

1. James Russell Lowell, *The Bigelow Papers* (Cambridge, MA, 1848), 23–25. For an excellent analysis of Lowell's work and the disillusionment and loss of belief that accompanied the soldiers' experience in Mexico, see Jaime Javier Rodriguez, *The Literatures of the U.S.-Mexican War: Narrative, Time, and Identity* (Austin: University of Texas Press, 2010), 110–28; and Rodriguez, "The U.S.-Mexican War in James Russell Lowell's *The Bigelow Papers,*" *Arizona Quarterly* 63 (Autumn 2007): 1–33.

2. Elizabeth Salas, *Soldaderas in the Mexican Military: Myth and History* (Austin: University of Texas Press, 1990), 32–33; Christopher Conway, "Ravished Virgins and Warrior Women: Gender and Literature of the U.S.-Mexican War," *Fronteras* 18 (Fall 2009): 3–4.

3. Donald Frazier, "Life in the Mexican Army," in *The United States and Mexico at War: Nineteenth-Century Expansionism and Conflict,* ed. Frazier (New York: MacMillan Reference Books USA, 1998), 28–29.

4. David Clary, *Eagles and Empire: The U.S., Mexico, and the Struggle for a Continent* (New York: Random House, 2009), 132; Mark Wasserman, *Everyday Life and Politics in Nineteenth Century Mexico: Men, Women, and War* (Albuquerque: University of New Mexico Press, 2000), 79, 82–83. For a detailed discussion of the nature and background of Mexican recruits, see Peter Guardino, "Gender, Soldiering, and Citizenship in the Mexican-American War of 1846–1848," *American Historical Review* 119 (February 2014): 23–46.

5. Christopher Conway and Gustavo Pellón, *The U.S.-Mexican War: A Binational Reader* (Indianapolis: Hackett, 2010), 78–80; Timothy J. Henderson, *A Glorious Defeat: Mexico and Its War with the United States* (New York: Hill & Wang, 2007), 76–81, 119, 162; K. Jack Bauer, *The Mexican War, 1846–1848* (1974; reprint with an introduction by Robert W. Johannsen, Lincoln: University of Nebraska Press, 1992), 393; Manuel Balbontín, *La Invasion Americana 1846 a 1848* (Mexico City, 1883), 12–18. For a general discussion of the organization and effectiveness of the respective armies, see Henderson, *Glorious Defeat;* Clary, *Eagles and Empire,* 130–32; Richard Bruce Winders, *Mr. Polk's Army: The American Military Experience in the Mexican War* (College Station: Texas A&M University Press, 1997); and John D. Eisenhower, *So Far from God: The U.S. War with Mexico, 1846–1848* (New York: Random House, 1989).

6. Frazier, "Life in the Mexican Army," 28–29; Clary, *Eagles and Empire,* 135–38.

7. Donald Frazier, "Soldaderas," in Frazier, *United States and Mexico at War,* 391.

8. "The Corporal," writing for the *New Orleans Bee,* June 27, 1846.

9. Ramón Alcaraz, *The Other Side, or Notes for the History of the War between Mexico*

and the United States (1850; reprint, New York: Burt Franklin, 1970); *Baltimore Sun,* May 13, 1847; *Constitution* (Middletown, CT), June 2, 1847; George Winston Smith and Charles Judah, eds., *Chronicle of the Gringos: The U.S. Army in the Mexican War, 1846–1848* (Albuquerque: University of New Mexico Press, 1968), April 28, 1847, 215–16; Tom Reilly and Manley Witten, *War with Mexico: America's Reporters Cover the Battlefront* (Lawrence: University Press of Kansas, 2010), 138–39; Salas, *Soldaderas,* 32.

10. Clary, *Eagles and Empire,* 271–72; William DePalo, *The Mexican National Army, 1822–1852* (College Station: Texas A&M University Press, 1997), 119–20.

11. Alcaraz, *Other Side,* 132–37. K. Jack Bauer contends that Santa Anna was solid at strategic conception but not execution. "He was not a good battlefield general." Bauer, *Mexican War,* 218.

12. Samuel Chamberlain, *My Confession: Recollections of a Rogue,* ed. William Goetzmann (Austin: Texas State Historical Society, 1996), February 24, 1847, 170–71.

13. Clary, *Eagles and Empire,* 282.

14. Ibid., 313, 351n26; James McCaffrey, *Army of Manifest Destiny: The American Soldier in the Mexican War, 1846–1848* (New York: New York University Press, 1992), 187.

15. *New Hampshire Sentinel* (Keene), December 9, 1846; *Niles' National Register* (Baltimore), December 19, 1846; *Maine Farmer* (Winthrop), November 26, 1846; *Ladies Repository and Gatherings of the West* (Cincinnati), April 1847; *Dwight's American Magazine and Family Newspaper* (New York), December 19, 1846; Smith and Judah, *Chronicle of the Gringos,* 90; Clary, *Eagles and Empire,* 199. The story remained critical to the narrative of the war and was retold a half century later in A. D. Hall's novel *Captain Impudence: A Romance of the Mexican War* (New York: Street & Smith, 1897), 13–14.

16. *Ohio Statesman* (Columbus), January 4, 1847.

17. "Heroine of Monterey," by James G. Lyons, Music for the Nation: American Sheet Music, 1820–1860, Library of Congress. The Americans spelled the city name Monterey, while the Spanish spelled it with an additional *r,* Monterrey. The latter form is used throughout.

18. Senator Thomas Corwin, speech, February 11, 1847, reprinted in *Niles' National Register,* February 27, 1847; Amy S. Greenberg, *A Wicked War: Polk, Clay, Lincoln, and the 1846 U.S. Invasion of Mexico* (New York: Alfred A. Knopf, 2012), 193.

19. J. H. Hewitt, "The Maid of Monterey," (1851), Music for the Nation: American Sheet Music, 1820–1860, Library of Congress (a very interesting version, sung by a woman, can be found on Youtube); Luis Senarens, *Old Rough and Ready, or The Heroine of Monterey* (New York: F. Tousey, 1886), available on microfilm at the University of Minnesota.

20. "Gwin Bernard, or the Escaped Soldier and the Dog," *Southern Patriot* (Charleston, SC), September 10, 1847.

21. "The Angels of Buena Vista" (1847), in John Greenleaf Whittier, *The Writings of John Greenleaf Whittier* (Boston: Houghton, Mifflin, 1892), 112–16; John H. Schroeder,

Mr. Polk's War: American Opposition and Dissent, 1846–1848 (Madison: University of Wisconsin Press, 1973), 102; Whittier, "Angels of Buena Vista," 173–76.

22. John Corey Henshaw, *Major John Corey Henshaw: Recollections of the War with Mexico,* ed. Gary Kurutz (Columbia: University of Missouri Press, 2008), 116.

23. Yolanda Romero, "María Josefa Zozaya," in Frazier, *United States and Mexico at War,* 490–91; Frazier, in a separate entry, ibid., 391, adopts Salas's argument, arguing that Zozaya, as the "Angel of Monterrey," was a *soldadera* who nursed Mexican soldiers and was killed by a bullet; Salas, *Soldaderas,* 31; Clary, *Eagles and Empire,* 199; Abner Doubleday, *My Life in the Old Army: The Reminiscences of Abner Doubleday from the Collections of the New York Historical Society,* ed. Joseph E. Chance (Fort Worth: Texas Christian University Press, 1998), 322n7.

24. Doubleday, *My Life in the Old Army,* 99; Daniel Harvey Hill, *A Fighter from Way Back: The Mexican War Diary of Lt. Daniel Harvey Hill, 4th Artillery, USA,* ed. Nathaniel C. Hughes Jr. and Timothy D. Johnson (Kent, OH: Kent State University Press, 2002), 27.

25. Salas, *Soldaderas,* 30–31.

26. General José Uraga, Monterrey, to General Pedro Ampudia, September 19, 1846, and Ampudia, Monterrey, to Minister of War, September 19, 1846, in Conway and Pellón, *U.S.-Mexican War,* 78–81; *Harbinger* (New York), November 13, 1847.

27. George Wilkins Kendall, "Irish Deserter and Mexican Joan of Arc," in *Spirit of the Times* (New York), January 2, 1847, reprinted in Chavez, *U.S. War with Mexico,* 104–5; William S. Henry, *Campaign Sketches of the War with Mexico* (New York: Harper Bros., 1847), 233–34. Kendall credits the remarks in his column to an Irish deserter. Almost concurrently, Henry, who was an officer in Monterrey in 1846, used the identical language to describe Doña Jesús in his memoir published in 1847. Clary, *Eagles and Empire,* 195, cites the Henry volume. Robert Johannsen, *To the Halls of Montezuma: The Mexican War in the American Imagination* (New York: Oxford University Press, 1985), 137–38.

28. Niceto de Zamacois, "Don Luis Martínez de Castro of the National Guard," in Conway and Pellón, *U.S.-Mexican War,* 188–90.

29. Frank S. Edwards, *A Campaign in New Mexico with Colonel Doniphan* (Philadelphia: Carey & Hart, 1847), 88; *Albion* (New York), November 27, 1847; McCaffrey, *Army of Manifest Destiny,* 158–59; Eisenhower, *So Far from God,* 234; John Frost, *Pictorial History of Mexico and the Mexican War* (Philadelphia: Thomas, Cowperthwait, 1849), 418; Doubleday, *My Life in the Old Army,* 322n7.

30. Hill, *Fighter from Way Back,* October 16, 1846, 29–30.

31. Salas *Soldaderas,* 35.

3. On the Santa Fe Trail

1. Sister Mary Loyola, *The American Occupation of New Mexico, 1821–1852* (Albuquerque: University of New Mexico Press, 1939), 28–30; Max Moorhead, *New Mexico's*

Royal Road: Trade and Travel on the Chihuahua Trail (Norman: University of Oklahoma Press, 1958), 59–66, 75–77, 85–88. Moorhead notes that mules rivaled oxen as the animals preferred to pull the wagons. They also served as pack animals and could travel fifteen to eighteen miles a day and carry up to four hundred pounds. Once in Missouri, the mules could be sold south to work on farms or plantations. Josiah Gregg, *Commerce of the Prairies* (1844; reprint, Norman: University of Oklahoma Press, 1954), 331–33, cites the statistics of the trade.

2. Loyola, *American Occupation,* 31–35. Bent indicates in a letter of January 30, 1841, to Manuel Alvarez, the US consul in Sante Fe, that more than twenty "American" men were living in Taos in 1841, although several clearly were French. Five are listed as "distillers." Loyola, *American Occupation,* 34. Ceran St. Vrain (1802–1870) was the son of aristocrats who escaped to the United States following the French Revolution. He partnered early with Charles Bent in the Santa Fe trade.

3. Stephen G. Hyslop, *Bound for Santa Fe: The Road to New Mexico and the American Conquest, 1806–1848* (Norman: University of Oklahoma Press, 2002), 295–99.

4. Loyola, *American Occupation,* 60–62.

5. Norma B. Ricketts, *The Mormon Battalion: Army of the West, 1846–1848* (Logan: Utah State University Press, 1996), June 26–27, 1846, 11–12.

6. Ibid., June 27–July 22, 1846, 13–17; Carl V. Larson and Shirley N. Maynes, *Women of the Mormon Battalion* (Providence, UT: Watkins, 1989), 46–47.

7. Daniel Tyler, *A Concise History of the Mormon Battalion in the Mexican War, 1846–1847* (Salt Lake City, UT, 1881), 124–30. Ricketts lists and documents thirty-four women on the march. *Mormon Battalion,* 31–33. Shirley N. Maynes, *Five Hundred Wagons Stood Still: Mormon Battalion Wives* (Sandy, UT: Corporate Edge, 1999), 15, 444–45.

8. Margrett Scott, Tennessee Dyer City, to J. Allen Scott, August 30, 1846, in David L. Bigler and Will Bagley, eds., *Army of Israel: Mormon Battalion Narratives* (Logan: Utah State University Press, 2000), 66–68. Margrett traveled from Nauvoo to a nearby Tennessee settlement, where she faced her own issues, including a swindler posing as a missionary.

9. Bigler and Bagley, *Army of Israel,* 196, 281. Deaths occurred both on the trail and at Pueblo, Colorado, where a number of Mormons had traveled after their discharge. For example, Celia Hunt lost her infant son, Parley, in Pueblo in January 1847. The cause of Lt. Col. Allen's death along the trail is unclear. Henry Standage, *The March of the Mormon Battalion from Council Bluffs to California: Taken from the Journal of Henry Standage,* ed. Frank A. Golder (New York: Century, 1928), October 14, 1846, 176; Larson and Maynes, *Women of the Mormon Battalion,* 1–2, 24–25, 41, 64–65, 102–3; Hyslop, *Bound for Santa Fe,* 360–62; George R. Gibson, *George R. Gibson: Journal of a Soldier under Kearny and Doniphan, 1846–1847,* ed. Ralph Bieber (Glendale, CA: Arthur H. Clark, 1935), 252.

10. Ricketts, *Mormon Battalion,* 29–31, October 14, 18, 1846, 68–69, 70–72; Philip St. George Cooke, *The Conquest of New Mexico and California* (New York: Putnam,

1878), 90–92. William Y. Chalfant's very readable *Dangerous Passage: The Santa Fe Trail and the Mexican War* (Norman: University of Oklahoma Press, 1994) offers particular insight regarding the Indians and the trail during the conflict.

11. Ricketts, *Mormon Battalion,* October 14, December 22, 1846, 69, 104. Coray was equally offended by the bare-breasted Pima women that he encountered in December in Arizona. They looked very "baudy" and "unnatural" wearing only breechcloths. Americans rarely found Indian women attractive, although they often praised them for their appearance and industriousness, contrasting them with the Mexican women. Frank S. Edwards, *A Campaign in New Mexico with Colonel Doniphan* (Philadelphia: Carey & Hart, 1847), 63; George Winston Smith and Charles Judah, eds., *Chronicle of the Gringos: The U.S. Army in the Mexican War, 1846–1848* (Albuquerque: University of New Mexico Press, 1968), 125.

12. Gibson, *George R. Gibson,* 258.

13. Bigler and Bagley, *Army of Israel,* 147; Ricketts, *Mormon Battalion,* October 18, 24, 29, 1846, 70–75. Sophia apparently later divorced Gribble in Salt Lake City and married another soldier, William Tubbs.

14. Ricketts, *Mormon Battalion,* October 24–27, 1846, 74–75.

15. Ibid., April 23–27, May 15–18, 1846, 136, 137; Standage, *March of the Mormon Battalion,* April 4, 1847, 216.

16. Deena J. Gonzalez, *Refusing the Favor: The Spanish-Mexican Women of Santa Fe, 1820–1880* (New York: Oxford University Press, 1999), 71–74.

17. Jane Dysart, "Mexican Women in San Antonio, 1830–1860: The Assimilation Process," *Western Historical Quarterly* 7 (October 1976): 369–72.

18. Ana Carolina Castillo Crimm, *De León: A Tejano Family History* (Austin: University of Texas Press, 2003), 187–211. See also Gerald Poyo, ed., *Tejano Journey, 1780–1850* (Austin: University of Texas Press, 1996).

19. Raymond S. Brandes, trans., *Times Gone By in Alta California: Recollections of Señora Doña Juana Machado Alipaz de Wrightington* (1878). *Historical Society of Southern California Quarterly* 41, no. 3 (September 1959): 195–97, 216–19. After losing her first husband, an otter hunter named William Curley, in a drowning accident, Ramona selected a most interesting spouse—"Cockney Bill" Williams, a farmer and rancher, who in 1857 advertised for a wife in the newspaper. He was rewarded with the hand of one of the most prominent widows in San Diego.

20. Ibid.,196, 216–19; Richard Henry Dana, *Two Years before the Mast and Twenty-Four Years After* (1840; reprint, New York: P. F. Collier, 1909), 113–14, 390.

21. Ricketts, *Mormon Battalion,* 222–25; Larson and Maynes, *Women of the Mormon Battalion,* 47. Eighty-two of the men of the Mormon Battalion chose to reenlist for an additional six months of service. They were mustered out in March 1848.

22. Winston Groom, *Kearny's March: The Epic Creation of the American West, 1846–1847* (New York: Alfred A. Knopf, 2011), 271. Groom offers the best and most readable recent account of the march. He credits Cooke for the brilliant engineering design of

the road west that is the present-day route of Amtrak's "Sunset Limited." Susan Easton Black, "Mormon Battalion," in *The United States and Mexico at War: Nineteenth-Century Expansionism and Conflict,* ed. Donald Frazier (New York: MacMillan Reference Books USA, 1998), 277. For a fine account of Doniphan's role, see Joseph G. Dawson III, *Doniphan's Epic March: The 1st Missouri Volunteers in the Mexican War* (Lawrence: University Press of Kansas, 1999).

23. Susan Shelby Magoffin, *Down the Santa Fe Trail and into Mexico: The Diary of Susan Shelby Magoffin, 1846–1847,* ed. Stella M. Drumm (New Haven, CT: Yale University Press, 1926), ix–xi. Scholars have long been aware of Susan Magoffin and her role. Bernard DeVoto recognized her in his classic *1846: Year of Decision* (1943), and a recent article by Monica Reyes, "'Within the little circle of my vision': Domesticity as the Catalyst for Acculturation in Susan Shelby Magoffin's *Down the Santa Fe Trail and into Mexico,*" appeared in *Coldnoon: Travel Poetics* 4 (January 2015): 108–35.

24. Magoffin, *Down the Santa Fe Trail,* xviii–xxi. The expedition soon increased dramatically in size, as several other merchants joined in, propelling the number of wagons to forty-five and creating "a village on a hill." Within a few weeks the total almost doubled, to eighty wagons of merchandise and 150 people. Susan referred to the presence of "Americans, Mexicans, and Negroes" on the wagon train but did not deal further with the black role or presence. Ibid., June 21, July 5, 1846, 20–21, 42–43. Gibson, *George R. Gibson,* 55; Mary J. Straw Cook, *Doña Tules: Santa Fe's Courtesan and Gambler* (Albuquerque: University of New Mexico Press, 2007), 23. For a penetrating look at the reaction of Mexican merchants to the conquest, see David A. Sandoval, "The American Invasion of New Mexico and Mexican Merchants," *Journal of Popular Culture* 35 (Fall 2001): 61–72.

25. Magoffin, *Down the Santa Fe Trail,* xxiv–xxv.

26. Ibid., June 11, July 5, 1846, xvii, 4–6, 55.

27. Ibid., June 16–17, 25–27, 30, August 8, 1846, 12–13, 20–21, 25–29, 34, 72–73. She seems to have been describing a grasshopper or a praying mantis.

28. Ibid., June 21–23, June 25, July 1, 3, 6, 1846, 21–23, 27, 35–39, 42–43.

29. Ibid., July 21, August 26, October 17, November 26, 1846, 56, 94, 157, 167–68.

30. Ibid., July 18, 29–31, August 6–7, 1846, 53, 65–68, 70–71.

31. Ibid., August 14, 26–28, 1846, 78–79, 92–95, 98.

32. Ibid., August 26–29, 1846, 93–102. *Cigarritos,* small, three-by-one-inch corn husks filled with tobacco, had the size and shape of cigarettes, while *cigarillos* featured tobacco wrappers enclosing tobacco, very much resembling small cigars.

33. Hyslop, *Bound for Santa Fe,* 281; James M. Lacy, "New Mexico Women in Early American Writings," *New Mexico Historical Review* 34 (1959): 41–48; Janet Lecompte, "The Independent Women of Hispanic New Mexico, 1821–1846," *Western Historical Quarterly* 1 (January 1981): 22–24. Lecompte contends that the moral outrage expressed by many American observers reflected their lack of understanding of New Mexican customs and culture. For example, she rejects Gregg's assumption in *Commerce of the Prairies* regarding the regularity of forced marriage.

34. Lewis Hector Garrard, *Wah-to-Yah and the Taos Trail* (1850; reprint, Norman: University of Oklahoma Press, 1973), 171, 174, 202–4.

35. A New Englander, "Scenes in the Rocky Mountains, Oregon, California, New Mexico, Texas, and the Grant Prairies," *Macon (GA) Weekly Telegraph*, March 9, 1847; Edwards, *Campaign in New Mexico with Colonel Doniphan*, 50–52, 59.

36. Matt Field, *Matt Field on the Santa Fe Trail*, ed. Clyde Porter and Mae Reed Porter (1960; reprint, Norman: University of Oklahoma Press, 1995), 213, 238–39; Richard Smith Elliott, *The Mexican War Correspondence of Richard Smith Elliott*, ed. Mark L. Gardner and Marc Simmons (Norman: University of Oklahoma Press, 1997), 170–71, 174.

37. Field, *Matt Field*, 238–39; Gibson, *George R. Gibson*, 195, 357. Gibson emphasized the disappointment of finding women in towns such as Las Vegas who looked more like frontier Indian squaws than Castilian beauties.

38. Gibson, *George R. Gibson*, 205, 216n355; James Josiah Webb, *James Josiah Webb: Adventures in the Santa Fe Trade, 1844–1847*, ed. Ralph Bieber (1831; reprint, Lincoln: University of Nebraska Press, 1995), 91–92; Field, *Matt Field*, 213.

39. Governor Armijo received scathing criticism for his withdrawal from Santa Fe but was acquitted of any charges. After the war, he returned to New Mexico as a merchant. Sandoval, "American Invasion of New Mexico," 71. Gibson, *George R. Gibson*, 215–16. For an older, traditional account see Ralph E. Twitchell, *The History of the Military Occupation of the Territory of New Mexico from 1846–1851* (Denver: Smith-Brooks, 1909).

40. Gibson, *George R. Gibson*, 215–16.

41. Ibid., 224–25; Cooke, *Conquest of New Mexico and California*, 49–50.

42. Magoffin, *Down the Santa Fe Trail*, September 11, 24, 1846, 119–21, 142–45; Smith and Judah, *Chronicle of the Gringos*, 118–19, 123–24.

43. Cook, *Doña Tules*, 1–2. *Tules* literally refers to reed or rushes in the local marshes of the region.

44. Ibid., 3–9. The best estimate for the arrival of Juan Ignacio Barceló in Sonora appears to be in the late 1760s.

45. Ibid., 12–14.

46. Ibid., 15–19. Tules's mother, Dolores Herrero, remarried in 1823 and lived in Santa Fe until 1841.

47. Ibid., 20–21; Ralph Adam Smith, *Borderlander: The Life of James Kirker, 1793–1852* (Norman: University of Oklahoma Press, 1999), 94–96, 275. A photograph of Kirker shows a powerful-looking man with large hands, stern visage, and burning eyes, someone rightfully feared if not admired in New Mexico. The sexual laxity of the society was commented upon in 1847 by an American doctor who noted the frequency of syphilis and the number of women who attended fandangos even when they were "far gone in pregnancy." Cook, *Doña Tules*, 30–31.

48. Field, *Matt Field*, 205–8, 238. "Nancy Dawson" is an eighteenth-century English song adapted in the United States as "Here we go round the Mulberry Bush."

49. Cook, *Doña Tules,* 20–23.

50. Ibid., 24–26.

51. Ibid., 26–28; Field, *Matt Field,* 209–11; Elliott, *Mexican War Correspondence,* 165–66. In August 1847, Elliott offered a fascinating and detailed look at the tavern environment and Tules in action.

52. Cook, *Doña Tules,* 21, 24–26; Smith, *Borderlander,* 94; Elliott, *Mexican War Correspondence,* 211; Cook, *Doña Tules,* 2, 22–23, 26–27, 42.

53. W. W. H. Davis, *El Gringo: or New Mexico and Her People* (New York: Harper & Bros., 1857). Davis, who errs in noting Doña Tules's birth in Taos, discusses her wealth and social position, labeling her the "most expert monte dealer in the city" (185).

54. Cook, *Doña Tules,* 34–36. Cook sees the amount awarded to Tules in the Coulter case as reflective of a rising tide of pro-American, anti-Tules sentiment in New Mexico by 1850.

55. Ibid., 42–44. The play *Pizarro,* performed by the soldiers in English, had debuted in St. Louis in 1821 and was very popular on the frontier. Magoffin, *Down the Santa Fe Trail,* 120. Frank Edwards complained about the lack of women for roles in *Pizarro* but allowed that three of the soldiers "made very good looking women when dressed in character." Edwards, *Campaign in New Mexico with Colonel Doniphan,* 70–71; Elliott, *Mexican War Correspondence,* 117–18, 211–15. Elliott coyly hints that Tules's vision of another conquest of an American officer failed to materialize. Gibson, *George R. Gibson,* 273n396; Hyslop, *Bound for Santa Fe,* 366. For a thoughtful examination of the relationship between Tules and Colonel Mitchell, see Janet Lecompte, "La Tules and the Americans," *Arizona and the West* 20 (Autumn 1978): 215–30.

56. Cook, *Doña Tules,* 41, 46–47.

57. David Clary, *Eagles and Empire: The U.S., Mexico, and the Struggle for a Continent* (New York: Random House, 2009), 246–47, 264–65.

58. The trapper James Beckwourth wistfully described Bent's wife as "a real Doña an' a beauty." "James Beckwourth," in Bruce Cutler, *At War with Mexico: A Fictional Mosaic* (Norman: University of Oklahoma Press, 2001), 106; Gibson, *George R. Gibson,* 242n376, 259, 275.

59. Cook, *Doña Tules,* 45–46. Stella Drumm reaffirms the credit due to Doña Tules's network for warning the Americans about a developing uprising in Taos in December. Magoffin, *Down the Santa Fe Trail,* xxxi n. 43.

60. Clary, *Eagles and Empire,* 265–67. Estimates of the population of Taos varied sharply. The trader and trapper Dick Wootton claimed that 5,000–6,000 people lived there. Teresina Bent recounted her childhood experience of the Taos Rebellion, especially the storming of her father's house and the escape of the women and children.

61. Lewis Hector Garrard recalled the trials and the sentencing of nine more Indians and Mexicans on April 30. Michael McNierney, ed., *Taos 1847: The Revolt in Contemporary Accounts* (Boulder, CO: Johnson, 1980),11–15, 76–77; Garrard, *Wah-to-Yah and the Taos Trail,* 181–82; "James Beckwourth," in Cutler, *At War with Mexico,* 106–8.

Excellent accounts of the Taos Rebellion can be found in Hyslop, *Bound for Santa Fe,* 381–403, and Cooke, *Conquest of New Mexico and California,* 111–24. See Sandoval, "American Invasion of New Mexico," 67–68, for the disenchantment of many Mexican merchants with the occupation. Dawson, *Doniphan's Epic March,* 129.

62. Cook, *Doña Tules,* 14, 95, 102–4. A sympathetic novel about Doña Tules is Anna Burr's *The Golden Quicksand* (New York: Appleton-Century, 1936).

63. Gibson, *George R. Gibson,* 243; Brian DeLay, *War of a Thousand Deserts: Indian Raids and the U.S.-Mexican War* (New Haven, CT: Yale University Press, 2008), 265–66, 278.

64. Magoffin, *Down the Santa Fe Trail,* September 25, October 1, 5, 1846, 146–49; Gibson, *George R. Gibson,* 252, 272–73.

65. Gibson, *George R. Gibson,* 273–75.

66. Magoffin, *Down the Santa Fe Trail,* July 30, October 14, 1846, February 12–13, 1847, 67, 156, 202–4; Gibson, *George R. Gibson,* 322–23.

67. Magoffin, *Down the Santa Fe Trail,* December 28, 1846, 190–91. See A. Brooke Caruso, *The Mexican Spy Company: United States Covert Operations in Mexico, 1845–1848* (Jefferson, NC: McFarland, 1991), 94–104, for a detailed description of the Magoffin mission. A solid biography that also explores the ill-fated intrigue is W. H. Timmons, *James Wiley Magoffin: Don Santiago—El Paso Pioneer* (El Paso: Texas Western Press, 1999), chap. 4.

68. Magoffin, *Down the Santa Fe Trail,* September 19, December 1, 1846, 134–36, 169.

69. Ibid., July 30, September 4, December 18, 1846, 66, 111, 177.

70. Ibid., February 21, 1847, 209–10.

71. Ibid., November 17, December 15, 1846, 163–65, 173.

72. Ibid., October 28, November 17, 1846, 163–65.

73. Gibson, *George R. Gibson,* 323n432.

74. Ibid., 356–57; Dawson, *Doniphan's Epic March,* 163–69; Journal of Marcellus Ball Edwards, in Abraham Robinson Johnston, Marcellus Ball Edwards, and Philip Gooch Ferguson, *Marching with the Army of the West, 1846–1848: Journal of A. R. Johnston, 1846, Journal of M. B. Edwards, 1846–47, Diary of P. G. Ferguson, 1847–48,* ed. Ralph Bieber (Glendale, CA: Arthur H. Clark, 1936), March 2, 1847, July 9, 1848, 271, 361.

75. Magoffin, *Down the Santa Fe Trail,* May 23, 1847, 228–29.

76. Ibid., July 4, 16, 21, August 23–25, 1847, 236, 239–41, 248–51. Maria Hunter's celebrity status in northern Mexico is discussed in some detail in chapter 4.

77. Ibid., August 24–26, 1847, 250–53.

78. Ibid., xxxi–xxxiii. Sam Magoffin continued to live in the St. Louis area until his death in 1888. *El Paso Times,* June 3, 2012.

4. Profiles in Courage

1. George Wilkins Kendall, *George Wilkins Kendall: Dispatches from the Mexican War,* ed. Lawrence Cress (Norman: University of Oklahoma Press, 1999), Matamoros, June 12, 1846, 50; Samuel Ryan Curtis, *Mexico under Fire: Being the Diary of Samuel Ryan Curtis, 3rd Ohio Volunteer Regiment during the American Occupation of Northern Mexico, 1846–1847,* ed. Joseph E. Chance (Fort Worth: Texas Christian University Press, 1994), September 2–3, 1846, May 3, 1847, 32–33, 230n32. Sutlers were independent traders who sold everyday goods, often at inflated prices, to soldiers in camp or in the field.

2. Curtis, *Mexico under Fire,* January 12, 1847, 96.

3. Ibid., November 15, 23, December 2, 1846, January 14, 1847, 62, 66, 97, 72, 244n122. Curtis noted in January 1847 that Miss Bowen's home was broken into and a trunk with all of her clothes and money stolen. The trunk was later found empty outside town.

4. Abner Doubleday, *My Life in the Old Army: The Reminiscences of Abner Doubleday from the Collections of the New York Historical Society,* ed. Joseph E. Chance (Fort Worth: Texas Christian University Press, 1998), March 1848, 128–34.

5. Napoleon Dana to his wife, Sue, September 30, October 1, 1845, in Napoleon Dana, *Monterrey is Ours! The Mexican War Letters of Lieutenant Dana, 1845–1847,* ed. Robert H. Ferrell (Lexington: University of Kentucky Press, 1990), 16–17.

6. Ibid., September 26, 30, October 6, 8, 15, 1845, 16–25.

7. Ibid., September 4, October 19, November 7, 1845, August 20, 1846, 8, 27–28, 32, 107. Dana grumbled about the number of pregnant women and children in camp in November 1845. With an overdose of Victorian sexism he observed, "Girls will do it, all of them, when you give them a chance, won't they?"

8. John McClanahan, October 25, 1846, to his sister, in George Winston Smith and Charles Judah, eds., *Chronicle of the Gringos: The U.S. Army in the Mexican War, 1846–1848* (Albuquerque: University of New Mexico Press, 1968), 303; John James Peck, *The Sign of the Eagle: A View of Mexico, 1830–1855; The Letters of Lieutenant John James Peck,* ed. Richard Pourade (San Diego: Union Tribune, 1970), December 27, 1846, 65; Cashion, "Women and the Mexican War," 111.

9. Helen Chapman, *The News from Brownsville: Helen Chapman's Letters from the Texas Military Frontier, 1848–1852,* ed. Caleb Coker (Austin: Texas State Historical Association, 1992), 344–45.

10. Paul Horgan, *Great River: The Rio Grande in North American History,* 4th ed. (Hanover, NH: Wesleyan University Press, 1984), 738. Wool and his fourteen hundred men marched out of San Antonio in September 1846 with the goal of capturing the interior city of Chihuahua. Three months later, the campaign was abandoned at Parras. Soon thereafter, in February 1847, Wool's troops fought with Taylor's forces in the difficult and celebrated Battle of Buena Vista.

11. Chapman, *News from Brownsville,* February 6, March 13, September 17, 1848, 20, 25, 76. Helen left her 7-year old son, Willie, behind with his grandmother. The family was reunited in 1849, when Willie came to Mexico.

12. Ibid., January 20, 26, 1848, 9, 13–14.

13. Horgan, *Great River,* 781–82; Chapman, *News from Brownsville,* February 13, April 6, May 15, July 3, August 26, September 15, 1848, January 22, February 5, 1849, 22–23, 33, 36, 41, 57, 68, 75, 110, 112. Helen Chapman found Taylor to be honest and genuine and also supported him for the presidency. William remained in the military and died in 1859 in Virginia. Helen expired in South Carolina in 1881. David Hunter rose to the rank of major general during the Civil War. He organized the first all-black regiment in federal service and presided over the commission that tried Lincoln's assassins in 1865. The Hunters passed away in Washington, DC, David in 1886 and Maria in 1887.

14. Kendall, *George Wilkins Kendall,* May 25, 1846, 45; Napoleon Dana to Sue Dana, August 20, 1846, in Napoleon Dana, *Monterrey is Ours!,* 107; E. Salas and Linda Vance, "Camp Followers," in *The United States and Mexico at War: Nineteenth-Century Expansionism and Conflict,* ed. Donald Frazier (New York: MacMillan Reference Books USA, 1998), 75. Reynosa, on the Rio Grande, is fifty-five miles west of Matamoros. The eventual destination of the women seems to have been New Orleans.

15. Smith and Judah, *Chronicle of the Gringos,* April 14, 1847, 304; Amy S. Greenberg, *A Wicked War: Polk, Clay, Lincoln, and the 1846 U.S. Invasion of Mexico* (New York: Alfred A. Knopf, 2012), 138; Robert E. May, "Invisible Men: Blacks and the U.S. Army in the Mexican War," *Historian* 49 (August 1987): 466–67. May does an excellent job of documenting the role of black men, especially as servants, but little has been written on black women and the conflict.

16. Richard Coulter and Thomas Barclay, *Volunteers: The Mexican War Journals of Private Richard Coulter, and Sargent Thomas Barclay, Company E, Second Pennsylvania Infantry,* ed. Allan Peskin (Kent, OH: Kent State University Press, 1991), May 9, 1848, 294; Peggy M. Cashion, "Women and the Mexican War, 1846–1848" (MA thesis, University of Texas at Arlington, 1990), 108–11.

17. D. H. Hill, January 5, 21, 1848, in Daniel Harvey Hill, *A Fighter from Way Back: The Mexican War Diary of Lt. Daniel Harvey Hill, 4th Artillery, USA,* ed. Nathaniel C. Hughes Jr. and Timothy D. Johnson (Kent, OH: Kent State University Press, 2002), 158, 164–66. The Americans often found themselves obliging requests from the English mining companies to provide armed escorts for the wagon-loads of bullion making their way to the coast. For a thorough account of the extent of British investment in Mexico, see Michael P. Costeloe, *Bonds and Bondholders: British Investors and Mexico's Foreign Debt, 1824–1888* (Westport, CT: Praeger, 2003).

18. S. F. Nunnelee, "Alabama and the Mexican War," *Alabama Historical Quarterly* 19 (Fall/Winter 1957): 431.

19. D. H. Hill, November 16, 1846, in Hill, *Fighter from Way Back,* 38.

20. D. H. Hill, November 23, 1846, ibid., 44. Abner Doubleday confirmed the

ongoing hostility and sullenness of the residents of Saltillo as late as March 1848, noting that they "frequently shut their doors and windows at the bare appearance of an American." Doubleday, *My Life in the Old Army,* 133.

21. "Yankee Girls at Saltillo," *Baltimore Sun,* January 20, 1847; D. H. Hill, February 5, 1847, in Hill, *Fighter from Way Back,* 63.

22. Samuel Chamberlain, *My Confession: Recollections of a Rogue,* ed. William Goetzmann (Austin: Texas State Historical Society, 1996), 170; Mark Crawford, "Caroline Porter," in Crawford, ed., *Encyclopedia of the Mexican-American War* (Santa Barbara, CA: ABC-CLIO, 1999), 220.

23. Chamberlain, *My Confession,* 170.

24. Though not well known outside of Western-history circles, the colorful Sarah Borginnis has been extensively studied by both academics and popular writers. The more thorough examinations are those of Brian Sandwich, *The Great Western: Legendary Lady of the Southwest* (El Paso: Texas Western Press, 1991), 4–5; J. F. Elliott, "The Great Western: Sarah Bowman, Mother and Mistress to the U.S. Army," *Journal of Arizona History* 30 (Spring 1989): 1–3; Suzann Ledbetter, *Shady Ladies: Nineteen Surprising and Rebellious American Women* (New York: Forge, 2006), 71–72; and Greta Anderson, *More than Petticoats: Remarkable Texas Women* (Guilford CT: Two Dot, 2002). 1–2. Also worth consulting are Arthur Woodward, *The Great Western: Amazon of the Army* (San Francisco: Johnck & Seeger, 1961); Nancy Hamilton, "The Great Western," in Western Writers of America, *Women Who Made the West* (New York: Doubleday, 1980), 186–97; Don Blevins, *A Priest, a Prostitute, and Some Other Early Texans* (Guilford, CT: Two Dot, 2008), 15–25; Lewis Leonidas Allen, *Pencillings of Scenes along the Rio Grande* (1848), in Smith and Judah, *Chronicle of the Gringos,* 304–7; "Sarah Borginnis," in *The United States and Mexico at War: Nineteenth-Century Expansionism and Conflict,* ed. Donald Frazier (New York: MacMillan Reference Books USA, 1998), 51; Mark Crawford, "Sarah Borginnis," in Crawford, *Mexican-American War,* 46–47; and Cashion, "Women and the Mexican War," 158–62. Historians are equally divided between her Clay County, Missouri, and Tennessee origins, with several, including Donald Frazier and Don Blevins, suggesting that she was born Sarah Knight.

25. Sandwich, *Great Western,* 5; Anderson, *More than Petticoats,* 2–3; Elliott, "Great Western," 2–3.

26. Sandwich, *Great Western,* 8; Elliott, "Great Western," 2–3; Blevins, *A Priest, a Prostitute,* 15 (claiming that Borginnis "gave solace to many . . . in many ways"); Robert Johannsen, *To the Halls of Montezuma: The Mexican War in the American Imagination* (New York: Oxford University Press, 1985), 139–41; Lewis Leonidas Allen, *Pencillings,* 304–7.

27. Sandwich, *Great Western,* 4–7.

28. Ibid., 8–9.

29. Lewis Leonidas Allen, *Pencillings,* 304–7; Sandwich, *Great Western,* 10.

30. Sandwich, *Great Western,* 11; Smith and Judah, *Chronicle of the Gringos,* 61–62.

31. George N. Allen, *Incidents and Sufferings in the Mexican War* (Boston and New York: Hall's, 1847).

32. John Corey Henshaw, *Major John Corey Henshaw: Recollections of the War with Mexico,* ed. Gary Kurutz (Columbia: University of Missouri Press, 2008), 56–57. Lucretia was a sixth-century BC noblewoman who was raped by the king's son. After exacting a vow of vengeance from her family, she courageously killed herself with a dagger. The incident is often marked as the beginning of the revolution to overthrow the monarchy and establish the Roman Republic.

33. Sandwich, *Great Western,* 12–13; Ledbetter, *Shady Ladies,* 74–75; Anderson, *More than Petticoats,* 3–4; Lewis Leonidas Allen, *Pencillings,* 307.

34. Sandwich, *Great Western,* 15–16; Samuel C. Reid, *The Scouting Expeditions of McCulloch's Texas Rangers* (1847; reprint, Freeport, NY: Books for Libraries, 1970), 135.

35. Sandwich, *Great Western,* 17, Blevins, *A Priest, a Prostitute,* 15–20; Anderson, *More than Petticoats,* 4–5.

36. Sandwich, *Great Western,* 17–18; Curtis, *Mexico under Fire,* 273n22; Anderson, *More than Petticoats,* 4.

37. Doubleday, *My Life in the Old Army,* 112; Curtis, *Mexico under Fire,* April 6, 1847, 179–80; Sandwich, *Great Western,* 18–19.

38. Doubleday, *My Life in the Old Army,* 326n11.

39. One very impressed soldier declared, "You can imagine how tall she was, she could stand flatfooted and drop these little sugar plums (her nipples) right into my mouth that way." Ledbetter, *Shady Ladies,* 75–76.

40. Sandwich, *Great Western,* 18–21; Chamberlain, *My Confession,* 242.

41. Curtis, *Mexico under Fire,* April 29, 1847, 185; Elliott, "Great Western," 6; Chamberlain, *My Confession,* 242; Sandwich, *Great Western,* 18–19.

42. Sandwich, *Great Western,* 18–21; Curtis, *Mexico under Fire,* 276n30.

43. Elliott, "Great Western," 8–9; Blevins, *A Priest, a Prostitute,* 21–25; Chamberlain, *My Confession,* 241–42; Sandwich, *Great Western,* 20.

44. J. F. Elliott offers evidence that seemingly challenges the tale of Sarah finding a "Hercules" and suggests that she was on her own and struggling when she reconnected with the army in the spring of 1849. Elliott, "Great Western," 8–9; Ledbetter, *Shady Ladies,* 77–79; Sandwich, *Great Western,* 20–21; Chamberlain, *My Confession,* 256.

45. Elliott, "Great Western," 9–10; Ledbetter, *Shady Ladies,* 78; Anderson, *More than Petticoats,* 7.

46. One trooper commented coldly, "Among her other good qualities she is an admirable pimp. She used to be a splendid looking woman and has done good service but is too old for that now." Ledbetter, *Shady Ladies,* 78. See also Sandwich, *Great Western,* 11–17; and Elliott, "Great Western," 18;

47. Anderson, *More than Petticoats,* 8; Elliott, "Great Western," 20–22; Lucia St. Clair Robson, *Fearless: A Life of Sarah Bowman* (New York: Ballantine Books, 1998).

48. John Crandall Glover, "Ann Chase, 'The Heroine of Tampico'" (MA thesis,

Southern Methodist University, 1947), 1–2; Cashion, "Women and the Mexican War," 162–64; T. Laidley, Tampico, to his father, March 11, 1847, in Theodore Laidley, *Surrounded by Dangers of All Kinds: The Mexican War Letters of Lieutenant Theodore Laidley,* ed. James McCaffrey (Denton: University of North Texas Press, 1997), 45; Shannon Baker, "Ann Chase," in Frazier, *United States and Mexico at War,* 93. Major John Corey Henshaw confused Ann's domestic situation, saying that she had arrived in Tampico with a previous husband (rather than her brother James) and "acquired a considerable fortune" and that upon his death she had married Franklin Chase. Henshaw, *Major John Corey Henshaw,* 108. Her brother James remained as a merchant in Tampico for a short time before leaving Mexico. Those reporting on Mrs. Chase employed the first names Ann and Anna interchangeably. Ann was probably the name she was christened with, while the Spanish derivative Anna was commonly used by those who knew her in Mexico. The name Anna appears on her gravestone, a stone presumably selected by her husband, in a Brooklyn cemetery. Cashion, "Women and the Mexican War," 162–64; Franklin Chase obituary, *New York Times,* December 28, 1890. Ann later reports letters from her brother James, who moved back to Europe, and a second brother in Havana. Journal of Ann Chase, July 16, 1846, Chase Family Papers, Dallas Historical Society.

49. Glover, "Ann Chase," 3.

50. Ann Chase, "History of Mexico," 361–62, Chase Family Papers, Dallas Historical Society. When Agustín de Iturbide returned from a year of European exile in July 1824, he was promptly executed. The Monroe administration recognized his government in 1822, but no US minister reached Mexico City until 1825, when a republic had been established. See Journal of Ann Chase, 349–467, for her examination of Mexico in this period. The constitutional analysis extends from 366 to 387. See 408–17 for a discussion of Yucatán and the military. Ann quite likely intended to publish her history but never did.

51. Chase, "History of Mexico," 416–21. Chase saw the mortality rate increase dramatically when raw recruits were brought in from the highlands to the tropical Tampico lowlands. Watching the five hundred troops parading on the plaza in August, Ann reiterated her contention that Mexican soldiers would follow their undeserving leaders and bravely meet death. Journal of Ann Chase, August 3, 1846.

52. Chase, "History of Mexico," 453, 421–32. Chase criticized the clergy, who grew to control both the church and "all the political movements of the country." For a lengthy discussion of the history of Roman Catholicism in Mexico, its organization into nine bishoprics, including a description of the churches in each, and business and financial issues, see ibid., 432–67.

53. Ibid., 421–32.

54. Glover, "Ann Chase," 7–10; Journal of Ann Chase, June 7, 1846. Glover points out an inconsistency in the reported value of the Chase inventory. The *Niles' National Register* (Baltimore), January 23, 1847, offers the figure of $80,000, while the *Philadelphia Ledger,* January 7, 1847, suggests a more modest $8,000.

55. Journal of Ann Chase, June 7–8, 21, 1846. The English, French, Germans, Dutch, Belgians, and Colombians maintained consulates in Tampico.

56. Glover, "Ann Chase," 11–13; Journal of Ann Chase, June 18–20, 1846; Baker, "Ann Chase," in Frazier, *United States and Mexico at War,* 93. James William Glass served as the British consul in Tampico. Gifford, who served as consul in Veracruz until 1858, did not directly mention Ann Chase in his correspondence but may have met her before the war. Francis Gifford, Veracruz, to Foreign Office, London, April 1, May 22, June 30, 1846, FO 50/203, National Archives, London.

57. Journal of Ann Chase, June 14, July 29, 1846.

58. Ibid., June 18, 23–26, 28, 1846. She later confided to her journal that John Bull evinced a friendship for Brother Jonathan whenever it served his purpose. The British did little to alleviate the difficulties between the United States and Mexico. Ibid., July 16, 1846. Conversely, her heart "throbbed" with national pride when she saw the flag of St. George waving on a royal steamer in mid-August. Ibid., August 16, 1846.

59. Ibid., June 28, August 1, 1846; *Philadelphia Ledger,* January 2, 1847.

60. Journal of Ann Chase, June 20, 21, 25, 1846; Glover, "Ann Chase," 10–11.

61. Glover, "Ann Chase," 10–11; Journal of Ann Chase, June 18, 23, July 21, 1846.

62. Journal of Ann Chase, June 26, July 11, 31, 1846.

63. Ibid., August 7, 31, September 2, 1846.

64. Ann received periodic "courtesy" invitations to Mexican balls in Tampico, some of which she accepted. Ibid., July 29, September 12, 1846. Her depression was an ongoing problem. She remarked about the "dark shadows which overcloud the heavy heart and the troubled mind." Ibid., July 30, August 1, 2, 1846. Amelia remained a trusted companion throughout Ann's ordeal, but she never provides her full name ("A.B.F."), nor, interestingly does Ann offer the name of her beloved small pet dog. Ibid., August 21, October 4, 1846.

65. Ibid., August 7, 1846.

66. Ibid., August 7, 27–28, 30, 31, 1846. Ann generally showed great sympathy and respect for Indians, allowing for their lack of Western civilization. Often referencing James Fenimore Cooper, she called them "children of the forest."

67. Ibid., August 16, 24, 1846. Cdr. Wm. J. McCluney to Ann Chase, August 16, 1846, Ann Chase Papers, Chase Family Papers, Dallas Historical Society. Ibid. Francis Gifford, Veracruz, to Lord Palmerston, January 1, 1847, FO 50/214, National Archives, London. Gifford reported that the *Somers* encountered a squall on December 8 and sank in minutes. British, French, and Spanish ships saved thirty-seven (one-half) of her crew.

68. Journal of Ann Chase, August 15–20, 1846. Santa Anna's return from exile infuriated Ann, who labeled his accomplices guilty of "folly and crime." She did not know that the blame rested at Polk's doorstep. Ibid., October 13, 1846. McCluney to Ann Chase, August 16, 1846, Ann Chase Papers.

69. Secretary of the Navy John Y. Mason to Commodore David Conner, Septem-

ber 22, 1846, in Philip Syng Conner, *The Home Squadron under Commodore Conner in the War with Mexico* (Philadelphia, 1896), 34–35.

70. *Niles' National Register,* January 23, 1847; Journal of Ann Chase, September 30, October 2, 1846.

71. Journal of Ann Chase, October 2, 1846. The losses were largely in textiles, including crepe bands and lace items. Ann reported more than four hundred armed foreign nationals, prepared to defend their property in the chaos that might follow an American landing. Ibid., October 13, 1846.

72. Baker, "Ann Chase," in Frazier, *United States and Mexico at War,* 93; Glover, "Ann Chase," 13–14; *Philadelphia Ledger,* January 7, 1847.

73. Ramón Alcaraz, *The Other Side, or Notes for the History of the War between Mexico and the United States* (1850; reprint, New York: Burt Franklin, 1970), 99–107, contains a detailed explanation of the confusing orders and dilemma Parrodi faced.

74. Journal of Ann Chase, October 6, 20, 23, 24, 1846. Parrodi was later court-martialed and acquitted for his decision to evacuate the town and abandon equipment. Glover, "Ann Chase," 13–16. Ann wisely made no mention of her interaction with officials in her journal. She reported that Santa Anna eventually concentrated eighty-five hundred troops in San Luis Potosí. Journal of Ann Chase, November 1, 1846. Ann reported her nefarious activities to a friend, B. M. Norman, and her letter of December 14 revealing the details was subsequently published in *Niles' National Register,* January 23, 1847.

75. Journal of Ann Chase, October 29–30, November 10, 1846. Ann also expressed her gratitude in her journal to Charles Droge, of the British consulate, who remained a loyal and supportive friend.

76. Ibid., November 7–8, 11, 14, 1846; Laidley, *Surrounded by Dangers of All Kinds,* January 19, 1847, 20; Glover, "Ann Chase," 15–16, 33; Mark Crawford, "Anna McClarmonde Chase," in Crawford, *Mexican-American War,* 76; *American Annual Cyclopedia and Register of Important Events,* vol. 14 (New York: D. Appleton, 1875), 662–63. It is uncertain whom Ann was referring to when she spoke of Americans remaining in Tampico who might have assisted her.

77. Journal of Ann Chase, November 14–16, 21, December 31, 1846; Glover, "Ann Chase," 15–16, 27–34. In a letter to a friend written a month after the incident and published in *Niles' National Register* on January 23, 1847, Ann extrapolated on the dialog with the councilmen. The situation appears to have been more threatening, and her behavior more aggressive, than recorded in the journal entry for November 14.

78. Mason to Commodore Conner, November 30, 1846, in Conner, *Home Squadron,* 35–36; Justin H. Smith, *The War with Mexico,* 2 vols. (New York: Macmillan, 1919), 1:279; Glover, "Ann Chase," 27–33; K. Jack Bauer, *Surfboats and Horse Marines: U.S. Naval Operations in the Mexican War* (Annapolis: US Naval Institute Press, 1969), 86–87. Bauer credits Ann for providing important information that persuaded Conner to speed up the timeline for the move against Tampico. Ibid., 54–55.

79. T. Laidley, Tampico, to his father, March 11, 1847, in Laidley, *Surrounded by Dangers of All Kinds,* 44–46. A photo of Ann taken in Mexico seemingly contradicts Laidley's physical description of her.

80. *Niles' National Register,* December 12, 1846, January 23, 1847; *Philadelphia Ledger,* January 2, 7, 1847.

81. W. W. Harrison, Tampico, to Franklin Chase, December 3, 1847, and Reverdy Johnson to Chase, January 28, 1847, Ann Chase Papers; Glover, "Ann Chase," 34.

82. *Clarion* (Sandusky, OH), August 10, 1847; *Niles' National Register,* October 9, 1847; *New Orleans Picayune,* December 15, 1847. The USS *Ann Chase* survived the explosion but was not back in service until the late fall of 1847. Glover, "Ann Chase," 29–31.

83. Glover, "Ann Chase," 32; Paul Coe Clark Jr., "Espionage," in Frazier, *United States and Mexico at War,* 146.

84. Cashion, "Women and the Mexican War," 164; *Godey's Magazine and Lady's Book* (Philadelphia) 34 (March 1847): 173. The brief Florentine poem quoted by Hale may be literally translated: "My house, my house, Though you are small, Thou to me equals an abbey."

85. *American Annual Cyclopedia,* 14:662–63. Franklin died in their Brooklyn home in 1890. Glover, "Ann Chase," 66–76; Journal of Ann Chase, October 24, 1846; K. Jack Bauer, *The Mexican War, 1846–1848* (1974; reprint with an introduction by Robert W. Johannsen, Lincoln: University of Nebraska Press, 1992), 120.

5. Women Editors Report the War

1. Tom Reilly and Manley Witten, *War with Mexico: America's Reporters Cover the Battlefront* (Lawrence: University Press of Kansas, 2010), 55, 121, providing an extensive list of about forty papers, along with their positions on the war; Mitchel Roth, "War Correspondents," in *The United States and Mexico at War: Nineteenth-Century Expansionism and Conflict,* ed. Donald Frazier (New York: MacMillan Reference Books USA, 1998), 472–73; Jesus Velasco-Marquez, "U.S. Press and the Mexican War," ibid., 294–95.

2. Bessie R. James, *Anne Royall's USA* (New Brunswick, NJ: Rutgers University Press, 1972), 158–62, 254–62. Elizabeth J. Clapp offers the most recent extensive biography, *A Notorious Woman: Anne Royall in Jacksonian America* (Charlottesville: University of Virginia Press, 2016).

3. *Huntress* (Washington, DC), April 26, 1845, May 23, July 25, 1846.

4. Ibid., April 17, 1847, September 19, 1846.

5. Ibid., July 25, August 15, 1846, April 10, September 11, 1847.

6. Ibid., July 25, October 24, 1846, May 15, 1847.

7. Ibid., October 31, 1846, January 23, 1847.

8. Ibid., July 4, 1846; James, *Anne Royall's USA,* 377.

9. *Huntress,* November 7, 1846, January 2, 1847.

10. Ibid., April 3, July 3, 1847; James, *Anne Royall's USA,* 376.

11. James, *Anne Royall's USA,* 370–75.

12. *Huntress,* July 10, 1847.

13. Ibid., March 13, 1847.

14. Sylvia D. Hoffert, *Jane Grey Swisshelm: An Unconventional Life, 1815–1884* (Chapel Hill: University of North Carolina Press, 2004), 36–53, 104.

15. Ibid., 46; Jane Grey Swisshelm, *Half a Century* (Chicago: Jansen, McClurg, 1880), 90.

16. Hoffert, *Jane Grey Swisshelm,* 104–5; Swisshelm, *Half a Century,* 91, 112. The pro-women's-rights Garrison argued that the Constitution was a proslavery document. Swisshelm disagreed and could not join his camp. See Michael D. Pierson, *Free Hearts and Free Homes: Gender and American Antislavery Politics* (Chapel Hill: University of North Carolina Press, 2003), chaps. 1–3, for Swisshelm's contribution to the Free Soil movement and for the controversy over gender roles in the party.

17. Swisshelm, *Half a Century,* 91–94.

18. Ibid., 93–94.

19. Ibid., 95–97. Swisshelm confused the battles of Veracruz and Buena Vista in 1847. The former involved a heavy and prolonged bombardment and loss of civilian lives. Amy S. Greenberg, *A Wicked War: Polk, Clay, Lincoln, and the 1846 U.S. Invasion of Mexico* (New York: Alfred A. Knopf, 2012), 196.

20. Swisshelm, *Half a Century,* 105–15, 121–23; Hoffert, *Jane Grey Swisshelm,* 105–7. Hoffert contradicts Swisshelm and claims that the *Visiter* was first issued on December 20, 1847.

21. Hoffert, *Jane Grey Swisshelm,* 107; Swisshelm, *Half a Century,* 112–15.

22. C.M., letter to the *Pennsylvania Freeman* (Philadelphia), April 22, 1847.

23. Swisshelm, *Half a Century,* 110–11.

24. Ibid.,121–25; Hoffert, *Jane Grey Swisshelm,* 107–8. Predictably, Swisshelm railed against the Compromise of 1850 as a sellout and the Fugitive Slave Act as "an infamous decision."

25. Hoffert, *Jane Grey Swisshelm,* 111.

26. Linda Hudson, "Jane Cazneau," in Frazier, *United States and Mexico at War,* 87–88. Jane McManus used her married name Storm until her divorce in 1831. Thereafter she reverted to her maiden name from ca. 1831 to 1839. She used Storm again from 1839 to 1849, and then her married name Cazneau from 1849 until her death. For clarity, in this volume I refer to her as Storm, although at some point she added an *s* to the end of her name.

27. Linda S. Hudson, *Mistress of Manifest Destiny: A Biography of Jane McManus Storm Cazneau* (Austin: Texas State Historical Association, 2001), 21–43; A. Brooke Caruso, *The Mexican Spy Company: United States Covert Operations in Mexico, 1845–1848* (Jefferson, NC: McFarland, 1991), 138; Robert E. May, "Plenipotentiary in Petticoats: Jane M. Cazneau and American Foreign Policy in the Mid-Nineteenth Century," in *Women and Foreign Policy: Lobbyists, Critics, and Insiders,* ed. Edward Crapol (Wil-

mington, DE: Scholarly Resources, 1992), 19–21; Hudson, "Jane Cazneau," in Frazier, *United States and Mexico at War,* 87–88.

28. Tom Reilly, "Jane McManus Storms: Letters from the Mexican War," *Southwestern Historical Quarterly* 85 (July 1981): 25; May, "Plenipotentiary in Petticoats," 21; Caruso, *Mexican Spy Company,* 139; Hudson, *Mistress of Manifest Destiny,* 57.

29. Hudson uses textual and word analysis of the "annexation" piece to argue for Storm's authorship of the term *Manifest Destiny.* Hudson, *Mistress of Manifest Destiny,* 60–62. O'Sullivan's biographer rejects both Hudson's methodology and her conclusions, although the matter remains open for historical debate. See Robert B. Sampson, *John L. O'Sullivan and His Times* (Kent, OH: Kent State University Press, 2003), 244–45. Megan Jenison Griffin, "Jane McManus Storm Cazneau, 1807–1878," *Legacy: A Journal of Women Writers* 27 (2010): 423.

30. Hudson, *Mistress of Manifest Destiny,* 57–59. Storm also contended in 1847 that annexation would be the salvation of the "long-suffering and hardly-treated working classes" of Mexico. Reilly and Witten, *War with Mexico,* 118.

31. Hudson, *Mistress of Manifest Destiny,* 58–59; Griffin, "Jane McManus Storm Cazneau," 416–17.

32. Hudson, *Mistress of Manifest Destiny,* 64–65; Reilly, "Jane McManus Storms," 24–26, 26n13; Reilly and Witten, *War with Mexico,* 114–15.

33. Hudson, *Mistress of Manifest Destiny,* 66, 72; May, "Plenipotentiary in Petticoats," 20; Reilly, "Jane McManus Storms," 25–26.

34. Hudson, *Mistress of Manifest Destiny,* 59; May, "Plenipotentiary in Petticoats," 20; Reilly, "Jane McManus Storms," 21–22; Reilly and Witten, *War with Mexico,* 114–15.

35. Reilly and Witten, *War with Mexico,* 114; May, "Plenipotentiary in Petticoats," 19–20.

36. Reilly, "Jane McManus Storms," 26n13; Hudson, *Mistress of Manifest Destiny,* 72–76.

37. Hudson, *Mistress of Manifest Destiny,* 77–78; Reilly and Witten, *War with Mexico,* 115–16. Caruso notes that Beach had a problem, since the isthmian concession had already passed to the British consul in Mexico City in January 1847. Beach had $50,000 in New York capital to establish a national bank in Mexico City to advance his and his partners' financial fortunes. Caruso, *Mexican Spy Company,* 139–43.

38. Anna Kasten Nelson, *Secret Agents: President Polk and the Search for Peace with Mexico* (New York: Garland, 1988), 75–79.

39. Hudson, *Mistress of Manifest Destiny,* 95–102.

40. Montgomery, "Tropical Sketches, No. 3," Charleston, SC, *New York Sun,* January 8, 1847; Montgomery, "Tropical Sketches, No. 9," Matanzas, Cuba, ibid., January 16, 1847.

41. Montgomery, "Tropical Sketches, No. 5," ibid., January 12, 1847; Montgomery, "Tropical Sketches, No. 6," ibid., January 13, 1847; Montgomery, "Tropical Sketches, No. 10," ibid., January 30, 1847.

42. Montgomery, "Tropical Sketches, No. 8," ibid., January 15, 1847; Montgomery,

"Tropical Sketches, No. 10"; Montgomery, "Tropical Sketches, No. 14," Havana, ibid., March 25, 1847.

43. Hudson, *Mistress of Manifest Destiny,* 79–81; Reilly, "Jane McManus Storms," 30–31; Reilly and Witten, *War with Mexico,* 116–17.

44. Michael P. Costeloe, "The Mexican Church and the Rebellion of the Polkos," *Hispanic American Historical Review* 46 (May 1966): 170–78. Pedro Santoni offers a most detailed account of the Polko crisis in *Mexicans at Arms: Puro Federalists and the Politics of War, 1845–1848* (Fort Worth: Texas Christian University Press, 1996), 168–69. Mexican politics is also closely studied by Dennis E. Berge, in "Mexican Response to United States' Expansionism, 1841–1848" (PhD diss., University of California, Berkeley, 1965), 238–51, and Jose Fernando Ramirez, in *Mexico during the War with the United States,* ed. Walter V. Scholes, trans. Elliott B. Scherr (1950; reprint, Columbia: University of Missouri Press, 1970). See also Reilly and Witten, *War with Mexico,* 116; and Reilly, "Jane McManus Storms," 32–34.

45. Hudson, *Mistress of Manifest Destiny,* 82–83; Reilly and Witten, *War with Mexico,* 117; Nelson, *Secret Agents,* 80–86; *New York Sun,* April 15, 1847; Reilly, "Jane McManus Storms," 34.

46. Hudson, *Mistress of Manifest Destiny,* 81–82; John Black, Mexico City, to Winfield Scott, March 12, 1847, in Bruce Cutler, *At War with Mexico: A Fictional Mosaic* (Norman: University of Oklahoma Press, 2001), 86–89.

47. Hudson, *Mistress of Manifest Destiny,* 81–82; Scott, Veracruz, to Black, March 29, 1847, in Cutler, *At War with Mexico,* 90–91; Nelson, *Secret Agents,* 87–90; *New York Sun,* May 6, 1847; Reilly, "Jane McManus Storms," 35. In seeming contradiction to logic, Black remained US consul in Mexico City even though the two nations were officially at war. Caruso maintains that in spite of Scott's derogation of Storm, "she provided him with very important firsthand information concerning the revolution, the peace possibilities, and the conditions of the Veracruz–Mexico City invasion route." Caruso, *Mexican Spy Company,* 143.

48. Hudson, *Mistress of Manifest Destiny,* 82–86; Reilly, "Jane McManus Storms," 34–35, 38.

49. Hudson, *Mistress of Manifest Destiny,* 71–74, 86–87. The "diffusion theory," a vestige of the Jeffersonians, argued that slavery might face extinction if slaves and free blacks were "diffused" thinly throughout the Southwest. Secretary of the Treasury Robert John Walker was most closely associated with the notion during this period.

50. Hudson, *Mistress of Manifest Destiny,* 87; James J. Polk, *The Diary of James K. Polk,* ed. Milo M. Quaife, 4 vols. (Chicago: A. C. McClurg, 1910), May 13, 1847, 3:22, 25.

51. Hudson, *Mistress of Manifest Destiny,* 87–90.

52. Ibid., 90–93; May, "Plenipotentiary in Petticoats," 22–24; Reilly, "Jane McManus Storms," 22, 41; Cora Montgomery [Jane Storm Cazneau], *Eagle Pass; or Life on the Border* (New York: Putnam, 1852), 187. While not ignoring correspondence that suggests otherwise, Hudson claims that Storm held fast to her commitment to a republic

of the Rio Grande and opposition to All Mexico. May believes that Storm evolved after witnessing the anarchy in Mexico in 1847: "Gradually, she concluded that total annexation would be best" (23).

53. Griffin, "Jane McManus Storm Cazneau," 424; May, "Plenipotentiary in Petticoats," 23; Reilly, "Jane McManus Storms," 38–44. Reilly asserts that "Storms constantly supported annexing all of Mexico" but desired a voluntary joining of dissident Mexican states with the United States. Ibid., 37–38.

54. Reilly, "Jane McManus Storms," 38–44.

55. Ibid., 22, 25, 40–44; Hudson, *Mistress of Manifest Destiny,* 202–3; Griffin, "Jane McManus Storm Cazneau," 417–18, 422–24.

6. The Señorita as Fantasy

1. Napoleon Dana to Sue Dana, November 6, 1845, in Napoleon Dana, *Monterrey is Ours! The Mexican War Letters of Lieutenant Dana, 1845–1847,* ed. Robert H. Ferrell (Lexington: University of Kentucky Press, 1990), 31; "The Conjugation of Mexico," *John-Donkey* (New York), January 22, 1848.

2. Nancy Isenberg, *Sex and Citizenship in Antebellum America* (Chapel Hill: University of North Carolina Press, 1998), xv; James McCaffrey, *Army of Manifest Destiny: The American Soldier in the Mexican War, 1846–1848* (New York: New York University Press, 1992), 76–79, 199–200; David J. Weber, *The Spanish Frontier in North America* (New Haven, CT: Yale University Press, 1992), 296.

3. John R. Kenly, *Memoirs of a Maryland Volunteer: War with Mexico in the Years 1846–1847* (Philadelphia: J. B. Lippincott, 1873), 369–70; Napoleon Dana to Sue Dana, August 27, 1846, in Napoleon Dana, *Monterrey is Ours!,* 112; Journal of Marcellus Ball Edwards, in Abraham Robinson Johnston, Marcellus Ball Edwards, and Philip Gooch Ferguson, *Marching with the Army of the West, 1846–1848: Journal of A. R. Johnston, 1846, Journal of M. B. Edwards, 1846–47, Diary of P. G. Ferguson, 1847–48,* ed. Ralph Bieber (Glendale, CA: Arthur H. Clark, 1936), August 14, 1846, 151–52. Theodore Laidley, *Surrounded by Dangers of All Kinds: The Mexican War Letters of Lieutenant Theodore Laidley,* ed. James M. McCaffrey (Denton: University of North Texas Press, 1997), 89.

4. Napoleon Dana to Sue Dana, May 22, 1846, February 14, 1847, in Napoleon Dana, *Monterrey is Ours!,* 81, 181; John Corey Henshaw, *Major John Corey Henshaw: Recollections of the War with Mexico,* ed. Gary Kurutz (Columbia: University of Missouri Press, 2008), 99, 108; William S. Henry, *Campaign Sketches of the War with Mexico* (New York: Harper Bros., 1847), September 26, December 22, 1846, 222–23, 274.

5. Rankin Dilworth, *The March to Monterrey: The Diary of Lieutenant Rankin Dilworth,* ed. Joseph E. Chance (El Paso: Texas Western Press, 1996), May 23, July 6, August 8, 1846, 19, 41, 45–46. Dilworth lost a leg at the Battle of Monterrey on September 19, 1846, and died eight days later.

6. John James Peck, *The Sign of the Eagle: A View of Mexico, 1830–1855; The Letters of Lieutenant John James Peck,* ed. Richard Pourade (San Diego: Union Tribune, 1970), June 22, December 13, 1846, 29–30, 63; *Niles' National Register,* July 11, 1846; George B. McClellan, *The Mexican War Diary and Correspondence of George B. McClellan,* ed. Thomas W. Cutrer (Baton Rouge: Louisiana State University Press, 2009), April 20, 1847, 122.

7. G. W. Kendall, Camargo, July 29, 1846, in George Wilkins Kendall, *George Wilkins Kendall: Dispatches from the Mexican War,* ed. Lawrence Cress (Norman: University of Oklahoma Press, 1999), 81–82; Napoleon Dana to Sue Dana, June 11, 1846, in Napoleon Dana, *Monterrey is Ours!,* 89; Abner Doubleday, *My Life in the Old Army: The Reminiscences of Abner Doubleday from the Collections of the New York Historical Society,* ed. Joseph E. Chance (Fort Worth: Texas Christian University Press, 1998), 75, 320n13.

8. Napoleon Dana to Sue Dana, June 11, August 2, October 11, 1846, in Napoleon Dana, *Monterrey is Ours!,* 89, 105, 142–46. Sue wanted her faults corrected, but she assured her husband that she responded better to a "rod of love than of iron." In a time of doubt, she also encouraged a disconsolate Napoleon to be steady and not resign his commission. Sue Dana to Napoleon Dana, 1847, Napoleon Dana Letters, US Military Academy, West Point, NY. Hill and Dana noticed that the women appeared to show no embarrassment in watching Mexican men swimming naked. Boys were also allowed to swim unclothed, but not girls. D. H. Hill, June 8, 1846, January 15, 1847, in Daniel Harvey Hill, *A Fighter from Way Back: The Mexican War Diary of Lt. Daniel Harvey Hill, 4th Artillery, USA,* ed. Nathaniel C. Hughes Jr. and Timothy D. Johnson (Kent, OH: Kent State University Press, 2002), 6, 59. Larger cities, such as Jalapa, offered the more discriminating individual stone and tile baths with separate bathing facilities for men and women. William J. Orr and Robert R. Miller, eds., *An Immigrant Soldier in the Mexican War* (College Station: Texas A&M University Press, 1995), 42.

9. John James Peck, "Sketches of Carl Nebel," in Peck, *Sign of the Eagle,* 28–29, 93.

10. Ibid., December 13, 1846, 63; Ernesto Chavez, *The U.S. War with Mexico: A Brief History with Documents* (New York: Bedford/St. Martin's, 2008), 94–95.

11. Helen Chapman, *The News from Brownsville: Helen Chapman's Letters from the Texas Military Frontier, 1848–1852,* ed. Caleb Coker (Austin: Texas State Historical Association, 1992), January 28, March 23, 1848, 15–16, 25; Peck, *Sign of the Eagle,* Matamoros, June 22, 1846, 29–30, from the *Panola,* July 24, 1846, 33; Hill, *Fighter from Way Back,* 6.

12. *Niles' National Register,* June 27, 1846; Ralph W. Kirkham to Kate Kirkham, June 1, 1847, in Ralph W. Kirkham, *The Mexican War Journal and Letters of Ralph W. Kirkham,* ed. Robert Ryal Miller (College Station: Texas A&M University Press, 1991), 20–21; Henshaw, *Major John Corey Henshaw,* 98–99.

13. De Lancey Floyd-Jones to his brother Ned, January 13, 1847, Floyd-Jones to his sister Cate, March 2, December 13, 1847, Floyd-Jones to his sister Nel, May 26, 1847, and Floyd-Jones to his sister Sarah, December 7, 1847, July 6, 1848, De Lancey

Floyd-Jones Letters, Special Collections, University of Texas at Arlington. Floyd-Jones determined that Mexico was far too dangerous for an American to remain there after the US Army departed. In spite of his disillusionment with the military and thoughts of an agrarian future, he continued in the service and led his men with distinction during the Civil War.

14. Kenly, *Memoirs of a Maryland Volunteer,* February 19, 1847, 238–39; Peter Guardino, "Gender, Soldiering, and Citizenship in the Mexican-American War of 1846–1848," *American Historical Review* 119 (February 2014): 40.

15. "Sketches by a Skirmisher," *Spirit of the Times* (New York), May 1, 1847; McCaffrey, *Army of Manifest Destiny,* 76–79.

16. Hill, *Fighter from Way Back,* July 1–8, 1846, 14–16; Kirkham, *Mexican War Journal and Letters,* July 17, 1847, 37–38; Arnoldo De León, *They Called Them Greasers: Anglo Attitudes toward Mexicans in Texas, 1821–1900* (Austin: University of Texas Press, 1983), 36–48.

17. Samuel Ryan Curtis, *Mexico under Fire: Being the Diary of Samuel Ryan Curtis, 3rd Ohio Volunteer Regiment during the American Occupation of Northern Mexico, 1846–1847,* ed. Joseph E. Chance (Fort Worth: Texas Christian University Press, 1994), December 26, 1846, 85.

18. Doubleday, *My Life in the Old Army,* 64.

19. Napoleon Dana to Sue Dana, June 14, 19, July 10, 1846, in Napoleon Dana, *Monterrey is Ours!,* 88–90, 93, 94–95.

20. Diary of Philip Gooch Ferguson, in Johnston, Edwards, and Ferguson, *Marching with the Army of the West,* 321–22; Franklin Smith, *The Mexican War Journal of Captain Franklin Smith,* ed. Joseph E. Chance (Jackson: University Press of Mississippi, 1991), October 27, November 5, December 8, 1846, 89, 113–14, 131. Smith had intended to leave the fandango at 3:00 a.m., but warned by his Mexican friends that robbers plagued the roads, he departed at sunrise after a breakfast of hotcakes and coffee.

21. Pedro Santoni, ed., *Daily Lives of Civilians in Wartime Latin America: From the Wars of Independence to the Central American Civil Wars* (Westport, CT: Greenwood, 2008), 66; *American Star* (Mexico City), October 10, 16, 1847, in Christopher Conway and Gustavo Pellón, *The U.S.-Mexican War: A Binational Reader* (Indianapolis: Hackett, 2010), 103–4.

22. *American Star,* October 5, 1847, in Conway and Pellón, *U.S.-Mexican War,* 103–4; *American Star,* November 6, 1847, in Chavez, *U.S. War with Mexico,* 114–16; T. Laidley to his father, May 19, 1847, in Laidley, *Surrounded by Dangers of All Kinds,* 88; Ramón Alcaraz, *The Other Side, or Notes for the History of the War between Mexico and the United States* (1850; reprint, New York: Burt Franklin, 1970), 415–17; *American Star,* October 15, 1847.

23. "La Pasadita," in Conway and Pellón, *U.S.-Mexican War,* 167–69; Alcaraz, *Other Side,* 415–17.

24. "Pardon Jones in Mexico," *Spirit of the Times,* September 19, 1846; Hill, *Fighter*

from Way Back, October 20, 1847, 138; Richard Coulter and Thomas Barclay, *Volunteers: The Mexican War Journals of Private Richard Coulter, and Sargent Thomas Barclay, Company E, Second Pennsylvania Infantry,* ed. Allan Peskin (Kent, OH: Kent State University Press, 1991), May 11, 1848, 295.

25. Henshaw, *Major John Corey Henshaw,* 17, 146–50.

26. Hill, *Fighter from Way Back,* Cerralvo, June 8; Monterrey, October 7; Saltillo, December 6, 1846–January 9, 1847, 14–15, 59, 28–29, 59, 48–57.

27. Grayson Prevost, Mier, to Charles Prevost, August 3, 1846, and to his sisters, from Saltillo, June 25, 1847, Grayson Prevost Papers, A Continent Divided: The U.S.-Mexico War, Occupation and Aftermath, Special Collections, University of Texas at Arlington.

28. Grayson Prevost, Saltillo, to his sisters, June 25, 1847, and to his sister, July 25, 1847, ibid.

29. Grayson Prevost, Saltillo, to his father, September 5, 1847, ibid.

30. Grayson Prevost, Saltillo, to his sister, September 19, 1847, to his mother, September 25, 1847, and to his sister, October 17, 1847, ibid.

31. Grayson Prevost, Saltillo, to his mother, September, October 11, 1847, to his sister, October 15, 17, 1847, and to his sisters, November 21, 1847, and Prevost, Monterrey, to his sister, January 25, 1848, ibid.; Chapman, *News from Brownsville,* May 18, July 12, 1848, June 19, 1850, April 15, 1852, 42, 62, 168, 284.

32. Hill, *Fighter from Way Back,* Monterrey, October 21–22, 1846, 30–31, 40–41.

33. *Farmer's Cabinet* (Amherst, NH), July 6, 1848; Tom Reilly and Manley Witten, *War With Mexico: America's Reporters Cover the Battlefront* (Lawrence: University Press of Kansas, 2010), 239–40; Samuel Chamberlain, *My Confession: Recollections of a Rogue,* ed. William Goetzmann (Austin: Texas State Historical Society, 1996), 237–38. Chamberlain contended that the collaboration with and affection for "Los Gringos" extended to all classes of Mexican women, not just the poor or the Margaritas.

34. *Hudson River Chronicle* (Ossining, NY), July 11, 1848; Peck, *Sign of the Eagle,* July 8, 1847, 97.

35. Rose Marie Beebe and Robert Senkewicz, trans., "Felipa Osuna: 'The Oldest Resident of Old Town in 1878,'" *Journal of San Diego History* 55 (Fall 2009): 231–44. Felipa's father, Juan María Osuna, filed a claim against the Americans in 1846 for destruction and confiscation of his property during the occupation of his house. He contended that they had destroyed his fence and orchard and stolen lard, salt, chilis, and onions, as well as a night pot valued at one dollar. Raymond S. Brandes, trans., *Times Gone By in Alta California: Recollections of Señora Doña Juana Machado Alipaz de Wrightington* (1878), *Historical Society of Southern California Quarterly* 41, no. 3 (September 1959): 222. The debate over the relative "virtue" of Californio women was not unlike that in other parts of the Mexican Republic. Husbands, sailors, and visitors might well hold conflicting views. The best source on this topic for the 1840s is David J. Langum, "Californio Women and the Image of Virtue," *Southern California Quarterly* 59 (1977): 245–50.

36. Chamberlain, *My Confession,* 210–17, 239–57. The rascally Chamberlain soon parted with Ellen, who wisely married someone more prone to fidelity.

37. Diary of Philip Gooch Ferguson, in Johnston, Edwards, and Ferguson, *Marching with the Army of the West,* 342–49.

38. Tennent Lomax, Orizaba, to Eliza, February 20, March 27, 1848, in "Letters to His Sister," *Alabama Historical Quarterly* 19 (Fall 1957): 461–64.

39. James McCaffrey, "Life in the U.S. Army," in *The United States and Mexico at War: Nineteenth-Century Expansionism and Conflict,* ed. Donald Frazier (New York: MacMillan Reference Books USA, 1998), 29–30; De Lancey Floyd-Jones to his brother Ned, February 27, 1847, De Lancey Floyd-Jones Letters.

40. Reilly and Witten, *War with Mexico,* 22–23, 48; Doubleday, *My Life in the Old Army,* 64–65; Smith, *Mexican War Journal,* October 27, 1846, 89; McClellan, *Mexican War Diary and Correspondence,* 3.

41. *Advocate of Peace and Universal Brotherhood* (Boston), May/June 1847; *National Police Gazette* (New York), February 13, 1847.

42. Reilly and Witten, *War with Mexico,* 48–49; Amy S. Greenberg, *A Wicked War: Polk, Clay, Lincoln, and the 1846 U.S. Invasion of Mexico* (New York: Alfred A. Knopf, 2012), 130–32. The most prominent Mexican source reports the panic among the women and children when Monterrey was attacked, but nothing about atrocities. Alcaraz, *Other Side,* 70.

43. Hill, *Fighter from Way Back,* Monterrey, September 1846, November 22, 1846, 28, 44; Laidley, *Surrounded by Dangers of All Kinds,* March 22, 1848, 150.

44. Reilly and Witten, *War with Mexico,* 48; *Albion* (New York), October 31, 1846; *Liberator* (Boston), December 18, 1846; Hill, *Fighter from Way Back,* December 2, 1846, 47.

45. Greenberg, *Wicked War,* 131, 190–91; Napoleon Dana to Sue Dana, October 18, November 29, December 7, 1846, in Napoleon Dana, *Monterrey is Ours!,* 145, 152–53.

46. Curtis, *Mexico under Fire,* January 25–28, 1847, 104–7.

47. David Clary, *Eagles and Empire: The U.S., Mexico, and the Struggle for a Continent* (New York: Random House, 2009), 293–304. The Mexicans employed women to spy on American activity during the siege, with George W. Kendall noting the capture close to camp of "a well-dressed female under suspicious circumstances." Kendall, *George Wilkins Kendall,* March 13, 1847, 161.

48. Francis Gifford, Veracruz, to Lord Palmerston, January 31, February 28, March 11, 22, 1847, FO 50/214, National Archives, London.

49. Ibid., March 29, 1847.

50. Ibid., April 6, 1847.

51. *Niles' National Register,* May 8, 1847; *New Orleans Delta,* April 17, 1847; George Winston Smith and Charles Judah, eds., *Chronicle of the Gringos: The U.S. Army in the Mexican War, 1846–1848* (Albuquerque: University of New Mexico Press, 1968), 192–94; Peck, *Sign of the Eagle,* 78; Napoleon Dana to Sue Dana, March 28, April 2, 1847, in Napoleon Dana, *Monterrey is Ours!,* 193, 196–97.

52. S. F. Nunnelee, "Alabama and the Mexican War," *Alabama Historical Quarterly* 19 (Fall/Winter 1957): 426–27; De Lancey Floyd-Jones to his sister, March 30, 1847,

De Lancey Floyd-Jones Letters; Clary, *Eagles and Empire,* 303; Greenberg, *Wicked War,* 169–70.

53. Greenberg, *Wicked War,* 169–70; Winfield Scott, *Memoirs of Lieutenant-General Scott,* 2 vols. (New York: Sheldon, 1864), 2:420–29; *Emancipator* (New York), June 9, 1847. Ramón Alcaraz offers the most detailed description of the devastating physical and psychological impact of the bombardment on the population in *The Other Side,* 184–95. *Christian Secretary* (Hartford, CT), April 23, 1847; *Pennsylvania Freeman* (Philadelphia), April 22, October 21, 1847.

54. K. Jack Bauer, *The Mexican War, 1846–1848* (1974; reprint with an introduction by Robert W. Johannsen, Lincoln: University of Nebraska Press, 1992), 249–53; Timothy D. Johnson, *Winfield Scott: The Quest for Military Glory* (Lawrence: University Press of Kansas, 1998), 174–80, which puts the estimate of Mexican casualties at "probably no more than 200." Relying upon a Mexican source, Johnson revised his estimate sharply upwards to 1,000 casualties and $5 million to $6 million in damages in *A Gallant Little Army: The Mexico City Campaign* (Lawrence: University Press of Kansas, 2007), 48–49. John D. Eisenhower, *Agent of Destiny: The Life and Times of General Winfield Scott* (New York: Free Press, 1997), 240–46; Allan Peskin, *Winfield Scott and the Profession of Arms* (Kent, OH: Kent State University Press, 2003), 159.

55. Greenberg, *Wicked War,* 169–70; Clary, *Eagles and Empire,* 303. In one of the greater ironies of the war, a Mexican woman solicited alms from G. W. Kendall to help rebuild the cathedral, which US guns had just destroyed. He donated a dollar. Kendall, *George Wilkins Kendall,* Veracruz, April 4, 1847, 196. Consul Gifford praised the American occupation forces for restoring order and tranquility in Veracruz and alleviating the suffering of the poor by distributing rations. Gifford, Veracruz, to Palmerston, April 1, April 13, May 31, 1847, FO 50/214, National Archives, London.

56. "Sketches of a Skirmisher," in *Spirit of the Times,* May 1, 1847.

57. Clary, *Eagles and Empire,* 303; *Emancipator,* June 9, 1847; Greenberg, *Wicked War,* 205, 209, 211; *New York Observer and Chronicle,* October 9, 1847; *Prisoner's Friend: A Monthly Magazine Devoted to Criminal Reform, Philosophy, etc.* (Boston), November 1847; Henry C. Wright, in *Liberator.* January 28, 1848; Guardino, "Gender, Soldiering, and Citizenship," 43–44; Amy Greenberg, *Manifest Manhood and the Antebellum American Empire* (Cambridge: Cambridge University Press, 2005), 8–14. Guardino and Greenberg discuss the shedding of a more restrained, moral, patriarchal masculinity for a more violent, physical, martial masculinity when the volunteers experienced Mexico.

58. *Soldaderas* continued to play a major role. D. H. Hill commented without emotion on the paroled Mexican Army leaving Veracruz, "There were a great many women with the Army, on foot and with heavy packs or children slung to their backs." Hill, *Fighter from Way Back,* March 29, August 18, 23, December 20, 1847, 91, 110–11, 152; Laidley, *Surrounded by Dangers of All Kinds,* October 24, 1847, 120.

59. Douglas Richmond, "Collaboration in Mexico, " in Frazier, *United States and Mexico at War,* 101; *Mobile (AL) Tribune,* September 14, 1846; Coulter and Barclay,

Volunteers, May 20–27, 1848, 298–99; Hill, *Fighter from Way Back*, October 6, 1847, 135–36; Mark Wasserman, *Everyday Life and Politics in Nineteenth Century Mexico: Men, Women, and War* (Albuquerque: University of New Mexico Press, 2000), 89; Santoni, *Daily Lives of Civilians in Wartime Latin America*, 73–77. British Consul Gifford contended that the "Texian Rangers were the worst part of the population of Texas—they shoot and destroy property without mercy." Gifford, Veracruz, to Palmerston, October 20, 1847, FO 50/214, National Archives, London; *American Star*, January 16, 25, 1848. The paper contended that the women received fair pay for their labors and that some earned "as good wages as any of our American women at home."

60. *Advocate of Peace and Universal Brotherhood*, May/June 1847; Paul Foos, *A Short, Offhand Killing Affair: Soldiers and Social Conflict during the Mexican-American War* (Chapel Hill: University of North Carolina Press, 2002), 121–23.

61. Richard Bruce Winders, *Mr. Polk's Army: The American Military Experience in the Mexican War* (College Station: Texas A&M University Press, 1997), 157.

7. Sensational Literature

1. Newton Curtis, *The Hunted Chief; or, Female Ranchero: A Tale of the Mexican War* (New York: W. F. Burgess, 1847), 4, 25. Curtis penned two other Mexican-American War romances, *Prairie Guide; or, Rose of the Rio Grande* (1847) and *The Vidette; or, The Girl of the Robber's Pass* (1848). Mexican guerrillas were particularly engaged against Winfield Scott in 1847. For a solid treatment of their activities, as well as local rebellions challenging the central government, see Irving W. Levinson, *Wars within War: Mexican Guerrillas, Domestic Elites, and the United States of America, 1846–1848* (Fort Worth: Texas Christian University Press, 2005).

2. Shelley Streeby, *American Sensations: Class, Empire, and the Production of Popular Culture* (Berkeley: University of California Press, 2002). Streeby offers a detailed and thorough analysis of the literature from the perspective of race, class, and gender. Jaime Javier Rodriguez, *The Literatures of the U.S.-Mexican War: Narrative, Time, and Identity* (Austin: University of Texas Press, 2010), explores many of the same sources but focuses more sharply on Mexico and sees the literature as offering more diverse themes. See also Jesse Aleman and Shelley Streeby, eds., *Empire and the Literature of Sensation* (New Brunswick, NJ: Rutgers University Press, 2007); Randi Lynn Tanglen, "Critical Regionalism, the US-Mexican War, and Nineteenth-Century American Literary History," *Western American Literature* 48 (Spring/Summer 2013): 180–99; Amy Greenberg, *Manifest Manhood and the Antebellum American Empire* (Cambridge: Cambridge University Press, 2005); and Greenberg, *A Wicked War: Polk, Clay, Lincoln, and the 1846 U.S. Invasion of Mexico* (New York: Alfred A. Knopf, 2012), 214–15.

3. Greenberg, *Manifest Manhood*, 11–12, 18–27, 51–52, 127–32. See also E. Anthony Rotundo, *American Manhood: Transformations of Masculinity from the Revolution to the Modern Era* (New York: Basic Books, 1993). Rotundo discusses shifting notions

of American masculinity, arguing that "self-made manhood" in the nineteenth century focused more on work and accomplishment than on family.

4. Streeby, *American Sensations,* 83–87; Robert Johannsen, *To the Halls of Montezuma: The Mexican War in the American Imagination* (New York: Oxford University Press, 1985), 175–79. Harry Hazel's three novels were *Inez the Beautiful: or, Love on the Rio Grande* (1846), *The Light Dragoon; or, The Rancheros of the Poisoned Lance* (1845), and *The Rival Chieftains; or, The Brigands of Mexico* (1845). Ingraham penned *The Texas Ranger; or, The Maid of Matamoras* (1846). Lippard wrote *Bel of Prairie Eden; A Romance of Mexico* (1848), which focuses upon Texas.

5. Johannsen, *To the Halls of Montezuma,* 175.

6. Jenny Franchot, *Roads to Rome: The Antebellum Protestant Encounter with Catholicism* (Berkeley: University of California Press, 1994), 9–15.

7. Ibid., 15.

8. Ibid., 38–47, quotation on 41.

9. John C. Pinheiro, *Missionaries of Republicanism: A Religious History of the Mexican-American War* (New York: Oxford University Press, 2014), 110–13.

10. Ibid., 116–22.

11. Streeby, *American Sensations,* 97–100, 104–12; Robert Ryal Miller, *Shamrock and Sword: The Saint Patrick's Battalion in the U.S.-Mexican War* (Norman: University of Oklahoma Press, 1989), 173–75. Miller points out the very high desertion rate (8 percent) in the Mexican-American War and that the vast majority of the five thousand Irishmen in uniform remained loyal. A minority of the San Patricios were Irish by birth, and most of those captured had served almost a year in the army. See also Tyler V. Johnson, *Devotion to the Adopted Country: U.S. Immigrant Volunteers in the Mexican War* (Columbia: University of Missouri Press, 2012), for a similarly positive view of the Irish soldier.

12. Curtis, *Hunted Chief,* 16–17; Streeby, *American Sensations,* 129.

13. Curtis, *Hunted Chief,* chap. 11.

14. Ned Buntline, *Magdalena, the Beautiful Mexican Maid: A Story of Buena Vista* (New York: Williams Bros., 1847), 24–33.

15. Ibid., chaps. 9–15.

16. Ibid., 96–97, 106.

17. Ned Buntline, *The Volunteer; or, The Maid of Monterey. A Tale of the Mexican War* (Boston: F. Gleason, 1847), 1–7; Streeby, *American Sensations,* 116, 120, 129.

18. Buntline, *Volunteer,* 8–11. Buntline's parallel between Edwina Canales and Doña Jesús Dosamentes (noted in chapter 2) and their heroism at Monterrey is remarkable.

19. Ibid., 54–57.

20. Ibid., 58–60.

21. Ibid., 105, 122–26.

22. Charles Averill, *The Mexican Ranchero; or, The Maid of the Chaparral: A Romance of the Mexican War* (Boston: F. Gleason, 1847); Streeby, *American Sensations,* 105–6, 110–12, 133; Rodriguez, *Literatures of the U.S.-Mexican War,* 29–30, 37–38, 41. Averill

perhaps gratuitously adds yet a third couple—Harold's younger brother William and Raphael's cousin Josefa—to the wedding list. They had both been kidnapped as youths and find each other in the novel.

23. Charles Averill, *The Secret Service Ship; or, The Fall of San Juan D'Ulloa: A Thrilling Tale of the Mexican War* (Boston: F. Gleason, 1848); Streeby, *American Sensations,* 117, 119, 123–24, 133.

24. Harry Halyard, *The Heroine of Tampico; or, Wildfire the Wanderer: A Tale of the Mexican War* (Boston: F. Gleason, 1847), 7–8. The particularly convoluted storyline with the subtitle "Wildfire the Wanderer" also involves a bearded frontiersman and his daughter, who aid Avaline. Their relationships to the main characters are resolved in a somewhat muddled conclusion containing revealed identities and unanticipated marriages. Halyard was the pseudonym for a still-unknown writer of the era who penned four additional Mexican-American War adventures in 1848—*The Chieftain of Churubusco, The Mexican Spy, The Ocean Monarch,* and *The Warrior Queen.*

25. Halyard, *Heroine of Tampico,* 49–100.

26. Eliza Allen, *The Female Volunteer; or the Life, and Wonderful Adventures of Miss Eliza Allen, a Young Lady of Eastport, Maine* (Eastport, 1851), 9–11.

27. Ibid., 11–14.

28. Ibid., 15–25.

29. Ibid., 25–36.

30. Ibid., 37–67.

31. Grace Greenwood, "The Volunteer," in *Greenwood Leaves: A Collection of Sketches and Letters* (Boston: Ticknor, Reed, & Fields, 1850), 100–121; Rodriguez, *Literatures of the U.S.-Mexican War,* 48–49.

32. Greenwood, "The Volunteer," 102.

33. Ibid., 103–6.

34. Ibid., 107–21.

35. John Roy Musick, *Humbled Pride: A Story of the Mexican War* (New York: Funk & Wagnalls, 1893), vi–vii.

36. Ibid., 2–3, 189–206.

37. Ibid., 207–10.

38. Ibid., 294–326, 385–412.

39. A. D. Hall, *Captain Impudence: A Romance of the Mexican War* (New York: Street & Smith, 1897), 12–13, 200–220; *Alumni Princetonian,* February 18, 1897.

40. The popular culture stereotypes in American film regarding the romantic fate of male protagonists and Latina women had begun to change by the mid-twentieth century, but only if the women remained fair-skinned and beautiful. The woman, still fiercely proud and patriotic, often found herself a contested object between competing men. Virtuously defending her nation and her cause, the woman could only hope that the often morally challenged man in her life would finally recognize the importance of honor.

In *One Man's Hero* (1999), a rare American film about the Mexican-American War, the plight of the aforementioned Irish deserters from the US Army who formed an element of the San Patricio Battalion is sympathetically outlined. The Mexican-born Daniela Romo plays the freedom fighter Marta, who eventually chooses a beaten but still honorable commander, John Riley, over his guerrilla rival.

As Nina, a secret agent of the 1860s revolutionary Benito Juarez, the Spanish actress Sara Montiel battles the forces of Maximilian in *Vera Cruz* (1954). Her lover, the soldier of fortune Ben Trane (Gary Cooper), has a moral dilemma as he debates whether to steal a cargo of French gold for himself or allow it to reach the Mexican revolutionaries. Ultimately, the reluctant Trane decides to do the right thing.

Cuban women might enjoy a similarly positive image and romantic fate. The novel *Santiago* (and the 1956 film) finds Cash Adams, a West Point graduate, dishonorably discharged from the service, running guns out of Tampa to Cuba and Jose Marti's revolutionaries on the eve of the Spanish-American War of 1898. The cynical Adams is only concerned about profit until he falls in love with the beautiful and idealistic Doña Isabella—played by the Italian actress Rossana Podesta—who raises funds to liberate her people from Spanish oppression. She is Cuba's Joan of Arc, "Passionaria," and a friend to Marti and General Antonio Maceo. The fiery Isabella opens Adams's eyes to justice, freedom, and a worthy cause. Her speech about love of country and defiant nationalism could have been made a half century earlier in another war and in another country. Adams's redemption is assured, and so is his romantic fate, as she chooses him over a dutifully evil fellow smuggler. The nation was prepared by the 1950s for a relationship that crossed ethnic boundaries, but within limits.

American film audiences had previously embraced classically attractive Mexican women such as Dolores Del Río, Lupe Vélez, and Katy Jurado. Sadly, Del Río's career suffered during the anticommunist McCarthy era, and Vélez committed suicide. Jurado remained consistently popular; however, it might be noted that her character in *High Noon* (1952) had no chance of wedding Gary Cooper's Marshal Will Kane when competing with her blonde rival, played by Grace Kelly.

41. Mrs. H. Marion Ward, "Lolah Montana," *Southern Patriot* (Charleston, SC), December 20, 1847.

42. Richard Bruce Winders, *Mr. Polk's Army: The American Military Experience in the Mexican War* (College Station: Texas A&M University Press, 1997), 175–76; Judge Zo Cook, "Mexican War Reminiscences," *Alabama Historical Quarterly* 19 (1957): 457–58; Rodriguez, *Literatures of the U.S.-Mexican War,* 40.

8. More Voices of Popular Culture

1. Kendall, *New Orleans Daily Picayune,* August 16, 1846; Robert Johannsen, *To the Halls of Montezuma: The Mexican War in the American Imagination* (New York: Oxford University Press, 1985), 231–39. The minstrel show, performed by whites in blackface, was a combination of music, humor, and theater. The composer Stephen Foster and

artists such as George Washington Dixon, Edwin Christy, and Daniel Emmett, with their traveling troupes, combined to win national and international reputations for their music. For a full discussion of the Anglo-American cultural conflict, see Sam Haynes, *Unfinished Revolution: The Early American Republic in a British World* (Charlottesville: University of Virginia Press, 2010). It should be noted that art, whether through oil, illustrations, or the increasingly popular lithography, generally involved military themes, scenes, and events and was created about men by men. Daguerreotype photography had been invented but was not readily available in Mexico, thus few photographs from the war period remain.

2. *The Rough and Ready Songster* (New York: Nafis & Cornish, 1848).

3. "Yankee Doodle in Mexico," 1847, Music for the Nation: American Sheet Music, 1820–1860, Library of Congress; "They Wait for Us," *Boston Uncle Sam,* June 20, 1846.

4. J. Wakefield, "Yankee Girls," in William McCarty, comp., *National Songs, Ballads, and Other Patriotic Poetry Chiefly Relating to the War of 1846* (Philadelphia: by the author, 1846), 81. Wakefield's patriotic comparison favored English, not Mexican, women.

5. "Away in Mexico," by Caroline Hiffert and the Alleghanians, 1847, Music for the Nation: American Sheet Music, 1820–1860, Library of Congress. Themes of glory and the women back home are also reflected in "Away to the Battle" and "Yankee Girls," in McCarty, *National Songs,* 60–61, 81. Johannsen, *Halls of Montezuma,* 230–40. For those who preferred to dance, Madame Anna Bishop composed "The Mexican Polka," Music for the Nation: American Sheet Music, 1820–1860, Library of Congress.

6. Thomas Haynes Bayley, "Oh, No! We Never Mention Him/Her," in Michael R. Turner, ed., *Victorian Parlour Poetry: An Annotated Anthology* (Mineola, NY: Courier-Dover, 1992), 91; "Uncle Sam in Mexico," in Christopher Conway and Gustavo Pellón, *The U.S.-Mexican War: A Binational Reader* (Indianapolis: Hackett, 2010), 165–66. Bayley was a popular English poet and songwriter best known for his phrase, "Absence makes the heart grow fonder."

7. "By a Lady," in McCarty, *National Songs,* 87.

8. "The Texian Camp Song," ibid., 104; "Uncle Sam's Song to Miss Texas," ibid., 100; "The Female Volunteer for Texas," ibid., 126–27.

9. "Song of the Memphis Volunteers," ibid., 8–9.

10. "Soldier's Death," ibid., 69; "Be Kind to the Loved Ones at Home" and "The Dying Soldier of Buena Vista," Music for the Nation: American Sheet Music, 1820–1860, Library of Congress.

11. Hiffert left the group in 1849. In the 1850s she embarked on a successful solo career as a singer and actress, including a blackface portrayal on Broadway in a parody of *Uncle Tom's Cabin.* Hiffert reunited with the Alleghanians for a New York tour in 1861. A rather lengthy cavatina entitled "The Soldier's Bride" was written after the war in 1850.

12. "The Storm," by Guadalupe Calderón, Josefa Teran, and Josefa Letechipia de González, in Conway and Pellón, *U.S.-Mexican War,* 171–73.

13. "To the Motherland," ibid., 170–71. Both "To the Motherland" and "The Storm" were published in *El Republicano* on November 27, 1846.

14. Christopher Conway, "Sisters at War: Mexican Women's Poetry and the U.S.-Mexican War," *Latin American Research Review* 47 (2012): 3–15. Conway explores the work of several other important poets, particularly Josefa Heraclia Badillo, at length.

15. Conway, "Sisters at War," 5–6; "When Women Oppose Cowardly Men," in Music and Poetry, A Continent Divided: The U.S.-Mexico War, Occupation and Aftermath, Special Collections, University of Texas at Arlington. Special thanks to Dr. Sam Haynes, of UTA, for providing the English translations of a number of the documents presented in this chapter.

16. María de la Salud García, in *El Republicano,* August 31, 1846, reprinted in Conway and Pellón, *U.S.-Mexican War,* 114–16.

17. "An Old Woman Calls for the Death of General Scott," in Music and Poetry, A Continent Divided: The U.S.-Mexico War, Occupation and Aftermath, Special Collections, University of Texas at Arlington.

18. "A Prayer that Yankees Recite to Shame Mexicans," ibid.; Peter Guardino, "Gender, Soldiering, and Citizenship in the Mexican-American War of 1846–1848," *American Historical Review* 119 (February 2014): 23–43.

19. "Federation or Death," in Music and Poetry, A Continent Divided: The U.S.-Mexico War, Occupation and Aftermath, Special Collections, University of Texas at Arlington; Guardino, "Gender, Soldiering, and Citizenship," 23.

20. "La Pasadita," Music for the Nation: American Sheet Music, 1820–1860, Library of Congress; Johannsen, *Halls of Montezuma,* 206–10. Johannsen's volume excels at exploring Mexican-American War poetry from a variety of angles. See 210–18.

21. Johannsen, *Halls of Montezuma,* 208–18.

22. Ibid., 215.

23. Caroline M. Sawyer, "The Warrior's Dirge," in McCarty, *National Songs,* 54–55.

24. Frances J. Crosby, *Monterey and Other Poems* (New York: R. Craighead, 1851).

25. Lydia Jane Pierson, *Forest Minstrel* (Philadelphia: J. W. Moore, 1847), 147–48; *Literary World,* November 6, 1847, 332–33; Johannsen, *Halls of Montezuma,* 210–11. Pierson, then in her forties, lived in Tioga, Pennsylvania.

26. Pierson, *Forest Minstrel,* 230.

27. Frances Dana Gage, *Poems* (Philadelphia: J. Lippincott, 1867), 125–29, 215–16; Nancy Isenberg, *Sex and Citizenship in Antebellum America* (Chapel Hill: University of North Carolina Press, 1998), 153.

28. Gage, *Poems,* 125–29. Frances Crosby similarly appealed for reconsideration in "To a Brother Going to California," in *Monterey and Other Poems,* 45.

29. Johannsen, *Halls of Montezuma,* 218–21; Haynes, *Unfinished Revolution,* 100–104.

30. Napoleon Dana to Sue Dana, February 3, 1847, in *Monterrey is Ours! The Mexican War Letters of Lieutenant Dana, 1845–1847,* ed. Robert H. Ferrell (Lexington:

University of Kentucky Press, 1990), 178. Americans also had a great affection for the circus, and promoters saw real profit to be made by performing before the troops. Some companies had been in Mexico before the war, while others followed the armies, often doing shows in one place for weeks at a time. Several soldiers mentioned the boyhood joy brought by the circus, especially the humor of the clowns and the performance of a monkey, "Dandy Jack," riding on the back of a pony. Possibly, women staged various acts with the shows in Mexico, but there is no specific comment to that effect. George Winston Smith and Charles Judah, eds., *Chronicles of the Gringos: The U.S. Army in the Mexican War, 1846–1848* (Albuquerque: University of New Mexico Press, 1968), 313; William S. Henry, *Campaign Sketches of the War with Mexico* (New York: Harper Bros., 1847), 254; John R. Kenly, *Memoirs of a Maryland Volunteer: War with Mexico in the Years 1846–1847* (Philadelphia: J. B. Lippincott, 1873), September 1846, 159, January 27, 1847, 381; Daniel Harvey Hill, *A Fighter from Way Back: The Mexican War Diary of Lt. Daniel Harvey Hill, 4th Artillery, USA,* ed. Nathaniel C. Hughes Jr. and Timothy D. Johnson (Kent, OH: Kent State University Press, 2002), 30. Hill complained that although they had defeated the Mexicans in battle (Monterrey), the locals were getting even by charging an exorbitant admission price of one dollar for the circus.

31. Smith and Judah, *Chronicles of the Gringos,* 313–14.

32. Hill, *Fighter from Way Back,* 135; George McClellan to his mother, Elizabeth, October 24, 1847, in George B. McClellan, *The Mexican War Diary and Correspondence of George B. McClellan,* ed. Thomas W. Cutrer (Baton Rouge: Louisiana State University Press, 2009), 132.

33. *La Somnambula* continued to be in demand in the United States. Jenny Lind, "the Swedish Nightingale," who earned a fortune on her P. T. Barnum–promoted American tour in 1850, played the lead role to great acclaim. John James Peck, *The Sign of the Eagle: A View of Mexico, 1830–1855; The Letters of Lieutenant John James Peck,* ed. Richard Pourade (San Diego: Union Tribune, 1970), 142; De Lancey Floyd-Jones to his sister, December 7, 1847, in De Lancey Floyd-Jones Letters, Special Collections, University of Texas at Arlington; McClellan to his mother, October 24, 1847, in McClellan, *Mexican War Diary and Correspondence,* 130–34; Will Fowler, *Santa Anna of Mexico* (Lincoln: University of Nebraska Press, 2007), 443n45.

34. Peck, *Sign of the Eagle,* 142; Michael P. Costeloe, *The Central Republic in Mexico, 1835–1846* (Cambridge: Cambridge University Press, 1993), 222; Malcolm D. McLean, ed., *Papers Concerning Robertson's Colony in Texas,* 19 vols. (Arlington: University of Texas at Arlington Press, 1974–93), 14:286.

35. Peck, *Sign of the Eagle,* 142; Ramón Alcaraz, *The Other Side, or Notes for the History of the War between Mexico and the United States* (1850; reprint, New York: Burt Franklin, 1970), 415.

36. John W. Brokaw, "A Nineteenth-Century Mexican Acting Company—Teatro de Iturbide, 1856–1857," *Latin American Theatre Review* 6 (Fall 1972): 6, 8, 11.

37. K. Jack Bauer, *The Mexican War, 1846–1848* (1974; reprint with an introduction by Robert W. Johannsen, Lincoln: University of Nebraska Press, 1992), 396–97.

Conclusion

1. Michael Van Wagenen, *Remembering the Forgotten War: The Enduring Legacies of the U.S.-Mexican War* (Amherst: University of Massachusetts Press, 2012), 41–46.

2. Ibid., 47–49.

3. Ibid., 50–58.

4. Ibid., 10–12.

5. Ibid., 13–21.

6. Ibid., 22–40. Santa Anna's leg, discovered in his carriage after the Battle of Cerro Gordo in 1847, is housed in the Illinois State Military Museum in Springfield. Both the state of Texas and the Mexican government have unsuccessfully attempted to have it returned.

7. K. Jack Bauer, *The Mexican War, 1846–1848* (1974; reprint with an introduction by Robert W. Johannsen, Lincoln: University of Nebraska Press, 1992), xvii, 392–93.

8. Silvia Marina Arrom, *The Women of Mexico City, 1790–1857* (Stanford, CA: Stanford University Press, 1985), 20–26; Mark Wasserman, *Everyday Life and Politics in Nineteenth Century Mexico: Men, Women, and War* (Albuquerque: University of New Mexico Press, 2000), 39.

9. Arrom, *Women of Mexico City,* 92–97, 252, 258; Wasserman, *Everyday Life and Politics,* 40.

10. Arrom, *Women of Mexico City,* 158–83.

11. Timothy J. Henderson, *A Glorious Defeat: Mexico and Its War with the United States* (New York: Hill & Wang, 2007), 188.

12. Arrom, *Women of Mexico City,* 259–68; Wasserman, *Everyday Life and Politics,* 86–87. For a fascinating look at the integration of *marianismo* with cookbooks, food, culture, and nationalism, see Jeffrey M. Pilcher, *¡Que vivan los tamales! Food and the Making of Mexican Identity* (Albuquerque: University of New Mexico Press, 1998), 45–70, 145–50.

BIBLIOGRAPHY

Primary Sources

MANUSCRIPT COLLECTIONS

Butler Family Papers. The Historic New Orleans Collection. Williams Research Center, New Orleans.

Chase, Ann, Papers. Dallas Historical Society.

Dana, Napoleon, Letters. US Military Academy, West Point, NY.

Floyd-Jones, De Lancey, Letters. Special Collections, University of Texas at Arlington.

Great Britain. Foreign Office Papers. National Archives, London.

Henry County Anti-Slavery Society Papers. Indiana State Library, Indianapolis.

Henry County Female Anti-Slavery Society Papers. Indiana Division, Manuscripts Collection, Indiana State Library, Indianapolis.

Howard Family Papers. Maryland Historical Society, Baltimore.

Hunter Letters. Louisiana State University Library, Baton Rouge.

McMillan, Alice, Papers. Ohio Historical Society, Columbus.

Music and Poetry. A Continent Divided: The U.S.-Mexico War, Occupation and Aftermath. Special Collections, University of Texas at Arlington.

Music for the Nation: American Sheet Music, 1820–1860. Library of Congress.

Prevost, Grayson, Papers. A Continent Divided: The U.S.-Mexico War, Occupation and Aftermath. Special Collections, University of Texas at Arlington.

PUBLISHED MEMOIRS AND DIARIES

Alcaraz, Ramón. *The Other Side, or Notes for the History of the War between Mexico and the United States.* Trans. and ed. Albert Ramsey. 1850. Reprint, New York: Burt Franklin, 1970. Originally published as *Apuntes para la historia de la guerra entre Mexico y los Estados Unidos* (Mexico City, 1848).

Allen, George N. *Incidents and Sufferings in the Mexican War.* Boston and New York: Hall's, 1847.

Allen, Lewis Leonidas. *Pencillings of Scenes along the Rio Grande.* New York, 1848.

Balbontin, Manuel. *La Invasion Americana 1846 a 1848.* Mexico City, 1883.

Beebe, Rose Marie, and Robert Senkewicz, trans. and ed. "Felipa Osuna: 'The Oldest Resident of Old Town in 1878.'" *Journal of San Diego History* 55 (Fall 2009): 231–44.

Berge, Dennis E., trans. and ed. *Considerations on the Political and Social Situation of the Mexican Republic, 1847.* El Paso: Texas Western Press, 1975.

Bigler, David L., and Will Bagley, eds. *Army of Israel: Mormon Battalion Narratives.* Logan: Utah State University Press, 2000.

Brandes, Raymond S., trans. *Times Gone by in Alta California: Recollections of Señora Doña Juana Machado Alipaz de Wrightington* (1878). *Historical Society of Southern California Quarterly* 41, no. 3 (September 1959): 195–240.

Chamberlain, Samuel. *My Confession: Recollections of a Rogue.* Ed. William H. Goetzmann. Austin: Texas State Historical Society, 1996.

Chapman, Helen. *The News from Brownsville: Helen Chapman's Letters from the Texas Military Frontier, 1848–1852.* Ed. Caleb Coker. Austin: Texas State Historical Association, 1992.

Cook, Judge Zo. "Mexican War Reminiscences." *Alabama Historical Quarterly* 19 (Fall 1957): 435–60.

Cooke, Philip St. George. *The Conquest of New Mexico and California.* New York: Putnam, 1878.

Coulter, Richard, and Thomas Barclay. *Volunteers: The Mexican War Journals of Private Richard Coulter, and Sergeant Thomas Barclay, Company E, Second Pennsylvania Infantry.* Ed. Allan Peskin. Kent, OH: Kent State University Press, 1991.

Curtis, Samuel Ryan. *Mexico under Fire: Being the Diary of Samuel Ryan Curtis, 3rd Ohio Volunteer Regiment during the American Occupation of Northern Mexico, 1846–1847.* Ed. Joseph E. Chance. Fort Worth: Texas Christian University Press, 1994.

Dall, Caroline Healey. *Daughter of Boston: The Extraordinary Diary of a Nineteenth-Century Woman, Caroline Healey Dall.* Ed. Helen Deese. Boston: Beacon, 2005.

———. *Selected Journals of Caroline Healey Dall, 1838–1855.* Ed. Helen Deese. Boston: Massachusetts Historical Society, 2006.

Dana, Napoleon. *Monterrey is Ours! The Mexican War Letters of Lieutenant Dana, 1845–1847.* Ed. Robert H. Ferrell. Lexington: University of Kentucky Press, 1990.

Dana, Richard Henry. *Two Years before the Mast and Twenty-Four Years After.* 1840. Reprint, New York: P. F. Collier, 1909.

Davis, W. W. H. *El Gringo: or New Mexico and Her People.* New York: Harper & Bros., 1857.

Dilworth, Rankin. *The March to Monterrey: The Diary of Lieutenant Rankin Dilworth.* Ed. Joseph E. Chance. El Paso: Texas Western Press, 1996.

Doubleday, Abner. *My Life in the Old Army: The Reminiscences of Abner Doubleday from the Collections of the New York Historical Society.* Ed. Joseph E. Chance. Fort Worth: Texas Christian University Press, 1998.

Edwards, Frank S. *A Campaign in New Mexico with Colonel Doniphan.* Philadelphia: Carey & Hart, 1847.

Edwards, R. M. *Down the Tennessee: The Mexican War Reminiscences of an East Tennessee Volunteer (R. M. Edwards).* Ed. Stewart Lillard. 1895. Reprint, Charlotte, NC: Loftin, 1997.

Elliott, Richard Smith. *The Mexican War Correspondence of Richard Smith Elliott.* Ed. Mark L. Gardner and Marc Simmons. Norman: University of Oklahoma Press, 1997.

Fennery, Thomas D. *The Mexican War Diary of Thomas D. Fennery.* Ed. D. E. Livingston-Little. Norman: University of Oklahoma Press, 1970.

Field, Matt. *Matt Field on the Santa Fe Trail.* Ed. Clyde Porter and Mae Reed Porter. 1960. Reprint, Norman: University of Oklahoma Press, 1995.

Frost, John. *Pictorial History of Mexico and the Mexican War.* Philadelphia: Thomas, Cowperthwait, 1849.

Garrard, Lewis Hector. *Wah-to-Yah and the Taos Trail.* 1850. Reprint, Norman: University of Oklahoma Press, 1973.

Gibson, George R. *George R. Gibson: Journal of a Soldier under Kearny and Doniphan, 1846–1847.* Ed. Ralph Bieber. Glendale, CA: Arthur H. Clark, 1935.

Gratz, Rebecca. *Letters of Rebecca Gratz.* Ed. David Philipson. Philadelphia: Jewish Publication Society of America, 1929.

Gregg, Josiah. *Commerce of the Prairies.* 1844. Reprint, Norman: University of Oklahoma Press, 1954.

Hill, Daniel Harvey. *A Fighter from Way Back: The Mexican War Diary of Lt. Daniel Harvey Hill, 4th Artillery, USA.* Ed. Nathaniel C. Hughes Jr. and Timothy D. Johnson. Kent, OH: Kent State University Press, 2002.

Henry, William S. *Campaign Sketches of the War with Mexico.* New York: Harper Bros., 1847.

Henshaw, John Corey. *Major John Corey Henshaw: Recollections of the War with Mexico.* Ed. Gary Kurutz. Columbia: University of Missouri Press, 2008.

Johnston, Abraham Robinson, Marcellus Ball Edwards, and Philip Gooch Ferguson. *Marching with the Army of the West, 1846–1848: Journal of A. R. Johnston, 1846, Journal of M. B. Edwards, 1846–47, Diary of P. G. Ferguson, 1847–48.* Ed. Ralph Bieber. Glendale, CA: Arthur H. Clark, 1936.

Kendall, George Wilkins. *George Wilkins Kendall: Dispatches from the Mexican War.* Ed. Lawrence D. Cress. Norman: University of Oklahoma Press, 1999.

Kenly, John R. *Memoirs of a Maryland Volunteer: War with Mexico in the Years, 1846–1847.* Philadelphia: J. B. Lippincott, 1873.

Kirkham, Ralph W. *The Mexican War Journal and Letters of Ralph W. Kirkham.* Ed. Robert Ryal Miller. College Station: Texas A&M University Press, 1991.

Laidley, Theodore. *Surrounded by Dangers of All Kinds: The Mexican War Letters of Lieutenant Theodore Laidley.* Ed. James M. McCaffrey. Denton: University of North Texas Press, 1997.

Lomax, Tennent. "Letters to His Sister." *Alabama Historical Quarterly* 19 (Fall 1957): 461–65.

Magoffin, Susan Shelby. *Down the Santa Fe Trail and into Mexico: The Diary of Susan Shelby Magoffin, 1846–1847.* Ed. Stella Drumm. 1926. Reprint, Lincoln: University of Nebraska Press, 1982.

Mansfield, Harvey, and Debra Winthrop, eds. *Democracy in America.* Chicago: University of Chicago Press, 2000.

McClellan, George B. *The Mexican War Diary and Correspondence of George B. McClellan.* Ed. Thomas W. Cutrer. Baton Rouge: Louisiana State University Press, 2009.

McLean, Malcolm D., ed. *Papers Concerning Robertson's Colony in Texas.* 19 vols. Arlington: University of Texas at Arlington Press, 1974–93.

McNierney, Michael, ed. *Taos 1847: The Revolt in Contemporary Accounts.* Boulder, CO: Johnson, 1980.

Nunnelee, S. F. "Alabama and the Mexican War." *Alabama Historical Quarterly* 19 (Fall/Winter 1957): 415–34.

Orr, William J., and Robert R. Miller, eds. *An Immigrant Soldier in the Mexican War.* College Station: Texas A&M University Press, 1995.

Peck, John James. *The Sign of the Eagle: A View of Mexico, 1830–1855; The Letters of Lieutenant John James Peck.* Ed. Richard Pourade. San Diego: Union Tribune, 1970.

Polk, James K. *The Diary of James K. Polk.* Ed. Milo M. Quaife. 4 vols. Chicago: A. C. McClurg, 1910.

Ramirez, Jose Fernando. *Mexico during the War with the United States.* Ed. Walter V. Scholes. Trans. Elliott B. Scherr. 1950. Reprint, Columbia: University of Missouri Press, 1970. Originally published as *Mexico durante su guerra con los Estados Unidos* (1850) and included in vol. 3 of *Documentos ineditos o muy raros para la historia de Mexico,* by Genaro Garcia (Mexico City, 1905).

Reid, Samuel C. *The Scouting Expeditions of McCulloch's Texas Rangers.* 1847. Reprint, Freeport, NY: Books for Libraries, 1970.

Robertson, John Blount. *Reminiscences of a Campaign in Mexico.* Nashville: J. York, 1849.

Scott, Winfield. *Memoirs of Lieutenant-General Scott.* 2 vols. New York: Sheldon, 1864.

Smith, Franklin. *The Mexican War Journal of Captain Franklin Smith.* Ed. Joseph E. Chance. Jackson: University Press of Mississippi, 1991.

Smith, George Winston, and Charles Judah, eds. *Chronicles of the Gringos: The U.S. Army in the Mexican War, 1846–1848.* Albuquerque: University of New Mexico Press, 1968.

Standage, Henry. *The March of the Mormon Battalion from Council Bluffs to California: Taken from the Journal of Henry Standage.* Ed. Frank A. Golder. New York: Century, 1928.

Swisshelm, Jane Grey. *Half a Century.* Chicago: Jansen, McClurg, 1880.

Tyler, Daniel. *A Concise History of the Mormon Battalion in the Mexican War, 1846–1847.* Salt Lake City, UT, 1881.

Webb, James Josiah. *James Josiah Webb: Adventures in the Santa Fe Trade, 1844–1847.* Ed. Ralph Bieber. 1931. Reprint, Lincoln: University of Nebraska Press, 1995.

Weber, R. B., ed. "The Mexican War: Some Personal Correspondence." *Indiana Magazine of History* 65 (June 1969): 133–39.

MEXICAN-AMERICAN WAR LITERATURE, POETRY, AND MUSIC

Aleman, Jesse, and Shelley Streeby, eds. *Empire and the Literature of Sensation.* New Brunswick, NJ: Rutgers University Press, 2007.

Allen, Eliza. *The Female Volunteer; or the Life, and Wonderful Adventures of Miss Eliza Allen, a Young Lady of Eastport, Maine.* Eastport, 1851.

Averill, Charles. *The Mexican Ranchero; or, The Maid of the Chaparral: A Romance of the Mexican War.* Boston: F. Gleason, 1847.

———. *The Secret Service Ship; or, The Fall of San Juan D'Ulloa: A Thrilling Tale of the Mexican War.* Boston: F. Gleason, 1848.

Buntline, Ned. *Magdalena, the Beautiful Mexican Maid: A Story of Buena Vista.* New York: Williams Bros., 1847.

———. *The Volunteer; or, The Maid of Monterey. A Tale of the Mexican War.* Boston: F. Gleason, 1847.

Crosby, Frances J. *Monterey and Other Poems.* New York: R. Craighead, 1851.

Curtis, Newton. *The Hunted Chief; or, Female Ranchero: A Tale of the Mexican War.* New York: W. F. Burgess, 1847.

———. *Prairie Guide; or, Rose of the Rio Grande.* New York: Williams Bros., 1847.

———. *The Vidette; or, The Girl of the Robber's Pass.* New York: Williams Bros., 1848.

Cutler, Bruce. *At War with Mexico: A Fictional Mosaic.* Norman: University of Oklahoma Press, 2001.

Fuller, Margaret. *Margaret Fuller: Critic.* Ed. Judith M. Bean and Joel Myerson. New York: Columbia University Press, 2000.

———. *The Writings of Margaret Fuller.* Ed. Mason Wade. New York: Viking, 1941.

Gage, Frances Dana. *Poems.* Philadelphia: J. Lippincott, 1867.

Greenwood, Grace. *Greenwood Leaves: A Collection of Sketches and Letters.* Boston: Ticknor Reed, & Fields, 1850.

Hall, A. D. *Captain Impudence: A Romance of the Mexican War.* New York: Street & Smith, 1897.

Halyard, Harry. *The Heroine of Tampico; or, Wildfire the Wanderer: A Tale of the Mexican War.* Boston: F. Gleason, 1847.

Hazel, Harry. *Inez the Beautiful; or, Love on the Rio Grande.* Boston: by the author, 1846.

———. *The Light Dragoon; or, The Rancheros of the Poisoned Lance.* New York: American News, 1848.

———. *The Rival Chieftains; or, The Brigands of Mexico.* Boston: Gleasons, 1845.

Ingraham, J. H. *The Texas Ranger; or, the Maid of Matamoras.* Boston: Henry L. Williams, 1846.

Lippard, George. *Bel of Prairie Eden: A Romance of Mexico.* Boston: Hotchkiss, 1848.
Lowell, James Russell. *The Bigelow Papers.* Cambridge, MA, 1848.
McCarty, William, comp. *National Songs, Ballads, and Other Patriotic Poetry Chiefly Related to the War of 1846.* Philadelphia: by the author, 1846.
Musick, John Roy. *Humbled Pride: A Story of the Mexican War.* New York: Funk & Wagnalls, 1893.
Pierson, Lydia Jane. *Forest Minstrel.* Philadelphia: J. W. Moore, 1847.
The Rough and Ready Songster. New York: Nafis & Cornish, 1848.
Turner, Michael R., ed. *Victorian Parlour Poetry: An Annotated Anthology.* Mineola, NY: Courier-Dover, 1992.
Whittier, John Greenleaf. *The Writings of John Greenleaf Whittier.* Boston: Houghton, Mifflin, 1892.

PERIODICALS

Advocate of Peace and Universal Brotherhood (Boston)
Albion (New York)
Alumni Princetonian
American Star (Mexico City)
Anti-Slavery Bugle (New Lisbon, OH)
Baltimore Sun
Boston Uncle Sam
Christian Secretary (Hartford, CT)
Cincinnati Weekly Herald and Philanthropist
Clarion (Sandusky, OH)
Constitution (Middletown, CT)
Dwight's American Magazine and Family Newspaper (New York)
El Paso Times
Emancipator (New York)
Farmer's Cabinet (Amherst, NH)
Godey's Magazine and Lady's Book (Philadelphia)
Harbinger (New York)
Hudson River Chronicle (Ossining, NY)
Huntress (Washington, DC)
John-Donkey (New York)
Ladies Repository and Gatherings of the West (Cincinnati)
Liberator (Boston)
Literary World (New York)
Macon (GA) Weekly Telegraph
Maine Farmer (Winthrop)

Mobile (AL) Tribune
Monthly Religious Magazine (Boston)
National Police Gazette (New York)
New Hampshire Sentinel (Keene)
New Orleans Bee
New Orleans Delta
New Orleans Picayune
New York Observer and Chronicle
New York Sun
New York Times
Niles' National Register (Baltimore)
Ohio Statesman (Columbus)
Pennsylvania Freeman (Philadelphia)
Philadelphia Ledger
Pittsfield (MA) Sun
Prisoners' Friend: A Monthly Magazine Devoted to Criminal Reform, Philosophy, etc. (Boston)
Southern Patriot (Charleston, SC)
Spirit of the Times (New York)
State Journal (Indianapolis, Indiana)
Union Magazine of Literature and Art (New York)
Western Citizen (Peoria, IL)

Secondary Works

American Annual Cyclopedia and Register of Important Events. Vol. 14. New York: D. Appleton, 1875.

Anderson, Greta. *More than Petticoats: Remarkable Texas Women.* Guilford, CT: Two Dot, 2002.

Arrom, Silvia Marina. *The Women of Mexico City, 1790–1857.* Stanford, CA: Stanford University Press, 1985.

Balducci, Carolyn. *Margaret Fuller: A Life of Passion and Defiance.* New York: Bantam Books, 1991.

Bauer, K. Jack. *The Mexican War, 1846–1848.* 1974. Reprint with an introduction by Robert W. Johannsen, Lincoln: University of Nebraska Press, 1992.

———. *Surfboats and Horse Marines: U.S. Naval Operations in the Mexican War.* Annapolis: US Naval Institute Press, 1969.

Belohlavek, John M. *Broken Glass: Caleb Cushing and the Shattering of the Union.* Kent, OH: Kent State University Press, 2005.

Berge, Dennis E. "Mexican Response to United States' Expansionism, 1841–1848." PhD diss., University of California, Berkeley, 1965.

Blevins, Donald. *A Priest, a Prostitute, and Some Other Early Texans.* Guilford, CT: Two Dot, 2008.

Brack, Gene M. *Mexico Views Manifest Destiny, 1821–1846.* Albuquerque: University of New Mexico Press, 1975.

Brokaw, John W. "A Nineteenth-Century Mexican Acting Company—Teatro de Iturbide, 1856–1857." *Latin American Theatre Review* 6 (Fall 1972): 5–18.

"Caroline Kirkland." www.scribblingwomen.org/ckbio.htm.

Caruso, A. Brooke. *The Mexican Spy Company: United States Covert Operations in Mexico, 1845–1848.* Jefferson, NC: McFarland, 1991.

Cashion, Peggy M. "Women and the Mexican War, 1846–1848." MA thesis, University of Texas at Arlington, 1990.

Chalfant, William Y. *Dangerous Passage: The Santa Fe Trail and the Mexican War.* Norman: University of Oklahoma Press, 1994.

Chavez, Ernesto. *The U.S. War with Mexico: A Brief History with Documents.* New York: Bedford/St. Martin's, 2008.

Clapp, Elizabeth J. *A Notorious Woman: Anne Royall in Jacksonian America.* Charlottesville: University of Virginia Press, 2016.

Clary, David. *Eagles and Empire: The U.S., Mexico, and the Struggle for a Continent.* New York: Random House, 2009.

Conner, Philip Syng. *The Home Squadron under Commodore Conner in the War with Mexico.* Philadelphia, 1896.

Conway, Christopher. "Ravished Virgins and Warrior Women: Gender and the Literature of the U.S.-Mexican War." *Fronteras* 18 (Fall 2009): 3–4.

———. "Sisters at War: Mexican Women's Poetry and the U.S.-Mexican War." *Latin American Research Review* 47 (2012): 3–15.

Conway, Christopher, and Gustavo Pellón, eds. *The U.S.-Mexican War: A Binational Reader.* Indianapolis: Hackett, 2010.

Cook, Mary J. Straw. *Doña Tules: Santa Fe's Courtesan and Gambler.* Albuquerque: University of New Mexico Press, 2007.

Costeloe, Michael P. *Bonds and Bondholders: British Investors and Mexican Foreign Debt, 1824–1888.* Westport, CT: Praeger, 2003.

———. *The Central Republic in Mexico, 1835–1846.* Cambridge: Cambridge University Press, 1993.

———. "The Mexican Church and the Rebellion of the Polkos." *Hispanic American Historical Review* 46 (May 1966): 170–78.

Crawford, Mark, ed. *Encyclopedia of the Mexican-American War.* Santa Barbara, CA: ABC-CLIO, 1999.

Crimm, Ana Carolina Castillo. *De León: A Tejano Family History.* Austin: University of Texas Press, 2003.

Dawson, Joseph G., III. *Doniphan's Epic March: The 1st Missouri Volunteers in the Mexican War.* Lawrence: University Press of Kansas, 1999.

DeLay, Brian. *War of a Thousand Deserts: Indian Raids and the U.S.-Mexican War.* New Haven, CT: Yale University Press, 2008.

del Castillo, Richard Griswold. "The U.S-Mexican War in San Diego, 1846–1847." *Journal of San Diego History* 49 (Winter 2003): 1–8.

De León, Arnoldo. *They Called Them Greasers: Anglo Attitudes toward Mexicans in Texas, 1821–1900.* Austin: University of Texas Press, 1983.

DePalo, William. *The Mexican National Army, 1822–1852.* College Station: Texas A&M University Press, 1997.

Dysart, Jane. "Mexican Women in San Antonio, 1830–1860: The Assimilation Process." *Western Historical Quarterly* 7 (October 1976): 365–75.

Eisenhower, John D. *Agent of Destiny: The Life and Times of General Winfield Scott.* New York: Free Press, 1997.

———. *So Far from God: The U.S. War with Mexico, 1846–1848.* New York: Random House, 1989.

Elliott, J. F. "The Great Western: Sarah Bowman, Mother and Mistress to the U.S. Army." *Journal of Arizona History* 30 (Spring 1989): 1–26.

Foos, Paul. *A Short, Offhand, Killing Affair: Soldiers and Social Conflict during the Mexican-American War.* Chapel Hill: University of North Carolina Press, 2002.

Fortier, Alcee, ed. *Louisiana: Comprising Sketches of Parishes, Towns, Events, Institutions, and Persons.* Vol. 3. Madison, WI: Century Historical Association, 1914.

Fowler, Will. *Santa Anna of Mexico.* Lincoln: University of Nebraska Press, 2007.

Franchot, Jenny. *Roads to Rome: The Antebellum Protestant Encounter with Catholicism.* Berkeley: University of California Press, 1994.

Frazier, Donald, ed. *The United States and Mexico at War: Nineteenth Century Expansionism and Conflict.* New York: MacMillan Reference USA, 1998.

Geary, Linda L. *Balanced in the Wind: A Biography of Betsey Mix Cowles.* Lewisburg, PA: Bucknell University Press, 1989.

Glover, John Crandall. "Ann Chase, 'The Heroine of Tampico.'" MA thesis, Southern Methodist University, 1947.

Gonzalez, Deena J. *Refusing the Favor: The Spanish-Mexican Women of Santa Fe, 1820–1880.* New York: Oxford University Press, 1999.

Greenberg, Amy S. *Manifest Manhood and the Antebellum American Empire.* Cambridge: Cambridge University Press, 2005.

———. *A Wicked War: Polk, Clay, Lincoln, and the 1846 U.S. Invasion of Mexico.* New York: Alfred A. Knopf, 2012.

Griffin, Megan Jenison. "Jane McManus Storm Cazneau, 1807–1878." *Legacy: A Journal of Women Writers* 27 (2010): 416–32.

Groom, Winston. *Kearny's March: The Epic Creation of the American West, 1846–1847.* New York: Alfred A. Knopf, 2011.

Guardino, Peter. "Gender, Soldiering, and Citizenship in the Mexican-American War of 1846–1848." *American Historical Review* 119 (February 2014): 23–46.

Hamilton, Nancy. "The Great Western." In Western Writers of America, *Women Who Made the West*. New York: Doubleday, 1980.

Haynes, Sam. *Unfinished Revolution: The Early American Republic in a British World.* Charlottesville: University of Virginia Press, 2010.

Henderson, Timothy J. *A Glorious Defeat: Mexico and Its War with the United States.* New York: Hill & Wang, 2007.

Hoffert, Sylvia D. *Jane Grey Swisshelm: An Unconventional Life, 1815–1884.* Chapel Hill: University of North Carolina Press, 2004.

Horgan, Paul. *Great River: The Rio Grande in North American History.* 4th ed. Hanover, NH: Wesleyan University Press, 1984.

Hudson, Linda S. *Mistress of Manifest Destiny: A Biography of Jane McManus Storm Cazneau.* Austin: Texas State Historical Association, 2001.

Hyslop, Stephen G. *Bound for Santa Fe: The Road to New Mexico and the American Conquest, 1806–1848.* Norman: University of Oklahoma Press, 2002.

Isenberg, Nancy. *Sex and Citizenship in Antebellum America.* Chapel Hill: University of North Carolina Press, 1998.

James, Bessie R. *Anne Royall's USA.* New Brunswick, NJ: Rutgers University Press, 1972.

Johannsen, Robert. *To the Halls of Montezuma: The Mexican War in the American Imagination.* New York: Oxford University Press, 1985.

Johnson, Timothy D. *A Gallant Little Army: The Mexico City Campaign.* Lawrence: University Press of Kansas, 2007.

———. *Winfield Scott: The Quest for Military Glory.* Lawrence: University Press of Kansas, 1998.

Johnson, Tyler V. *Devotion to the Adopted Country: U.S. Immigrant Volunteers in the Mexican War.* Columbia: University of Missouri Press, 2012.

Kaplan, Amy. "Manifest Domesticity." *American Literature* 70 (March 1998): 581–606.

Klassen, Teri. "Polk's Fancy: Quiltmaking, Patriotism, and Gender in the Mexican War Era." *Uncoverings* 27 (2006).

Lacy, James M. "New Mexico Women in Early American Writings." *New Mexico Historical Review* 34 (1959): 41–51.

Lander, Ernest M. *Reluctant Imperialists: Calhoun, the South Carolinians, and the Mexican War.* Baton Rouge: Louisiana State University Press, 1980.

Langum, David J. "Californio Women and the Image of Virtue." *Southern California Quarterly* 59 (1977): 245–50.

Larson, Carl V., and Shirley N. Maynes. *Women of the Mormon Battalion.* Providence, UT: Watkins, 1989.

Lavan, Spencer, and Peter Hughes. "Caroline Healey Dall." *Dictionary of Unitarian and Universalist Biography.* March 12, 2004. uudb.org/articles/carolinedall.html.

Lecompte, Janet. "The Independent Women of Hispanic New Mexico, 1821–1846." *Western Historical Quarterly* 1 (January 1981): 17–35.

———. "La Tules and the Americans." *Arizona and the West* 20 (Autumn 1978): 215–30.

Ledbetter, Suzann. *Shady Ladies: Nineteen Surprising and Rebellious American Women.* New York: Forge, 2006.

Levinson, Irving W. *Wars within War: Mexican Guerrillas, Domestic Elites, and the United States of America, 1846–1848.* Fort Worth: Texas Christian University Press, 2005.

Loyola, Sister Mary. *The American Occupation of New Mexico, 1821–1852.* Albuquerque: University of New Mexico Press, 1939.

MacLean, Maggie. "Caroline Kirkland." *History of American Women* (blog), May 2, 2013. www.womenhistoryblog.com/2013/05/caroline-kirkland.html.

Masterson, Rosemary. "The Machado-Silvas Family." *Journal of San Diego History* 15 (Winter 1969): 1–2.

May, Robert E. "Invisible Men: Blacks and the U.S. Army in the Mexican War." *Historian* 49 (August 1987): 463–77.

———. "Plenipotentiary in Petticoats: Jane M. Cazneau and American Foreign Policy in the Mid-Nineteenth Century." In *Women and American Foreign Policy: Lobbyists, Critics, and Insiders,* ed. Edward Crapol. Wilmington, DE: Scholarly Resources, 1992.

Maynes, Shirley N. *Five Hundred Wagons Stood Still: Mormon Battalion Wives.* Sandy, UT: Corporate Edge, 1999.

McCaffrey, James. *Army of Manifest Destiny: The American Soldier in the Mexican War, 1846–1848.* New York: New York University Press, 1992.

Melder, Keith. "Aspects of the Changing Status of New England Women, 1790–1840." teachushistory.org/detocqueville-visit-united-states/articles/aspects-changing-status-new-england-women.

Meyer, David. "The Roots of American Industrialization, 1790–1860." *EH.Net Encyclopedia of Economic and Business History.* March 16, 2008. eh.net/encyclopedia/the-roots-of-american-industrialization-1790-1860/.

Miller, Robert Ryal. *Shamrock and Sword: The Saint Patrick's Battalion in the U.S.-Mexican War.* Norman: University of Oklahoma Press, 1989.

Moorhead, Max. *New Mexico's Royal Road: Trade and Travel on the Chihuahua Trail.* Norman: University of Oklahoma Press, 1958.

Nelson, Anna Kasten. *Secret Agents: President Polk and the Search for Peace with Mexico.* New York: Garland, 1988.

Peskin, Allan. *Winfield Scott and the Profession of Arms.* Kent, OH: Kent State University Press, 2003.

Pierson, Michael D. *Free Hearts and Free Homes: Gender and American Antislavery Politics.* Chapel Hill: University of North Carolina Press, 2003.

Pilcher, Jeffrey M. *¡Que vivan los tamales! Food and the Making of Mexican Identity.* Albuquerque: University of New Mexico Press, 1998.

Pinheiro, John C. *Missionaries of Republicanism: A Religious History of the Mexican-American War.* New York: Oxford University Press, 2014.

Poyo, Gerald, ed. *Tejano Journey, 1780–1850.* Austin: University of Texas Press, 1996.

Reilly, Tom. "Jane McManus Storms: Letters from the Mexican War." *Southwestern Historical Quarterly* 85 (July 1981): 21–44.

Reilly, Tom, and Manley Witten. *War with Mexico: America's Reporters Cover the Battlefront.* Lawrence: University Press of Kansas, 2010.

Resendez, Andres. *Changing National Identities at the Frontier: Texas and New Mexico, 1800–1850.* Cambridge: Cambridge University Press, 2005.

Reyes, Monica. "'Within the little circle of my vision': Domesticity as the Catalyst for Acculturation in Susan Shelby Magoffin's *Down the Santa Fe Trail and into Mexico.*" *Coldnoon: Travel Poetics* 4 (January 2015): 108–35.

Ricketts, Norma B. *The Mormon Battalion: Army of the West, 1846–1848.* Logan, UT: Utah State University Press, 1996.

Robertson, Stacey. *Betsey Mix Cowles: Champion of Equality.* Boulder, CO: Westview, 2014.

Robson, Lucia St. Clair. *Fearless: A Life of Sarah Bowman.* New York: Ballantine Books, 1998.

Rodriguez, Jaime Javier. *The Literatures of the U.S.-Mexican War: Narrative, Time, and Identity.* Austin: University of Texas Press, 2010.

———. "The U.S.-Mexican War in James Russell Lowell's *The Bigelow Papers.*" *Arizona Quarterly* 63 (Autumn 2007): 1–33.

Rotundo, E. Anthony. *American Manhood: Transformations in Masculinity from the Revolution to the Modern Era.* New York: Basic Books, 1993.

Salas, Elizabeth. *Soldaderas in the Mexican Military: Myth and History.* Austin: University of Texas Press, 1990.

Sampson, Robert B. *John L. O'Sullivan and His Times.* Kent, OH: Kent State University Press, 2003.

Sandoval, David A. "The American Invasion of New Mexico and Mexican Merchants." *Journal of Popular Culture* 35 (Fall 2001): 61–72.

Sandwich, Brian. *The Great Western: Legendary Lady of the Southwest.* El Paso: Texas Western Press, 1991.

Santoni, Pedro, ed. *Daily Lives of Civilians in Wartime Latin America: From the Wars of Independence to the Central American Civil Wars.* Westport, CT: Greenwood, 2008.

———. *Mexicans at Arms: Puro Federalists and the Politics of War, 1845–1848.* Fort Worth: Texas Christian University Press, 1996.

Schroeder, John H. *Mr. Polk's War: American Opposition and Dissent, 1846–1848.* Madison: University of Wisconsin Press, 1973.

Senarens, Luis. *Old Rough and Ready, or the Heroine of Monterey.* New York: F. Tousey, 1886.

Sewell, Richard H. *John P. Hale and the Politics of Abolition.* Cambridge, MA: Harvard University Press, 1965.

Smith, Justin H. *The War with Mexico.* 2 vols. New York: Macmillan, 1919.

Smith, Ralph Adam. *Borderlander: The Life of James Kirker, 1793–1852.* Norman: University of Oklahoma Press, 1999.

Stansell, Christine. *City of Women: Sex and Class in New York City, 1789–1860.* Urbana: University of Illinois Press, 1987.

Stewart, James Brewer. *Joshua R. Giddings and the Tactics of Radical Politics.* Cleveland, OH: Press of Case Western Reserve University, 1970.

Streeby, Shelley. *American Sensations: Class, Empire, and the Production of Popular Culture.* Berkeley: University of California Press, 2002.

Tanglen, Randi Lynn. "Critical Regionalism, the US-Mexican War, and Nineteenth-Century American Literary History." *Western American Literature* 48 (Spring/ Summer 2013): 180–99.

Timmons, W. H. *James Wiley Magoffin: Don Santiago—El Paso Pioneer.* El Paso: Texas Western Press, 1999.

Tutorow, Norman E. *The Mexican-American War: An Annotated Bibliography.* Westport, CT: Greenwood, 1981.

Twitchell, Ralph E. *The History of the Military Occupation of the Territory of New Mexico from 1846–1851.* Denver: Smith-Brooks, 1909.

Van Wagenen, Michael Scott. *Remembering the Forgotten War: The Enduring Legacies of the U.S.-Mexican War.* Amherst: University of Massachusetts Press, 2012.

Varon, Elizabeth R. *We Mean to Be Counted: White Women and Politics in Antebellum Virginia.* Chapel Hill: University of North Carolina Press, 1998.

Wasserman, Mark. *Everyday Life and Politics in Nineteenth Century Mexico: Men, Women, and War.* Albuquerque: University of New Mexico Press, 2000.

Weber, David J. *The Spanish Frontier in North America.* New Haven, CT: Yale University Press, 1992.

Winders, Richard Bruce. *Mr. Polk's Army: The American Military Experience in the Mexican War.* College Station: Texas A&M University Press, 1997.

Woodward, Arthur. *The Great Western: Amazon of the Army.* San Francisco: Johnck & Seeger, 1961.

Zboray, Ronald J., and Mary S. Zboray. *Voices without Votes: Women and Politics in Antebellum New England.* Hanover, NH: University Press of New England, 2010.

Ziegler, Valarie H. *The Advocates of Peace in Antebellum America.* Bloomington: Indiana University Press, 1992.

INDEX